Story and History

Story and History

Narrative Authority and Social Identity in the Eighteenth-Century French and English Novel

William Ray

Basil Blackwell

Copyright © William E. Ray, Jr. 1990

First published 1990

Basil Blackwell, Inc.
3 Cambridge Center
Cambridge, Massachusetts 02142, USA

Basil Blackwell Ltd
108 Cowley Road, Oxford, OX4 1JF, UK

Library of Congress Cataloging in Publication Data

Ray, William E., Jr.
    Story and history: narrative authority and social identity in the eighteenth-century French
and English novel/William Ray.
        p.   cm.
    Includes bibliographical references.
    ISBN 0-631-15436-1   0-631-17512-1 (pbk.)
    1. French fiction – 18th century – History and criticism. 2. English fiction – 18th century
– History and criticism. 3. Identity (Psychology) in literature. 4. Social history in literature.
5. Literature, Comparative – French and English. 6. Literature, Comparative – English and
French. 7. Narration (Rhetoric) I. Title.
PQ648.R38   1990
843'.509353—dc20   89-16035
                                                                                    CIP

British Library Cataloguing in Publication Data

A CIP catalogue record for this book is available from the British Library.

Typeset in 10 on 12 pt Plantin
by Graphicraft Typesetters Ltd., Hong Kong
Printed in Great Britain by Billing & Sons Ltd., Worcester.

Contents

Preface

This study did not start out as a general reconsideration of the French and English novel in the eighteenth century. It began, in fact, with a relatively benign observation that the relationship between personal story and public account, between the social act of relating one's perceptions or events to some listener and the collective narrative or history that framed such acts, seemed to form an essential component of the thematic structures and even plots of several novels of the period. As I expanded my investigation, I was struck by the pervasiveness of this theme and its clear affiliation with the emergence of a decidedly metaliterary tendency in the later works. Inevitably I was led to try to account for this pattern in terms of the function which critics and theoreticians of the period assign to narration and narratives – and to fiction in particular – and to see if the pattern applied to the major works in both the French and English traditions. The result is a set of readings and speculations which themselves form a story, namely that of the eighteenth-century French and English novels' evolving conceptualization of narration and narratives, as they relate to selfhood, identity, society, and culture through the structures of authority subtending such categories. These questions are explicitly treated in the novels in question; indeed, I will argue that many of the individual works express microcosmically in their plots and thematic structure the patterns of development which I perceive in the genre's collective evolution. But these themes are not *all* the novels contain, and the reader should be forewarned that my interpretations are of necessity partial, in both senses of the word. They do not attempt to provide comprehensive views of the works in question, and, unfortunately, they cannot take into consideration the enormous amount of fine scholarship that each of the novels has provoked. These shortcomings are the unhappy consequence of the study's scope and format.

The conviction that my arguments could only be useful, and my analytic perspective validated, if they could be shown to pertain to most of the major works of the period, led me to re-examine a substantial portion of the canon; my ambition to enclose within a single account two national traditions expanded still further the list of works I felt obliged to treat. At the same time, the nature of my thesis required me to consider the works in their entirety: I could not demonstrate that the relationship of narration to authority was fundamental to the thematic structure of a work without providing a free-standing reading of that work. These considerations, along with my desire to produce a work useful to readers interested primarily in only one or two authors or novels, compelled me to choose a rather unimaginative format but one which I hope avoids the extremes of coercive synthesis or disconnected exegetic fragments. Following an introductory chapter which, like the ubiquitous "Author's preface" or narrative frame so popular in the eighteenth century, sets down the terms in which I wish my publication to be read, I treat each of the major works in (roughly) chronological order, recapitulating and developing the conceptual framework and the historical argument at the beginning of each chapter and in two short interchapters designed to clarify the theoretical notions and patterns of development that emerge from those readings, taken collectively.

Many of the issues I touch upon merit more attention than I can give them in this study, and the conclusions I draw should be understood as self-consciously provisional. My goal has not been to elaborate a comprehensive account of the eighteenth-century novel, but rather to explore some questions about how fiction relates to reality that seem to me fundamental to the genre's evolution during that period. Similarly, it was a conscious decision to seek a theory of narration and the novel within the stories the novels themselves tell about narration. There are many theoretical texts in the eighteenth century concerned with language, discourse, social hierarchies, political organization, or law, but nowhere does the practical use of narration to alter social identity and shared reality receive more sustained attention than in the novel – and nowhere is this attention more pertinent than in the very genre which, as a developing model of social reality, derives its own increasing authority over culture from its progressive refinement of narrative representation.

Accordingly, I have extrapolated my theoretical arguments primarily from the plots of the works themselves, and from other literary discussions concerned with fiction, rather than evaluating the novels against theories imported from other disciplines. Different portraits of the way the eighteenth century thought about fiction, history, and individual identity can no doubt be drawn on the basis of different documents and methodologies, and it is futile to argue the superiority of disciplinary biases. I would say only that my decision to use novels as evidence is based on the observation that there is no more logical place to learn about the status of fiction, history, and narrative than in the texts where those notions converge most explicitly. In the best of all possible cases, those who cannot bring themselves to accept the analysis of fictional texts as a firm ground for theoretical and historical generalizations will at least find in this book a series of interesting speculations they can explore subsequently with the investigative conventions of their choice.

Because I am dealing with two national traditions, thus including novels which may be unfamiliar to some readers, I have taken little for granted in my analyses and structured my exposition so that even the uninitiated reader should be able to follow the argument. I have also drawn my citations from readily accessible editions of the novels. Similarly, I have provided translations of the voluminous citations in French, taken in several cases from the contemporary translations with which an eighteenth-century English reader would have been familiar. I would hope that the length of the resulting volume is at least partially offset by the conceptual unity of the readings, which, if nothing else, have the merit of bringing together within a single interpretive framework two traditions that in my opinion have been artificially separated by the critical canon, in spite of fundamentally similar preoccupations and strategies.

Support for completion of this book was provided by Reed College, the National Endowment for the Humanities and the Camargo Foundation.

1

Introduction

The Muses wove, in the loom of Pallas, a loose and changeable robe, like that in which Falsehood captivated her admirers; with this they invested Truth, and named her Fiction.

Samuel Johnson, *The Rambler*

In the mid- to late eighteenth century there occurred in both France and England a remarkable reassessment of the function and truth value of fictional narratives. Increasingly relegated since the Renaissance to a position of mere amusement in comparison to factual accounts – "le Roman ne pense qu'à plaire, & l'Histoire ne pense qu'à instruire"[1] (the novel seeks only to please and history seeks only to instruct) – fiction suddenly emerges in the critical discourse as the primary vehicle for representing contemporary social reality, and even shaping that reality. As part of this reassessment, the commonplace that fiction exercised an influence on the morals of its readers received substantial re-examination and refinement, at the hands of the novel's proponents and detractors alike. One of genre's most rabid opponents in France implicitly concedes that social usage is determined by contemporary fiction – "où les jeunes gens en apprendront-ils les usages, si ce n'est dans la lecture des bons romans?"[2] (where will young people learn usages, if not in good novels?). The same writer attributes to the genre a pernicious, almost subliminal effect on personal beliefs and feelings which is equal to that of social intercourse:

> Les livres & les sociétés font les hommes... l'impression qu'ils font, même malgré nous, sur notre esprit & sur notre cœur, y porte toujours un germe de justesse ou de fausseté, de vertu ou de vice, quoique dans le moment de la lecture que nous en faisons, nous ne nous sentions que très-médiocrement affectés.[3]

> People are shaped by books and by the company they keep... the impression they [books] make on our minds and hearts inevitably plants, even in spite of

us, a seed of propriety or falseness, virtue or vice, even though at the time of our reading we may feel only moderately affected.

Similar ideas can be found in English essays of the time. Lord Kames, for instance, attributes to narrative an evocative force equivalent to that of actual perception: "A lively and accurate description . . . raises in me ideas no less distinct than if I had been originally an eye-witness."[4] Such ideas form what Kames calls "ideal presence" and he goes on to explain that "even genuine history has no command over our passions but by ideal presence only; and consequently . . . it stands upon the same footing with fable."[5] In fact, since the effect of both fictional and historical narratives "depends on the vivacity of the ideas they raise: . . . fable is generally more successful than history."[6] Kames' analysis further specifies that narrative representation does not merely affect one's feelings or passions; it also shapes our beliefs, since "when events are related in a lively manner, and every circumstance appears as passing before us, we suffer not patiently the truth of the facts to be questioned."[7]

Fiction, in other words, not only has an affective impact superior to that of factual accounts, it has the very capacity to generate "truth" and "facts" – provided, at least, the description it provides is "accurate." As Dr Johnson specifies, the single distinguishing feature about the new fiction, and the trait upon which all of its privileges are founded, is its representational accuracy with respect to contemporary social reality: "the works of fiction, with which the present generation seems more particularly delighted, are such as exhibit life in its true state, diversified only by accidents that daily happen in the world, and influenced by passions and qualities which are really to be found in conversing with mankind."[8] Johnson assumes that fiction reflects actual social interactions, and his further delineation of the author's task makes clear that the portrait of life presented by the novel must have a certain degree of historical specificity:

> The task of our present writers . . . requires, together with that learning which is to be gained from books, that experience which can never be attained by solitary diligence, but must arise from general converse and accurate observation of the living world.

> The chief advantage which these fictions have over real life is, that their authors are at liberty, though not to invent, yet to select objects, and to cull from the mass of mankind those individuals upon which the attention ought most to be employed.[9]

Writing thirty-five years later, Clara Reeve will insist more aggressively on the novel's historical referentiality, noting at one point that "the Novel is a picture of real life and manners, and of the times in which it is written,"[10] and later citing one of her contemporaries: "if you wish in a Novel to inculcate some moral truth ... there should always be a reference to the manners and the time in which it is written."[11] The French author Baculard d'Arnaud puts it more bluntly: "la vérité débarrassée de l'alliage imposteur est du nombre de ces phénoménes qui n'ont point encore été visibles à nos yeux: notre meilleure histoire, j'excepte nos livres sacrés, est le roman le moins grossier & le plus vraisemblable"[12] (unadulterated truth figures among those phenomena which have never yet been visible to our eyes: our best history, leaving aside the sacred scriptures, is the least crude and most realistic novel).

Arnaud overstates the case perhaps, but his assumption that truth is always mediated by some motivation or agenda, and hence beyond perception in a pure state, is representative of the skepticism that pervaded the age. The notion of the simple fact, and the simple narrative of such facts, had been under attack since the seventeenth century, as part of the reaction to what Michael McKeon has characterized as "naive empiricism,"[13] and its theoretical debunking reached a high point in the early eighteenth century as part of the critique of history. The foundations for this critique had been articulated by René Rapin in 1677, when he stipulated that "ce n'est pas écrire l'Histoire que de conter les actions des hommes, sans parler de leurs motifs; c'est faire le Gazetier, qui se contente de dire les évenemens des choses, sans remonter à leur source"[14] (it is not writing history to relate human actions without discussing their motives; it is emulating the news reporter, who is content to report the occurrence of things without tracing them back to their source). Rapin's insistence that causal explanation is a precondition for capturing the reader's interest and assuring the moral benefits of history will persist throughout the eighteenth century. Lenglet Du Fresnoy, for instance, will reaffirm that "l'histoire ne doit pas être seulement un narré fidèle des choses arrivées pour nous servir d'instruction, elle doit encore découvrir les causes & les motifs secrets des grands évenements, les ressorts & les intrigues que l'on a mis en œuvre pour y réüssir"[15] (to provide us instruction, history must not be simply an accurate account of things that have happened, it must also reveal the causes and secret motives of great events, the mechanisms and intrigues which were put into play in order to make them succeed). When Bolingbroke produces his analysis of the discipline of history, he correlates not only the ethical benefits but also the epistemological status of historical accounts to their contextualization and motivation: "Naked facts, without the causes that produced them and the circumstances that accompanied them, are not sufficient to characterize actions or counsels."[16] Rousseau states the case even more strongly:

Mais qu'entend-on par ce mot de faits? ... Croit-on que la véritable connaiss-ance des événements soit séparable de celle de leurs causes, de celle de leurs effets, et que l'historique tienne si peu au moral qu'on puisse connaître l'un sans l'autre? Si vous ne voyez dans les actions des hommes que les mouve-ments extérieurs et purement physiques, qu'apprenez-vous dans l'histoire? Absolument rien ... [17]

But what do people mean by this word "facts"? ... Do they believe that the genuine knowledge of events is separable from that of their causes, from that of their effects, and that the historical is so unrelated to the moral that one could know one without the other? If you see in human action only external, purely physical movements, what are you learning in history? Absolutely nothing ...

The interrogation of historical writing reveals an implicit assumption in the second half of the century that the human partitioning of reality which we call "events" can only be grasped in the form of a complex economy of intentions, causes, and moral contexts. In its broadest sense as a cultural matrix, such a contextual framework accounts for the specific patterns of behavior that characterize a given society and color its construals of the world. The eighteenth century's interest in such notions is attested to by numerous theoretical essays on culture, as well as by works such as Montes-quieu's *Lettres persanes*, Argens' *Lettres juives*, or Johnson's *Rasselas*. By depicting the mores of their epoch and nation from the "outside," as they might be seen by someone from another land, and juxtaposing these mores to those of other civilized nations, these works put into question the assumption that human events are simply "given"; they reflect a growing fascination with the idea that much of what people take for granted as "normal" or true is merely the reflection of shared cultural biases – pre-judices that are inherited through tradition, reinforced by structures of authority, and inculcated through habit. A similar notion of cultural relativ-ism pervades the theories of history of the period in the form of those inherited prejudices which vitiate the historian's objectivity. As Bolingbroke puts it, "the accidental and other causes, which give rise and growth to opinions, both in speculation and practice, are of infinite variety; and where ever these opinions are once confirmed by custom and propagated by education, various, inconsistent, contradictory as they are, they all pretend (and all their pretences are backed up by pride, by passion, and by interest) to have reason, or revelation, or both on their side."[18]

I would argue that the novel's promotion as a representational vehicle is linked to the increasing conviction that both individual and social truths are rooted in continually evolving codes of behavior, contexts of belief, religious biases, and ethical assumptions, most of which are beyond the scope of traditional historical accounts. For the eighteenth century, classical history's fascination with military and political upheavals and the careers of great figures that shape the human record, blinded it to the crucial dimension of cultural determination, the subtle codes which evolve over time under the pressure of re-expression and reinterpretation, changing what counts as facts for their society and historical epoch. As Voltaire laments,

> après avoir lu trois ou quatre mille descriptions de batailles, et la teneur de quelques centaines de traités, j'ai trouvé que je n'étais guère plus instruit au fond. Je n'apprenais là que des événements. Je ne connais pas plus les Français et les Sarrasins par la bataille de Charles Martel, que je ne connais les Tartares et les Turcs par la victoire que Tamerlan remporta sur Bajazet. ... quiconque veut lire l'histoire en citoyen et en philosophe...recherchera quel a été le vice radical et la vertu dominante d'une nation...les changements dans les mœurs et dans les lois seront enfin son grand objet. On saurait ainsi l'histoire des hommes, au lieu de savoir une faible partie de l'histoire des rois et des cours[19]

> after having read three or four thousand descriptions of battles, and the equivalent of a few hundred treatises, I found that basically, I was scarcely more knowledgeable. I was only learning events there. The battle of Charles Martel teaches me no more about the French and the Sarrasins than Tamerlan's victory over Bajazet tells me about the Tartars and the Turks.... whoever wants to read history as a citizen and a philosopher will try to learn what the fundamental vice and dominant virtue of a nation have been... changes in behavior and in the laws will ultimately be his primary object. In this way one could know the history of mankind, instead of knowing a small part of the history of the kings and courts.

However, the very idea of an informing cultural matrix puts into question the historian's claim of factuality. The narration of the remote past necessarily expresses and rationalizes the collectively validated usages and conventions of the history writer's own epoch, but cannot be assured of perceiving those of the "target" society or period.

It is just such collectively maintained assumptions which the realistic fiction of the period undertakes to represent on two fronts, by focusing its attention on the social practices *of which it is itself an expression*.[20] Freed from the limitations of factual fidelity, assured of representing the biases of the culture it depicts by virtue of its own enclosure within that culture, the novel can formulate, analyse, and illustrate general paradigms of social interaction explicitly through its plot structure, at the same time that it exemplifies in its gesture of narration the conventions of communication and representation underlying such interactions. In other words, the eighteenth-century novel instantiates or stands for the culture it depicts; in this sense the novel can claim to "be" history: it represents the system it represents.[21]

One might argue that all modes of mimesis more or less explicitly partake of this double sense of representation, in which the ordering gesture's exemplification of norms overlays or seconds the order represented. But the eighteenth-century novel makes the double mode of representation a self-conscious practice, deliberately aligning its own narrational practice with the one it depicts – and vice versa. The great works which were instrumental in the genre's consecration as social record do not casually, or merely theoretically, express the cultural model that infuses them with their authority; they explicitly and insistently portray social reality as driven by a cultural engine that functions as the novel itself functions, specifying and coordinating private and collective experience through narrative mechanisms. The plot structure, thematic fabric, and mode of presentation of eighteenth-century fiction all work together to assimilate the idea of truth, its human correlate identity, and the instrumental conjunction of the two – authority – to the narrative processes which that fiction deploys in its structuring and re-presentation of social reality.

Most accessible at the level of plot and theme, this "narrativation" of reality becomes increasingly apparent as the century progresses. It pervades the early novels of individualism in the form of the accounts of personal experience which the protagonists use to combat or internalize the systems of authority and social hierarchy limiting their mobility. In later works the merger of private and collective reality, and frequently the manipulation or structuring of the community by the individual, form the backbone of more ambitious agendas of narrative organization. All of these novels foreground the way in which the narration or relating of experience legislates through representation, by imposing an order on reality and an identity on the narrator(s). But while the early novels focus primarily on the use of narration as a means of self-assertion and the local, provisional subversion of authority systems, subsequent works dramatize how the narratives which result from such acts of narration can shape collective behavior by literally becoming part of shared history. Assimilated to the public discourse of the community in the form of circulated stories, narratives of exemplary conduct redefine the social hierarchy and modify the script of acceptable behavior to which the exercise of authority looks for its rationalization. Eventually, the novel comes to acknowledge its own exemplification of this process of circulation and dissemination – and even its function as an authoritative expression of, and template for, the contemporary world. However, this acknowledgment occurs only within the context of a dialectical reformulation which forecloses on the possibility of cultural domination by any single narrative or author.

My alternating reliance here on metaphors of imitation and instrumentality is meant to convey my own intention that the novel's representative function be neither reduced to mere reflection of a pre-existing state of affairs, nor inflated to a role of direct legislation. Studies of the eighteenth-century novel have frequently assumed that the imitation of complex social reality is a natural objective, in the pursuit of which the novel developed its strategies of "realistic" narration; and one can naturally conceptualize the tendencies I trace in the following readings as mere responses to evolving attitudes about reality. However, given the novel's phenomenal popularity in the period, and the amount of ink devoted in the eighteenth century to analysing its effect on the moral and intellectual fibre of both France and England, it seems naive to assume that realistic fiction did not itself contribute to those evolving attitudes. In fact, the case for mere imitation collapses, if taken literally, since the world the novel portrays, and the model of narrative transaction it promotes (both of which must be assumed to be essentially accurate, within the logic of the imitation argument) come to postulate a dialectical relationship of mutual determination between individual construal and shared construct. Read as successive emplotments of a larger trend, the period's most influential works demonstrate, albeit with local variations, that personal initiatives, and *a fortiori* narration, are both framed by and react to, a cultural matrix of scripts, codes, and conventions from which they draw their authority, but which they in turn reconfigure, however slightly, if only through their own innovations of usage. Within the context of such a model, which will be dramatized repeatedly and graphically within the plots of the period, the novel is neither simply the product nor the producer of the patterns it depicts and exemplifies, but both at all moments.

Michael McKeon's monumental study of the origins of the English novel provides a useful framework for understanding the double function of representation which I attribute to the novel, and which I think informs its evolution. McKeon postulates that " 'the novel' must be understood as what Marx calls a 'simple abstraction,' a deceptively monolithic category that encloses a complex historical process. It attains its modern, 'institutional' stability and coherence at this time because of its unrivaled power both to formulate, and to explain, a set of problems that are central to early modern experience. These may be understood as problems of categorical instability, which the novel, originating to resolve, also inevitably reflects."[22] The categorical instabilities which concern McKeon involve shifts during the seventeenth and eighteenth centuries in attitudes about how to signify or tell truth and how to signify virtue, and his thesis, to oversimplify it, is that the novel ultimately attained pre-eminence and generic coherence because of its ability to mediate (express, render intelligible, and hence in some measure reconcile within a broadly accommodating form) the conflicting narrative strategies and ideologies which succeeded one another during the period of transition from romance idealism and aristocratic ideology to the modern era.

One of the ways of "signifying the truth" with which McKeon deals in depth is the "claim to historicity" which becomes widespread in the seventeenth century and which functions in his argument as romance's response to the early modern historicist revolution (*Origins*, p. 53). By claiming to be factual, early prose fiction, like the various news sheets, official gazettes, travel accounts, exotic biographies, and pseudo-historical genres which proliferated during the period, attempts to capitalize on the naive empiricist assumption that history can be separated from romance in narrative – that fact can be distinguished from fable. As McKeon sees it, this claim to historicity competes during the early modern period with the Aristotelian notion of verisimilitude, and while he casts their competition in terms of a provisional domination by the claim to historicity during the seventeenth century and an eventual victory by verisimilitude "as the reformulated doctrine of 'realism,'" his overall theory of fictional mediation specifies that both could co-exist within the genre of the novel conceived as an abstract category.[23] The moment and phenomenon which interest me in the present study can be conceptualized in somewhat similar terms as the novel's coming to terms with its incompatible identities as fiction and truth – private construct and public structure – by formulating a dialectic of personal narration and narrative truth that grounds each in the other.

In the terms of my discussion above, the claim to historicity, which persists in an increasingly vestigial form in the prefaces of the novels which I will be studying, predicates a merely "imitative" form of narrative as a simple reflection of reality – a narrative which, to the extent it purports to be unadulterated by personal motive, denies the history of its own production in an interested act of narration. Fable, conversely, is a narrative postulated to have no referent other than its narration: it produces a simulacrum of reality behind which there is no historical reality. History is a story *produced by* reality, fable a story *productive of* reality, and both are presumed to stand *outside of* reality. Such pure forms are of course reciprocal delusions, limiting cases of theoretical value which, if implemented, would lead to self-cancelling excesses. The historicist delusion is that there can be an account *of* human reality that is not mediated by an act situated *in* human reality and vitiated by the biases of that situation – that there can be a narrative produced directly by reality that is immune to the processes of change it chronicles. The converse delusion is that there could be a narrative having no origins in reality, but capable of modifying – or, as is generally the charge, corrupting – reality. Like the radical claim to historicity, the radical charge of fictionality denies the framing of the text (and its producer) *in* reality or history, and the consequent "representative" nature of that narrator's postulates.[24]

Both of these excessive conceptualizations resist what we might call the historical situation of history and historians, narration and narratives, authoritative orders and gestures of ordering; and it is the varieties of such resistance, and the consequences to which it leads, which the eighteenth-century novel systematically explores, then ultimately rejects, in its ongoing interrogation of how individual story relates to collective history. One of the implicit theses of the readings making up this book is that the thematic evolution of the eighteenth-century French and English novel can be understood as a gradual coming to terms with the complexities of a genuine historical consciousness, one which conceives of the identity of individuals and societies, and the orders of authority that modulate their behavior, in terms of a continual process of recounting and rearticulation that is regulated by, and derives its authority from, the accumulating context of its own past narratives. Within such a model, (reconfiguring) narration and (grounding) narrative, story and history, are but different faces/phases of the same equation, as are, from the perspective of the social economy underwritten by that equation, individual behavior and collective norm. To that extent, the gradual emergence of historical consciousness entails a concomitant reassessment of personal freedom and collective authority.

At first glance the French and English novels of the eighteenth century seem rather different: the rarified atmosphere of stylized posturing, marivaudage, *esprit*, social codes, and worldliness that is typically associated with the French novel, and which prompted Ian Watt to dismiss the entire tradition from *La Princesse de Clèves* to *Les Liaisons dangereuses* as being peripheral to the mainstream development of the realistic novel, seems to have as little in common with the matter-of-fact coupling and commercial maneuvering of Moll Flanders and Roxana, or Richardson's dramas of tyrannical authority and struggling virtue, as with Fielding's earthy comic epics.[25] This apparent discordance is reflected in the critical tradition as well. While critics of the English novels have by and large approached them thematically, focusing on their moral and psychological dimensions, their treatment of selfhood, and the interpersonal relationships of the characters within the plot, students of the French tradition have, as often as not, been drawn to purely technical questions of formal affiliation, technique, and style.[26] And, until recently, few studies of one tradition seemed to take the other into consideration.[27]

Such partiality is all the more remarkable in light of the intense fascination which the French and English exercised for each other during the eighteenth century, each functioning as the essential "Other" against which national achievements or generalizations were elaborated. Beyond their political and religious differences, they seemed to exemplify for each other alternative paradigms of honor, citizenship, and national character, and different ways of envisioning the individual's relationship to the collective. Comparisons between the two nations – which tellingly incline to a favorable judgment of the rival in almost every case – abound in the critical and moral literature of the period, from Voltaire's remarks on the English in the *Lettres philosophiques* or d'Argens' extended comparison of the two cultures in the *Lettres juives*, to John Brown's tirade against the effeminization of the English character and praise of the French sense of honor, in *An Estimate of the Manners and Principles of the Times*, or even Sterne's accounts of his French journeys in *Tristram Shandy* and *Sentimental Journey*.[28] As concerns the novel's development, there is ample evidence that if the novelists of the two countries were not as well acquainted with each other personally as were the historians and philosophers, they were nonetheless acutely aware, and appreciative, of their counterparts across the channel. All of the works I will be covering in this study were translated into the other language, some appearing almost simultaneously.[29] Many enjoyed a success across the channel equal to their influence at home. English authors of the period regularly refer to the work of their French contemporaries, and the latter acknowledge the influence of the English not only in their theoretical essays, but also in their own novels, several of which openly borrow techniques and themes from British precedents.[30]

However I have no intention of formulating any theories of influence in this study. My consideration of French and English works within a single argument is based solely on the observation that whatever their formal differences, the most popular and influential novels of both countries share a common insistence on the act of narrative representation broadly construed. In both traditions the *relating* of acts and facts – the organization, articulation, and reconciliation of private experience and shared reality within a narrative structure – provides a mainspring for similar agendas of individualism and a paradigm for the emerging notion of a shared cultural script. Narration and narratives are not the only things these novels talk about, nor even in most cases the central theme of the plot. Moreover, as the century progresses, the practice of representation is linked to different projects, varying from the internalization of divine authority to the creation of elaborate masks and plots to destroy one's social rivals. But all of the novels explicitly thematize the extent to which social existence and the social order are regulated by acts of relating and ordering, accounting and recounting, as well as by the narratives which circulate in society as a result of such acts. Whatever else they may be, these novels are stories about stories, representations of representation; and they all implicitly argue that reality – the assumptions, rules, and beliefs which are shared by all members of a society – is elaborated through constant narration and sustained as a shared narrative. The consistency of this emphasis, and the fact that in both countries the genre evolves toward narrative self-consciousness and explicitly metanarrative works which put into question the mechanism of fiction itself as an exemplary form of narrative, seems to suggest a far stronger affinity than the critical tradition has heretofore acknowledged.

In the readings that follow, I shall try to show that taken collectively the novels can be seen as episodes in the larger story of an evolving relationship in the eighteenth century between individual acts of representation and the systems of authority that frame them – parental, Divine, political, economic, and increasingly, I shall argue, historical-cultural. As the genre of the novel matures, it tends to portray authority in more explicitly consensual and narrative terms, as an interaction between the postulates of identifiable acts of narration – personal relations which impose a structure on experience – and the evolving horizon, or composite narrative of reality regulating social values and framing such individual instances of narration. This shared narrative will develop in scope and formality from the gossip of a small social cohort, which delimits shared experience at some junction in time, to the all-encompassing script of usages, beliefs, and origins which defines the society as a whole and frames its members' expressions of experience within a network of competing meanings and construals of reality. Eventually, after testing several scenarios of domination of one side of the narrative equation by the other, the novel will reconcile them in an unstable dialectic, which, as intimated above, can be grasped as the tension between history's two identities: an ordering of events and an order of reality; an ongoing act of narration linking individual to collective in a mutual construal of reality, and a shared narrative structure of experience that both results from and enables that construal.[31]

Recently critics have begun to enlarge the definition of narration to include the fundamental ordering activity of consciousness, as it makes sense out of the world and asserts its identity.[32] One can make a similar case for narration as the indispensable complement of analysis or reflection: the act by which, whatever the genre of our discourse – scientific, philosophical, artistic, historical, or moral – we posit the entities to be analyzed. This is a notion which emerges in the theoretical literature of the eighteenth century. L'Abbé Trublet, for instance, points out in 1735 that analysis and narration are complementary phases of the conceptualization of reality; all logical analysis builds on *related* events, every account of the past implies an analysis of reality:

> on peut rapporter tout ce qui se dit dans la conversation à ces deux chefs, conter & raisonner. On raisonne sur les affaires, sur les sciences, sur les moyens de venir à bout de quelque chose: on conte des nouvelles; on fait le récit d'une aventure arrivée à soi-même, ou à un autre; on cite un trait d'histoire. Ces deux manières de converser se mêlent et se succedent: on raisonne sur un fait, sur une nouvelle, & on appuye un raisonnement d'un fait, d'un exemple.[33]

We can assign everything that is said in conversation to the two categories of telling and reasoning. We reason on affairs, the sciences, the means of achieving something: we relate news; we tell the story of an adventure that befell us, or someone else; we cite an historical anecdote. These two means of conversing mingle and alternate: we reason on the basis of a fact, a piece of news, and we substantiate our reasoning with a fact, an example.

This sense of narration as the positional phase (or face) of discourse and the complement of reflection hovers in the background of the works I will be studying, some of which postulate explicitly that to recount feelings, actions, plans, or judgments, or even just to describe an event, is to impose oneself on the world. Through speech people body themselves forth and consolidate their identity in the social environment, and in this sense all discourse precipitates an historical residue: "je parle, & dans l'instant mes idées & mes sentiments se communiquent à celui qui m'écoute; toute mon âme passe en quelque sorte dans la sienne"[34] (I speak, and instantly my ideas and feelings are communicated to the person listening to me; my whole soul passes into his in a sense). To *relate* events is to determine their relationship in the mind of the listener, and to the extent the listener participates in the conversation, he or she sanctions a way of organizing reality as well as the very existence of the components making up that reality.

This dialogical dimension of narration forms one of the central concerns of the eighteenth century. Whether narration aims at characterizing a person or event, seducing a victim, formulating an abstract rule, pronouncing judgment, or even simply amusing the reader, it necessarily looks to an Other for its endorsement or ratification. The Other can be a single person, a group of people, an anonymous collective, or a well-defined public; it can be present in the dialogue, as a partner in conversation, or removed in space or time, as the recipient of a letter, a reading public, or the posterity to which an author appeals. But an Other there must be, acknowledging and corroborating – or resisting – the narrational initiatives. Although the limits which the Other poses for narration seem at first glance more immediate than those of the accumulated conventions framing the narrative, they are in fact only enactments of those rules, as the later novels will come to understand. In the dialogical transaction, the narrator structures the narratee's world, while the narratee validates the narrator's formulations; but this transaction, which prefigures the integration of the individual into the community, merely expresses an interpersonal correlate of the more abstract dialectical relationship of story to history that figures the assimilation of personal account into shared truth.

Finally, the dialogical relationship of individual and Other is inextricable from the play between narration and narrative. Conversation is narration in its most evanescent form, but even conversation produces a narrative residue, or *representative order* which is placed into circulation by virtue of being articulated by the narrator and validated by the interlocutor. If narration is the act of relating, narrative can be thought of as the order which results from such acts and which can be transmitted to another individual: a story that is retold, a judgment that is reiterated, a rumor that is repeated. Narrative relates to narration in the same way a story does to its telling or reading, or a song to its singing. In the books we will be looking at, narratives are frequently disseminated by a material document – letters that are passed around, a diary that is reread, or even a literary work that is published, but they need not be: *viz.* the nearly ubiquitous collective narrative of reputation which regulates individual identity in the eighteenth century. Nor do they always retain as part of their referential field the moment of their narration or the identity of their author. This is the case with those narratives which transmit or maintain collective usages and protocols, such as public records. Typically, the exercise of authority involves appeals to such anonymous scripts.

The novels I examine in this work will propose various construals of the rapport between personal and public experience, individual will and collective authority, entailing different formulations of how personal narration, with its interpretation of events and expression of personal values, interacts with the shared, evolving script of collective assumptions. While the novels do not present a neat linear development in their handling of these questions, and in fact occasionally propose, as part of their moral deliberations, contrasting and incompatible models, certain trends are discernable. These trends form the line of argument of my study, which I present less as a demonstration piece for a current methodology or theoretical credo, than as an extended reading of one type of fictional discourse. In keeping with the implicit assumption of this discourse that truth is a function of the *relations* one produces (in both senses of that word), I have chosen to present my readings as a story, whose thematics – and persuasiveness as a viable way of understanding the eighteenth century – gradually unfold out of its episodes. Current critical discourse abounds in theories of history and theories of narrative, as well as theories of how each relates to the other, and many of these texts provide rich contexts for reassessing the eighteenth century's thought on the subject.[35] However, my objective in this study has not been to formulate a theory of narrative and history, much less a history of such theories, but rather to re-animate a distinctive eighteenth-century model of discourse which uses representation to subvert the distinction between story and theory.

At the same time, since one of the lessons of the stories of narration permeating the eighteenth-century novel is that all gestures of relating derive from, and tend toward, totalizing narratives or systems of ordering the world, I shall not pretend to have perceived no historical patterns in my readings. At the heart of my story lies the question of the extent to which individual acts of representation can alter the perceptions of other people, but the question rapidly expands in the century as it becomes apparent that narrative representation motivates not only personal action and the identity or rank of the individual within society, but also the collective values, laws, institutions of authority, and traditions which are assumed to limit such acts. In general as the century advances, the thematization of narration and narrative becomes more explicit and the models of their relationship more abstract.

The earliest works – those of Lafayette, Chasles, Defoe, Prévost, and Marivaux – focus primarily on the individual's relationship to the collective systems of authority that assign social identity and limit the range of personal initiative. The very notion of social identity, or the particular mix of station, function, rights, and privileges which is assigned to each individual by the collective and which determines the range of action and freedom of that individual, emerges in these novels as distinct from, but subject to re-evaluation on the basis of, the more rigorous concept of identity involving the intrinsic moral character of the individual.[36] Increasingly, the allocation of public esteem is associated with a reassessment of the individual's true worth, as manifest in the account of his or her past actions. Within this context, self-representation provides a strategy for determining one's own identity: by producing more compelling accounts of one's self than those presumed by the existing hierarchy, the distinctive protagonist generates a frame of identity capable of displacing the established order.[37] The most fundamental form of such self-representation, and the variety that dominates in the early novels of individualism, is that of immediate, oral narration, directed at particular interlocutor in view of producing a specific effect.

A more refined model of instrumental narration, adumbrated by Marivaux but epitomized by Richardson's works and present in a more ambitious, abstract form in Rousseau's, associates the narration of selfhood with a stable narrative or textual record which represents the protagonist in a larger community long after its initial formulation. More precisely defined as meticulous chronicles of personal experience, the narratives generated in these works by the attempt to "account" for oneself merge into the order of shared history as they are validated by an ever-expanding readership whose deliberations and discussions legislate moral standards. As an embodiment of ideal moral behavior, the individual's story assumes the function of a template or exemplar for the reconfiguration of collective values by the larger community, whose informal negotiations and re-presentations of that story explicitly constitute the society's moral authority. Self-representation thus acquires a formative function with respect to the discourse of the community even as it engineers its assimilation as narrative into the shared record.

The volatility of this model becomes apparent in the novels of Fielding, Rousseau, and Diderot, where rather than being limited to a few virtuous or vicious, but similarly gifted, individuals, representation is extended to society at large and becomes the paradigmatic social act. The result is an environment of intense narrative competition where truth is relativized and the triumph of the virtuous can only be insured through the postulation of a higher, more informed level of narrative authority capable of penetrating the motives of the individual and orchestrating the social interaction. Such authority, predictably, is associated with uninvolved narration – namely that of the professional Author or law-giver, who, with the cooperation of the Reader, establishes and guides the relationships of the narrative economy depicted in the novel in view of extracting moral lessons.

The Author and Reader are not to be confused with the real author or reader: hence the use of the uppercase, which I shall maintain throughout the study. They are metacharacters emplotted within the novel, though at a higher level of consciousness overseeing – and seeing through – the self-interested ploys of the "characters." Proposing rival construals of fictional events, but dependent on each other's sanction for the validation of their postulates, they "relate" to each other according to the paradigm of rivalry and dependence that reigns in the emplotted world, exemplifying in the more literal terms of the literary transaction, the dialogical structure of selfhood and authority. I would suggest, however, that their appearance simultaneously with the postulation of a generalized narrative economy, functions as an oblique acknowledgment of the problems implicit in the notion of narratively generated truth, and as an even more oblique proposition for remedying those problems.

Rendering explicit the power of the fictional author even as they ironize it, the metanovels intimate the need for a dispassionate, detached representation of the world – one that could, by virtue of its omniscient disinterest, represent various social behaviors and types in their true colors. The Author, precursor to the omniscient narrator of the nineteenth century, provides just such a form of authority – at least that is what these novels imply, through their gradual displacement of personal narration with professional narrative. However, the claim of cultural authority is one they dare not articulate explicitly, for fear of compromising their claim of detached representation and opening themselves to charges of moral subversion.

They thus use the Author/Reader dialogue as a prototype for a dialectical recasting of the relationship between personal narration and shared narrative which will shield the novelist from any such charges by postulating a law of cultural enclosure.

The Author and Reader do not only depend on each other; they are also culturally bound: their structuring of reality occurs according to a set of narrative conventions that functions as a microcosmic equivalent of the cultural grammar enclosing the emplotted characters. In other words, the framing of their rivalry and mutual determination within a framework of narrative conventions, upon which both rely even as they strive to revise it, provides a precise model of the dialectical enclosure of personal and collective action within the process and structure of history. Even individuals possessed of a dispassionate command of the conventions governing human interactions, these novels seem to say, are themselves necessarily framed by rules of construal which enable their gestures. More to the point, even negative thematizations of conventional fields obligatorily rely on the grammars they subvert: this is what the Authors demonstrate, in their obsession with undermining established fictional conventions.

The lesson of cultural enclosure which the Author and Reader enact in literary terms reiterates the more graphic and brutal stories of deluded narrative mastery which the plots depict. From *Clarissa* to *Les Liaisons dangereuses* the figure of the master narrator forms a recurrent motif in the novel's plot, either in the form of a social manipulator intent on destroying rivals, or an epistemological buffoon, attempting to organize history or reality. The libertine monsters, in particular, indulge in the delusion that having mastered the codes of their society they can orchestrate history to their own advantage; and the repeated drama of their self-destruction as a consequence of plots they initiate but can no longer control serves to drive home the point that every articulation of reality, even the most averted, is enabled by, and subject to, grammars it cannot understand. This truth is one the novel cannot state as such, without compromising its validity: it cannot claim to *comprehend* the specifics of its historical enclosure without presupposing a transcendence or bracketing of that enclosure. But it is a truth which can be dramatized, both in the plot and in the relationship of the Author and Reader to that plot; and in that form it functions strategically to disarm any accusations of cultural hegemony that might be levelled at the novel. By thematizing the impossibility of a culturally authoritative narrative that would not itself reflect the frame of the culture in which it is produced, the novel can exercise its authority even as it denies it: it makes a recurrent theme of the impossibility of the task it performs, namely the understanding and predication of the social and cultural codes which enable it.

With time, the formal imposture of the omniscient, detached Author(ity) will become conventionalized, and the insistence on the framing matrix which limits personal initiative will undercut the dialectic model itself, by demoting personal acts of structuring to a position of relative impotence in comparison to the increasingly impersonal systems perceived to govern human reality. When, in 1842, Balzac roundly declares his ambitions in the "Avant-Propos" to the *Comédie humaine*, he takes for granted that even though the constitutive trait of the human animal is its representational bent, individual acts of representation have only a local function of expressing their agent. The complexity of social reality is tautologically attributed to the impersonal environmental system of "Society," the human equivalent of "Nature," which determines the shape of the individual species making it up, but exceeds determination by any individual.[38] Predictably, Balzac declines responsibility for the stereotypes he proposes, declaring himself the mere secretary of Society. His novels, though, will continue to function referentially, under the umbrella of their impartiality, by providing the history of social behavior which history has never written ("Avant-Propos," p. 5). For if it is given, by the time Balzac writes, that novels are the vehicle for knowledge about society and a primary repository of cultural values, it is also taken for granted that they deny their hand in the organization of the world.

NOTES

1 René Rapin, *Instructions pour l'histoire* (1677) 2nd edn (Paris: Claude Cellier, 1690), p. 30.
2 Armand-Pierre Jacquin, *Entretiens sur les romans: Ouvrage moral et critique* (Paris: Duchesne, 1755), p. 354.
3 Jacquin, *Entretiens sur les romans*, pp. 104–5.
4 Henry Home, Lord Kames, *Elements of criticism* (1761), 11th edn (London: B. Blake, 1839), p. 35.
5 Ibid. p. 36.
6 Ibid. p. 37.
7 Ibid. p. 39.
8 *Rambler*, no. 4 (March 31, 1750) 4 vols. (London: W. Suttaby, 1809), vol. 1, p. 18.
9 Ibid., pp. 18–19, 21.
10 Clara Reeve, *Progress of Romance* (1785), 2 vols in one (New York: New York Text Facsimile Society, 1930), vol. 1, p. 111.
11 Ibid., vol. 2, p. 92, the quote is from *The Trial, or the History of Charles Horton, Esq.*
12 F. M. Baculard d'Arnaud. "Préface aux *Nouvelles Historiques*" (1774), in *Œuvres complètes*, 5 vols (Amsterdam: Michel Rey, 1775), vol. 4, p. 8.

13 Michael McKeon, *Origins of the English Novel 1600–1740* (Baltimore: Johns Hopkins University Press, 1987). Although I only became acquainted with McKeon's study after completing the bulk of this book, I have attempted in the following discussion to situate my own argument with respect to his thesis, with which I essentially agree.

14 Rapin, *Instructions pour l'histoire*, p. 63.

15 Nicolas Lenglet Du Fresnoy, *De l'usage des romans*, 2 vols (Amsterdam, 1735), vol. 1, p. 53. For Rapin's correlation of causal explanation and moral efficacy, see *Instructions pour l'histoire*, p. 65.

16 Henry St John, Lord Viscount Bolingbroke, *Letters on the Study and Use of History*, a new edition, corrected (London: A. Millar, 1752), p. 135.

17 Jean-Jacques Rousseau, *Emile* (1762), ed. François et Pierre Richard (Paris: Garnier, 1961), p. 106.

18 Bolingbroke, *Letters*, p. 405.

19 Voltaire, "Nouvelles considérations sur l'histoire," in *Œuvres historiques*, ed. René Pomeau (Paris: Gallimard "Editions de la Pléiade," 1957), pp. 47–8.

20 Fiction is of course not the only mode of expression of those collective codes. The rapid growth in the eighteenth century of periodicals such as the *Tatler* and the *Spectator* testifies to a lively interest in identifying the shared assumptions, codes, and shifting fashions of one's society, as does, more generally, the growth of the institution of coherent collective discourse which Jürgen Habermas has called the public sphere; *Strukturwandel der Öffentlichkeit* (1962), 17th printing, Darmstadt: Hermann Luchterhand, 1987; see also Terry Eagleton, *The Function of Criticism* (London: Verso Editions and New Left Books, 1984).

21 This is an aspect of the genre we now take for granted. But in the eighteenth century it only gained currency gradually with the conviction that society was regulated by a "body of customary beliefs, social forms, and material traits constituting a distinct complex of tradition," to borrow part of Webster's definition of "culture"; *Webster's Third New International Dictionary* (Springfield, Mass.: G. and C. Merriam, 1966), s.v. "culture."

22 McKeon, *Origins*, p. 20.

23 Ibid. p. 53.

24 In his discussion of the notion of fiction, Jean-François Marmontel dubunks the correlative delusion of an imagination capable of creating anything of nothingness, arguing instead that fiction consists of an origianl configuration or "mosaic" of elements which are necessarily drawn from nature; *Eléments de littérature* (1787), 3 vols (Paris: Firmin Didot, 1846), vol. 2, pp. 173–85.

25 For a excellent definition of worldliness and its role in the French novel, see Peter Brooks, *The Novel of Worldliness* (Princeton: Princeton University Press, 1969). Ronald Rosbottom, *Marivaux's Novels: Theme and Function in Early Eighteenth-Century Narrative* (Rutherford, New Jersy: Fairleigh Dickinson University Press, 1974), also provides a good analysis of worldliness in the French novel as it is exemplified by Marivaux. Brooks cites Watt's neglect of the French tradition in *The Rise of the Novel* (London: Chatto and Windus, 1957; citations are from the Peregrine Press reprint of 1985), and convincingly argues that Watt's idea of "le réel écrit" is too narrowly focused on the material

circumstances of human existence and fails to take into account the importance of social relations and the "consciousness of society as a system of values, forces, choices" in defining human reality. It is this social dimension which interested the French *moralistes*, and their role in the development of the novel, particularly the novel of manners, is far more important than Watt acknowledges; *Novel of Worldliness*, pp. 88–90. English Showalter feels simply that Watt "does not offer much more than his own subjective impressions of what is 'real' in a novel," *The Evolution of the French Novel 1641–1782* (Princeton: Princeton University Press, 1972), p. 7, while Georges May, whose heavily documented *Le Dilemme du roman au XVIIIe siècle* (New Haven: Yale University Press, 1963), traces the evolution of the French novel in terms of the pressure exerted by a reactionary critical establishment in the first half of the century, singles out Watt's strange assessment of the French tradition as a good example of the misprisions to which a poor understanding of the contemporary historical conditions could lead (p. 7). If Watt's theory ignores the entire French tradition, it also has difficulty accounting for the presence of Fielding in the middle of the century and for the persisting popularity of romance, with its many reactionary, non-middle class tendencies: cf. McKeon, *Origins*, pp. 1–4. McKeon's account of the genre's rise in terms of dialectical reversals of larger epistemological and ethical trends is not only more compelling than Watt's, but has the added virtue of being applicable in many respects to the French tradition as well as the English.

26 May's book, almost exclusively concerned with historical evaluations of the novel, is a case in point. Vivienne Mylne, *The Eighteenth-century French Novel: Techniques of Illusion* (Manchester: Manchester University Press, 1965) catalogues the technical advances towards "accurate representation and . . . creating an illusion of reality" (p. 2); while English Showalter, one of the few critics to appreciate the importance of Robert Chasles, takes as his objective in *Evolution* to demonstrate how various techniques of realism transformed the seventeenth-century romance into its more realistic eighteenth-century successor. Philip Stewart, *Imitation and Illusion in the French Memoir-Novel, 1700–1750* (New Haven: Yale University Press, 1969), is similarly concerned with techniques of illusion, with particular attention to the memoir novels of the period. Geoffrey Bennington, *Sententiousness and the Novel: Laying Down the Law in Eighteenth-century French Fiction*, (Cambridge: Cambridge University Press, 1985), provides a fresh perspective on early French fiction by examining the tradition and form of maximal or sentential writing from the perspective of structuralist and post-structuralist theory. Peggy Kamuf's *Fictions of Feminine Desire* (Lincoln, Nebraska: University of Nebraska Press, 1982), while not strictly speaking a general account of the eighteenth-century French novel, nonetheless contains some valuable feminist/post-structuralist readings of the period's major works. A classic example of the English thematic approach can be found in Dorothy Van Ghent, *The English Novel: Form and Function*, (New York: Rinehart and Company, 1953). More recently, Terry Castle's interesting *Masquerade and Civilization* (Stanford: Stanford University Press, 1986) examines the sociological implications of the masquerade in eighteenth-century England and its

function in the period's fiction. Eve Tavor, *Scepticism, Society, and the Eighteenth-century Novel* (New York: St Martin's Press, 1987) reads Defoe, *Clarissa*, *Tom Jones*, and *Tristram Shandy* as embodiments of the sceptical tradition. Two studies that pivot on the idea of selfhood are Patricia Meyer Spacks, *Imagining a Self*, (Cambridge, Mass.: Harvard University Press, 1976), and John Preston, *The Created Self: the Reader's Role in Eighteenth-century Fiction*, (London: Heinemann, 1970), which examines the image of the reader which Defoe, Richardson, Fielding, and Sterne "created" as a projection of their narrative gesture.

27   Recent exceptions are Nancy K. Miller, *The Heroine's Text: Readings in the French and English Novel, 1722–1782*, (New York: Columbia University Press, 1980); Rita Goldberg, *Sex and the Enlightenment: Women in Diderot and Richardson*, (Cambridge: Cambridge University Press, 1984); and Marie–Paul Laden, *Self-Imitation in the Eighteenth-Century Novel*, (Princeton: Princeton University Press, 1987). Laden uses recent French theory to examine the "problem of the subject," as embodied in the impossibility of coincidence between the enunciating "I" and the enunciated "I" it recounts, in the works of Lesage, Defoe, Marivaux, Richardson, and Sterne.

28   Voltaire, *Lettre philosophiques*, in *Mélanges*, ed. Jacques Van Den Heuvel (Paris: Gallimard "Bibliothèque de la Pléiade," 1961). The letters appeared in 1734 bearing the imprint "Amsterdam: E. Lucas," but were actually published in Rouen by Jore, according to Van Den Heuvel (p. 2, n.1). An excellent example of the close relations of the two cultures, the work appeared in English translation several months before its publication in French. Jean Baptiste de Boyer, marquis d'Argens, *Lettres juives*, new edn 8 vols (The Hague: Pierre Paupie, 1754), letters 133–6, 192. John Brown, *An Estimate of the Manners and Principles of the Times* (London: L. Davis and C. Reymers, 1757), pp. 135–45.

29   Rousseau's *Julie, ou la nouvelle Héloïse* was published more or less simultaneously in 1761 in French and in an English translation overseen by the author. The first four books of Marivaux's *Paysan parvenu* were published in English even before the fifth book appeared in French. *La Princesse de Clèves* and *Les Liaisons dangereuses* appeared in translation within a year or so of their publication, as did *Joseph Andrews* and *Tom Jones*.

30   Diderot's "borrowing" of *Tristram Shandy* for *Jacques le fataliste* or Laclos' incorporation of motifs from *Clarissa* in *Les Liaisons dangereuses* are cases in point. The best known French theoretical pronouncement on the novel is perhaps Diderot's "Eloge de Richardson," which makes clear enough the English influence on the continent, but Rousseau's "Entretien sur les romans," published as a postface to *Julie, ou la nouvelle Héloïse* (itself one of the most influential novels in England) also refers explicitly to the contemporary English tradition, as do his *Confessions*. A different sort of measure of reciprocal influence can be found in the inventories of the major private libraries of the period undertaken by Daniel Mornet. He found that *Pamela*, *Tom Jones*, *Clarissa*, and *Joseph Andrews* all appeared more frequently (as did a number of

other English works) than did the novels of such popular French authors as Marivaux and Prévost; see "Les Enseignements des Bibliothèques Privées," *Revue d'Histoire Littéraire* 17 (1910), pp. 449–96. Conversely, Clara Reeve in the *Progress of Romance*, vol. 1, p. 28ff., devotes more attention to *Julie* than to any English novel and includes in her analysis substantial discussion of the French novelists' influence in England.

31   There are obvious similarities between this idea of narrational ordering against a horizon of orders and M. M. Bakhtin's concepts of heteroglossia and dialogism. Bakhtin holds that "for any individual consciousness living in it, language is not an abstract system of normative forms but rather a concrete heteroglot conception of the world"; *The Dialogic Imagination: Four Essays by M. M. Bakhtin*, ed. Michael Holquist, trans. Caryl Emerson and Michael Hohlquist (Austin, Texas: University of Texas Press, 1981), p. 293. The world gains shape and meaning through the language which represents it to consciousness, and that language, unique to every concrete instance or individual, is in turn constituted out of various socially typifying "languages" which are themselves the product of prior socially significant verbal performances whose traces they bear, in the form of semantic nuances, axiological overtones, accentuation tendencies, and vocabulary patterns (pp. 289–91). Bakhtin sees the ordering of the world, the making of meaning, as a function of the continual intersection or collision of such "languages" within the concrete situation of any utterance, such that any meaning is always conditioned by the competing languages and pre-existing systems of meaning with which it relates dialogically. The novel, in turn, is the genre which interrogates as it exemplifies this discursive economy: "the human being in the novel is first, foremost and always a speaking human being; the novel requires speaking persons bringing with them their own unique ideological discourse, their own language. The fundamental condition, that which makes a novel a novel, that which is responsible for its stylistic uniqueness, is the *speaking person and his discourse*" (ibid. p. 332). My specification of the eighteenth-century novel differs from Bakhtin's global theoretical definition in that it focuses on the rudimentary or incipient stages of the genre's developing sense of itself, in which the ordering of the world and the instantiation of ideology had not yet come to be understood as inhering in *any* language use, but were correlated to the more specifically organizing gesture of narrating past experience. Similarly, the underlying dialogical structure of meaning which Bakhtin rightly sees as inherent in all discourse, emerged in the eighteenth century in the literal dialogical relationship of narrator to listener, author to reader. As the century progresses, this literal conceptualization of the dialogical situation as an interpersonal exchange will give way to more intrapersonal and intertextual paradigms tending toward a dialectical understanding of how discursive instance relates to the Other of culture.

32   For instance, Peter Brooks, *Reading for the Plot* (New York: A. A. Knopf, 1984), p. 3, prefaces his study of plot with the observation that "Our lives are ceaselessly intertwined with narrative, with the stories that we tell and hear

told, those we dream or imagine or would like to tell, all of which are reworked in that story of our own lives that we narrate to ourselves in an episodic, sometimes semi-conscious, but virtually uninterrupted monologue." Barbara Hardy states the case even more forcefully: "We cannot take a step in life or literature without using an image. It is hard to take more than a step without narrating. Before we sleep each night we tell over to ourselves what we may also have told to others, the story of the past day.... We begin the day by narrating to ourselves and probably to others our expectations, plans, desires, fantasies and intentions.... We meet our colleagues, family, friends, intimates, acquaintances, strangers, and exchange stories, overtly and covertly. We may try to tell all, in true confession, or tell half-truths or lies, or refuse to do more than tell the story of the weather, the car, or the food.... The stories of our days and the stories in our days are joined in that autobiography we are all engaged in making and remaking, as long as we live, which we never complete, though we all know how it is going to end"; *Tellers and Listeners* (London: The Athlone Press, University of London, 1975), p. 4. M. M. Bakhtin's characterization of real life as permeated by speech about speech makes much the same point in different terms: "in real life people talk most of all about what others talk about – they transmit, recall, weigh, and pass judgment on other people's words, opinions, assertions, information; ... At every step one meets a 'quotation' or a 'reference' to something that a particular person said, a reference to 'people say' or 'everyone says,' to the words of the person one is talking with, or to one's own previous words, to a newspaper, an official decree, a document, a book and so forth"; *Dialogic Imagination*, p. 338. My choice of the term "narration" in this study is predicated on the observation that such speech about speech is fundamentally narrative in nature: it reports past (verbal) actions or events and arranges them in causal sequences.

33   Nicolas-Charles-Joseph Trublet, *Essais sur divers sujets de littérature et de morale* (Paris: Briasson, 1735), pp. 29–30.

34   Trublet, *Essais*, p. 20.

35   Lionel Gossman's study of the development of historiography in eighteenth-century France, *Medievalism and the Ideologies of the Enlightenment: the World and Work of La Curne de Sainte-Palaye* (Baltimore: Johns Hopkins University Press, 1968), includes a useful account of changing attitudes during the eighteenth century toward both the contemporary historian's act of narrative ordering and the narrative documents of former periods which formed the basis for history writing. For a discussion of current and eighteenth-century theories of history as they relate to each other see Suzanne Gearhart, *The Open Boundary of History and Fiction*. (Princeton: Princeton University Press, 1984). See also Guy Bourdé and Hervé Martin, *Les Ecoles historiques* (Paris: Seuil, 1983), and Henri-Irénée Marrou, *De la connaissance historique* (Paris: Seuil, 1954).

36   For a study of this latter notion of identity as it relates to the gesture of autobiography see Spacks, *Imagining a Self*. For a thorough examination of major eighteenth-century theories of the self, see Stephen D. Cox, *"The Stranger Within Theè" Concepts of the Self in Late Eighteenth-Century Literature* (Pittsburgh: University of Pittsburgh Press, 1980).

37 Spacks' analysis of how protagonists in some eighteenth-century novels "change the world by their dreams of it" (*Imagining a Self*, p. 307), approaches the question of self-determination somewhat differently, focusing on the private, psychological dimension of imagination and the autobiographical impulse.

38 Honoré de Balzac, *La Comédie humaine*, ed. Marcel Bouteron, 11 vols ("Bibliothèque de la Pléiade" Paris: Gallimard), vol. 1, pp. 4–5. Subsequent citations are from this edition.

2

Private Lives and Public Stories
(*La Princesse de Clèves*)

It may seem strange to start a study of the eighteenth-century novel with a work published in 1678, but *La Princesse de Clèves* is in many respects the first novel of the tradition that interests me. As Peter Brooks remarks, it is "the model to which the eighteenth-century novels of worldliness all implicitly refer,"[1] and it sets out in extraordinarily graphic terms not only the framework of social determination which will become a central theme in the following century, but also the essential differences between the French tradition and its English counterpart. Published anonymously, it was translated almost immediately into English, and it embodies in an exceptionally pure form the conflict between the genres of history and fiction which preoccupy all of the novelists for the next century.[2]

La Princesse de Clèves is frequently cited as the first modern novel in the French language, on the basis of its subtle psychological analysis of love and realistic portrayal of character. Its publication triggered a controversy, though, which was centered primarily on its blatant distortion of history and its frequent lack of verisimilitude – features which would still be drawing fire from critics three-quarters of a century later.[3] Indeed, in its attentiveness to its own status, the work differs markedly from most of its contemporaries: in plot structure, narrative technique, and thematic content, it dramatizes the relationship of personal account to public history, and, by extension, the status of fictional accounts such as itself. This play between history and story is perhaps most evident in the novel's technique of multiple framing.

The work commences with a lengthy historical description of the court of Henri II and intersperses the recounting of its protagonist's adventure with historical anecdotes and portraits from the period. With the exception of the protagonist (for whom the book is named), and her mother (Mme de Chartres), the primary actors in the drama are historical figures, and the political events portrayed correspond roughly to accepted accounts of the period.[4] Stylistically, moreover, the expositional and transitional portions of the narrative strongly resemble the monotonous reportage of seventeenth-century history writing, with its treaties, wars, marriages, and alliances.[5]

This historical narrative is interwoven with a series of framed anecdotes which various courtiers relate to the protagonist during the course of the story. These accounts concern the amorous liaisons and political intrigues of the courtiers; they involve both historical and fictional characters and events; and they have a substantial impact not only on the concerned parties, whose fortunes they directly affect, but on the behavior of the Princesse as well, whose attempt to stand clear of the collective chronicle forms one of the novel's main themes.

Finally, at a more private level, and framed by the impersonal narrative of political history and the tales of courtly intrigue which the characters recount, there is the story of the Princesse de Clèves and her struggle to conceal and overcome a growing attraction to the duc de Nemours – a story to which we have access primarily through the voice of the omniscient narrator and the private dialogues of the Princesse.

The personal, emotional struggle of the protagonist is thus framed by an ongoing semi-public drama of gossip and local reportage which mediates between the private realm of affect and personal experience, and the public domain of politics and history. Part obvious invention, part accepted historical fact, this mediate order straddles the division between the genres of fiction and history and underscores the complex relationship of personal invention to collective record. These two extremes, the public or historical and the private or individual, do not simply co-exist in the novel. Nor does the historical tableau serve as a mere backdrop to provide verisimilitude for the fictional portions of the narrative. Indeed, the novel elicited an immediate protest from a contemporary critic, Jean-Henry du Trousset de Valincour, who argues rather persuasively that the admixture of historical fact and blatant invention could hardly pass unnoticed by a public all too familiar with the main figures of the court of Henri II. The invention of a major "historical" character like the Princesse, or a fictitious event, such as the marriage of the Prince de Clèves, can only be read as a challenge to the traditional subordination of personal account to collective record.[6]

As part of his critique, which appropriately takes the form of a debate between a conservative pedant shocked by the author's revision of history and an enthusiastic reader who finds such liberties compensated by the pleasure the book procures, Valincour articulates a number of presuppositions about the relationship of historical fact to personal account which go to the very heart of *La Princesse de Clèves*' thematics. The pedant's argument, that while authors have the right to embellish general historical events, they must never go against accepted accounts of those events, explicitly equates historical fact with shared public knowledge and subordinates all independent reconstructions of the past to this collective discourse.[7] At the same time, he proposes an ideal form of fiction which would exercise its invention at a level of detail that exceeds the general account, by depicting the causal mechanisms underlying famous events and persons, the specifics of whose conduct were not known. Such fiction would not just appear to be the record of reality, but its cause, and it would be indistinguishable from truth: "Enfin, je voudrais que mes fictions eussent un rapport si juste et si nécessaire aux événements véritables de l'histoire, et que *les événements parussent dépendre si naturellement de mes fictions*, que mon livre ne parût être autre chose que l'histoire secrète de ce siècle-là, et que personne ne pût prouver la fausseté de ce que j'aurais écrit"[8] (Finally, I should desire my fictions to have such an exact and necessary relationship to the real events of history, and have the events seem to depend so naturally on my fictions, that my book would appear to be nothing other than the secret history of that century, and that nobody would be able to prove the falseness of what I had written). The injunction against rewriting history addresses, finally, not the presumption of the author, but her double refusal to conform to the collective account and to conceal her gesture, so as to spare the public the pain of acknowledging the fictional bases of history: "il n'y a rien qui choque davantage un lecteur, que de voir qu'on lui propose comme véritable une chose qui ne l'est point, et qui est même entièrement fausse"[9] (nothing shocks a reader more than to see that he is being given as genuine something which is not at all and which is even completely false).

This double imperative of conformity and dissimulation both acknowledges and denies the authority of individual fiction, and if the author of the novel seems to resist it, by foregrounding her fictional creations, it nonetheless reappears as the infrastructure of the plot of *La Princesse de Clèves*. A reading that would take both that law and its rejection into account needs to seek the concealed gesture of the author behind the surface thematics of that plot, and in particular beneath the "fictional" psychological causes which it foregrounds in the person of its obviously invented protagonist.

In effect, while the subordination of private account to public record forms an underlying theme of all the anecdotes in the novel, it finds its strongest enactment in the fictional sequences of the Princesse's story. There the relationship of the public and personal planes can be visualized as one of repeated engulfment or assimilation, each attempt at private action or a personal plot being swallowed up into the public narrative and re-counted in ways that subvert the heroine's intentions. But just as Valincour's pedant articulates his program for fictional authority within a defense of history, the fictitious protagonist's attempts to preserve herself from entrapment in a collective discourse repeatedly articulate the primacy of that discourse. Ironically, the authority of collective narration over individual identity is established by the fictional account of a nameless author, who, by figuring the domination of private story by shared history in precisely those portions of the plot that are most obviously contrived, slyly – and invisibly – recoups her autonomy. While the protagonist's substitution of a private world for the social arena, as with her ultimate withdrawal from that social world, merely adumbrates a response to the tyranny of the collective, the author achieves a measure of mastery over the mechanisms of the collective by enclosing them in her fiction and introducing them – anonymously – into her culture's narrative.[10]

This subtle mechanism relies on a relatively straightforward plot. Married to a man for whom she feels no passion, the Princesse de Clèves falls inexorably in love with the duc de Nemours, against whose advances and declarations she struggles valiantly, going even to the point of confessing her inclination to her husband and enlisting his aid. When the latter misinterprets the report of a spy and dies of a broken heart, convinced that his spouse has betrayed him, the Princesse rejects the duc definitively, alleging that it would be impossible to realize their passion in the face of her guilt. She then withdraws from society and leaves for the provinces, where she eventually retreats to a convent.[11]

Thus paraphrased, the plot is deceptively simple, and aside from the capital scene of the confession to her husband, the various episodes that chart its progression are adapted from a repertory of love *topoi* going back to the Middle Ages.[12] Indeed, the Princesse's growing sense of her story's predictability, and of the probability that it will terminate unhappily, plays no small role in her refusal to cede to the duc's passion. Even before it begins to enclose her, she has learned her "plot line." This is partly the result of her mother's way of educating her and partly the result of her exposure to a series of narratives that chart love's pitfalls and demonstrate the difficulty of insuring the privacy of one's story in the public world of the court. Her mother inaugurates a series of four controversial digressions dealing with love,[13] by recounting for her the career of the duchesse de Valentinois; this initial account establishes the importance of narratives of courtly affairs as a principle of education:

> La plupart des mères s'imaginent qu'il suffit de ne parler jamais de galanterie devant les jeunes personnes pour les en éloigner. Mme de Chartres avait une opinion opposée; elle faisait souvent à sa fille des peintures de l'amour; elle lui montrait ce qu'il a d'agréable pour la persuader plus aisément sur ce qu'elle lui en apprenait de dangereux; elle lui contait le peu de sincérité des hommes, leurs tromperies et leur infidélité, les malheurs domestiques où plongent les engagements . . . (P. 248)[14]

Most mothers imagine that it suffices never to speak of love in front of young people in order to discourage them from it. Mme de Chartres was of the contrary opinion; she frequently depicted love for her daughter; she showed her its agreeable side so as to persuade her more easily of what she revealed of its dangers; she related men's lack of sincerity, their deceits and infidelity, the domestic misfortunes which involvements occasion.

Designed to pre-empt her daughter's involvement in an adulterous affair that might damage her reputation, Mme de Chartres' accounts take advantage of the courtly gossip she fears: her ominous vision of adultery's dangers finds natural confirmation in the stories of disastrous love affairs that form the daily fare of the king's entourage. Indeed, the tiny, ingrown society that is depicted in *La Princesse de Clèves* finds its whole *raison d'être* in the management of reputations, and a large part of this enterprise – particularly for the women, who are barred from direct forms of action such as military exploits – consists in the dissemination of stories about the private liaisons of friends, rivals, and public figures.

The four framed digressions are capital in this regard. While their plots do not directly address Nemours and the Princesse, their themes motivate the latter's eventual refusal of involvement. The short recapitulation of the career of the duchesse de Valentinois is matched by an account of the life of Ann Boleyn, similarly stressing the instability of love, the disastrous results it can lead to, and the political turmoil that inevitably accompanies courtly liaisons. Two long stories each recount involved tales of deception and infidelity that awaken the Princesse to the pain of jealousy and convince her of the unreliability and ephemerality of personal relationships at court – particularly those consisting of verbal commitments.

While all of these narratives are concerned with love, they also have political repercussions and illustrate the degree to which, within the context of courtly society, personal affect is indissociable from political effect: "L'ambition et la galanterie étaient l'âme de cette cour, et occupaient également les hommes et les femmes. Il y avait tant d'intérêts et tant de cabales différentes, et les dames y avaient tant de part que l'amour était toujours mêlé aux affaires et les affaires à l'amour" (p. 252)[15] (ambition and love affairs were the soul of this court, and occupied men and women alike. There were so many interests and so many different cabals, and women had such a large part in them, that love was always mixed with political affairs and politics with love). To thrive in the court of France means, in a very real sense, to have the ear of the king or, lacking that, someone close to him, and, as the history of Mme de Valentinois confirms, no one has the king's ear more frequently than his mistress. At the center of the courtly universe, the monarch retains the ultimate narrative, as well as political, authority. Like an absolute version of the family father, whose authority over his children will emerge as a dominant theme in eighteenth-century fiction, the king must be obeyed by his children: "si un bon roi doit être le père de ses Sujets, ils doivent avoir pour lui la soumission des enfans"[16] (if a good king must be the father of his subjects, they must have for him the submission of children). Sanctioned by divine right, his decisions determine the fate not just of individuals, but of the entire kingdom, and his words are literally predicative: what he says, becomes reality. When Henri II expresses disapproval of a proposed marriage, that marriage cannot take place (p. 255); when he decides that his daughter will marry the king of Spain, marry him she must, whether she likes the idea or not (p. 292); when he declares astrology devoid of substance, it immediately loses credibility (pp. 296–7); when, against the wishes of the queen, the comte de Montgomery, and the duc de Savoie, he demands a final joust, his demands must be met (pp. 355–6).

The individuals immediately surrounding the king and enjoying a certain influence over his pronouncements benefit from a similar, if proportionately attenuated, authority. Mme de Chartres fails in her initial ambitions to find a match for her daughter, because her allies are not as close to the king as is her enemy, the duchesse de Valentinois (p. 255). Conversely, the latter instantly loses all of her power – indeed, her entire courtly identity – when the king dies. In such an environment, survival, not to mention self-advancement, becomes a matter of ingratiating oneself with those higher on the social ladder and knowing the positions of one's rivals.[17]

In *La Princesse de Clèves* these two imperatives converge in the courtly practice of gossip. By exchanging stories about their peers, the courtiers at one and the same time increase their mastery of the ever-changing web of alliances at the court and ingratiate themselves with their accomplices in the exchange – who are always pleased to hear new stories, if only because it increases their control over the collective discourse. At least that is what they assume, and it would seem self-evident that a knowledge of all current cabals and a careful regulation of information would carry with it a strategic advantage. Conversely, a loss of control over information can cost one's influence and fortune, as the longest digression in the *La Princesse de Clèves* vividly demonstrates. When the vidame de Chartres – the queen's confidant, but also an incorrigible Don Juan – loses a letter from one of his ex-mistresses, his infidelity becomes known to the queen, and he gains an implacable enemy who ultimately avenges herself by implicating him in a plot against the king (p. 329). In like manner, lesser episodes recounted in the course of the novel, such as Sancerre's inadvertent disclosure of his affaire with Mme de Tournon (pp. 282–3), or Nemours' ill-advised confidences to the vidame de Chartres (pp. 338, 346), demonstrate the extent to which poorly managed information can turn up in unexpected places to the great discomfort of the concerned parties.

In the court, where "personne n'était tranquille, ni indifférent; on songeait à s'élever, à plaire, à servir ou à nuire" (p. 252) (no one was calm or indifferent; one thought of advancing, pleasing, or doing harm), there are few moves one can make without becoming part of the public account and literally losing (control over) one's reputation. That is why Mme de Chartres exhorts her daughter to isolate herself from the web of intrigue by attaching herself entirely to her husband:

> elle lui faisait voir, d'un autre côté, quelle tranquillité suivait la vie d'une honnête femme, et combien la vertu donnait d'éclat et d'élévation à une personne qui avait de la beauté et de la naissance; mais elle lui faisait voir aussi combien il était difficile de conserver cette vertu, que par une extrême défiance de soi-même et par un grand soin de s'attacher à ce qui seul peut faire le bonheur d'une femme, qui est d'aimer son mari et d'en être aimée. (P. 248)

> on the other side she gave her to see what tranquility accompanied the life of a virtuous woman, and how much luster and superiority virtue gave a person who had beauty and good blood; but she gave her to see also how difficult it was to conserve this virtue, other than by a diffidence in one's self and a serious application to attach oneself to that which alone can bring a woman happiness, which is to love one's husband and be loved by him.

Mme de Chartres intends for her daughter to obtain distinction quite literally: by remaining distinct from the common practice of seeking one's identity in love affairs, but her prescription for chastity in fact conceals a conventional subordination of woman to man that undermines this agenda of difference. The goal of all courtiers is to obtain celebrity. However, since women lack direct access to renown through participation in battles, diplomatic missions, or political and ecclesiastical responsibilities, their reputation is necessarily mediated by the men associated with them, which is to say both the men they attract sexually, and can therefore influence, and the men attracted to them because of their perceived influence. At the same time, they are prevented by their society's residual allegiance to the principle of female chastity from actively courting men and thus promoting themselves.[18] Their only means of compensating for this inequity is to expose more aggressively the continually shifting amorous liaisons at the court, crippling or disabling secret lines of influence by making them public. Unfortunately, this purely negative practice affords no positive enhancement of one's own reputation. Although *La Princesse de Clèves* prefigures subsequent agendas of narrational self-definition, by correlating individual fortune and political power to the stories, fanciful or true, that circulate through the court, the novel does not envision any direct authority over those stories by the parties most concerned: one cannot tell one's own story, or control its evolution in the hands of others. The aristocratic woman inhabits a world regulated by a collective narrative in which she may participate, but always only after the fact and as narrator of the Other.

The Princesse's story is that of resistance to this role and the logic that subtends it, as epitomized in the duc de Nemours. In this, she conforms to her mother's wish. But Mme de Chartres' program is flawed from the outset by its reliance on a logic of derivative identity indistinguishable from that which motivates adultery: when alliance with another person is the only means of establishing one's identity, and identity is conceived of in terms of celebrity, it becomes difficult to resist the overtures of a person as renowned as the duc de Nemours. If selfhood comes only with the grafting of one's self to a splendid male, one can scarcely ignore the attentions of the superlative man – a man next to whom all others, including the Prince de Clèves, pale. This is why, in spite of his reputation as a womanizer, the duc de Nemours is the envy of every woman in the court:

> Il n'y avait aucune dame dans la cour dont la gloire n'eût été flattée de le voir attaché à elle; peu de celles à qui il s'était attaché, se pouvaient vanter de lui avoir résisté, et même plusieurs à qui il n'avait point témoigné de passion, n'avaient pas laissé d'en avoir pour lui. (P. 244)

> There was no woman in the court who would not have prided herself on seeing him devoted to her; few of those to whom he had devoted himself could boast of having resisted him, and even several for whom he had never exhibited any inclination nevertheless could not forebear having one for him.

As "nature's masterpiece" and the most remarkable man of his time (even Elizabeth I of England expresses interest), Nemours offers any woman capable of holding him assured resplendency. Any woman, that is, except the Princesse de Clèves, who, similarly superlative, and thus a logical match, recognizes – and this is what sets her apart from her peers – that the splendor he, or any man, can offer is only transitory in comparison to the absolute distinction that would come with asserting her difference from all women and rejecting the entire mechanism of derivative identity, along with the practice of collective narration that underwrites it.

Just as the duc de Nemours stands out among the male courtiers, so is the Princesse exceptional among the women. She is the most beautiful woman in the court – "l'on doit croire que c'était une beauté parfaite, puisqu'elle donna de l'admiration dans un lieu où l'on était si accoutumé à voir de belles personnes" (p. 247) (one must assume that she was a perfect beauty, since she elicited admiration in an environment where one was so accustomed to seeing beautiful people); the most virtuous – "une vertu austère, qui n'a presque point d'exemple" (p. 388) (an austere virtue that has almost no precedent); and the most sincere – "Mme de Chartres admirait la sincérité de sa fille, et elle l'admirait avec raison, car jamais personne n'en a eu une si grande et si naturelle" (p. 259) (Mme de Chartres admired the sincerity of her daughter, and rightly so, for never had any-one's been so great and so natural).[19] Nemours qualifies her as simply "la plus estimable personne du monde" (p. 386) (the person most worthy of esteem in the world).

However, Mme de Clèves is not merely superlative according to the conventional criteria of her culture. She is *qualitatively* different as well, and in this respect she prefigures a long tradition of heroines and heroes in both the English and French novel, whose primary identifying characteristic is that they are not just quantitatively exemplary, but *exceptional*.[20] Being exceptional is something the Princesse quite consciously cultivates, even when she is engaged in conventional social relations. In her long interview with Nemours, she herself points out how remarkable her sincerity is (p. 383), and she is careful to preface her famous confession to her husband with a scene that foregrounds her unparalleled virtue and honesty while at the same time dramatizing her exemplary subordination to her spouse: "Eh bien, monsieur, lui répondit-elle en se jetant à ses genoux, je vais vous faire un aveu que l'on n'a jamais fait à son mari; mais l'innocence de ma conduite et de mes intentions m'en donne la force" (p. 333) (well, Sir, she replied to him, throwing herself at his knees, I am going to make an admission no one has ever made to her husband; but the innocence of my conduct and my intentions gives me the force to do it). This is a point she will reiterate in even stronger terms when her story is circulated (anonymously) in the court: "il n'y a pas dans le monde une autre aventure pareille à la mienne; il n'y a point une autre femme capable de la même chose. Le hasard ne peut l'avoir fait inventer; on ne l'a jamais imaginée et cette pensée n'est jamais tombée dans un autre esprit que le mien" (p. 349) (there is not another adventure similar to mine in the world; there is no other woman capable of the same thing. Chance could not have brought its invention; nobody has ever imagined it, and this thought has never occurred to a mind other than mine).

Extraordinary behavior is of course in line with her mother's original agenda of difference, which Mme de Chartres reiterates on her deathbed:

> songez ce que vous vous devez à vous-même, et pensez que vous allez perdre cette réputation que vous vous êtes acquise et que je vous ai tant souhaitée.... si quelque chose était capable de troubler le bonheur que j'es-père en sortant de ce monde, ce serait de vous voir tomber comme les autres femmes" (P. 278)[21]

> think about what you owe yourself, and think that you are going to lose this reputation which you have acquired and which I so wished for you.... if anything were capable of troubling the happiness I hope for in leaving this world, it would be to see you fall like the others.

It is within the context of this agenda that one can understand the Princesse's remarkable resistance to Nemours. She is determined not to accept passively the fate which her culture prescribes for her – that of being the superlative mistress of the superlative courtier. Reading literally her mother's admonition to be loyal to *herself*, she determines to resist the pull of convention and forego any sexual attachment whatsoever. This self-imposed duty, which, as she reveals to Nemours at their final interview, "me défend de penser jamais à personne" (p. 385) (forbids me ever to think of [becoming involved with] anyone), and which, she admits, "ne subsiste que dans mon imagination" (p. 389) (subsists only within my imagination), will pit her against an inexorable discursive economy that repeatedly takes her story out of her hands, forcing her towards the role of Nemours' mistress.

In his own way, which is much more in line with the usages of the court, the duc is also remarkable. As resolutely as the Princesse avoids involvement in *galanteries*, he gives himself over to them, but in fact he never "distinguishes" anyone. He flirts indiscriminately with all women who express an interest, because he knows he must be indiscriminate in his attention to avoid the wrath of the scorned: "Il avait tant de douceur et tant de disposition à la galanterie qui'il ne pouvait refuser quelques soins à celles qui tâchaient de lui plaire: ainsi il avait plusieurs maîtresses, mais il était difficile de deviner celle qu'il aimait véritablement" (p. 244) (he had such sweetness and such a disposition for love that he could not refrain from paying court to those who tried to please him: thus he attended several ladies, but it was difficult to guess which he truly loved). A free agent in a system where no one remains unaligned, Nemours epitomizes the instability of courtly relationships and, by avoiding any real commitment, preserves himself from the unpleasant side effects of alliances. This gives him a definite privilege in the social economy of despotism (in fact, he is the only character in *La Princesse de Clèves* that no one seems to hate[22]), but it also disqualifies him from the Princesse's agenda of distinction, since his entire identity is bound up in the economy which the Princesse rejects. He exists not as a private individual, endowed with intimate qualities he might share in private with a single partner, but as the very embodiment of public opinion, a construct of reputation born of, sustained by, and belonging to, the collective.

The ever-attentive Mme de Chartres sees to it that her daughter is made aware of this fact early on: "Elle se mit un jour à parler de lui; elle lui en dit du bien et y mêla beaucoup de louanges empoisonnées sur la sagesse qu'il avait d'être incapable de devenir amoureux et sur ce qu'il ne se faisait qu'un plaisir et non pas un attachement sérieux du commerce des femmes" (p. 274) (She started talking about him one day; she said some good things about him and mixed in much venomous praise of his wisdom for not being able to fall in love and of the fact that he made of his commerce with women only a pleasure and not a serious attachment). Her lesson does not fall on deaf ears: when the death of M. de Clèves finally opens the way to their marriage, the Princesse will cite the duc's gallant achievements as proof that he could not long love her:

> Rien ne me peut empêcher de connaître que vous êtes né avec toutes les dispositions pour la galanterie et toutes les qualités qui sont propres à y donner des succès heureux. Vous avez déjà eu plusieurs passions, vous en auriez encore; je ne ferais plus votre bonheur; je vous verrais pour une autre comme vous auriez été pour moi. (Pp. 387–8)

> Nothing can prevent me from knowing that you were born with all of the dispositions for love and all of the qualities appropriate to assuring success in that domain. You have already had several passions, you would have still others; I would no longer be the source of your happiness; I would see you become for another what you would have been for me.

The Princesse understands that Nemours' identity is inseparable from the courtly commerce he epitomizes: he cannot fulfill his role as superlative courtier if he attaches himself to a single woman; nor can he maintain his identity without the structure of public expression that defines him and compels him to ever greater conquests. Within this framework, her own role could only be one of passive reaction and disenfranchizement. Yet however much she fights his attraction and attempts to maintain control of her fate, she is swept towards involvement with him by social transactions, accounts, and rituals she cannot avoid. The mechanism of this involvement is blatantly narrative, and it occurs on several levels.

La Princesse de Clèves abounds in scenes that emblematize the structural subordination of private relationship to public narrative. The ballroom scene – where the two protagonists first meet and dance under the watchful eyes of the entire court – precisely states the mode of expression of courtly liaisons as well as the shape of the two protagonists' future relations. Although the entire court knows who they are and has already begun the narrative of their relationship, Nemours and the Princesse have yet to be introduced to each other and thus cannot be absolutely certain of their respective partner's status: "Quand ils commencèrent à danser, il s'éleva dans la salle un murmure de louanges. Le roi et les reines se souvinrent qu'ils ne s'étaient jamais vus, et trouvèrent quelque chose de singulier de les voir danser ensemble sans se connaître" (p. 262) (When they started to dance, a murmur of praise rose in the hall. The king and the queens remembered that the couple had never seen each other, and found it unusual to see them dancing together without knowing each other). Already embedded in the text of courtly discussion, the two dancers can neither confess their suspicions about the other's identity (as the duc chooses to do) nor conceal them, as the Princesse does, without revealing to the court the degree to which they find each other remarkable. As Marie Stuart remarks to the Princesse, "il y a même quelque chose d'obligeant pour M. de Nemours à ne vouloir pas avouer que vous le connaissez sans l'avoir jamais vu" (p. 262) (there is even something flattering for M. de Nemours in the fact that you do not want to admit knowing who he is without ever having seen him).

The "private" relationship of the Princesse and Nemours is thus mediated from the beginning by courtly gossip. Subsequent episodes, such as the discussion about Nemours' preference that his mistress not go to balls (pp. 271–4), the explanation of the colors worn by each jouster (p. 355), the riding accident where Nemours is slightly injured (p. 306), or the episode concerning astrology (pp. 296–7), all underline the degree to which sexual attraction and attachment enact themselves publicly, within a collectively elaborated record of personal alliances. In truth, the book contains no examples of a successful private relationship. Attempts at intimacy are inevitably uncovered by the courtiers and assimilated into the ongoing collective narrative. Even the most careful mastery of the social economy is of no ultimate benefit, since one cannot share one's knowledge without inaugurating yet another alliance for the public discourse to explore and expose. The two fictional framed episodes concerning Sancerre and the vidame de Chartres demonstrate this quite forcefully, documenting the inability of lovers and confidants to keep their relationships secret from society and from one another.

However, the most striking illustrations of the dysfunction of private discourse involve Mme de Clèves herself. The earliest and most subtle expressions of her interest in Nemours – the episodes where she herself is not completely aware of how deeply infatuated she has become – establish the degree to which her actions are influenced by courtly gossip. As if to underline the dependency of personal feeling on public account, the novel casts the Princesse's awakening to her feelings in terms of her identification with figures in public anecdotes. For instance, when the prince de Condé recounts Nemours' displeasure upon seeing his mistress attend a ball, the Princesse immediately assumes *she* must be the woman in question (p. 272). Later, when her husband relates the story of Sancerre, he mentions that he advised the latter to relinquish the role of lover in order to be a friend to his mistress. The Princesse cannot help but note the resemblance between Mme de Tournon's situation and hers: "ces paroles firent rougir Mme de Clèves, et elle y trouva un certain rapport avec l'état où elle était, qui la surprit et qui lui donna un trouble dont elle fut longtemps à se remettre" (p. 284) (these words made Mme de Clèves blush, and she found in them a certain relationship to her own state, which surprised her and caused an inner turmoil which she was some time in getting over). Similarly, the Princesse has no difficulty associating herself with the "other woman" mentioned in the letter to the vidame de Chartres which she mistakenly believes destined for Nemours (pp. 310–11).

These episodes link the Princesse's private behavior to publicly circulated stories in a very concrete way: upon hearing each anecdote, she re-enacts that portion of its plot with which she identifies, thereby literally *realizing* the story. After the discussion of Nemours' preference that his mistress not go to the ball, she decides not to go to the ball; after reading the jealous mistress's letter to the vidame, she becomes violently jealous of Nemours.[23] Most important of all, it is her recollection of her husband's remarks to Sancerre concerning sincerity (cf. pp. 303, 311) that precipitates her confession to her husband.

While the protagonist of *La Princesse de Clèves* recapitulates, under the guise of "original" behavior, moves already inscribed in the narratives defining her environment, the collective voice continually appropriates her attempts at private communication and re-presents her with the degraded, vulgar, public version of her own story. When she fails to go to the ball, Marie Stuart immediately determines her motives – and confronts her with them in the presence of the other courtiers:

> Vous voilà si belle, lui dit Mme la dauphine, que je ne saurais croire que vous ayez été malade. Je pense que M. le prince de Condé, en vous contant l'avis de M. de Nemours sur le bal, vous a persuadée que vous feriez une faveur au maréchal de Saint-André d'aller chez lui et que c'est ce qui vous a empêchée d'y venir. (P. 273)

> You are looking so beautiful, the Dauphine said to her, that I cannot believe you have been sick. I think that in relating to you M. de Nemours' opinion about the ball, the Prince de Condé persuaded you that you would be showing a preference for the Maréchal de Saint-André if you went to his dance, and that is what prevented you from attending.

Although the Dauphine imputes the Princesse's behavior to the wrong man, her remarks are still devastating. Modelled on a collective account, the Princesse's attempt at a private gesture of affection is taken up by the collective, within whose ongoing narrative it returns to confront her as public anecdote. Her own story exceeds her control.

A more subtle version of the same phenomenon occurs in the two scenes when the Princesse hears the story of Nemours' changed behavior and identifies herself as the unknown woman in the public accounts who has wrought such wonders (pp. 275–7, 289–91). Yet the most striking example of the absorption of private gesture into public narrative comes when the

Princesse confesses her inclination for Nemours to her husband. Overhearing the confession, Nemours, true to character, carelessly relates it to his best friend, only to find that it has become the central topic of discussion in the court the following day. This episode is especially troubling because of the delicacy of the subject and the lack of any plausible explanation for its dissemination,[24] and it subjects Nemours to the same shock as the Princesse: "Le trouble et l'embarras de Mme de Clèves était au delà de tout ce que l'on peut s'imaginer, et, si la mort se fût présentée pour la tirer de cet état, elle l'aurait trouvée agréable. Mais M. de Nemours était encore plus embarrassé, s'il est possible" (pp. 345–6) (The agitation and embarrassment of Mme de Clèves were beyond anything one could imagine, and if death had presented itself as a way out of this state, she would have found it agreeable. But M. de Nemours was even more embarrassed, if that is possible).

This episode confirms the Princesse's inability to articulate her life privately and, because it throws a cloud of distrust over her relationship with the Prince (each believes the other to be lying and to have divulged the secret), it also establishes the extent to which narratives determine behavior. The Princesse is not just distressed at being the central – if anonymous – character in the stories recounted in the salon of the reine dauphine, and at the duplicity of her situation and the further deceit which suppressing her shock requires, she must also come to grips with the fact that her story – and her marriage – are no longer under her control. Stripped of its original context and the motives that justify it, her behavior is open to any number of interpretations and assessments; even the reality of her remarkable confession becomes a subject of debate. From the private expression of non-conformity, her conversation with her husband has been transformed into a narrative whose rapid dissemination in the court alienates her husband from her and embodies the very appropriation of self by collective that she fears.

The episode of her husband's death provides a final, and brutal, confirmation that her story is out of her control. Fleeing society, the Princesse isolates herself in her country home, where, one evening, she finally gives expression to her love for Nemours, albeit in a private, symbolic mode: she goes alone to a garden pavilion, where, weaving ribbons around a cane that formerly belonged to Nemours, she gazes in rapture at his representation in a tableau of the siege of Metz. The privacy of this expression is doubly ironized, for not only is Nemours observing this rite of adoration from a hiding spot in the hedge, but he himself is being observed by a spy sent by the Prince. When the latter hears his man's vague report that the duc spent the night in the estate, he suspects the worst and dies of a broken heart. Thus even the Princesse's most radically enclosed gesture of self-expression is overseen, appropriated, and reinterpreted by others. The Prince dies because of a report that is blown out of proportion, and because he will not believe his wife's account, and his death dramatizes microcosmically the distortions to which self-expression is subject, and the unforeseen effects it can have, once re-counted within collective discourse.

Later novels will show a happy symbiosis of individual discourse and world order in a dialectic whereby the cultural narrative continually reshapes itself to admit the self-defining narrations of its members, which narrations in turn adjust themselves to the grammar of their culture. *La Princesse de Clèves* relates no such collaboration, but rather a darker transaction, in which every attempt at self-definition is appropriated by the collective, circulated, disfigured, and used against its author. Mme de Clèves cannot still the collective voice, or contain her own story, in spite of her vigilance. Powerless to resist entrapment in an intrigue with Nemours as long as she remains within the court, she elects flight as a final means of taking her identity out of its hands. Since the collective account is the ground of identity, however, this necessarily implies a loss of character: after briefly tracing her withdrawal from society, the narrative abruptly stops. Having disappeared from the public eye, the Princesse disappears from reality and ceases to function as an embodiment of the courtly ideal. Once she has transgressed the bounds of the collective history, her story becomes un-knowable, her behavior inimitable; thus the novel's dismissive last sentence: "sa vie, qui fut assez courte, laissa des exemples de vertu inimitables" (p. 395) (Her life, which was rather brief, left inimitable examples of virtue).

Yet if *La Princesse de Clèves* refuses the possibility of *self*-definition, it does point the way towards a more subtle form of interaction between personal narration and collective narrative. Even as it seals the doom of the protagonist's marriage, the famous scene of the garden house allegorizes the *symbolic* representation of the *Other* as a strategy for self-expression. Rather than seeking to articulate her love for the duc directly, or repress it entirely, the Princesse expresses it symbolically through the creation of a fetish object (the cane) which she embellishes lovingly. In this process, it is an artistic representation, the painting of the duc, which bodies forth for the Princesse the duc's person. This private resymbolization of the desired person resonates in the duc's similar gesture some time later. Having failed to gain access to the Princesse in person, he retreats to his own private copse in the garden where he re-presents the entirety of his love for the Princesse to his imagination and engages a dialogue with this more tractable object of adoration:

> Il s'éloigna le plus qu'il lui fut possible, pour n'être vu ni entendu de personne; il s'abandonna aux transports de son amour . . . Il se mit à repasser toutes les actions de Mme de Clèves depuis qu'il en était amoureux . . .

Laissez-moi voir que vous m'aimez, belle princesse, s'écria-t-il, laissez-moi voir vos sentiments; pourvu que je les connaisse par vous une fois en ma vie, je consens que vous repreniez pour toujours ces rigueurs dont vous m'accabliez. Regardez-moi du moins avec ces mêmes yeux dont je vous ai vue cette nuit regarder mon portrait; pouvez-vous l'avoir regardé avec tant de douceur et m'avoir fui moi-même si cruellement? Que craignez-vous? Pourquoi mon amour vous est-il si redoutable? Vous m'aimez, vous me le cachez inutilement; vous-même m'en avez donné des marques involontaires. Je sais mon bonheur; laissez-m'en jouir, et cessez de me rendre malheureux. (Pp. 368–9)

He removed himself as far as possible, in order to be neither seen nor heard by anyone; he gave himself over to the transports of his love... He began to go over all of Mme de Clèves' actions since he had been in love with her... Let me see that you love me, beautiful princess, he exclaimed, let me see your feelings; provided I hear them from your mouth once in my life, I will consent that you resume that severity with which you overwhelmed me. At least look at me through those same eyes with which I saw you gaze at my portrait that night; can you have looked upon it with such sweetness and yet have fled me so cruelly? What are you afraid of? Why is my love so fearsome? You love me, it is useless trying to conceal it from me; you yourself have given me involuntary indications of it. I am aware of my good fortune; let me enjoy it, and stop making me miserable.

In this remarkable passage, Nemours for the first time articulates a goal at variance with the conventional script of *galanterie*: having observed the Princesse's symbolization of her desire, he expresses his own willingness to renounce possessing her in return for a single visionary moment in which he might see his love confirmed directly. Upon returning to Paris he will further implement this displacement of public display by private vision: in an urban reiteration of the garden scene, he rents a room with a view over her courtyard and, on the pretext of painting the beautiful courtyard, spends his afternoons gazing in rapture, yet unseen, at his cherished mistress across the way (pp. 378–9).

In the next episode, the Princesse reiterates the same gesture of symbolization, when she spies Nemours in a public garden "couché sur les bancs... enseveli dans une rêverie profonde" (p. 379) (lying on the benches... absorbed in a deep reverie). Echoing his covert contemplation of her and the trance which it elicits, the Princesse extracts from her brief glimpse of the duc a spectacular internal vision which is all the more remarkable for the narrative elaboration it receives:

Ce prince se présenta à son esprit, aimable au-dessus de tout ce qui était au monde, l'aimant depuis longtemps avec une passion pleine de respect et de fidélité, méprisant tout pour elle, respectant jusqu'à sa douleur, songeant à la voir sans songer à en être vu, quittant la cour, dont il faisait les délices, pour aller regarder les murailles qui la renfermaient, pour venir rêver dans des lieux où il ne pouvait prétendre de la rencontrer; enfin un homme digne d'être aimé par son seul attachment, et pour qui elle avait une inclination si violente qu'elle l'aurait aimé quand il ne l'aurait pas aimée; mais, de plus, un homme d'une qualité élevée et convenable à la sienne. Plus de devoir, plus de vertu qui s'opposassent à ses sentiments; tous les obstacles étaient levés, et il ne restait de leur état passé que la passion de M. de Nemours pour elle et que celle qu'elle avait pour lui. (P. 380)

This prince appeared to her mind attractive beyond anything in the world, having loved her for a long time with a loyal and respectful passion, disdaining everything for her, even respecting her pain, thinking of ways to see her without thinking of making himself seen by her, leaving the court, whose delight he was, to go and look at the walls that enclosed her, to come and daydream in places where he could not hope to meet her; a man, finally, whose mere devotion made him worthy of love, and for whom her attraction was so violent that she would have loved him even if he had not loved her; but in addition, a man of quality and rank equal to hers. No longer would duty or virtue conflict with her feelings; all obstacles had been removed, and there remained of their previous situation only M. de Nemours' passion for her and hers for him.

This abstract assessment of her passion for the duc marks the Princesse's formulation of an ideal relationship unhampered by the constraints of society, but it also foreshadows her decision to leave Nemours. Knowing that her ideal vision could never survive the confrontation with Nemours' infidelity, and that his infidelity is a near certainty, given the power of the social framework, the Princesse elects to content herself with the contemplation of her dream, rather than testing its durability in reality. As she explains in their first, and last, conversation about their relationship:

la certitude de n'être plus aimée de vous, comme je le suis, me paraît un si horrible malheur que, quand je n'aurais point des raisons de devoir insurmontables, je doute si je pourrais me résoudre à m'exposer à ce malheur. (P. 387)

the certainty of no longer being loved by you the way I am now, appears to me a misfortune so terrible that even if I had no insurmountable reasons of duty, I doubt that I could bring myself to suffer exposure to this unhappiness.

Par vanité ou par goût, toutes les femmes souhaitent de vous attacher. Il y en a peu à qui vous ne plaisiez; mon expérience me ferait croire qu'il n'y en a a point à qui vous ne puissiez plaire. Je vous croirais toujours amoureux et aimé et je ne me tromperais pas souvent. (Pp. 388)

Whether from vanity or inclination, all women hope to have you. There are few whom you do not please; my experience would lead me to believe there are none whom you could not please. I would always suspect you of being in love and loved, and I would not often be mistaken.

Ultimately, it is the Princesse's imagination that wins out: rather than remain at court to witness the repudiation of her ideal, she retreats to the seclusion of the provinces where her vision of Nemours' perfect love will risk no contradiction. At the same time, Nemour sees the fulfillment of the wish he formulated in the woods: he receives Mme de Clèves' unabashed declaration of love in the single interview they have together, after which he never again sees her. Deprived of its main characters, the novel abruptly stops.

Although private representation emerges in these final scenes as an alternative to social reality, it is an alternative that is only obliquely proposed. The conclusion of the novel does not retract the dominance of cultural narrative: the Princesse may elaborate a version of love at odds with that of her culture, but she cannot enact this love within the culture. Nor, for that matter, does she attempt *self*-depiction in her ideal vision: she idealizes the duc but makes little effort to redefine herself in an equally positive way. This reticence to narrate the self is consistent with the form of the novel: the story is narrated in an anonymous third person omniscient voice, takes place in a setting temporally removed from that of the author or reader, and was published anonymously.

All of these features reiterate the plot's negation of self-expression: while the establishment of facts and fortunes is everyone's business, and in this sense history is a collective enterprise in which all are free to participate, the individual enjoys only an indirect mode of self-presentation. The tales one spreads about others in a sense represent one's self, but only in the form of an Other's story, the meaning of which is continually shifting. Moreover, the stories one puts into circulation metamorphose so rapidly under the pressure of successive recounting that one can never be certain what stories they tell: once taken up by the collective, they exceed the intentions of their author, and whatever effect they have can no longer be traced to a particular intention. This mechanism, and the strangely impersonal form of self-expression it predicates, find striking thematization in the successive scenes of representation that close the novel.

The series of symbolization episodes mentioned above all stress the fluidity of meaning by insisting on the shifts which come with the recontextualization or reiteration of a story. Thus the duc's despair in the park becomes the object of the Princesse's joyful vision and the catalyst for her reawakening passion, while the vision of her grief during her mourning of her husband nourishes his adoration from across the courtyard. Of course, the most spectacular version of this paradigm is the garden scene. Blatantly gesturing towards its allegorical dimensions, and hence the reader's share in the events, through the device of the garden, this scene piles up no less than four levels of framed observers. The Princesse is contemplating the duc, who is framed in the canvas and embodied in the cane. The duc is observing the Princesse framed in her garden house window. The Prince de Clèves' spy is outside the garden, watching the duc, who is framed by its walls and hedges. And the reader is contemplating all of these characters framed by the scene and, on a larger plane, the novel and the period it depicts.

There are other scenes of framing in the novel (such as the ballroom scene cited above, where the duc and the Princesse are observed by the court as they dance), and one might conceptualize the system of collective narrative as a structure of permanent recontextualization, in which each individual's acts and identity undergo continual reinterpretation at successive levels of observation. In the case of the garden scene, for instance, the same set of events takes a different meaning at each level of observation: what for the Princesse seems a perfectly secure moment of safety from the duc's presence, functions for the duc as a declaration of love, for the spy as an ambiguous episode of voyeurism, for the Prince de Clèves as the proof of his wife's adultery, and for the reader as an emblem of the novel's thematic infrastructure.

Because it underlines the contingency of "facts" on their context and moment of interpretation, the theme of the frame opens a possibility for narrational intervention which is latent in earlier scenes but consistently denied by the catastrophes that accompany personal expression. By accumulating multiple levels of framed observation, the garden scene forces the analogy between the situation of the characters and that of the reader, compelling the latter to realize the degree to which his or her perception of events is conditioned by the context of their reception. At the same time, the scene insists on the fact that the first link in the chain of this perception is an artistic representation – an historical portrait painted by a professional artist with a particular goal in mind. As an emblem of the author's private ideation, as well as that of the reader who contemplates it and weaves her/his own fantasies around it, the scene of the painting and of Mme de Clèves' embellishment of the cane asserts the literary narrative's recuperation of the narrational prerogatives which are denied to individual expression within the plot. This scene in particular not only portrays the flexibility of facts and their ultimate contingency on acts of individual interpretation, but, by underlining the fact that the novel's lesson of collective primacy is grounded in an *artistic artifact* masquerading as historical account, it recuperates for the author (and to a lesser degree the reader) the privileges which the surface plot rescinds. While direct intervention in one's own story may be impossible, one can nonetheless gain leverage over the collective narrative by creating a fiction that *represents* that narrative. What the Princesse cannot do – oppose her version of Nemours' love to the version her culture has elaborated – the novel accomplishes, by putting into circulation within the collective a story that *relates* its mechanisms and thus surpasses them.[25]

True to the strictures on self-expression that it lays down, the novel conceals its personal origins under the mask of history, which, as the ultimate order framing reality, relieves the novelist of responsibility for the worldly vision she advances. Yet the insertion of a blatantly personal fiction into the discourse of history challenges the primacy of the collective record even as it affirms it, reclaiming for fiction and its agents, the author and reader, the rights which the plot abrogates.[26] This gesture will become standard in the novels of the eighteenth century, where "authentic histories" repeatedly merge into personal accounts of individuals manipulating the collective record to their advantage.

One can of course explain such thematic discretion in terms of the political climate. Generating a model of society whose resemblance to contemporary reality implicitly defines and codifies social behavior, but which, unlike "live" narration, and given the interpretive function of the reader, cannot be linked to any single origin, the discourse of *La Princesse de Clèves* subverts the structures of authority it depicts: it destabilizes the hierarchy of power by birthright or personal attachment through the introduction of an "impersonal," "historical" authority the personal origins of which one can posit but not locate. By thus disguising their remappings of reality under the guise of history, early novelists could usurp an authority otherwise reserved for the empowered aristocracy. In this sense, the narrative oligarchy Mme de Lafayette depicts is precisely that which works like *La Princesse de Clèves* were destined to disrupt.[27]

A more straightforward thematic treatment of how individual construals of reality relate to the order that grounds them – and which they inevitably try to comprehend – can be found in the early English fiction of the eighteenth century. I have chosen as a starting point Defoe's remarkable allegory *Robinson Crusoe*, not only because it draws in particularly clear lines the gradual comprehension of grounding order within personal plot, but because it graphically illustrates that order's providential, divine basis in the English tradition. The grounding authority for personal identity in the French tradition as prefigured by *La Princesse de Clèves* is resolutely secular and collective: a restricted social cohort whose discursive activities delimit the role and status of each of its members according to a highly conventionalized code of behavior. If in the English tradition self-definition will also ultimately invoke the confrontation between individual and collective discourse, this confrontation evolves out of a framework of solitary exchanges or dialogues – which in the early works are frequently subtended by the dialogue between one's self and one's God. It is the movement from this highly private relationship with divine authority to a relationship linking individual to society, which *Robinson Crusoe* portrays.

NOTES

1   Brooks, *Novel of Worldliness*, p. 68. The influence and prestige of *La Princesse de Clèves* extended far beyond the tradition of worldliness. Even Rousseau used it as a standard of comparison when boasting of the excellence of his own *Julie, ou la nouvelle Héloïse*; cf. *Les Confessions*, in vol. 1 of *Oeuvres complètes*, ed. Bernard Gagnebin et Marcel Raymond (Paris: Gallimard, "Bibliothèque de la Pléiade," 1959), p. 546.

2   *La Princesse de Clèves* is generally attributed to Mme de Lafayette, a remarkably versatile woman of letters who, in addition to running her household singlehandedly and defending the interests of her husband's estate, was a *demoiselle d'honneur* to the queen, former habituée of the literary salons of Mlle de Scudéry and l'hôtel de Rambouillet, and friend of Mme de Sévigné and La Rochefoucauld. It is generally accepted that the latter, and probably also Jean-Regnauld de Segrais, with whom she had collaborated on an early novel, *Zaïre*, participated in the work's composition. An English translation appearing in 1679 reflected the possible multiple authorship of the novel: *The Princess of Cleves. The Most Famed Romance. Written in French by the greatest Wits of France*, Rendered into English by a Person of Quality at the Request of some Friends (London: A. Bentely and M. Magnes).

3   See for example Trublet, *Essais*, pp. 225–8, and Jacquin, *Entretiens*, pp. 161ff. In clear testimony to the work's seminal role in redefining French fiction, Jacquin classes *La Princesse de Clèves* with the more recent realist works of Prévost and Crébillon fils as having played a decisive role in the obsolescence of the romance; p. 96.

4   In their critical editions of *La Princesse de Clèves*, Antoine Adam and Emile Magne identify a great number of the historical personages mentioned in the novel, as well as many of the sources for the historical portions of the plot; cf. *Romanciers du XVIIe siècle*, ed. Antoine Adam (Paris: Gallimard, "Bibliothèque de la Pléiade", 1958) pp. 53–4; Mme de Lafayette, *Romans et nouvelles*, ed. Emile Magne (Paris: Garnier, 1961), p. 426, n. 43. In addition, Adam lists several possible historical and fictional sources for the fictional episodes of the text; *Romanciers*, pp. 54–6. For more detailed analysis see H. Chamard and G. Rudler, "Les Sources historiques de la *Princesse de Clèves*," *Revue du XVIe Siècle*, 2 (1914), pp. 92–131, and "Les Episodes historiques," ibid, pp. 289–321, and "La Couleur historique dans *La Princesse de Clèves*," *Revue du XVIe Siècle*, 5 (1917), pp. 1–20. While several of the main characters are based on historical individuals, the events recounted by Mme de Lafayette in the personal story of the Princesse are her own creation, as are the characters of the Princesse and her mother.

5   Mme de Lafayette wrote two histories herself, *Histoire de Madame Henriette d'Angleterre*, dating from 1665–9, and the *Mémoires de la cour de France pour les années 1688 & 1689*, written two decades later. While the former text, which reports Mme de Lafayette's first-hand experience of the death of her friend Henriette, is considered the more interesting of the two documents because of

its lively presentation of the personal dramas of the court, the latter, with its unrelenting attention to military developments and the larger political sphere, is probably more typical of the histories of the period. For an appreciation of the two works and their relationship to Mme de Lafayette's fictional works, see Gilbert Sigaux's introduction to his critical edition, *Histoire de Madame Henriette d'Angleterre, suivie de Mémoires de la cour de France pour les années 1688 & 1689* (Paris: Mercure de France, 1982).

6   Jean-Henry du Trousset de Valincour, *Lettres à Madame la marquise *** sur le sujet de la "Princesse de Clèves"* (1678), ed. Albert Cazes (Paris: Bossard, 1925); see esp. pp. 132–43. In the eighteenth century, l'abbé Jacquin will also object to Mme de Lafayette's fanciful vision of the court of Henri II in his diatribe against novels, without, however, grasping the function of the invention within a historical context; *Entretiens*, p. 160.

7   Speaking of the epic Greek poets, for instance, Valincour asserts, p. 133: "ils ont travaillé sur un sujet véritable; ... Je n'examine point ici s'il y a jamais eu une véritable guerre de Troie; si les Grecs prirent cette ville, ou s'ils y furent battus: il suffit que le fond de cette histoire, de la manière dont les poètes l'ont écrite, était répandu parmi le peuple comme une chose véritable; ainsi ils pouvaient le prendre pour fondement de leurs ouvrages" (they worked on a real subject ... I am not debating here whether there ever really was a Trojan war; whether the Greeks took that city or whether they were defeated there: it is enough that the fundamentals of the story as the poets wrote them were widely accepted among the people as a genuine thing: in that case they can use them as the basis of their works). Two pages later he will invert the equivalence: "les noms et les événements étant tirés de l'histoire ... ils sont connus de tout le monde" (the names and the events being taken from history ... they are known by everyone).

8   Valincour, p. 142; my italics. See also p. 139, where, citing Castelvetro in his admonition against abusive invention, Valincour backhandedly envisions a fiction which would carry positional authority over reality: "si l'on permettait aux auteurs d'inventer ainsi de nouveaux personnages, lorsqu'ils en auraient besoin dans leurs histoires, l'on devrait aussi leur permettre d'inventer de nouveaux fleuves, de nouveaux pays, et enfin de faire un nouveau monde, si cela leur est utile" (if one were to permit authors to invent new people in this way, whenever they needed them in their histories, one should also permit them to invent new rivers, new countries, and finally to fabricate a new world, if it is useful to them).

9   Ibid., p. 135.

10 In my reading of the novel, I am of course intermixing two perspectives, one that analyses the events of the book as events and one that reassesses them as the products of a narration. It is precisely such a mixing, I would contend, that the book invites through its own melding of history and fiction.

11 Several of the episodes and themes of this plot, such as the role of love in courtly intrigues, the inadvertent revelation of a secret passion, the nocturnal visit to the garden, the jealous but misinformed husband, the confession to the husband, and the death from heartbreak of a rejected lover, can be found in

Mme de Lafayette's other stories, *La Princesse de Montpensier* and *La Comtesse de Tende*, but neither of these shorter works has the complexity nor the attention to the sociology of the courtier that mark *La Princesse de Clèves*.

12   The general stages of the Princesse's passion (first sight, visual captivation, symbolic declarations, the lover's timidity and fear of compromising his beloved, the pain of jealousy, the jealous husband, the fear of discovery by local gossips, the nocturnal "rendez-vous," the separation of the lovers, the grief of the abandoned lover) correspond to *topoi* of courtly love, as celebrated in the poetry of the troubadours and *trouvères* and reiterated in a variety of genres spanning the centuries, from the immensely successful *Roman de la rose*, and the fixed form love poetry of the fifteenth century, up to the pastoral love stories of Mme de Lafayette's own times.

13   Valincour is particularly critical of the digressions; cf. *La Princesse de Clèves; Romans et Nouvelles*, pp. xxvii, 428 n.58, 429 n.71. For a discussion of other reactions to the digressions, both contemporary and modern, see Jean Rousset, *Forme et signification* (Paris: José Corti, 1962), pp. 28ff.

14   All citations are from Magne (ed.), *Romans et nouvelles*. Translations are my own.

15   The oblique political influence of women and love is a central theme of later eighteenth-century French critics of history, who single out the lack of details concerning the role of women in shaping great events as one of the discipline's most obvious shortcomings, and an area where novels provide a more accurate vision of reality; see Lenglet Du Fresnoy, *De l'usage des romans*, 1:223–30; d'Argens, *Lettres juives*, letter 39; Johnson, *Rambler*, no 34 (July 14, 1750).

16   Argens, *Lettres juives*, letter 27; see also letter 55, where d'Argens reiterates the analogy and reaffirms the king's divine exemption from retribution at the hands of his subjects.

17   Mme de Lafayette's chronicle of the intrigues in the court of the young Louis XIV, *Histoire de Madame Henriette d'Angleterre*, provides abundant examples of the complexity and the stakes involved in the web of courtly intrigue. As the account of one particularly obnoxious courtier, Vardes, illustrates, a single imprudent snide remark could easily trigger a sequence of events culminating in a sojourn in the Bastille, banishment from the court, permanent imprisonment, or even exile and the stripping of charges (cf. *Histoire*, pp. 77–8). Even more dramatic is the fate of Henriette d'Angleterre's daughter by Monseigneur (the brother of Louis XIV). As reported by Mme de Lafayette, *Mémoires de la cour de France*, pp. 156–7, she is poisoned at the court of Spain by counselors to the king of Spain (her husband) eager to stop her influence. Similarly, when her mother, Henriette, dies, she too will claim on her death bed to be poisoned (cf. *Histoire* pp. 80–91). The accounts that are put into circulation at the court do not simply influence individuals, though. In his discussion of the way rumors and embellished accounts metamorphose into facts through repetition, Pierre Bayle emphasizes that state interest can be advanced by a fictitious report which is allowed to circulate for a few days, or suffer from an inopportune revelation of political secrets; *Dictionnaire historique et critique*, 3ème édition revue, cor-

rigée, et augmentée par l'auteur, 4 vols. (Rotterdam: Michel Bohm, 1720), vol. 4, 2953.

18 Michael McKeon elegantly traces the gradual transvaluation of honor into the two separate categories of virtue and aristocratic rank which culminates in England during the seventeenth century and results, subsequently, in both the valorizing of female chastity as a locus of honor-as-virtue and a literary "fascination with the constancy of common women, pursued by corrupt aristocrats" (p. 158). The French are substantially more tolerant of adultery and bastardy, possibly because their inheritance procedures make the strict monitoring of offspring less crucial than in England, but they still value at least a nominal adherence to chastity on the part of their noblewomen. As portrayed both in *La Princesse de Clèves* and in the eighteenth-century novels, this nominal chastity consists primarily in discretion – again, concealing one's involvement in social reality. There are stories, however, that depict extra-marital engagements in remarkably open terms, suggesting that in practice little opprobrium was attached to co-habitation, and even raising children out of wedlock: cf. Robert Chasles' *Les Illustres Françoises* (1713), ed. Frédéric Deloffre, 2 vols (Paris: "Les Belles Lettres," 1967). The fact that at least one influential critic, Lenglet Du Fresnoy, reproached Chasles, whom I discuss below at more length, for presenting a picture of sexual reality too close to history and too little idealized, suggests that his representation of the French attitude toward chastity is reasonably accurate; cf. *De l'usage des romans*, vol. 1, pp. 295–6.

19 The Princesse de Montpensier, in Mme de Lafayette's story of the same name, exhibits the same superlative beauty and charm: "la beauté de la princesse effaça toutes celles qu'on avait admirées jusques alors. Elle attira les yeux de tout le monde par les charmes de son esprit et de sa personne" (p. 14). Superlative characters are of course a hallmark of the romance tradition to which Mme de Lafayette's earlier works belong and within whose shadow *La Princesse de Clèves* appeared.

20 As the following discussion intimates, to be exceptional is both to excel according to the conventions of a culture *and* to stretch the limits of those conventions through behavior so remarkable that it forces a redefinition or rethinking of conventionality itself. It is thus the ground for virtually all programs of individualism portrayed in the eighteenth-century novel, and particularly those of the great (im)moral heroines: Moll, Roxana, Pamela, Clarissa, Julie, Mme de Merteuil. A striking early English example of an exceptional individual, and one that exploits the familiar strategy of cultural self-scrutiny through comparison with the "outside" or exotic, is the character of Oroonoko, in Aphra Behn's short novel of the same name, published in 1688. Combining a distinctly European sense of virtue, honor, and bravery with the exotic cultural usages of an African prince, Oroonoko, a black nobleman enslaved and abused by the British, embodies the conjunction of the familiar and the "other," the conventional and the different, and his story contains an implicit critique of the culture within which it appeared. It is interesting to note in passing that another of Behn's novels, *The History of Agnes de Castro*, contains many of the same plot

elements as *La Princesse de Clèves*, including the attraction to the spouse's best friend, resistance to this attraction, its confession to one's spouse, the death of the spouse upon receiving a false report of adultery, and the retreat to a solitude in a public garden, where the loved one in encountered. However, Behn's tale inverts the sexes, making the husband the enamored one and the wife the one who dies, and she extends the tale to include a secret marriage of the lovers following the wife's death. The story depicts, finally, a courtly economy similarly regulated by narrative, and includes examples of narrative manipulation far more graphic than those in Mme de Lafayette's work: forged letters, blatant lies and misrepresentations, etc.; Aphra Behn, *All the Histories and Novels Written by the Late Ingenious Mrs. Behn*, 2 vols, 7th edn (London: Mr Charles Gildon, 1722).

21 Peggy Kamuf, *Fictions of Feminine Desire* (Lincoln, Nebraska: University of Nebraska Press, 1982), pp. 67–96, associates this agenda of inviolability with "the mother's fantasy of impervious womanhood" (p. 94) and Mme de Chartres' enclosure of the Princesse in a mother–daughter dialogue that pre-empts the daughter's sexual desire by representing it as a function of the mother's (educational) narrative. Kamuf's reading of a "mother's construction and a daughter's excess" (p. 69), while decidedly psychoanalytic in its approach, confirms the central role of coercive narratives in the novel.

22 The Chevalier de Guise, who is hopelessly in love with the Princesse and resents the Duc's favor, might be the one exception. The relationship of these two young rivals, each of whom is the most perceptive observer of the other precisely because of their love for the same woman, corresponds to that of the duc d'Anjou and the duc de Guise in *La Princesse de Montpensier* (cf. *Romans et nouvelles*, pp. 12–13, 19–20).

23 Even the Princesse's overall, if repressed, plan to have her love and hide it too, finds a precedent in the mention her mother makes, while recounting the story of the duchesse de Valentinois, of a noble woman whose virtue was compromised, but who nonetheless managed to keep it secret throughout her life.

24 A variation on the same theme can be found in the scene of the masked ball in *La Princesse de Montpensier*, where the Princesse inadvertently, and without recognizing she has done so, reveals her love for the duc de Guise to his rival the duc d'Anjou (pp. 18–22).

25 I am assuming, of course, that the social mechanisms described in *La Princesse de Clèves* are those of the culture within which it was written. Indeed the similarities between the social mechanisms described in *La Princesse de Clèves* and those chronicled in Mme de Lafayette's *Histoire de Madame Henriette d'Angleterre* make clear that the culture in question is that of the court of Louis XIV – as does Mme de Lafayette's own evaluation of the novel: "surtout, ce qu'on y trouve, c'est une parfaite imitation du monde de la cour et de la manière dont on y vit" (cited by Adam, pp. 54–55, Rousset, *Forme et signification*, p. 18) (What one finds there is especially a perfect imitation of the courtly world and of the manner in which one lives there). At the same time, the consistent preoccupation with jealousy, repressed passion, and marital stress in all of Mme de Lafayette's works indicates to what degree the vision of reality

presented in her novel is particular to its author. The world of *La Princesse de Clèves* is thus incontestably a *mise en scène* of the reality framing both author and work, in spite of its historical setting.

26 One of the few commentators sensitive to the subtlety of the novel's subversion of collective authority is Barbara Jones Guetti, who figures Mme de Lafayette's fiction as a kind of forgery seeking "to usurp historical truth, replacing it with an alternative, rival truth," which gesture she in turn links to a feminist agenda which "supplements the silence of real women with fictions designed to usurp the priority (and the propriety) of all modes of discourse – legal, fictional, or historical – that have, so effectively, imposed that silence upon them"; "'Travesty' and 'Usurpation' in Mme de Lafayette's Historical Fiction," *Yale French Studies*, 69 (1985), pp. 211–21; pp. 213, 221.

27 This subversion is particularly remarkable as the work of a woman, since it succeeds in overturning, or inverting, the pattern of surveillance of women which the novel dramatizes. As Jean Rousset notes, "Mme de Lafayette proclame à travers ses romans que l'on ne pénètre pas au fond de son propre cœur, et que le seul regard perspicace est le regard d'autrui. . . . Le roman est une parfaite démonstration, par sa structure même, que la connaissance objective est avantagée aux dépens de la connaissance interne" (*Forme et signification*, p. 23) (Mme de Lafayette proclaims through her novels that one does not penetrate to the bottom of one's own heart, and that the only perspicacious gaze is the gaze of the Other. . . . The novel is a perfect demonstration, by its very structure, that objective knowledge is favored at the expense of internal knowledge), and although he extends this generalization to men as well as women, it is clear from the structure of the plot, which repeatedly places Nemours in a position of the unseen spectator of the Princesse (ibid., p. 26), and only once gives her the same privilege, that the repressive force of the permanently surveying eye falls primarily on women. Barred from codified, symbolic expressions of their passion, such as wearing the loved one's colors in jousts, women are also deprived of their privacy, and thus inhibited from any mode of self-expression. Assuming the novel is in fact the work of a woman, it reverses this pattern by enclosing and penetrating this mechanism of surveillance with its own analytic gaze.

3

Personal Ordering and Providential Order
(*Robinson Crusoe*)

Daniel Defoe's *Robinson Crusoe* is as firmly entrenched in bourgeois materialism as is *La Princesse de Clèves* in the rarified world of French nobility. Yet while they start from different sociopolitical and cultural bases, both works are concerned to define the structures of authority overseeing individual endeavor within their respective cultures, and both dramatize the apprenticeship of those structures by the self-assertive individualist. Coming a half-century before the heyday of individualism, *La Princesse de Clèves* can only gesture covertly toward the narrational strategies of self-definition that will emerge with more clarity in later works, but its articulation of a secular, social system of authority prefigures the tendency under consideration here and underlines the single most important difference between the French novelists of the eighteenth century and their English counterparts. For the French the various forms of authority confronting the individual are grounded primarily in the secular order of social practices, even at the outset. Divine authority may be assumed to underlie social institutions, but only nominally so. The major determining force against which protagonists will have to assert themselves is that of the collective voice, and their most pressing task will be finding a voice of their own, a means of expressing themselves within the competitive economy of social discourse.

The early English protagonists have a relatively easier time getting their versions of things into circulation, perhaps because they do not perceive collective discourse to be the sole ground of their identity. Especially in *Robinson Crusoe*, the individual's struggle with the social order is assumed to figure a more fundamental dialogue between that individual and the Creator. In Defoe's subsequent novels this private dialogue will be supplanted by the struggles of the individual against the hostile Other which is constituted by society in opposition to personal autonomy. Still later in the century, first in the works of Richardson, then even more graphically in those of Fielding, the different members of this hostile community will emerge as individuals in their own right – the other players in a game of social antagonism which pits the protagonist against rival, equally assertive, individuals following plans of their own which have little or nothing to do with divine agency. Ultimately, the French and English traditions will both lead to a vision of social reality as the product of a competitive economy of collective narration, in which various individuals momentarily seem to gain the upper hand, by virtue of a superior grasp of the grammar of that economy, but which eventually forecloses on all such delusions of mastery.

In Defoe's Puritan world, though, we find only the earliest stages of this evolution. The world he depicts is one of an isolated self constantly threatened by an undifferentiated collective "other,"[1] yet answerable to a higher order of divine authority accessible solely through a private, singular dialogue of self and providence. *Robinson Crusoe* addresses both of these relationships by showing how the internalization of divine authority by the individual provides a paradigm for the successful reconciliation of personal will and social demands. Both relationships, moreover, are mediated narratively by the protagonist's account of his experience, prefiguring subsequent stories of how individuals "come to terms" with both their experiences and the contexts of those experiences by setting them down in a logical order and reassessing their meaning.[2]

If, as Ian Watt says, Robinson Crusoe personifies "three associated tendencies of modern civilization – absolute economic, social and intellectual freedom for the individual"[3] he also correlates these projects – especially the latter two – with narration and narratives. Citing Rousseau, Watt defines intellectual freedom as the possibility one has to "raise oneself above prejudices, and order one's judgement on the real relationship between things . . . to put oneself in the place of an isolated man, and to judge of everything as that man would judge of them according to their actual usefulness" (p. 96). As Crusoe's own behavior testifies, this definition is impractically naive in its assumption that one could ever conceive of a totally culture-free state of mind: even at the height of his self-sufficiency, much of the marooned seaman's judgments and wants – such as the obsession with wearing clothing or the desire for a tobacco pipe – bespeak an obvious cultural bias. These vestiges of Crusoe's heritage underline Rousseau's implicit acknowledgment that it is culture that dictates the "relationship between things" for social man. The exact form and utility of this predication can be found late in *Robinson Crusoe*, when Robinson prepares to abandon the mutinous English sailors on his island and return to Europe. Having obtained the agreement of the sailors to carry on his practice of colonization, Crusoe quite literally initiates them into the reality of his domain:

> When they had all declared their willingness to stay, I then told them I would let them into the story of my living there, and put them into the way of making it easy to them. Accordingly I gave them the whole history of the place, and of my coming to it; shewed them my fortifications, the way I made my bread, planted my corn, cured my grapes; and in a word, all that was

necessary to make them easy. I told them the story also of the sixteen Spaniards that were to be expected; for whom I left a letter, and made them promise to treat them in common with themselves.

I left them my fire arms, viz. five muskets, three fowling pieces, and three swords. I had above a barrel and half of powder left; for after the first year or two, I used but little, and wasted none. I gave them a description of the way I managed the goats, and directions to milk and fatten them, and to make both butter and cheese.

In a word, I gave them every part of my own story. (Pp. 272–3)[4]

Covering many of the functions of the collective accounts that ground specific cultures and give them their identity – history, inventory of property, delineation of boundaries, definition of tools, technological instruction, moral exemplum ("I used but little, and wasted none"), collective contract ("I made them promise . . .") – Crusoe's account furnishes the sailors with both a role in life and the technology to fulfill it. It thus provides a vastly simplified functional equivalent of the cultural narrative that orders social reality and guides our actions. At the same time, Crusoe omits instructing his successors in the reality-ordering practice that generated this rich set of procedures and usages in the first place, namely his self-conscious program of innovation, invention, and ritualization. For the world he passes on to posterity owes its coherence – indeed, its very being – as a set of goals, activities, monuments, and routines, to a sustained narrational drive that draws its energy for ordering reality from the vision of order provided by its past accomplishments. Crusoe does not passively assimilate a ready-made world the way he would have his successors do: he creates one. His entire reality – architecture, defenses, shelter, boatbuilding, carpentry, animal husbandry, agriculture, artisanship, and, ultimately, social organization of the other humans that come to the island – reflects, and thus funds, his personal history. It is the image of its maker and his incentive to future endeavor. Each of his successive accomplishments adds another episode to a story whose recounting and contemplation not only furnishes him with his major inspiration, but ultimately obtains for him the fortune considered beyond his reach at the beginning of his wanderings. In fact, Crusoe's story encapsulates both of the "fortunes" his father rejects for him at the outset of his manhood: "he told me it [a wandering, seafaring life] was for men of desperate fortunes on one hand, or of aspiring, superior fortune on the other, who went abroad upon adventures, to rise by enterprize, and make themselves famous in undertakings of a nature out of the common road" (p. 28).

In his reconstitution of a system of authority and program of human endeavor to replace the culture he rejects, and then loses, Crusoe's story provides an allegory of how individualism that is essentially historical in its reliance on narrative strategies of self-representation can displace the paternalistic authority of the established order by internalizing the divine authority of providence which that order claims to represent. *Robinson Crusoe* redefines selfhood against the authority of paternal ambition by outlining an apprenticeship of self-guidance articulated around an intimate dialogue with providence. And this association of personal action with divine decision sets the stage for a properly historical perspective in which the providential order can be subsumed by the historical order that is established by the record and ritualization of individual enterprise.[5] As rehearsed and refined by successive generations of eighteenth-century novelists, this process will entail the displacement of the retainers of cultural authority whose arbitration has been muddled by self-interest – typically the father, the sovereign, or the social superior (nobleman, or Master) – through a personal, more rigorous *re-presentation* of the principles underlying this authority. By both re-counting and acting out those principles within the context of his or her motives and logic, the individual will create an account of personal virtue which represents the laws of the culture in their unadulterated form and thus provides grounds, once circulated and validated by other members of society, upon which to base that individual's promotion or re-evaluation within the social order. *Robinson Crusoe* defines the first stage of this process by showing how a deliberate account of personal achievement can appropriate the authority of providence and ground social authority.

The story of *Robinson Crusoe* is well known in its general traits: a young man rejects his father's desires for him to settle into business and assume his rightful place in the "middle station" of society, choosing rather to satisfy his wanderlust and go to sea. After a series of adventures, he settles on a plantation in Brazil, where he achieves prosperity, only to go to sea once more in search of wealth on a slaving voyage. Shipwrecked on an uninhabited island, he re-enacts the domestication of nature and the establishment of human civilization through his ingenious inventions and agricultural exploits, all the while maintaining a careful record of his daily activities in a journal for that purpose. After many years, his idyll is disturbed by the discovery that cannibals periodically invade his domain, but when he rescues one of their victims, Friday, he rediscovers the pleasures of society. Eventually other Europeans come to the island, which Robinson declares to be his own empire. He initiates them into its maintenance, entrusts them with it, and returns to England with Friday.

While Robinson's clever domestication of nature is the part of his story that has captured the popular imagination, it should be remembered that his story is not just a tale of individual ingenuity, but also his account of how he *came to terms* with his situation through a deliberate sustained narrative representation to himself of his plight. The most obvious artifact of this dimension of the novel is his journal – a narrative within the narrative, which backtracks and recapitulates his experience in an effort to situate it within the context of his entire stay on the island, twenty-seven years. This journal underlines the fact that Robinson's story is above all the record of a man's representation of his situation, the story of his learning how to *give an account* of his life that is acceptable to both his eyes and those of society.

There are several stages to this process. Up to Robinson's shipwreck, the story traces primarily his rejection of mediated authority. The first, and strongest, incarnation of such authority is Robinson's father, whose defense of the "middle station" of life as that having the fewest disasters and vicissitudes, and as that into which Robinson had been born and ought to remain, personifies passivity in the face of the existing order. If Robinson sees his rejection of this paternal advice as "my wicked leaving my father's house, and abandoning my duty" (p. 31), it is not only because his repudiation of the "middle station" is an affirmation of self-interest against cultural prescription, but also because he associates his father's will with that of God, as he makes clear in the reference to his disobedience as "the breach of my duty to God and my father" (p. 31).[6] His father's admonition "that if I did take this foolish step, God would not bless me, and I would have leisure hereafter to reflect upon having neglected his counsel when there might be none to assist in my recovery" (p. 29) is precise in the ambiguity of its reference: "*his* counsel" might well refer to either the father or God, since paternal authority is synonymous with that of providence. This is underlined by the reaction of the second father figure whose counsel Robinson rejects. After suggesting that the lad ought to take his first disaster in the storm at Yarmouth as a "plain and visible token that you are not to be a seafaring man" (p. 37), the Master of the foundered ship (and the father of Robinson's sailing comrade) inquires on "what account" he went to sea in the first place. Upon hearing Robinson's story of filial disobedience, he "burst out with a strange kind of passion. 'What had I done,' says he, 'that such an unhappy wretch should come into my ship? I would not set my foot in the same ship with thee again for a thousand pounds'" (p. 37). Later he admonishes Crusoe "if you do not go back [home], where-ever you go, you will meet with nothing but disasters and disappointments till your father's words are fulfilled upon you" (p. 38). Clearly, paternal premonition has the weight of divine ordinance, and Robinson's own access to his *fortune*, whether one thinks of that notion as the greater order of things, or as the particular destiny he wishes for himself, is blocked by the authority of his parents. As Robinson later remarks, it is "in order to act the rebel to their authority" (p. 60) that he leaves home.[7]

A similar pattern of rebellion against authority and complacency continues throughout the book. Robinson's refusal to accept the order of things asserts itself twice more before his shipwreck: first, he undertakes to escape from his Moorish master, in spite of the improbability of success in the venture; then he abandons his plantation activities in favor of a slaving voyage. As a motive for his discontent in the second case, he specifically cites the resemblance of his life to the existence he could have led in England, had he heeded his father's counsel: "I was gotten into an employment quite remote to my genius, and directly contrary to the life I delighted in, and for which I forsook my father's house and broke thro' all his good advice; nay, I was coming into the very middle station, or upper degree of low life, which my father advised me to before" (pp. 55–6). Rather than taking his advancement as confirmation of his father's conviction that middle-class prosperity is his lot, Robinson determines once again to disrupt the "natural" order determining him and take his fate into his own hands:

> Had I continued in the station I was now in, I had room for all the happy things to have yet befallen me, for which my father so earnestly recommended a quiet retired life, and of which he had so sensibly described the middle station of life to be full of; but other things attended me, and I was still to be *the wilful agent of all my own miseries*; and particularly to *encrease my fault and double the reflections upon my self*, which in my future sorrows I should have leisure to make; all these miscarriages were procured by my apparent obstinate adhering to my foolish inclination of wandring abroad and pursuing that inclination, in contradiction to the clearest views of doing my self good in a fair and plain pursuit of *those prospects and those measures of life which nature and Providence concurred to present me with, and to make my duty*. (P. 58, my emphasis)

This passage sums up Crusoe's dilemma and prefigures his future strategy. He is an individual torn between two conflicting exigencies. On the one hand, he remains convinced of a higher order of reality, which he alternately refers to as providence, fortune, or nature, and which is manifest in his culture's structures of authority. Thus, the place society assigns him in the middle station, while the result of *cultural* institutions such as the family, which he braves without hesitation, are nonetheless associated with a *divine* order of things whose design he cannot hope to overcome. On the other hand, neither can he resist the imperative of his personal desire which opposes him to his family and culture. His particular mode of self-expression – the urge to wander – does not jibe with the values of society, and since he cannot dissociate those values from the divine authority they invoke, he cannot reconcile himself to his behavior. Neither, however, can he curtail that behavior without stifling his self-expression.

The resolution of this dilemma depends on the realignment of providence: if it can be made to coincide not just with the dictates of society but also with Crusoe's own "self-destructive" behavior, then he can be freed to follow his personal inclinations in the certitude that, as the will of a higher order, they are *a priori* justified. This would seem a reasonable task; since divine order necessarily includes everything Robinson does – as the reference above, "other things attended me," hints – Robinson already (and contradictorily) thinks of his own "disobedience" to God as inscribed in the design of providence. But while he is in society, whose competing values claim the authority of providence, he cannot correlate his own priorities with the will of God. It will require an outrageous *deux ex machina*, encompassing not only the shipwreck and sole survival of Crusoe, but the convenient availability of an entire ship's store of supplies, for Crusoe to align his activity with a divine design.

Making individual initiative and divine will congrue is only the first step in Crusoe's itinerary, however. By plotting his activities in a careful narrative account, he will overlay the script of providential design with his personal history, which history will eventually emerge as an authoritative script in its own right once other humans come to his island.[8] To this end, he establishes both a calendar and his journal (pp. 81, 86). He starts the latter only after more than a year on the island, during which time he has salvaged all the materials from the shipwreck, built himself a cavelike habitation in the side of a hill, surrounded it with a stockade, organized all of his provisions, and fashioned some pieces of furniture (pp. 82–6). It is therefore less an actual day-to-day journal, than a parallel or alternative account of his adventure – one which retrospectively encloses his experience in a strict chronological progression, permitting him to maintain his position within time and comprehend his existence in historical terms.[9] However, the boundaries between the journal and the autobiography soon become muddled, since the journal, which commences formally within the framework of that autobiography as a series of dated entries, and which backtracks to the beginning of Crusoe's island sojourn, recapitulating material already recounted, never actually ends: gradually the notations of dates become more sporadic and merge into a continuous, yet chronologically linear narrative which continues until the end of the book. The autobiographical framing narrative is thus assimilated into Crusoe's deliberate ongoing record of how he took account of his adventure.

Because it documents each successive labor or reassessment of his situation in terms of the amount of time, material, and energy such episodes require, as well as the period of Crusoe's life they occupy, the journal serves as a foundational script: it provides him with both a means of measuring his accomplishment and a frame of reference for future activity. This historical-narrative framework necessarily evolves in conjunction with the articulation of the providential scheme, since Robinson takes each of the accomplishments it records as further evidence of an overarching divine intentionality. Thus when he finds some barley growing on the island, he first takes it as a miracle, then discovers a rational explanation – he had "shaken a bag of chickens' meat out in that place" – before coming on an explanation that takes both his activity and divine intervention into account: "for it was really the work of providence as to me, that should order or appoint, that 10 or 12 grains of corn should remain unspoiled . . . as also, that I should throw it out in that particular place . . ." (p. 95).

Thus Robinson's gradual imposition of human order on the island advances in step with, and finds its correlate in, a properly narrational gesture of self-historization which is simultaneously an exegesis of providential authority. By the time he comes once again into contact with Europeans, Robinson will have completely assimilated the intent of providence into the structure of his history, which story will then serve as the vehicle of his reintegration into society in precisely the middle station he originally fled. His history, in both the sense of his life and its narrative, brings about the merger of individual experience, providential design, and social imperative which eluded him at the outset of his adventure. And in that sense *Robinson Crusoe* can be read not just as an allegory of economic individualism and freedom, as Watt would have it, or as an allegory of suffering and salvation, as Defoe would later argue,[10] but also as an allegory of the transition from a providential to an historical framework of reality. The individual stages in this process merit examination.

Early on, Crusoe has a revelation of his place within the overseeing plan of God, and his ensuing reflections articulate the problems raised by the conflict of providence with self-determination:

> I had great reason to consider it as a determination of Heaven, that in this desolate place and in this desolate manner I should end my life; the tears would run plentifully down my face when I made these reflections, and sometimes I would expostulate with my self, why Providence should thus compleatly ruine its creatures, and render them so absolutely miserable, so without help abandoned, so entirely depressed, that it could hardly be rational to be thankful for such a life. (P. 80)

To the extent that his situation does not correspond to his desires, Crusoe's motivation to act is crippled: there is no point in action if providence dictates that all of one's efforts shall only aggravate one's misery. Human striving only becomes rational when its objectives and practice can be construed to accord with a greater teleology, a larger plan of which it is part. Since all of Crusoe's goals are thwarted, since his existence is uniformly miserable, he can only conclude that his objectives do not coincide with any such greater design, and that his striving is thus in vain. Tears of self-pity are the only logical response in such a case.

Almost immediately, however, the solution to his dilemma occurs to him; it comes with his realization that reality, including the reality of his plight, is not a simple given, but rather a form of knowledge resulting from the interpretation of experience according to perceived needs. The marooned sailor discovers his situation is wretched only to the extent he perceives it to be so; his alienation from providence is the result of his own reading of experience. To modify his plight and move from despair and loneliness to tranquil bliss, he need only inaugurate a rereading of his situation as an example of extraordinary good fortune.[11] The first step in this program entails the *recontextualization* of his situation – its re-evaluation not in the light of all human experience, and particularly not that of the contented bourgeois Englishman which Crusoe has consistently associated with providence, but with respect to the much narrower range of history comprised by Crusoe's *own* adventures:

> I was very pensive upon the subject of my present condition, when reason as it were expostulated with me t'other way, thus: Well, you are in a desolate condition, 'tis true, but pray remember, where are the rest of you? Did not you come eleven of you into the boat? where are the ten? Why were not they saved and you lost? Why were you singled out? Is it better to be here or there? and then I pointed to the sea. All evils are to be considered with the good that is in them, and with what worse attends them. (P. 80)

Crusoe goes on to reconsider his extraordinary good fortune in having the ship with all of its supplies float in to where he could unload it. This active interpretation of reality opens the possibility of complicity with providence, but more importantly it triggers Crusoe's decision to establish a context for understanding his situation by recapitulating his adventure in the journal. Having discovered that it suffices to narrate events in a favorable light in order to persuade himself that providence really has his good fortune in mind, he formalizes the process narratively: "And now being to enter into a melancholy relation of a scene of silent life, such perhaps as was never heard of in the world before, I shall take it from its beginning, and continue it in its order" (p. 81).

The discovery that reality can be related into a form congruent with one's happiness opens the door to Crusoe's rapprochement with the order of providence, and it is only logical that his decision to narrate his situation coincides with an increasing devotional activity: indeed, the first two accounts of Crusoe's praying conclude with an abrupt return to his journal, underlining the close correlation between the two gestures (cf. pp. 106, 111). Provoked by an acute illness to cry out to the Lord for help, he rediscovers the possibility of immediate access to the divine order through prayer. Subsequent reflections on the omniscience of God convince him that his situation is indeed inscribed within a higher will, the benevolent protection of which becomes his major preoccupation. As Crusoe notes, it is the dialogue with providence that replaces human society for him: "as for my solitary life, it was nothing; I did not so much as pray to be delivered from it, or think of it; it was all of no consideration in comparison to this [deliverance]" (p. 111). Alone with God, suffering no competition from other parties claiming divine will for their own agendas, Crusoe can align the design of providence with his own actions. When he delights in the beauty of the island, for instance, an integral part of his pleasure comes from his conviction that while God may have created it, it now belongs to him: "I descended a little on the side of that delicious vale, surveying it with a secret kind of pleasure (tho' mixt with my other afflicting thoughts) to think that this was all my own, that I was king and lord of all this country indefeasibly, and had a right of possession; and if I could convey it, I might have it in inheritance as compleatly as any lord of a mannor in England" (pp. 113–14).

A key part of Crusoe's happiness thus hinges on *exclusivity*: his interpretations of reality, like his establishment of particular routines and procedures, succeed so completely only because they suffer no competition from other humans. At the same time, he requires a structure of authority against which to situate his efforts. His "civilization" of the island, which is also an articulation of his identity, hinges on his conviction that a greater scheme, a vaster, "other" intentionality, underwrites and comprehends his actions. Such an answering, authorizing "Other" will form an indispensable component of all eighteenth-century models of self-affirmation, the great majority of which associate it with one or more individual interlocutors or dialogical partners: a lover, sidekick, or rival, whose reception and response to "my" construal of reality serve as its validation. *Robinson Crusoe* is remarkable in that it conceptualizes the mechanism of this authorizing "Other" in abstract terms that already prefigure its dialectical formulation forty years later in the metanovels of Rousseau, Sterne, and Diderot, where, in addition to its incarnation in the person of an interlocutor, it takes on the shape of an accumulating text of past representations and the conventions they modulate. As in the case of such a text, which is explicitly that of history, the comprehensive "outer" intentionality that frames Robinson's narrational gesture is articulated and posited from within that gesture; it is the ground, but also the product, of his ongoing interpretation and reformulation. Naturally, the Puritan voice downplays the reciprocity of this relationship – the fact that the Other order of authority is sustained by "my" continual gloss of its design. But what Robinson calls providence displays roughly the same structure and function as the secular notion of history: it both motivates and is revealed by the narrational gesture of the individual seeking to come to grips with the larger order that frames personal experience.

Robinson's earliest essays in this regard content themselves with demonstrating that the specifics of his experience are indeed the will of the Lord: "if nothing happens without His knowledge, He knows that I am here, and am in this dreadful condition; and if nothing happens without His appointment, He has appointed all this to befal me" (p. 107). Recovery from sickness is a further example of God's intercession, the continuance of which might well be contingent on the benefactor's expression of gratitude: "Have I not been delivered, and wonderfully too, from sickness? . . . Had I done my part? God had delivered me, but I had not glorify'd Him; that is to say, I had not owned and been thankful for that as a deliverance, and how cou'd I expect greater deliverance?" (p. 110). Having concluded that divine intercession might hinge on his own activity, Crusoe now begins to pray in earnest and "to have hope that God would hear me" (p. 111). And to convince himself of the link between his story and God's, he turns to the Bible for descriptions of his situation, appropriating as part of his own narration the authoritative narrative of providence. Ultimately, he comes to conclude that the words of the Scripture are actually addressed to him: "I opened the Bible upon these words, *I will never, never leave thee, nor forsake thee*; immediately it occurred that these words were to me; why else should they be directed in such a manner, just at the moment when I was mourning over my condition, as one forsaken of God and man?" (p. 126). There is of course nothing in this behavior that is inconsonant with good Puritan doctrine, but such doctrine also underwrites individualism. Robinson's actions merely emphasize the extent to which the glorification of individual initiative relies on the writing of oneself into a larger script, the scope of which confirms the extraordinary status of the individual in question. As Crusoe's criticism of his earlier ways implies ("I do not remember that I had in all that time one thought that so much as tended either to looking upwards toward God, or inwards towards a reflection upon my own ways" (p. 103), reflection upon one's own experience and reflection upon a greater order go hand in hand, whether one calls that order providence, history, or even culture.

Crusoe's conviction that he plays the central role in the narrative design of providence – there being no other human beings in his world who might dispute him this place – allows him to dispense with society:

He could fully make up to me the deficiencies of my solitary state, and the want of humane society, by His presence and the communications of His grace to my soul, supporting, comforting, and encouraging me to depend upon His providence here, and hope for His eternal presence hereafter. (P. 125)

This made my life better than sociable, for when I began to regret the want of conversation, I would ask my self whether thus conversing mutually with my own thoughts, and, as I hope I may say, with even God Himself by ejaculations, was not better than the utmost enjoyment of humane society in the world. (P. 146)

What Crusoe realizes is that society functions primarily as the collective voice of the cultural narratives that situate and enable our individual projects of self-actualization. Isolated from society, he supplants this voice with that of the Lord, who, as the above quote makes obvious, speaks to Crusoe in Crusoe's voice ("with even God Himself by ejaculations"). Thus Crusoe founds a completely self-sufficient personal/providential history: he narrates the narrative within which his own narrational gesture is determined.

Of course this extraordinary self-determination and the intellectual freedom that goes with it are made possible and sustained by an extraordinary exemption from the imperatives of competing narration. Unlike any other fictional character we shall be examining, Crusoe lives in a controlled environment, one that is devoid of world-ordering narratives other than his own – with one exception: the Bibles saved from the wreck. The word of the Gospel, the absolute narrative of authority, the all-inclusive history of man's origins and aspirations, survives to temper Crusoe's egocentricity – and make it possible. For however obvious his part in the design of reality and providence, Robinson must attribute it to the Other. The divine order to which he appeals is the product of his *need* and the guarantor of his right; he could not survive its subordination to his own efforts. Just as the first tentative expressions of individualism in the French tradition deploy themselves negatively, by asserting the primacy of collective discourse and thereby enclosing its mechanisms within their own fictional structure, so too the Puritan self consolidates its dominion through the negation of its authority, attributing its excesses of the ego to a greater power who thereby absolves the individual of responsibility for them. That is why Crusoe's most exalted expressions of absolute dominion generally occur in tandem with the glorification of the Lord's power:

I had nothing to covet; for I had all that I was now capable of enjoying; I was lord of the whole manor; or if I pleased, I might call my self king or emperor over the whole country which I had possession of. There were no rivals; I had no competitor, none to dispute sovereignty or command with me.... I frequently sat down to my meat with thankfulness, and admired the hand of God's providence, which had thus spread my table in the wilderness. (Pp. 139–40)

How mercifully can our great Creator treat His creatures, even in those conditions in which they seemed to be overwhelmed in destruction! How can He sweeten the bitterest providences, and give us cause to praise Him for dungeons and prisons! What a table was here spread for me in a wilderness, where I saw nothing at first but to perish for hunger!

It would have made a stoick smile to have seen me and my little family sit down to dinner; there was my majesty the prince and lord of the whole island; I had the lives of all my subjects at my absolute command; I could hang, draw, give liberty, and take it away, and no rebels among all my subjects. (P. 157)

These two extremes of attitude, that of absolute mastery and that of complete enclosure within a system beyond one's control, correspond to two perspectives on the same phenomenon – the shaping of history by individuals/the shaping of individuals by history – and they will repeatedly find expression in the eighteenth-century novel as complementary moments in the self's definition. Just as economic individualism and Puritan devotion become complementary once one conceives of the exploitation of the earth's riches in terms of a divine agenda, so even in this early work, Crusoe's swings between despair and hubris turn out ultimately not to be in conflict with one another. Crusoe can only sustain his Edenic agenda of total mastery because he is certain of enclosure within the authoritative paternal script, which provides a positive model for his activities, in the mastery of Adam in the garden. To the extent that he remains convinced of the divine script's coincidence with his own, and he will, as long as there are no competing exegetes inhabiting his island, it can function as the justification for everything he does.

Like *La Princesse de Clèves*, *Robinson Crusoe* confirms that society, whether construed as a collective narrative or a collection of narrators, poses problems for individuals intent on self-determination. But rather than exploring the dynamics of a plurality of competing accounts or analyzing how, precisely, individual destiny is informed by collective discourse, the first half of *Robinson Crusoe* outlines an "ante-social" account of how a single self-narration can reconcile itself to, and eventually appropriate, the divine narrative of world order. The subsequent portion of Defoe's story, which relates how Robinson's unique relationship with God is modified by the advent of other humans, follows individuality beyond its genesis into the post-lapsarian world of social man.

Although *Robinson Crusoe* achieves its clarity of analysis through the device of isolation, its lesson would be incomplete if it failed to follow Robinson back into society after his attainment of mastery. Were his idyll to continue undisturbed, the novel would not only languish as a perverse solipsistic utopia, it could not serve as a paradigm for social behavior and make good on its didactic pretensions. Accordingly, the happy collusion of Robinson's dominion and that of providence is broken by a *deus ex machina* as radical as that which initiated it: after fifteen years of solitude and assured exclusivity in the Lord's eye, Robinson is stunned one morning to discover a human footprint in the sand. The mere thought that there might be other people on his island suffices to unsettle in an instant his entire sense of self:

> like a man perfectly confused and out of my self, I came home to my forti-fication, not feeling, as we say, the ground I went on, but terrify'd to the last degree.... When I came to my castle, for so I think I called it ever after this, I fled into it like one pursued; whether I went over by the ladder as first contrived, or went in at the hole in the rock which I called a door, I cannot remember; no, nor could I remember the next morning...(P. 162)

The ensuing "wild ideas" and "strange unaccountable whimsies" (p. 162) that take over Robinson's fancy banish his complacent self-narration and plunge him into a state of anguish that lasts several years. There are multiple stages to his ensuing crisis, which in many respects can be read as an allegory of the confrontation with history as a *social* enterprise. Because Crusoe's sense of self constitutes itself reciprocally with his belief in God's power, it is not surprising that his initial "loss of self" occasions a loss of faith: "Thus my fear banished all my religious hope; all that former con-fidence in God, which was founded upon such wonderful experience as I had had of His goodness, now vanished, as if He that had fed me by miracle hitherto, could not preserve by His power the provision which He had made for me by His goodness" (p. 164).

It is prolonged reasoning about the nature and frequency of the savages' visits, rather than contemplation of his own situation and the glory of God, that eventually affords Crusoe a degree of faith and calm. His program of self-glorification based on exclusive communion with providence will never regain its original intensity. Similarly, his ongoing imperial enter-prise falters, then ceases entirely:

> the frights I had been in about these savage wretches, and the concern I had been in for my own preservation, had taken off the edge of my invention for my own conveniences. (P. 174)

> these anxieties, these constant dangers I lived in, and the concern that was now upon me, put an end to all invention, and to all the contrivances that I had laid for my future accommodations and conveniences. (P. 182)

Abandoning his relentless domestication of the island along with his delu-sions of mastery, he channels all his energy for the next two years into fortification and the concealment of his property. When he discovers traces of cannibalism on the beach, he withdraws into a near hermitlike existence;

his former manor, having been militarized into a castle, now becomes a prison cell: "I kept my self, as I said, more retired than ever, and seldom went from my cell" (p. 180).

As Robinson's history metamorphoses from a chronicle of self-realization and conquering individuality to a journal of paranoid hermitage and obsession with the Other, his attention to the divine Other also falters:

> the discomposure of my mind had too great impressions also upon the religious part of my thoughts, for the dread and terror of falling into the hands of savages and canibals lay so upon my spirits, that I seldom found my self in a due temper for application to my Maker. (P. 170)

To conquer his paralysis, Crusoe turns to reinterpretation, revising his experience into a more tractable history. His first impulse, betraying his enduring egocentricity, is to convince himself that the offending footprint is actually his own (p. 165). As the sole inhabitant of his realm, his natural tendency is to attribute all phenomena – including his terror – to his own actions. This "appropriation" of the footprint heartens him sufficiently for a sortie out of doors: "Now I began to take courage, and to peep abroad again; for I had not stirred out of my castle for three days and nights" (p. 166). Unfortunately, measurement reveals the footprint could not be his, and a second loss of composure ensues: "these things filled my head with new imaginations, and gave me the vapours again to the highest degree; so that I shook with cold, like one in an ague" (p. 166). This crisis culminates, appropriately, in a veritable paroxysm of self-negation: "I proposed to my self . . . to throw down my enclosures and turn all my tame cattle wild . . . digging up my two corn fields . . . [and] then to demolish my bower and tent" (p. 167), but eventually Robinson confronts the loss of his exclusivity and, through a dialogue with himself, not God, begins to re-evaluate his situation: "now I began to think sedately; and *upon the utmost debate with my self*, I concluded that this island, which was so exceeding pleasant, fruitful, and no farther from the main land than as I had seen, was not so entirely abandoned as I might imagine" (p. 167, my emphasis).

Yet Robinson's "self" is loath to relinquish its domain. He is willing to concede the existence of other beings, but only as *visitors* to his realm, and not necessarily *intentional* visitors at that: "altho' there were no stated inhabitants who lived on the spot, yet . . . there might sometimes come boats off from the shore, who either with design, or perhaps never but when they were driven by cross winds, might come to this place" (pp. 167 – 8). This interpretation helps Robinson avoid the possibility of competing designs on his own reality, and after two more years of defensive improvements and furtive existence, he is able to accommodate his visitors into his version of providence:

I was presently convinced that the seeing the print of a man's foot was not such a strange thing in the island as I imagined; and but that it was a special providence that I was cast upon the side of the island where the savages never came, I should easily have known that nothing was more frequent than for the canoes from the main, when they happened to be a little too far out at sea, to shoot over to that side of the island for harbour. (P. 171)

Compelled to accommodate the activities of other humans in his order, Crusoe learns that interpretations need not be definitive: the re-evaluations of his situation which he formulated early during his sojourn as the basis for aligning his will and God's, and which had acquired in the interim the status of immutable history and the grounding narrative of reality, now reveal themselves to be only stages in a continuing process of reconfiguration, the fluidity of which is the condition of adaptability to shifting social exigencies. Accordingly, when his fury is aroused by the confirmation of the savages' cannibalism, Robinson will rethink his initial urge to ambush and destroy them. He admits that "night and day I could think of nothing but how I might destroy some of these monsters in their cruel bloody entertainment," and that "it would take up a larger volume than this whole work is intended to be, to set down all the contrivances I hatched, or rather brooded upon in my thought, for the destroying these creatures" (p. 175). Yet after preparing himself for the slaughter and waiting three months for their return, he re-appraises his design – and that of providence – asking himself "what authority or call I had, to pretend to be judge and executioner upon these men as criminals, whom Heaven had thought fit for so many ages to suffer unpunished ... How do I know what God Himself judges in this particular case?" (p. 177).

This uncertainty as to the will of God is a function of social competition. When designs other than our own appear as part of the greater order of things – particularly when they are practiced by large groups of people – we must either adopt those designs as our own (this is, looking ahead, what Friday and all the European visitors to the island will do, faced with Robinson's authority) or postulate a providential narrative so vast it can enclose both our reality and that of the competing society. Crusoe elects this latter strategy and consoles himself with the imperialist assumption that the encounter of a different cultural order is an invitation from providence to convert or subjugate it as proof of his primacy.

It is significant, though, that when he relinquishes his plans of massacre, it is not because of a divine revelation, but because he tires of the routine of vigilance: "As long as I kept up my daily tour to the hill to look out, so long also I kept up the vigour of my design ... But now, when, as I have said, I began to be weary of the fruitless excursion, which I had made so long, and so far, every morning in vain, so my opinion of the action it self began to alter" (p. 177). This is an important acknowledgment, for it introduces the idea that just as former events can change their aspect when reinterpreted, so too can current action provoke reinterpretation. Increasingly, Crusoe will rely on such historical logic, tailoring his behavior to conform to his current account of reality and modifying that account in accordance with his experience. His story evolves in response to its telling and vice versa.

A fine example of this new posture is provided by the long consideration of the savages, where, for the first time, Crusoe analyzes a cultural Other. In the course of his reflection, he employs all of the techniques he previously brought to bear on his own situation, namely *comparison* ("these people were not murtherers in the sense that I had before condemned them in my thoughts; any more than those Christians were murtherers who often put to death the prisoners taken in battle" (p. 177–8); *contextualization* ("albeit the usage they thus gave one another was thus brutish and inhumane, yet it was really nothing to me: these people had done me no injury" p. 178); and the *adaptation of reality to self-interest* ("this really was the way not to deliver my self, but entirely to ruin and destroy my self; for unless I was sure to kill every one . . . I should only bring upon my self a certain destruction" (p. 179). Fully cognizant of the criteria upon which he bases his decision, Crusoe concludes "that neither in principle or in policy, I ought one way or other to concern my self in this affair" (p. 179), and only after such a conclusion, does he seek confirmation in the design of providence: "Religion joyned in with this prudential, and I was convinced now many ways, that I was perfectly out of my duty when I was laying all my bloody schemes for the destruction of innocent creatures" (p. 179).

In spite of its religious trappings, this moment of reconsideration marks the emergence of an incipient historical conscience. To accept such behavior and beings as these, no models for which can be found in the order of things to which Crusoe is accustomed, is to accept the possibility of a potentially unlimited number of orders and thus to open the door to virtually any form of behavior. To make the cannibals' behavior a function of history, and a cultural, rather than divine plan, one would need only to grant them a self-representational drive of their own; their ghastly behavior would then appear the result of cultural assertion and be on a par with Crusoe's. Defoe excludes this possibility by making the acquisition of language commensurate with the recognition of the sin of cannibalism and the virtual repudiation of the heathen life. As soon as Friday masters language, for instance, (and it is significant that he is never allowed to do so completely, speaking until the end a crude pidgin), Robinson communicates to him his story and that of his narrative authority, the Bible, which Friday unquestioningly accepts.

At the same time that it signals his re-entry into history as a plurality of narratives, Robinson's acceptance of the cannibals' existence reconfigures his relationship to God. While he still retains a place in the divine scheme of things, he is no longer certain of his privilege. Implicitly recognizing that his earlier visions of mastery were flawed by their failure to *take into account* the existence of other beings in the providential order, he now acknowledges that there may be schemes other than his own, and that he must write the stories of other people into his history and assimilate them to his design, if he is to consolidate and retain his primacy in the larger story uniting them all. In concrete terms he needs to learn all about the savages without them learning about him. His new agenda – to find "some-body to speak to, and to learn some knowledge from of the place where I was, and of the probable means of my delivrance" (p. 202) – seeks guidance not through dialogue with providence, but in the culture of another society. More precisely, he adopts a goal that comes to him – no doubt as proof of his continuing good grace – in a dream where a savage slated to be consumed by his enemies eludes his captors, seeks refuge in Robinson's cave, and offers himself up as servant. Robinson's immediate reaction, in the dream, testifies to his simplistic program of subjugation, but it also reiterates his new respect for the narratives of other cultures: "as soon as I had gotten this man, I said to my self, 'Now I may certainly venture to the main land; for this fellow will serve me as pilot, and will tell me what to do, and whether to go for provisions; and whether not to go for fear of being devoured, what places to venture into, and what to escape'" (p. 202).

In fact, once the dream is fulfilled, Robinson does most of the telling, marching Friday through a crash course in island etiquette that includes lessons on how to eat, dress, abhor cannibalism, till land, make bread, and, in short, "every thing that was proper to make him useful, handy, and helpful; but especially to make him speak, and understand me when I spake" (p. 213). Having taught "his" man "to do all the work for me, as well as I could do it myself" (p. 215), Crusoe sets about pumping him for useful information: "I asked Friday a thousand questions about the country, the inhabitants, the sea, the coast, and what nations were near; he told me all he knew with the greatest openness imaginable" (p. 217). "Openness" is not, however, the predominant characteristic of Crusoe's narration. At the outset, when he undertakes to mystify Friday as to the way firearms function, he takes care to fashion a narrative for his servant that will keep him subjugated to his master. In good colonial fashion, he initially imparts only that part of his own story concerned with toil and production, omitting the personal history of his adventures and provenance which will prove all-important in his later transactions with Europeans. When he explains religion, he is careful to debunk Friday's own cultural beliefs, while at the same time evading direct answers to the "savage's" pertinent questions about the existence of the devil (pp. 218–21). As time passes, however, and Friday becomes increasingly like Crusoe, the latter imparts ever greater portions of his own cultural narrative to him, including his (Crusoe's) own origins and shipwreck, the mysteries of gunpowder and how to shoot, the techniques of navigation and sailing, and the description of the European countries and their practice of trading.

This prolonged program of instruction, which lasts several years and reinstates for Crusoe a second age of happiness on the island, provides a simple paradigm of reciprocal narration and shared narrative in a social setting, much in the way Crusoe's earlier period of happiness sketched the relationship of individual narration to history. The notion of a divine order does not disappear, but the continual communion with the Lord that characterized Robinson's presocial period on the island is replaced with a mutually instructive cross-cultural exchange of human narratives. Naturally, given the Puritan context, Crusoe must think of his cultural imperialism as the duty of a good Christian:

> my habitation grew comfortable to me beyond measure; and when I reflected that in this solitary life which I had been confined to, I had not only been moved my self to look up to heaven, and to seek to the hand that had brought me there, but was now to be made an instrument under Providence to save the life, and, for ought I knew, the soul of a poor savage, and bring him to the true knowledge of religion . . . a secret joy run through every part of my soul, and I frequently rejoyced that ever I was brought to this place. . . .
>
> In this thankful frame I continued all the remainder of my time, and the conversation which employed the hours between Friday and I was such as made the three years which we lived there together perfectly and compleatly happy, if any such thing as compleat happiness can be formed in a sublunary state. (P. 222)

The social intrusion of Friday's arrival that disrupted Robinson's idyll of divine communion thus comes to furnish the mainstay of a more culturally mature practice of narration. Society is articulated around collective stories, of mythical, divine, or historical nature, and Robinson's own story of achievement can only function in a social context to the extent he imparts it to others and expands it to absorb theirs. However convinced he may be that the ultimate scheme of things lies in the hands of a power beyond human reach, he must nevertheless engage his social peers in reciprocal narration and persuade them to adopt his personal narrative if he hopes to succeed in society. It is precisely this sort of persuasion of his version of things that he was unable to practice with his father, and which he performs so adeptly with Friday and the Europeans that subsequently come to his island.

First with the arrival of a Spanish prisoner and later with that of some English sailors, the importance of this narrative exchange becomes evident, as does the precise mechanism of domination – which one can readily see in the fact that Friday becomes a Christian, rather than Crusoe a cannibal, but which is not immediately clear in its underpinnings. Having rescued the Spaniard and Friday's father, Crusoe immediately sets to interrogating them, adding to his own store of information all that they provide. Of his own story, however, he offers little, preferring to present himself through the propositions he makes the Spaniard concerning his marooned compatriots and which Crusoe handles as contracts offered by a benefactor to those in worse circumstances than his:

> he would make conditions with them upon their solemn oath, that they should be absolutely under my leading, as their commander and captain, and that they should swear upon the holy sacraments and the Gospel, to be true to me, and to go to such Christian country as that I should agree to, and no other; and to be directed wholly and absolutely by my orders, 'till they were landed safely in such country as I intended; and that he would bring a contract from under their hands for that purpose. (P. 244)

Crusoe can impose such conditions only to the extent that the Spaniard accepts his version of reality – a version which Friday is certain to second, and which Crusoe himself sums up quite straightforwardly:

> My island was now peopled, and I thought my self very rich in subjects; and it was a merry reflection which I frequently made, how like a king I looked. First of all, the whole country was my own meer property; so that I had an undoubted right of dominion. 2dly, my people were perfectly subjected: I was absolute lord and lawgiver; they all owed their lives to me...(Pp. 240–1)

By presenting himself as proud ruler and proffering no accounts of his wretchedness in years past, Robinson imposes on the Spaniard a near fiction (why else would it inspire merriment in its author?) which the latter can either take or leave, but which, once accepted, is necessarily consolidated into reality.

An even more striking application of the same procedure is used to intimidate – and dupe – the mutinous English sailors that arrive shortly thereafter. Again, Robinson interrogates his benefactors before revealing anything about himself; this time he exacts formal promises that his authority will be respected on the island and that he will have the ship at his disposal for passage to England, even before he agrees to deliver the English captain and his mate from the mutineers (p. 253). More amusing than this reiteration of a set pattern is his gradual assumption of a purely fictional role: that of an English colony's governor, with an entire army at his disposal. Robinson sets the tone for this penchant for fiction when he first addresses the prisoners, whom he knows to be English, in Spanish – the language he least knows. And when, in the midst of duping the mutineers into thinking fifty men surround them, the captain refers to Crusoe as the "governor," Crusoe immediately plays along, remaining out of sight as the all-powerful lawgiver for the duration of the Englishmen's sojourn.

During the subsequent negotiations with the mutineers, "the Governor" is promoted to the level of absolute sovereign, deciding life or death on the basis of his own judgment. Simultaneously, Robinson's hut and cave attain a rather more grandiose status:

> When I shewed my self to the two hostages, it was with the captain, who told them I was the person the governour had ordered to look after them, and that it was the governour's pleasure they should not stir any where, but bv my direction; that if they did, they should be fetched into the castle, and be lay'd in irons; so that as we never suffered them to see me as governour, so I now appeared as another person, and spoke of the governour, the garrison, the castle, and the like, upon all occasions. (P. 267)

It is on the basis of this fiction that Crusoe coerces the most recalcitrant mutineers to replace him as the inhabitants of the island, offering them the choice between *his* life or certain death as mutineers in England. A fictional narrative thus becomes at once the vehicle for Robinson's deliverance and for the perpetuation of his personal cultural narrative on the island, through its assimilation by the new inhabitants as a foundational history and statement of procedures.

The startling thing about this sequence of events is that it is based on sheer narration: it is Crusoe's story that first impresses the captain and consolidates Crusoe's authority over the island and those that inhabit it. Surprisingly, however, whereas Crusoe stressed his *European* culture in his relationship with Friday and omitted all mention of his past in the account of the Spaniard, he here emphasizes his history on the island – and does so with little urging from the captain: "It now remained that the captain and I should enquire into one another's circumstances. I began first, and told him my whole history, which he heard with an attention even to amazement ... and indeed, as my story is a whole collection of wonders, it affected him deeply" (p. 255). This shift in narrational strategy reveals the mechanism by which Crusoe maintains his authority, and which can be summed up in the dictum "make the other person Other." With Friday, Robinson gains the upper hand by insisting on the prevalence of English, Puritan values; with the captain, it is the island's regime that he claims for his own: he is never the homesick, shipwrecked sailor, but always the governor of a colony the strangeness of which they cannot immediately assimilate into their maritime culture. As Crusoe modestly puts it: "All I shewed them, all

I said to them, was perfectly amazing" (p. 256). Overwhelming the interlocutor with a narrative so alien as to thwart his own efforts at assimilation thus appears to be a fundamental strategy for cultural domination, and it serves Crusoe repeatedly once he returns to "civilization."

There is a further feature of narrative that only begins to emerge in the episodes on the island: its commodity value in a capitalist environment. Friday and Crusoe teach each other things that not only make them more similar, but which also are valuable as a means of obtaining future goals and wealth in societies sharing that story. In terms of sheer technology, and within the framework of the island, Crusoe's narrative contains the knowledge of how to make things, and thus re-enact the subordination of reality to man, the master: it is in this sense that it is valuable to the seamen he leaves on the island. But in the context of his original society, Robinson's story states his mastery of history and assures his identity, which in turn provides him his ultimate monetary fortune. He becomes rich by accumulating an adventure, the recounting of which convinces his friend the Portuguese captain that he is indeed the Robinson Crusoe that disappeared twenty-eight years ago. It is on the basis of his account that he receives the wealth which has accrued at his plantation during his absence. In this sense, Crusoe's story is particular because it shows the fundamental and most valuable content of narrative to be the story of its narration, the account of how it was produced.

NOTES

1 Homer O. Brown, "The Displaced Self in the Novels of Daniel Defoe," in Harold E. Pagliaro, ed., *Studies in Eighteenty-century Culture*, vol. 4 (Madison, Wisconsin: University of Wisconsin Press, for the American Society for Eighteenth-Century Studies, 1975), p. 88.
2 See Patricia Meyer Spacks, *Imagining a Self*, p. 33.
3 Watt, *Rise of the Novel*, p. 96.
4 All references are to the 1985 reprint of Angus Ross's 1965 edition of *Robinson Crusoe*, published by Penguin Books, which is based on the first edition but incorporates alterations made in the third edition.
5 Robinson's adventure can of course be read as a dramatization of other themes and historical developments, many of which overlap my concerns with narration. Homer Brown, "Displaced Self," for instance, emphasizes the relationship between symbolic narrative, the doubled self it produces, and the need in Defoe's world for a continual, recurrent conversion. John Richetti, *Defoe's Narratives* (Oxford: Clarendon Press, 1975), pp. 54–5, expresses Crusoe's story in terms of freedom and contingency, as the realization of the "dream of freedom perfectly reconciled with necessity, the self using necessity to promote

its freedom." Going beyond the traditional association of the story with the genre of spiritual autobiography, Michael McKeon associates Crusoe's "internalization not only of divinity but of sociopolitical authority" (p. 333) with Defoe's mediation of the secularization crisis – his demonstration "that the metaphysical realm of the Spirit may be accommodated and rendered accessible as the psychological realm of Mind" and his specification of this lesson "to the concrete dimension of material and social ambition" (p. 336).

6   John Brown, *Estimate*, pp. 82, 138, specifies "those of the middle Life" as the only social class maintaining respect for the clergy, and he associates their effeminized "high life" counterparts with the scourge of self-interest afflicting the nation.

7   Concerning Robinson's rebellion, Watt, *Rise of the Novel*, maintains that "the argument between his parents and himself is a debate, not about filial duty or religion, but about whether going or staying is likely to be the most advantageous course materially: both sides accept the economic argument as primary" (p. 72). The text does not support this account. Robinson at no point advances economic gain as his motive, and aside from his acknowledgment of a need to rebel against authority, he claims only a compulsion to wander: "my head began to be filled very early with rambling thoughts ... I would be satisfied with nothing but going to sea" (p. 27) Later he tells his mother "my thoughts were so entirely bent upon seeing the world, that I should never settle to any thing with resolution enough to go through with it" (p. 30). Moreover, even Robinson's father sees no other motives for his son's behavior: "he asked me what reasons more than a meer wandring inclination I had for leaving my father's house and my native country" (p. 27) – a question to which the boy has no answer.

8   Brown, "Displaced Self," pp. 87–90, provides a good analysis of the merger between providence and Crusoe's narrative, which "removes the contingency and absurd inconsequence of the lived moment by abstracting that moment from the field of open possibility and directing it toward a certain outcome which will define it and give it significance" (p. 89).

9   In line with her reading of Defoe's works as embodiments of skepticism, Eve Tavor, *Scepticism*, pp. 8–16, reads the relationship between the journal, the narrative framing it, and the journal which Robinson did not write – the record of chaotic reactions following upon his shipwreck – as a strategy of narrative stratification corresponding to the "progressive layering over of the immediate data of sensation and reflection with increasingly complex and comprehensive strata of thought" (pp. 10–11). Her interpretation of the book as inconclusive and open to multiple evaluations, while running counter to most readings, reflects the variety of those readings as well as Crusoe's lesson that every phenomenon is susceptible to further assessment within new contexts; see n. 11, below.

10   See *Serious Reflections During the Life and Surprising Adventures of Robinson Crusoe: with his Vision of the Angelick World* (1720).

11   The conviction that reality is the product of our interpretative efforts, and that those efforts take as their vehicle a process of narration, plays a central role in

projects of self-actualization in the eighteenth-century novel. It is through the negotiated re-evaluation of situations, identities, and conduct, that later protagonists, from Marivaux's Marianne and Jacob, or Richardson's Pamela, to Fielding's Tom Jones and Laclos' Merteuil, will obtain their desired ends and modify their social identity. *Robinson Crusoe* provides a striking example of the interpretive underpinnings of this process, which correlates more generally to the demystification of objectivity which Michael McKeon notes *à propos* of *Gulliver's Travels* and associates with the development of skeptical epistemology in the seventeenth and eighteenth centuries; see *Origins*, pp. 348–50.

4

Negotiating Reality
(*Moll Flanders* and *Roxana*)

Considered chronologically, Defoe's novels portray a world in transition from the theocentric authority of Puritanism to the historical authority of culture, a world where divine order by itself no longer suffices to constrain the individual, but where "culture" and "history" have not yet attained sufficient conceptual clarity to take its place as the acknowledged frame of human destiny. The aggregate social experience, which as shared history and behavioral code will later in the century supplant providence as a limiting factor on self-determination, begins to make itself felt in *Moll Flanders* (1722) and *Roxana* (1724); and the differing outcomes of the novels reflect Defoe's repressed but increasing awareness of the excesses and internal inconsistencies to which individualism leads, as well as his progressively clearer understanding of the role the collective record plays with respect to personal enterprise. While *Moll Flanders* builds on *Robinson Crusoe* by providing a tentatively optimistic – but somewhat simplistic – vision of the individual's ability to negotiate her own destiny within a social environment, *Roxana*, Defoe's last novel, portrays the ultimate failure of self-determination to manage its own history. The loose ends of the protagonist's story which the earlier work so tidily wraps up, return in *Roxana* to torment the heroine and give the lie to her ambitions.[1]

Both novels are written as retrospective confessional autobiographies which claim to tell the history of a life gone astray. But in each case the heroine seems to find a sustaining sense of self in the practices of self-representation she develops to survive. These practices involve managing social contingencies through the projection of various assumed identities, and they explicitly rely on narration. At the outset of their adventures the two heroines are cast adrift in society by a *deus ex machina* similar to that which separates Robinson from the world: within the first few pages, Moll is made an orphan, Roxana a poverty-stricken abandoned wife. With this pre-emptory gesture, the narrative situates itself within the question of how individuals having no property or family can nonetheless make their way in the world. Deprived of these two sources of social rank, such individuals make perfect test cases for the possibility of self-fabrication, since within a society that evaluates identity on the basis of inherited rights and property, they literally have none.[2]

Each heroine allies herself with a variety of men in the course of her life, assumes a multiplicity of identities, and eventually attains a point of relative material comfort. But Moll's adventures occur on the margins of society, taking her through successively more outrageous roles – mistress, whore, incestuous wife, bigamist, thief, condemned criminal. Her most consistent trait is her protean ability to assume any identity she chooses, and she comes to cultivate such masquerading for the sheer thrill of it. Eventually brought to justice and condemned to death, in part because of her own notoriety, she represents her case, and her repentance, to a sympathetic clergyman, who obtains clemency for her in exchange for her reform and repudiation of her past. The autobiographical narrative presents itself as one instrument of her repentance – a confession whose didactic value for others will aid her in expiating her sins.

Roxana, in contrast, develops her identity *within* the (corrupt) institutions of bourgeois and aristocratic society as the kept mistress of a succession of rich supporters, from each of whom she gathers further wealth and, consequently, independence. After a colorful career in Paris and Holland, she returns to London, where she gains notoriety in the debauched aristocratic society of the court after a risqué dance she performs in the costume of the Turkish courtesan "Roxana." Eventually deciding to retire to a life of ennobled respectability with a wealthy husband, she finds herself entrapped by her own history: threatened with exposure by one of her abandoned children, who recognizes her as the famous courtesan, she is forced to choose between killing the child or relinquishing her own life of privilege. Unable to resolve her dilemma, and fearing that her maid Amy has murdered the daughter, she becomes increasingly deranged, and her story ends inconclusively, in a state of confusion reflective of its heroine's madness.

In spite of their divergent conclusions, both novels emphasize the role of individual self-representation in the everyday negotiation of one's social identity and material fortunes.[3] The two heroines consistently attribute their misfortune to their own flawed characters and appetites, rather than to a grander divine scheme,[4] and indeed, many of the things that befall them, such as Moll's inadvertent marriage to her brother, cannot readily be explained in terms of providential purpose. Failing to find an overarching order in the events that affect them, the heroines learn to order their own actions more deliberately, compensating for the loss of stable world order with an enhanced consciousness of their own behavior.[5] Each develops a sense of self concomitantly with her refinement of a survival strategy, which starts in both cases with procuring male support through sexual favors, but evolves rapidly toward a more autonomous mode of selfhood which exploits the social and economic system by means of deceit and the fabrication of convincing personal histories.

Initially, Moll and Roxana rely on the conventional strategy of seeking protection and support from a man – frequently a husband in Moll's case, generally a wealthy lover in that of Roxana. But the minimal attention the heroines accord the everyday pleasures of conjugal security suggests that their men carry little interest as emotional partners; they are simply a means toward the end of securing financial autonomy.[6] Financial independence is in turn only a means to the greater end of controlling their own destinies. As their stories progress, self-determination becomes an end in itself: both Moll and Roxana occasionally attribute their bad conduct to poverty, yet neither gives up her deviant behavior even when financial circumstances would permit an easy retirement. At the height of their mastery – when Moll has become the legendary protean thief and Roxana acquired notoriety as the infamous "Turkish" dancer – their quest for conjugal security has been displaced by a larger relationship with society in which the identity of the heroine is at once grounded in, yet unknown in its particulars by, the larger collective of Greater London.

More than *Robinson Crusoe*, these two novels are concerned with the relationship of individualism to social order – a relationship which they dramatize in antagonistic terms as the conflict between social institutions and the behavior that subverts them: marriage versus adultery and prostitution; commerce and trade versus theft and fraud; legal work versus crime. Taken collectively, the three novels re-enact the same progressive socialization of the individual and authority which *Robinson Crusoe* allegorized in the gradual reintegration of its protagonist into society: Moll Flanders elaborates her identity in the urban environment of London, but she remains until the end of her story an outsider with respect to the social order; Roxana acts out her life within the established social order and ultimately seeks respectability within that order.[7] In this increasingly social context for identity, the various structures and practices of social intercourse form the effective ground for Moll's and Roxana's deviations in much the same way that paternal-providential law serves as a horizon for Robinson's travels.

If, as John Richetti says, "the real movement of Defoe's novels is not simply towards the determinants of character but rather towards the depiction of a dialectic between self and other which has as its end a covert but triumphant assertion of the self,"[8] the "other" in the three novels covered by this study evolves steadily toward a social order, whose otherness expresses itself in the competitive versions of events and characters which its members promote. Moll's obsession with penetrating all quarters of the city to perform ever more daring thefts and Roxana's desire for celebrity as a royal mistress are eminently social projects. These are not gestures one can envision on a desert island, and to the extent they provide a sense of power or mastery, they also necessarily reinforce the dependency of the self on a social standard by which it can gauge its impact. This collective Other is the nominal victim of the individualistic heroines' self-(mis)representations; but it also, by virtue of that fact, exercises a structural restraint on their mastery: to the extent that Moll and Roxana deploy their individuality through impersonation, they are dependent on the validating responses of their public. The multiple identities which they devise for themselves can procure the benefits associated with such roles only to the extent that they receive accreditation by a responsive public. Even as it founds the autonomy of the individual, the practice of self mis-representation incurs a dialogical dependence on an Other. The versions of themselves which the heroines promote, and which form the impetus for many of their projects, require validation by some other party – minimally construed as a devoted husband, lover, or accomplice, but capable of embracing all of society, or even the reader.[9]

In *Moll Flanders* the link is quite explicit between this Other who responds to the heroine's stories and the authority systems regulating her world. Frequently the Other functions as the immediate detainer and agent of that authority, as in the cases of testimony, false witness, and legal judgment which confront Moll. Though more immediately perceptible in its effects, since it can entail immediate imprisonment, or even death, such straightforward exercise of authority is also more susceptible to control than either divine law or the diffuse authority of reputation. For instance, when Moll is faced with a death sentence – the ultimate repression of identity – she regains control of her destiny by giving a Newgate minister the full account of her past history and promising repentance: her new ally then obtains her reprieve.

The dialogical structure of individualism will remain a constant throughout the century, but it will not always be so unproblematic. Moll Flanders minimizes her dependence on the Other by maintaining her mobility and keeping her relationships on the level of a practical structural contingency rather than a personal involvement: she goes through a large number of husbands, lovers, victims, accomplices, and accusers, but seldom has any deep emotional interaction with them.[10] But such a strategy is incommensurate with a stable social identity, and it assumes a passive, or at least thick-witted Other, whose distance from the self is never seriously questioned.[11] Later novels reject this simplification, insisting rather that the Other is a necessary component of selfhood and, in the most extreme cases of individualism, of an equivalent intelligence: for Richardson, Diderot, and Laclos, in particular, the Other is always simultaneously an object of attraction and rivalry, lover and enemy, accomplice and adversary. *Roxana* prefigures this trend, and the delicate equilibrium it presupposes, in the person of Amy, Roxana's lifelong maid, friend, and *Doppelgänger*. Roxana's ultimate inability to control Amy, who is the active principle in their partnership – the one who implements the things Roxana only dares think about – will ultimately bring about her madness.

Read as the protagonist's problems with the "other" side of her story, the final episodes of the novel elucidate the close relationship between the interpersonal self/Other exchange and the "internarrative" relationship of current (personal) story to cumulative (collective) history. In both *Moll Flanders* and *Roxana*, history, in the sense of an accumulating collective narrative to which each individual contributes and which conversely accords a place to each individual, begins to emerge as a competitive order to the providential script as both the frame and the means of selfhood. As a *comprehensive* order – that is, one which is both all-inclusive and infinitely understanding and accommodating – the accumulating record of experience, both personal and public, opens the door to extraordinary programs of self-determination, since it responds to, and can be manipulated by, individuals who understand its workings. But as an enduring record within which all events and stories must be situated, it exercises a determining influence on those same programs, and thus functions in tandem with, or as a cumulative temporal analog to, the law of the collective Other.

Moll Flanders is the story of an individual who succeeds in managing the play between these two functions – between the stories she contrives for her profit and the history which accumulates as a result of her exploits, between her momentary fictions and her growing notoriety, between the public identities she invents and the inner narrating identity which invents them in response to shifting social exigencies. She thus provides a compelling, if somewhat crude, prototype for the more polished versions of dialectical individualism that dominate the next generation. As John Richetti puts it, "*Moll Flanders* is about eighteenth-century social and economic realities, but it is also about the superior reality of a self which moves through them, mastering them with a powerful dialectic rhythm and never succumbing to their full implications as cumulatively limiting realities."[12] Roxana, conversely, fails to manage the two sides of her identity or the two identities of her (hi)story: an identity and life that she claims as her own creation but which conflicts with her current persona will persist in the collective memory and coerce her into an increasingly narrow frame of options. Her eventual ambiguous madness allegorizes both the dangers of individualism conceived as a mastery of history and, by extension, Defoe's resistance to the secular self-determination which begins to emerge in the place of providence. In this sense, his last novel does not relate the ultimate victory of virtue or any similar moral order, but rather the slipperiness of history – even history that one writes personally.

At the core of the program of self-determination which structures *Moll Flanders* and *Roxana* lies a subset of interpersonal discourse we can call *negotiation*, and a form of interpersonal relationship we can call *transaction*. Personal relationships are in these novels incidental to the main business of negotiating one's place and fortune in the world. In the place of Robinson Crusoe's contemplative retrospection and philosophical speculation, Moll and Roxana embody selfhood as an ongoing activity of bargaining, planning, and representation. Although they share the earlier work's retrospective autobiographical mode, they devote little energy to the assessment of previous events and the contemplation of current comfort. Rather, all their attention is absorbed by the intricate management of their material situation and appearance.

Moll Flanders establishes the pattern early on: the heroine relates in minute detail the complex negotiations leading up to her first marriage, but devotes only one paragraph to the ensuing five years of conjugal existence (p. 76). Two pages later, she disposes of her second marriage with similar efficiency.[13] On the other hand, she recounts with great care the justifications for deceit in an age dominated by material interest, and illustrates her theory immediately with two similar anecdotes, one concerning the strategy of defamation she orchestrates for a young neighbor seeking to avenge herself for a suitor's scorn, and one that deals with Moll's own deception of the suitor that will become her third husband (pp. 85–9, 91–6).

The attention to negotiation is even more pronounced in *Roxana*: the heroine's vacillations concerning her landlord's offer to make her his kept woman occupy over twenty pages, but the years of cohabitation themselves are briefly disposed of in a few vague paragraphs. An even better example can be found in her relationship with the Dutch merchant, which both in Holland before their marriage and in London later on, is taken up almost entirely by negotiation. When they are not arranging for the maintenance of Roxana's estate (p. 150), or planning how to manage a Jew who has intimations of Roxana's real identity and continually threatens to expose her fraudulent claim to the inheritance of her "husband" (pp. 155–9), they are reckoning debts (pp. 178–80) or exchanging proposals and counter-proposals concerning matrimony and cohabitation (pp. 183–97). Even after their marriage, the relationship remains dominated by negotiation, particularly when Roxana finds herself pursued by her daughter and needs to shift her own and her husband's whereabouts frequently without letting the latter know why.

Negotiation is not the same thing as narration, but taken narrowly, as a means of striking contracts, it answers many of the same needs as relating events narratively, and taken broadly, as a paradigm of social relationships, it subtends all narrative situations. In the narrow sense, negotiation has as its goal agreement between two or more people on the shape of things to come. Like narration, it aims at fixing reality, stabilizing events and providing a basis for further planning, but whereas narration foregrounds its organization of the past, and only implicitly predicates the future, negotiation claims to schematize the future and only implicitly concretizes the past. One might envision negotiation in this sense as the mutual determination of the future past, of what one will be able to cite, at some future date, as a pre-existing, stable order and grounds for action.

This process of negotiation suffuses the later novels of the century, particularly those of Richardson, Rousseau and Laclos, in the form of the various agreements, compacts, and projects which friends, lovers, and rivals elaborate as part of their dialogical exchange, but it can be found earlier as well – in the interview between the Princesse de Clèves and Nemours, for instance, or, more graphically, in the late episodes of *Robinson Crusoe*, where Robinson extracts a variety of promises, agreements, and compacts from the English and Spaniards concerning his future treatment and the future maintenance of his island. In its most extreme form such negotiation gives rise to the concept of the *contract*, which in *Moll Flanders* and *Roxana* generally takes the form of a promise of financial reimbursement or support by a seducer, suitor, mother, or friend, in exchange for services rendered. With the possible exception of Moll's initial seduction at the hands of her master's oldest son, neither Moll nor Roxana ever ally themselves with anyone without first carefully establishing the precise conditions of the alliance. In the same way that later protagonists will secure their future through the presentation of a story likely to elicit the support of the listener, Moll and Roxana attempt to gain control over their destiny through the careful negotiation of contracts.

In its larger sense as a paradigm of social interaction, negotiation embraces the situation of give and take that is inherent in the narrative situation. Storytelling implies an agreement, on the part of the teller, to provide a coherent version of some reality and, on the part of the listener, to grant attention to that relation of events and thus to ground, at least minimally as an event of narration, its coherence. Reality itself, like history, is under constant negotiation: the essential qualities and historical situation we assign various phenomena are always elaborated in conjunction with our social partners' versions of those phenomena, and it is through our constant and reciprocal relating of the world that we establish the relations that comprise it. To agree to listen to someone is already to grant her story a place in history – and to shift the locus of her identity to the resultant narrative.

Such is in any case the version of social reality that *Moll Flanders* and *Roxana* adumbrate. Without formulating it as explicitly as will Diderot or Sterne, Defoe's works nonetheless portray social identity and personal fortune as the product of an ongoing process of narrative negotiation in which one's history, character, and fate hinge on one's rhetorical energy. When Moll succeeds in talking her way out of arrest in a silver shop, it is because she can produce a convincing story of innocence that is consistent with the details of the incident and her general demeanor (pp. 254–7). When she bilks a wealthy woman whose home is aflame into turning over her valuables (pp. 200–1), or gains the confidence of a wealthy young girl (pp. 245–6), it is on the basis of the flawless explanations of things she gives, the likelihood of her stories. It is her "abridgement of this whole history . . . the picture of my conduct for fifty years in miniature" (p. 271) that convinces the Newgate ordinary of her repentance and ultimately proves instrumental in obtaining her reprieve. Similarly, Roxana's narrow escape from the Jew in Paris hinges on the relative truth of her version of events and the resultant "unconcern'd Easiness" with which she tells her story (p. 153), just as her ability to manipulate her Dutch husband and Quaker friend likewise derives from their acceptance of her version of things. Unlike the world of *La Princesse de Clèves* where authority over reality depends almost entirely on one's social rank, Defoe's universe is one increasingly regulated by historical verisimilitude, which is to say that the story most apparently congruent with existing versions of events (i.e., the negotiation that finds agreement among the largest number of parties) is the story that gains acceptance.[14]

Moll and Roxana are, of course, superior narrators/negotiators. Careful management of their personal history, liberally spiced with fiction when necessary, permits them to present themselves as wealthier and of a better background than they really are, and thus to negotiate from a position of strength when they confront other people. Moll knows this instinctively when, following the ruin and flight of her second husband, she goes into the Mint, changes her name, and assumes the identity of a widow (p. 81). When she later takes up residence with a captain's widow and discovers that "marriages were here the consequences of politic schemes for forming interests, and carrying on business" (p. 83), she makes no scruples about shedding her identity of poor widow in favor of a more attractive role. Allowing her friend to spread the word that she has a fortune of £1,500, she soon finds herself surrounded by admirers, among whom she need only "single out . . . the properest man that might be for my purpose; that is to say, the man who was most likely to depend upon the hearsay of a fortune, and not inquire too far into the particulars" (p. 93). Although she openly qualifies such tactics as "the fraud of passing for a fortune without money, and cheating a man into marrying" (p. 98), they form the cornerstone of her strategy for obtaining her fourth husband as well, and for the duration of her life, even to the final episodes with her (now refound) fourth husband and (also refound) son, she carefully monitors and adjusts the information she passes along about her past and present situation.

From a "subtle game" imposed by necessity (p. 93), to the sport of a self-assured seductress ("I played with this lover as an angler does with a trout" p. 145), Moll's role-playing evolves towards full-time deceit and perfect fluidity of identity. During her career as a thief she assumes the costume and manners of everything from widow or helpful neighbor to beggar woman and even a middle-aged man, exploring all the nooks and crannies of London street life and adopting the identity appropriate to the moment – and to the goods she hopes to purloin. Increasingly, she turns from simple theft to complex trickery, depending on her costume and discourse to bilk people out of their property (pp. 228–9, 244–6, 249–54). As she succinctly puts it, "I took up new figures, and contrived to appear in new shapes every time I went abroad" (p. 249). Even once she no longer needs to steal, she continues her one-woman show, making deceit and role-playing not only her profession, but her avocation: "I could not forbear going abroad again, as I called it now, than any more I could when my extremity really drove me out for bread" (p. 241).[15] Her identity gradually establishes itself within this ongoing game of metamorphosis, fascinated not merely with deceiving people, but with deceiving them with *new* disguises and ploys. As Marie-Paul Laden aptly puts it, "in Moll's case, disguise and successive rejections of the past self (as it becomes fixed, alien, other) *constitute* the self."[16]

Roxana's story is more tightly bound to a narrow conception of negotiation, and can be read as the attempt to manage history through contracts. Unlike her predecessor, she is more intent on arresting the flux of change than exploring it. Built on an initial lie – that she has left her house and fled her creditors – her career commences with a pre-meditated illicit liaison whose rules, conditions, and moral implications are thoroughly hashed out well before the adulterous act itself. Her sham marriage to her landlord provides Roxana with her first assumed identity, for once in Paris, she passes as his wife and claims his property upon his death. In her subsequent roles as mistress to a German prince, friend and mistress to a Dutch merchant, "Roxana" of London society, mistress to a nameless Lord, and pseudo-Quaker widow, she progressively revises her past as she accumulates wealth, developing, frequently at the insistence of her sidekick and accomplice, Amy, careful schemes for surveying and controlling her past while structuring a profitable future. Like Moll, she claims poverty as her initial motivation to sin (pp. 73–9) but fails to change her ways even once she has accumulated enough capital to retire. And like Moll, she is ultimately undone by her own obsessive ambition, when her own daughter connects her to the infamous Roxana and threatens her current bourgeois idyll. Her deceits and stories are not born out of need, much less a flare for virtuosity, but rather an obsession with gaining control over her future and attaining a glorious station immune to interference from other parties.

This first emerges in her long tirade against marriage, upon receiving a proposal from her Dutch merchant friend. Extolling her independence and her aversion to parting with it or her fortune (p. 185), she states that "a Woman gave herself entirely away from herself, in Marriage. ... the very Nature of the Marriage-Contract was, in short, nothing but giving up Liberty, Estate, Authority, and every-thing, to the Man, and the Woman was indeed, a meer Woman ever after, that is to say, a Slave" (p. 187).[17] The give and take of negotiation as Moll practiced it, is for Roxana an abnegation of the authority one has over one's destiny; only the single woman enjoys "the full Command of what she had, and the full Direction of what she did. ... she was controul'd by none, because accountable to none, and was in Subjection to none" (p. 188). In a more than simply etymological sense, not wanting to share one's accounts implies a refusal of the negotiative economy of narration. Roxana does not just keep her money to herself, she keeps her story to herself as well, for she knows that relating it to another individual gives that individual a say in her destiny:

> Then I consider'd too, that *Amy* knew all the Secret History of my Life; had been in all the Intriegues of it, and been a Party in both Evil and Good, ... so it must be only her steddy Kindness to me, and an excess of Generous Friendship for me, that shou'd keep her from ill-using me in return for it; which ill-using me was enough in her Power, and might be my utter Undoing.
> (P. 365)

In fact, Roxana almost is undone by the Jew in Paris whose familiarity with her husband's history allows him to tie Roxana to the latter's death (pp. 150–2). With the device of foreign language, this scene underlines the vulnerability that comes with the circulation of one's story beyond one's control: Roxana cannot challenge the Jew's version of her past, because she cannot understand his language and thus what, precisely, is being said of her. Similarly, the Dutch merchant's sympathetic reaction to Roxana is marked by his use of English, a language the Jew cannot understand. Not surprisingly, given such experiences, Roxana learns to be extremely parsimonious with her history and makes a general principle of secrecy. Even her dear friend, and infinitely patient defender, the Quaker lady, does not merit confidence: "you must not understand me as if I let my Friend the QUAKER into any Part of the Secret History of my former Life; ... it was always a Maxim with me, *That Secrets shou'd never be open'd, without evident Utility*" (p. 375).

Roxana's obsession with absolute control is a response to the discovery that social identity carries its risks: having made a name for herself, she senses her vulnerability to muckraking and tries to minimize it. But her reluctance to share her history places her program of self-definition in an untenable position. Once the self is defined through the relationships it entertains with society – rather than in a private dialogue with its Maker – it can no longer dispense with "telling itself." Like Moll, Roxana must "ex-propriate" her self through narration in order to realize her goals; she must give her identity, in the form of a story, to the people whose help she requires. Unlike Moll, whose social marginality and mobility allow her to shed her past as she fabricates it, Roxana must live with the history she constructs. The consolidation of her identity and the attainment of her ends depend on her entry into the social economy. Relating her story to other individuals provides them with the cultural and social markers they need in order to relate her to their own worlds. In concrete terms, she must share her story with the Prince (or the Dutch Merchant, or her Quaker friend) in order to obtain assistance. But this sharing is in a very real sense a giving up of authority, since, as a narration, it generates a narrative persona that can be maintained beyond the control of the original narrator through further narrations by the parties to whom the history is recounted.

Self-determination in *Roxana* thus evolves into a double bind. Like the Princesse de Clèves, Roxana cannot manage her destiny without sharing her history, but she cannot share her history without losing control over her destiny. There are at least two responses to this dilemma, two attitudes the self can adopt, and both will find more graphic dramatization in later eighteenth-century novels. One can give one's self over to the economy completely, by saturating it with a relation of one's conduct that omits virtually nothing. Such total expropriation carries with it its own encoded "instructions for reading," since it promotes an image of spontaneity, innocence, and openness that encourages a sympathetic response in the listener and promotes the subject's cause through the agency of others. Richardson's heroines, Pamela and Clarissa, personify this strategy. Alternatively, one can limit one's history to a few select episodes and tailor the account to fit specific listeners. This approach draws on appropriation more than expropriation: it subordinates the content and form of the narrative to the identity of the listener and thus assimilates his or her identity into that of the narrator. This is the strategy of the self-interested or resolutely immoral person, most strikingly exemplified by Lovelace, in *Clarissa*, or Valmont and Merteuil in Laclos' *Les Liaisons dangereuses*, but present also in the novels of Fielding and Diderot, in characters such as Blifil, Mme de la Pommeraye, or the Chevalier de Saint-Ouin.

In *Roxana* these two divergent attitudes take the form of a schizophrenic ambivalence between two distinct personalities and principles of behavior, as embodied in the relationship between Roxana and her *Doppelgänger*, Amy. The latter functions not only as a validating Other who supports and seconds Roxana's projects, but also as an extension of Roxana's selfhood, her embodiment as a principle of action in the social world. As Roxana herself points out, Amy is "not only...a Servant, but an Agent; and not only an Agent, but a Friend, and a Faithful Friend too" (p. 365). Amy quite literally shares Roxana's life: when Roxana starves, she starves too (although she could simply leave); when Roxana prostitutes herself to her landlord, Amy likewise accepts deflowering (although the landlord does not request it) and even furnishes the household its first child; when Roxana takes up with a foreign prince in Paris, Amy naturally takes up with his attendant gentleman; when Roxana becomes terrified in the storm at sea, Amy goes nearly berserk. In fact, Amy as frequently precedes her mistress's example as she follows it. It is Amy who first suggests that one of them will have to sleep with the landlord – and generously offers to do so if need be. It is Amy who first goes to the Dutch merchant in Paris (p. 149); who arranges Roxana's transformation into a Quaker in an unknown part of London (pp. 251–2); who re-establishes contact with the prince in Paris and arranges Roxana's marriage with him (pp. 259–60, 275–6); who disposes of, and later recovers, Roxana's children. It is even Amy who is first misidentified by Roxana's daughter as her mother. And it is of course Amy who gets rid of the daughter at the end of the book. As Roxana accurately puts it, "*Poor* Amy! *What art thou, that I am not?* what hast thou been, that I have not been?" (p. 164).

Yet if the two characters share the same fate, they react to it differently. Amy complements and completes her mistress, by providing the agency for action that the latter, for all her talk about independence, frequently lacks. The contrast between the two appears almost at the beginning of the novel. While Roxana plays the innocent and refuses to see the designs of her landlord, Amy not only states the case with characteristic bluntness ("you may have a handsome, charming Gentleman, be rich, live pleasantly, and in Plenty; or refuse him, and want a Dinner, go in Rags, live in Tears; in short, beg and starve" (p. 74)), but offers herself to lie in her mistress' place, and justifies the illicit relationship on the basis of practices in other cultures. Later during the storm at sea, Roxana casts the difference between the two temperaments in terms of violent expression versus repression:

> this Difference was between us, that I said all these things within myself, and sigh'd, and mourn'd inwardly; but *Amy*, as her Temper was more violent, spoke aloud, and cry'd, and call'd out aloud, like one in an Agony. (P. 164)

> *Amy* was much more penitent at Sea, and much more sensible of her Deliverance when she Landed, and was safe, than I was; I was in a kind of Stupidity, I know not well what to call it; I had a Mind full of Horrour in the time of the Storm, and saw Death before me, as plainly as *Amy*, but my Thoughts got no Vent, as *Amy's* did; I had a silent sullen kind of Grief, which cou'd not break out either in Words or Tears, and which was, therefore, much the worse to bear. (P. 167)

More verbal in nature, Amy functions as the active agent or manipulative principle of selfhood, and she embodies the dynamic negotiation of narration to the extent that she is always ready to revise her stories and alter current plans at a moment's notice. She mediates most of Roxana's relationships with the past, keeping tabs on her first husband, returning to France to check on the whereabouts of the Dutch merchant, re-establishing contact with the prince, and handling all the arrangements concerning her mistress's children. As part of this ongoing activity, she also initiates most of Roxana's various fictional alibis, such as the stories she tells her mistress's first husband (pp. 124–30), relatives and children (pp. 232–7, 376), and tenacious daughter pp. 359–63). In fact, she even lies to Roxana, when she judges it expedient – as when she tells the latter that her first husband has died, in order to encourage her to marry again (p. 170).[18]

Possessing all of the parts of Roxana's past, and in a very real sense the personification of her history as an active principle structuring the present, Amy increasingly takes over the management of her mistress's life. When Roxana's daughter begins her dogged inquiry on the basis of "but a broken Account of things" (p. 315), Amy blithely mentions – with her usual decisive foresight – that "she began to think it wou'd be absolutely necessary to murther her" (p. 316), a suggestion that provokes the first argument between the two friends. Later, Amy becomes "next-door to stark-mad" about the daughter (p. 358) and increasingly difficult to control, while Roxana progressively withdraws from the world. Though she admits that she, too, secretly longs for her daughter's death (p. 350), she can neither bear the thought of being party to her murder, nor, on the other hand, of confronting her.

Roxana's ultimate paralysis and breakdown dramatizes the inability of the self to cope with its history, both in the sense of the enduring public record of identity that comes back to haunt it (the daughter) and in the sense of the coercive logic of its accumulated experience (Amy). Roxana refuses both the anachronistic, static identity predicated by her public story, and the desperate flight from that identity which is pressed upon her by the logical pattern of her past initiatives. Not surprisingly, the result is a breakdown of sorts which signals the final loss of control over the self's own mechanisms:

Amy abandons her mistress after a second dispute, and Roxana, upon hearing a report that she has "taken care" of the daughter, falls into a "Fit of trembling" and runs "raving about the Room like a Mad-Woman" (p. 372). Now totally alienated from her more active half by the violence of the maid's (supposed) act, she quite literally withdraws from history: the autobiography abruptly ends within a few pages, the daughter's disappearance unaccounted for, Roxana's (and Amy's) reunion left dangling in an unfinished flashback.[19] Rather than a dénouement, the novel concludes in a knot of impossibility.

That *Roxana* should culminate so catastrophically is built into the conflict between the heroine's desires and her strategy of tampering with her story. It is Roxana's wish to change her way of life and "put myself into some Figure of Life, in which I might not be scandalous to my own Family, and be afraid to make myself known to my own Children, who were my own Flesh and Blood" (p. 249) which triggers the disintegration of her identity, by proposing to arrest the very economy of notoriety upon which her self-hood had established itself. When she first thinks of "putting a new Face upon" her "Manner of Living" (p. 250), she quite naturally turns to Amy, who provides and executes a "Scheme" that, as she puts it, will allow her mistress to "begin, and finish a perfect entire Change of your Figure and Circumstances, in one Day" (pp. 251–2). Unfortunately, although it is born of a desire for stable respectability, this scheme reiterates the practices of deceit and fabulation – this time it is the Quaker lady who is the victim – that are at the base of Roxana's problems in the first place. Each successive attempt to paper over the discrepancies in her stories requires further fabulations that are themselves susceptible to exposure and will require further repair. Likewise, every such episode, to the extent it requires enlisting the support of further witnesses, adds another layer to the already mushrooming economy of her story that the protagonist strives to control. Short of exposure, humiliation, and submission to a greater authority, such as Moll undergoes when she is arrested, there can be no stopping this process, since any attempt to control Roxana's history only adds to that history and increases the problem. Having appropriated the authority of the law, history cannot be arrested: *Roxana* cannot, and does not, really end.

Moll Flanders not only concludes her story, she does so on a relatively happy note, having settled all her accounts in both senses of the word. She has reconciled all the conflicting accounts of her past, revealed the essential truth to both her husband and her son, served her sentence for theft, and retired to England at the ripe old age of seventy. Having demonstrated her autonomy, she repudiates its logic – at least nominally – accepting reintegration into the social order. The offspring she leaves behind greet her with open arms, her leftover Lancashire husband reappears in her life to their mutual benefit, and she arrives in America to find her mother has graciously left her a substantial inheritance.

If Roxana has no such luck it is precisely because she is unwilling to give herself over to the mechanism she exploits. She wants to write history without being written by it, make a name for herself without giving up control of that name, negotiate a juicier destiny for herself without giving her self over to the vicissitudes of social negotiation. Her joyless bargaining, like her avowed avarice and vanity (p. 244) – and unlike Moll's dynamic social interaction – aims only at securing the future and accumulating an excess of glory. While Moll, even in her most outlandish shenanigans as a thief, never yearns to be known publicly – indeed does everything in her power to remain anonymous even among her fellow thieves – Roxana's wildest dream runs rather to "being a *Princess* . . . being surrounded with Domesticks; honour'd with Titles; be call'd HER HIGHNESS; and live in all the Splendor of a Court" (p. 278). Moll cedes to grander pretensions only once, when she chooses, as her second husband, a "gentleman-tradesman" who "might become a sword, and look as like a gentleman as another man; and not be one that had the mark of his apron-strings upon his coat" (p. 78). But at the end of her story she no longer lays any claim to respectability and obtains her peace of mind with a partner who shares her past and her profession. Roxana demands a life not just of comfort, but of prestige and glory in the public eye: confronted with "all the Gayety and Glory" associated with becoming a princess (p. 280), she does not hesitate to abandon her wealthy, worthy merchant (pp. 277–81), and even once this dream evaporates, she maintains her pretentions by demanding her husband purchase both English and Dutch titles of nobility.

Yet it is precisely this assurance of identity which contracts are unable to provide. As Roxana's story illustrates, their ideal rigor conflicts with their negotiative, narrative underpinnings: the process out of which contracts are born always lurks in the background as a threat to their survival, just as the opportunistic conduct of Amy conflicts with the image of nobility it has helped purchase. To the extent they do succeed, contracts, like narratives, remain in circulation as historical records of past action long after the transactions they were to regulate have expired: the glory as as a courtly mistress which Roxana negotiates with such skill remains as a document of her character long after it has ceased to describe her conduct, just as on a more concrete level, Roxana's own daughter persists as the residue of a previous "contract." Just as every successful negotiation produces a transitory contract, every shift in identity leaves its rules imprinted in the memory of those that sanction it. Such historical traces can themselves at any moment resurface as the content of a further negotiation and revision of identity: it is because she succeeds so well in impressing her persona of "Roxana" on London society, that Roxana's daughter remembers her so clearly; it is the very distinctiveness of the jewels which she shows the Dutch merchant in Paris that permits the Jew to recognize them and associate Roxana with the death of her lover years earlier. Such is the drawback of social identity: when one weaves one's self into the fabric of public discourse, one's history becomes public property. This is a pattern we have already seen at work in *La Princesse de Clèves*, with the difference that in Defoe's work the heroine herself does the weaving.

To the extent that Roxana's individualism proves unable to extricate the heroine from her dilemma, the book would seem to invalidate the mechanisms of self-definition it dramatizes. Just as *Moll Flanders* tries to undercut its dramatization of social mastery and hard-won autonomy by framing Moll's story in her belated repudiation of individualism, *Roxana* engineers its heroine's ruin by engaging her in an attempt at self-negation from which there is no return. At the very least, *Roxana* depicts not the triumph of individualism, but rather the complications posed for it by the strategy of historical negotiation it exploits. In this sense the novel prefigures the generation to come. In particular, the splitting of the self into two distinct psychological comportments, one that enters aggressively into negotiation with other individuals, revising its past freely as it adapts itself to new identities, and one that withholds accounts, conceals its past and strives to control the future, foreshadows the cleavage of selfhood into public performance and private scheme which is later associated with incarnations of anti-social evil. In its most benign manifestation, this duplicity is called hypocrisy:

> How did my Blood flush up into my Face! when I reflected how sincerely, how affectionately this good-humour'd Gentleman embrac'd the most cursed Piece of Hypocrisie that ever came into the Arms of an honest Man? His was all Tenderness, all Kindness, and the utmost Sincerity; Mine all Grimace and Deceit; a Piece of meer Manage, and fram'd Conduct ... (*Roxana*, p. 348)

In its more deliberate versions, the same "meer Manage, and fram'd Conduct" states the terms of social mastery and erotic coercion personified by narrational monsters such as Lovelace, in *Clarissa* and Valmont, in *Les Liaisons dangereuses*. Their agendas of narrative mastery are ultimately unfulfillable for much the same reasons as are Roxana's ambitions of controlled infamy. Yet they will exercise substantial fascination over the novelists of the succeeding generations.

Defoe differs significantly from his successors in his refusal to acknowledge a positive model of historical selfhood. While Marivaux will associate the coy self-consciousness and transparent hypocrisy of his characters with, among other things, their erotic attraction, and Richardson will balance the negative agendas of Lovelace and Mr B. with a positive mastery of the public record by his virtuous heroines (Fielding and Diderot similarly), Defoe seems reticent to acknowledge the increasingly secular model of selfhood he depicts. *Roxana* aligns authority more explicitly with shared history than did *Robinson Crusoe* and *Moll Flanders*, but it also seems to argue that any programs of self-definition based on such a notion can only lead to schizoid obsession and self-destruction. Subsequent authors will indeed maintain the negative side of self-definition with characters such as Lovelace, Blifil, Valmont, and the scores of lesser villains that people the works of Fielding and Diderot, but they will also seek an alternative model of self-expression that accommodates the self to the collective record without compromising the integrity of either. I will argue in coming chapters that this alternative model draws on the notion of self-narrativation, or the transposition of identity into a written textual order, whose representation of the self is both limited at the outset by the author yet subject to continual modulation by the successive readers that constitute its public. Such textualization of the self would no doubt be as repugnant to Defoe as the lies of Roxana, since it implicitly reinforces the authority of the continually elaborated social narrative at the expense of the authoritative providential script; it nonetheless builds on the very paradigm of reality as the product of negotiation which his novels, perhaps in spite of themselves, advance.

NOTES

1   Nancy K. Miller, *The Heroine's Text*, reads *Moll Flanders* in similarly positive, although feminist, terms of a "quest for (female) autonomy" (p. 19), in which the heroine systematically progresses from the status of an object of desire to that of the "determining agent of her destiny" (p. 20). My reading likewise assumes, against Watt, who asks skeptically "Is there – either in *Robinson Crusoe* or in *Moll Flanders* – any design whatsoever in the usual sense of the term?" (p. 135), that however flawed it may be in comparison with later "realistic" fiction, *Moll Flanders* deliberately and coherently adumbrates a strategy of self-determination. John Richetti, *Defoe's Narratives*, interprets the book even more strongly as concerned with the freedom and power which come with the mastery of sociological relationships by a consistent self standing apart from those relationships. His reading, perhaps more persuasively than mine, demonstrates the extent to which Defoe's works prefigure the later agendas of social mastery which pervade the French and English traditions alike.

2   Defoe is clearly not the only author to use the orphan as a test case for self-determination. Among the authors covered in this study, Marivaux, Fielding, and Diderot will exploit the device.

3 It is obvious that the heroines' tactics can be understood in a variety of ways, drawing as they do on seduction, marriage, prostitution, frugality, careful investment, even hard work (in Moll's case). I do not mean to downplay the validity of any of these perspectives through my neglect of them, but as my goal is to demonstrate the fundamental role self-fabulation plays in the novels, I must necessarily forego extended treatment of the many economic and social systems with which it interacts.

4 Roxana in particular remarks on her lack of a "Sence of a Supreme Power managing, directing, and governing in both Causes and Events in this World" (p. 159); citations are from *Roxana*, ed. David Blewett (Penguin Books, 1982), which reproduces the first edition of 1724. Citations of *Moll Flanders* are from the Juliet Mitchell edition (Penguin books, 1978), which is based on the text of the January, 1722, first edition.

5 Cf. Tavor, *Scepticism*, pp. 33–34.

6 Moll's eventual reunion with one of her husbands, Jemy, is the one exception. But coming at the end of Moll's adventures, and marking her repudiation of her former ways, and her reintegration into the social order, this relationship necessarily contrasts with her behavior throughout her life; cf. Blewett, *Defoe's Art of Fiction* (Toronto: University of Toronto Press, 1979), pp. 82–3.

7 Cf. David Blewett, pp. 146–7; also Richetti, *Defoe's Narratives*, pp. 96, 112, 122.

8 *Defoe's Narratives*, p. 96.

9 John Preston, *Created Self*, p. 33, notes that Moll in fact stands in closer relationship to her reader than to any of the other characters in the novel.

10 Watt, *Rise of the Novel*, pp. 122–9 devotes considerable energy to explaining Moll's apparent shallowness in her relationships with other people, eventually favoring the hypothesis that she is essentially a projection of Defoe's own personality.

11 Cf. Richetti, *Defoe's Narratives*, p. 108.

12 Ibid.

13 As Ian Watt points out, Robinson Crusoe holds the record for narrational discretion as regards family life: his marriage, two sons, daughter, and wife's death are sandwiched into a single sentence that commences with his settling in England and concludes with his departure for the Indies, many years later (Watt, *Rise of the Novel*, p. 75).

14 This is not to say that rank disappears as an important criterion for assigning truth value, since both Moll and Roxana are careful to maintain an appearance of respectability consistent with their stories, as discussed below.

15 In his reading of Moll as a "bourgeois picaroon," Robert Alter states that she is uncomfortable with disguise and that "her variety of extralegal activities is not in the least a game for her; . . . she certainly never gives the faintest hint of any pleasure or emotional involvement in connection with it"; *Rogue's Progress* (Cambridge, Mass.: Harvard University Press, 1964), pp. 46–7. Above and beyond the fact that Moll frequently refers to her sorties as a "game," and that the great variety of disguises she assumes testify to a predilection for assuming false identities and are in keeping with her general tendency to fabricate social

identities for herself in her dealings with suitors, passages like the one quoted clearly indicate that she *is* emotionally involved with her role as Proteus, and cannot stop, even when her wealth makes such behavior absurd. Her discomfort when disguised as a beggar or a man is simply due to the danger involved: a beggar invites suspicion, as does a woman dressed like a man. Marie-Paul Laden persuasively argues Moll's predilection for "the Trade" on narrative grounds: her delight in relating her various exploits, and detailing her "Art" and "Invention," belie the disclaimer that she stole for money; *Self-Imitation*, pp. 58–9.

16 *Self-Imitation*, p. 67.

17 Earlier, Roxana will compare marriage unfavorably to the state of being a mistress (pp. 170–1). Although she claims to be primarily interested in preserving her wealth, Roxana's arguments against marriage cover the whole gamut of conjugal relations and make of her a person as exceptional and "contrary to the general Practice" (p. 193) as the Princesse de Clèves or Pamela.

18 In fact, although she preaches self-reliance, Roxana seldom takes credit for any of her major decisions. The landlord sets the terms of her first relationship, the Prince those of the second. Likewise, the Dutch merchant contrives the elaborate plan of her escape to Holland and the means of transmitting her fortune to England. Later, her anonymous Lord will set her up in a private house in London, from which she will move to the Quaker's lodging at the insistence of Amy. At the conclusion of the novel even the Quaker has taken a more active role than Roxana, helping her to avoid her daughter and perpetuating her deceit in spite of her (the Quaker's) religious convictions.

19 When the flashback begins, Roxana is established in Holland, at the height of her "Glory and Prosperity" (p. 307), many years after the episode of the nosey daughter, and on good terms with Amy, who furnishes her what little comfort she can during her bouts of guilt (p. 310). When the book ends, this flashback has only just barely been brought back to the main narrative. Amy has disappeared, being completely estranged from Roxana, who leaves for Holland alone and in a state of permanent anxiety. A few sentences in the last pages of the book again allude to Amy's disposal of the daughter as a *fait accompli*, to her eventual arrival in Holland, and to a "Dreadful Course of Calamities" that befalls both women and is interpreted by Roxana as a "Blast of Heaven" to avenge "the Injury done the poor Girl, by us both" (p. 379).

5

Individualism and Authority

However different in class and aspiration, the Princesse de Clèves, Robinson Crusoe, Moll, and Roxana all have one thing in common: in a culture where birth, station, and social code define the scope of action of the individual, they attempt to determine their own destiny in spite of the institutions of authority regulating society. Like their predecessors in the seventeenth-century heroic romance or *roman*, they are *extraordinary*, but more literally so. They do not exemplify the values of their society, they take exception to them, establishing their identity outside of ordinary patterns of behavior and in opposition to the undifferentiated otherness of competing intentions which continually menaces them. The Princesse's refusal to conform to the codes of *galanterie*, Crusoe's disinterest for middle-class prosperity, Moll's refusal to live by the law, or Roxana's rejection of marriage and morals, are but the first instances of an interrogation of authority and an assertion of self-determination that will in one guise or another permeate virtually all of the plots we will be examining.

In the first third of the eighteenth century, this self-assertion expresses itself primarily as resistance to the station or status prescribed by the social order, which the protagonist superficially repudiates by her or his behavior, but ultimately internalizes and reasserts through the gesture of self-representation: the confessional narrative both affirms individuality and atones for past sins by rearticulating as part of the individual's story the systems of authority he or she violated. Thus *Robinson Crusoe* challenges paternal (and Paternal) authority before internalizing and re-expressing it, while *Moll Flanders* and *Roxana* rebel against collective codes, both criminal and moral, and ranging from the formal statutes regarding theft or murder to pervasive social institutions such as marriage, before ultimately reaffirming those codes as the lesson of their personal experience.

A similar pattern of self-assertion and resistance to authority informs some of the most influential French fiction of the period. Two French works spanning the period of Defoe's activity that had a substantial impact on the future form and thematics of the novel are Robert Chasles' *Les*

Illustres Françoises, 1713, and l'Abbé de Prévost's *Histoire du Chevalier des Grieux et de Manon Lescaut*, 1731, known popularly as *Manon Lescaut*.

Although extremely successful in its time,[1] *Les Illustres Françoises* has attracted less critical attention than *La Princesse de Clèves* or *Manon Lescaut*, possibly because it was published anonymously and could not be correlated to any known author's *œuvre*.[2] Nor does it conform to the formal conventions of the novel: it is composed of a series of different personal accounts by the various members of a group of old friends recently reunited in Paris and eager to bring each other up to date on their respective situations. Unlike their counterparts in traditional collections of framed stories, these narrators are also the characters in the accounts,[3] and they relate their histories to other individuals involved in them not in order to pass the time, but as means of clarifying dubious or strange behavior that has been attributed to them.[4] Several of the narrators are unjustly assumed to have wronged their spouses or lovers prior to their story; one was thought to be dead; one has been acting bizarrely because of his wife's cruel death under circumstances which are first revealed in his story. Their narratives not only clear their names by setting the record straight but, in two cases, effect a reconciliation.

Within each story, a young couple desirous of marrying struggles against the will of parents and social institutions which oppose them. There are a number of variations in this pattern – tyrannical or sympathetic fathers, mothers, uncles, and siblings; women of a fortune and class inferior to their lover, and lovers inferior to the woman they pursue; secret marriages, surprise marriages, illegitimate children, and abductions – but in all cases, the relationship of authority to personal freedom remains in the foreground: in the parent's censure of the child's inclination, in the use of inheritances to influence the choice of a fiancé, in the complex regulations governing marriage without the parents' consent, in the legal manœuverings that play a central role in several stories, in the clergy's omnipresence as the right arm of the law, and in the pressure exercised by social conventions of accepted behavior.[5] The violent revolt that is necessary to break the hold of these institutions and which in a sense marks the protagonists as outlaws, finds its redemption in the subsequent detailed account of the characters' motivations and specific actions. When they explain what they did, and why, their story absolves them of wrongdoing and obtains their reintegration into the community and its moral codes. In this sense, narrative self-representation functions as a rival mode of authority capable of intervening directly in the collective record and rehabilitating the individuals whose reputations have been slighted by the collective record.

Where attempts to relate one's own story inevitably misfired in *La Princesse de Clèves*, the narrators in *Les Illustres Françoises* succeed in

mediating their own history, and they do so in a world where the negotiation of individual identity has become a frankly narrative ritual: the characters listen to each other's stories, comment on them, pose questions, and,
together, arrive at a conclusion concerning the individual's past conduct
and, hence, true character.[6] While their tales depict a social system predicated on the avaricious, selfish, and often cruelly capricious authority of a
father (or mother) over his or her offspring, their own miniature society is
one in which individuals are allowed to define themselves and select their
destiny according to their own reason. The enclosure of the individual
within an authoritarian social order is thus mitigated or superseded by the
open narrative economy of the circle of friends, and to that extent the tales
allegorize the emergence not only of self-definition, but of a community
of discourse whose authority both informs and is informed by individual
self-representation. As we shall see, this same paradigm of mutual determination will inform more mature expressions of individualism and eventually lead to a dialectical conceptualization of selfhood and history.

Manon Lescaut is closer to Defoe's works in tone and structure. Presented
as a retrospective confessional autobiography similar to those of Defoe's
characters, and narrated by the Chevalier des Grieux, a young man of
superior birth and intelligence destined for the order of Malta, it recounts
how he encounters, elopes with, and ultimately ruins the life of, Manon
Lescaut, a rather warm-blooded fifteen-year old with a decided penchant for
sensual pleasure and comfort. Throughout their tempestuous relationship,
during which Manon abandons des Grieux for a wealthier man each time his
resources dwindle, the chevalier progressively debases himself in order to
satisfy his mistress, resorting to gambling, fraud, theft, and even murder in
order to elude the law and obtain money enough to satisfy her. Both are
repeatedly apprehended by the law, and Manon is eventually deported to
Louisiana as a prostitute. Following her there, des Grieux poses as her
husband, and they live contentedly until he decides they should really
marry, at which time, upon learning of their deceit, a rival demands
Manon's hand. Des Grieux injures him in a duel and flees with Manon into
the bayou, where she promptly dies of exposure. The entire drama is
recounted by des Grieux to a third party as an oral autobiography not unlike
that of Moll Flanders or Roxana.

The form of the narrative in fact gives the lie to both the superficial plot
and the shortened title which has been given the novel and the operas based
upon it: it is not the story of Manon Lescaut, who scarcely ever says
anything in the work and barely has enough texture as a character to justify
des Grieux's passion, but of des Grieux, whose shuttling back and forth
between his identity as a member of the privileged classes, with all of the
obligations that implies, and his identity as a romantic hero, which is largely

a construct of his own devising, forms the backbone of the novel's thematics. As systematically as Moll Flanders, des Grieux violates his culture's codes of conduct and institutions of authority, but he does not do so out of a desire for sheer survival. Rather he fabricates a persona for himself out of literary commonplaces, which he tenaciously maintains in spite of both Manon and his family. He is determined to see himself as a tragic lover and victim of destiny, and he not only repeatedly invokes this scenario in his defense, when confronted by figures of authority with the record of his infractions of the law, but also uses it to coerce Manon toward a role for which she has no natural inclination, which is that of the devoted mate. Each time she abandons him for a more lucrative situation, des Grieux plays on her guilt with the image of his fidelity and sacrifice, drawing her into a betrayal of her new protector in order to prove her loyalty. Since these betrayals are the cause of their successive imprisonments and Manon's ultimate deportation – the chevalier's dishonest gambling and his murder of a servant are never held against him – it is no exaggeration to say that the chevalier's obsession ultimately destroys his mistress. It is not society's institutions of authority that eradicate Manon, but her lover's compulsion to cast his life in terms of ill-starred passion and tragic destiny: even in New Orleans, where the same institutions do not exist, where des Grieux could have lived out his life contentedly with Manon, having finally through the fiction of their marriage obtained the exclusive possession of her favors, and where, even after the duel with his rival, nothing forces them to flee into the wilderness, the chevalier persists in electing the most romantic course of action and the one most likely to procure his misery. Only after his fiction has finally cost Manon her life, and permanently associated her with the role of sacrificing lover to which he has always pushed her, does he renounce his scenario and, having contributed to the death of both his father, the figure of authority against which he rebelled, and his lover, the vehicle for that rebellion, return to the fold of the virtuous life.

More graphically than the other works we have examined, *Manon Lescaut* juxtaposes personal scenario to cultural script, individual desire to institutional authority. To the extent that she personifies complete receptivity, or the willingness to conform to the projects of the highest bidder, Manon is also a figure for social reality, as it is determined by the conflicting demands of different individuals and the collective in general. Two mutually exclusive versions of her contend within the novel for supremacy: the chevalier's vision of her as a perfect object of love, uniquely charming, but susceptible to the projects of other men; and his father's idea of her as a recognizable social type, the self-interested prostitute who feeds on the illusions of young men. Because these two versions do not address each other – neither des Grieux's father nor the authority figures in the novel who imprison and deport her ever confront her in person, and des Grieux never sees her alone with other men – they can both define Manon with equal success, reading her admittedly paradoxical behavior in the light most favorable to their conception of her character. As the point of intersection and product of two conflicting scripts and modes of reality construal, she figures the conflict between individual and institution, the locus of their discord and the obstacle to their reconciliation. For the chevalier to find his place once again in his society and class, for his family and class to find in him a worthy representative of their interests, Manon must be removed. Her death, like Moll's arrest or Roxana's exposure, is a necessary preamble to the reaffirmation of the moral order at the end of the book.[7]

Significantly, Prévost's novel casts the reassertion of institutional authority in the paradoxical terms of its rejection: des Grieux can only reaffirm the values of virtue once he has pursued his personal fiction to its inevitable conclusion. The apparent paradox is simply a function of the paradigm of individualism that is at work here, and which subordinates the validation of collective norms to their revelation in personal experience. Here, as in *Robinson Crusoe*, the authority of the Other emerges only as a component of the self's story: it is within the very gesture of organizing one's private history that the order of the public world becomes manifest. The revelation of authoritative order through personal history traditionally pertains to spiritual autobiography – a genre to which *Robinson Crusoe* is closely related. Subsequent novels, however, shift the focus of the personal revelation toward the purely secular order of society, and they also gradually abandon the spiritual autobiographer's demurral of responsibility for the order and ordering power thus revealed.[8] The value and inevitability of moral order become apparent within the process of structuring personal experience as a narrative order; the structuring force of narration welds the external system of the world to the internal vision of the narrator by making the former appear as a consequence of the latter. Thus self-representation, in the form of a confessional narration, brings external order into accordance with internal ordering: the form of the private history unites personal author with public authority.

Within the context of this paradigm it is clear that programs of individualism feed on the conventions they resist, not only in the sense that the Other forms the indispensable backdrop for the self's expression of its difference, but also because, for that very reason, the project of self-expression necessarily finds its vocabulary and syntax within the cultural lexicon: Crusoe's self-sufficiency, Roxana's rejection of marriage, and the chevalier's vision of tragic love only make sense to the extent that they address recognized economic and legal constraints and that they do so in familiar terms. *Manon Lescaut* comes close to making this dependence – and its repression by the individualist – explicit: in its formulaic language and familiar logic of passion, the hero's fiction announces at every turn its indebtedness to seventeenth-century literary models. The tragic lover to whom he increasingly compares himself near the end of his adventure, the heroic victim of the combined forces of his passion and an implacable destiny, is a commonplace of French classicism – of that culture within which a young man of his station would necessarily have been schooled. Likewise, the form of his narration parodies in broad strokes that of *Les Illustres Françoises*, by undercutting the story of pure love thwarted by corrupt social convention with that of Manon's shameless love for money, resistance to marriage, and casual sexual infidelity. Des Grieux's tenacious defense of his personal fiction may function as an expression of individual freedom, but that fiction reflects a pattern of cultural determination which reinforces the case of his opponents – which may be one reason he never succeeds in convincing them that his actions are anything other than the familiar pattern of adolescent excess they perceive.

More developed versions of individualism in the middle third of the century address the relationship of personal experience and collective authority positively, aligning individualism with the conscious interrogation and renovation of institutions of authority, and redefining authoritative discourse as consensus opinion modeled on exemplary personal narrative. The works of Richardson, Fielding, and Rousseau develop positive models of personal rebellion: characters who expose by contrast, and eventually disarm, the corruptions of authority that threaten their autonomy. By re-presenting, in the form of their exemplary behavior, the principles which underlie institutional authority and which have been perverted through self-interest, these individuals simultaneously bring the authority of the collective within the frame of their personal experience and assert the enclosure of that experience within shared norms. This appropriation of authority by the individual goes against the very notion of authoritative discourse, which, as Bakhtin puts it, demands of the subject "unconditional allegiance" and not "a free appropriation and assimilation of the word itself."[9] If individualism attains its most optimistic expression in the plots of this period, it is precisely because they relocate the authority for individual action in a collective discourse made up of personal accounts and therefore susceptible to appropriation and redefinition by the individual.

Typically, the order of authority which has been subverted in these novels, and against which the protagonists rebel, is that of the self-interested father, or his institutional equivalent: paternalistic, but self-serving, law.[10] By relating the abuses of the empowered to the ideals embodied in the law, the individualist makes her voice the voice of authority; by exemplifying those ideals in her conduct, she wins over the collective, whose sanction confirms her authority; and by advancing her written record of experience as documentary proof of her exemplarity, she also promotes textual narratives to a central role in the emendation of culture.

Thus Richardson's heroine Pamela asserts herself against the (degenerate) (but not permanently) paternalistic tyranny of her lusting master, Mr B, by articulating her indenture to her father (and Father) and the principles of chastity underwritten by her society; and by literally giving a good account of herself, she wins over her master and his entire social cohort, becoming the embodiment of moral authority for their micro-society. A similar paradigm regulates *Clarissa*, although the degenerate authority against which the heroine first rebels is that of her father, and the benefits of her gesture do not accrue to the heroine, but society in general. In a similar manner, the abuses exposed by Suzanne, the heroine of Diderot's *La Religieuse*, whose cruel confinement in a nunnery by selfish parents and insensitive ecclesiastics produces a graphic account of complicity between corrupt paternal and civil law, benefit only society – and the authority of the Author, whose invention the account turns out to be. In Rousseau's *Julie, ou la nouvelle Héloïse*, the rebellion against paternal authority serves as the prologue for the most ambitious program of exemplification of all: the founding of an ideal community in the image, and according to the principles of, the protagonist.

Narratively speaking, these characters literally *take into (their) account* the principles they wish to reaffirm, citing them in their defense and making them the basis for their resistance. In this way they not only appropriate for themselves the authority formally associated with the collective, they also achieve their (both the protagonist's and the principles') reintegration into society. For this to occur, the protagonist's account needs to function as documentary evidence of both her and her adversary's behavior, rather than a retrospective recollection of past experience. The eventual redemption which des Grieux or Moll obtain by repudiating the past they recount has little in common with the ongoing relation of identity which the more active individualists of Marivaux, Richardson and Rousseau effect. The latter do not take their distance from misdeeds and earn their nominal reintegration into the reader's society after the fact; they mediate their personal reality at all moments with their social contemporaries, by making self-presentation to these contemporaries their sole preoccupation. They narrate themselves to those around them, and their narration structures their social identity by modulating the image they project for these Others: by presenting themselves in specific ways, they obtain specific reactions on the part of the social cohort and open specific opportunities for future action, which opportunities are in turn related in and to the narrative. Narration thus becomes the explicit foundation of social interaction, and, by extension, the ordering force behind the destiny of the character. At the same time, (self)-representation becomes the object of novelistic representation; the deliberate plotting of one's life becomes the centerpiece of the plot.

This program implies the association of authority with collective discourse, as well as the precise identification of abusive paternalistic institutions of authority. The pattern of a struggle between paternal authority and the child's revolt has become common enough to deserve parodying in Fielding's *Tom Jones*, Sterne's *Tristram Shandy*, and Diderot's *Jacques le fataliste*.[11] However the novels of Fielding and Diderot reserve the brunt of their irony for the more diffuse but equally self-interested and cruel authority of collective practice. Indeed it rapidly becomes apparent that the field of social discourse is as susceptible to contamination by self-interest as is the exercise of paternal or paternalistic authority.

If the abusive father or master tends to be superseded in later works by the collective to which the individualist appeals, that collective in turn takes on the aspect of a generalized narrational competition, in which every individual seeks to represent events in the light most favorable to his or her projects. The final stage in the progression I am charting, represented by the metanovels of Sterne, Diderot, and Laclos, explores this abuse of narrational authority, both on the personal level and on the institutional, in the form of fiction. For hand in hand with the progression of individualism, the genre of the novel itself accumulates authority: the process of exposure, rearticulation, and exemplification of moral codes and systems of authority which the protagonist acts out within the plot is nothing other than the microcosmic dramatization of the moral exemplification, both negative and positive, which is provided by fiction. As the conventionality and conventions of social interaction become more explicit, so too does the growing conventional stability of the novel, and its growing reputation as a significant moral force within its culture. And just as the generalization of personal accounting leads to increasingly daring displays of narrational authority, so too does the acknowledgment of the novel's growing influence invite ever more extravagant explorations of the literary author's (and reader's) authority over the script of their culture. The internalization and redefinition of authority which the novels portray as a fictional plot increasingly allegorizes the internalization and redeployment of cultural authority which realistic fiction achieves by dint of its own gesture of re-presentation; and like the virtuoso narrators within the plots, such as Lovelace, or the libertines in *Les Liaisons dangereuses*, for whom their own gesture of fabulation becomes so fascinating as to exclude all other considerations, the novels of the last third of the century will increasingly promote their own strategies of representation and reader manipulation to positions of thematic pre-eminence.

The compulsion to manage the collective narrative seems to grow in intensity with the conviction that that narrative is not only the prime ground of authority within the culture, but an impersonal mechanism or economy whose rules can be mastered. Even in the early works, the collective ground of authority is evident. Already in *Moll Flanders*, where the word of the mob or the false testimony of a shopkeeper can make the difference between life or death, it is no longer providence, but *what people say* that carries authority over one's fate and social identity – a situation which Marivaux will exploit with bemusement and delicacy, but the abusive potential of which quickly becomes apparent in the libertine agenda of Lovelace in *Clarissa* and the play of malice that saturates *Tom Jones*. *Tristram Shandy*, *Jacques le fataliste*, and *Les Liaisons dangereuses* present even more extensive visions of a world dominated by narrative competition – so much so that the notion of individualism no longer retains its original valences.

As long as the collective voice is considered to be a mere plurality of personal voices, it is easily manipulated by the exceptional individual, such as Marivaux's Jacob or Pamela, or Richardson's Pamela, whose representation of the principles of honesty and virtue, along with a bit of sex appeal, can overcome the self-interested contrivances of the adversary. More difficult to master is the completely impersonal authority of what we might call social grammar, which appears with *Clarissa* and becomes the dominant theme by the time of Diderot and Laclos. Social grammar can be thought of as a subset of culture; it is made up of the principles or unspoken rules which regulate all interpersonal interactions, the great majority of which are verbal, and it makes itself felt especially in the conventions which regulate the way personal accounts are produced and received. Social grammar is ubiquitous and permanent in all of the novels we will consider, from the warnings that Mme de Chartres gives her daughter in *La Princesse de Clèves*, to the calculations of her effect which Moll makes, the moral maxims that permeate Marivaux, and the schemes of the libertines and rakes. But it emerges as an abstract thematic preoccupation only in the wake of individualism – and logically so, since the generalization of self-representation brings with it a necessary attentiveness to the systems of convention governing collective narration.

Ironically, the awareness of such conventions seems to trigger the compulsion to deploy them in the service of personal predominance. Having formulated rules of social interaction, the individual cannot resist putting them to the test. In some cases the experiment is a positive one: the ideal community which Rousseau's master figure Wolmar constructs in *Julie, ou la nouvelle Héloïse* purports to further the happiness of its inhabitants and not just the vanity of its author. But elsewhere, the illusion of detachment, of being outside of the compass of the cultural grammar, becomes the primary ground of the protagonist's selfhood, as is the case with Lovelace in *Clarissa*, or Merteuil and Valmont, in *Les Liaisons dangereuses*. In such cases the codification of social relationships leads to perverse experiments in manipulation and enslavement. The gesture of self-representation that first appeared as an antidote to degenerate authority rapidly develops into the dispassionate construction of fictional identities for the sheer joy of asserting one's superiority over other less averted individuals and, more importantly, the social code in general. This is a pattern which is first adumbrated in *Moll Flanders* and *Roxana* in conjunction with strategies of survival. In later novels such representational virtuosity becomes the sole ground of selfhood negatively conceived: it is the expression of a self sustained by its destruction of the Other.

The ultimate Other, however, is the code that underwrites all initiatives, if only because the code is precisely that which cannot be mastered. To base one's authority on codes is to state one's subservience to a system of conventions which by definition cannot be mastered, since it necessarily encapsulates all instances of its implementation. As Lovelace discovers in *Clarissa*, or Valmont in *Les Liaisons dangereuses*, one cannot adopt a role taken from the scripts regulating social intercourse without playing the part, and thus subordinating one's self to the script. Selfhood which would express its exceptional status through mastery of an underlying grammar and thereby assert its personal authority over not only the fate of others, but the economy of fate itself, inadvertently reaffirms the primacy of impersonal grammar and acts out its own enclosure in that grammar. The more methodical and detached the codification of social reality, the more untenable the assertion of personal control.

Carried to excess, the practice of individualism, through its dependence and subscription to a narrative model of authority, culminates in its own negation and a reaffirmation of authority under the new guise of an impersonal historical economy: a permanently developing collective narrative and script of possibilities that accommodates and responds to individual instances of narration or self-determination, but can never be enclosed or comprehended by such instances. It is with this impersonal economy, under a variety of guises (history, culture, society, science, nature, literary myth, etc.), that the individual of the following century will negotiate his or her identity, rather than with the personal figures of authority such as the father, the master, or the author. And with this depersonalization of authority, the authoritative voice of the self-defining narrator fades: not only the autobiographical narrator, but that narrator's institutional correlative in the later metanovels, the Author. The voice of truth in the next century will be that of the impersonal system, the Other, the so-called third person that is neither me nor you.

As an introduction to the more active variety of self-narration that inaugurates this development – one that acts on the protagonist's present circumstances and facilitates his or her immediate redefinition within society – I have chosen the works of Pierre Carlet de Marivaux. His novels take the form of an autobiography, but unlike those of Defoe or *Manon Lescaut*, they are written by parvenus, that is, individuals who have risen from humble origins to positions of ease and influence. Further, these narrators address a public familiar with the protagonist, who consequently can intersperse her/his narration of the past with current reflections on him- or herself and references to a common culture. The narration serves no redemptive purpose, then, and rather than asserting a distance between the narrator's current character and past sins, revels in the convergence between past and present which it occasions. The revolt against authority, in other words, has already been absolved, the rebel integrated into the structures of authority which sanction his or her story. These novels complement the earlier tales of resistance to authority, by describing precisely how individuals who refuse to be defined or coerced by self-interested authorities or corrupt institutions can take their fate into their own hands, *relating* themselves to both the empowered members of society and the principles underlying that society's culture.

NOTES

1 In his edition of *Les Illustres Françoises*, Frédéric Deloffre identifies fifteen certain editions, from 1713 to 1780, including seven between 1713 and 1725, noting that the total number of eighteenth-century printings of the work must have reached nearly twenty, a number that makes *Les Illustres Françoises* nearly as successful as Marivaux's novels and more so than all but a handful of other similar works. The stories were translated into English in 1727, under the title of *The Illustrious French Lovers*, and into German the following year; (vol. 2, pp. 555–63).

2 The author's identity remained a complete mystery until 1748, when an editor of a new edition of the work, Marc-Michel Rey, contacted a former collaborator of the review and publishing house associated with *Les Illustres Françoises* and obtained the approximate name of the author and the list of his other works. Basing his investigation on this information, Deloffre uses a variety of historical records to identify the author as Robert Chasles, a visionary but unsuccessful colonial entrepreneur in Acadia who subsequently worked as a ship's writer and parlementary lawyer distinguishing himself primarily for his *Journal de Voyage aux Indes* (3 vols, 1721), a detailed diary of a royal expedition to the East Indies. Frédéric Deloffre's re-edition of *Les Illustres Françoises*, with its extensive introduction and critical evaluation, inaugurated something of a critical revival of Chasles. English Showalter, pp. 196–261, devotes a major chapter to him, as does Jean Rousset, *Narcisse romancier* (Paris: José Corti, 1972),

pp. 92–102; see also Henri Coulet, *Le Roman jusqu'à la révolution*, 2 vols (Paris: Armand Colin, 1967), vol. 1, pp. 309–15. Chasles' formal innovations are also discussed by Philip Stewart, *Imitation*.

3 As Jean Rousset specifies, the collection presents three different degrees of narrative presence: immediate first person, mediated first person (that is, a first person narration transmitted by a transparent agent who speaks in an "I" that is not his own), and impersonalized first person, transposed into a third-person format; *Narcisse romancier*, pp. 97–8.

4 Coulet, *Le Roman jusqu'à révolution*, vol. 1, p. 313.

5 English Showalter construes the theme of *Les Illustres Françoises* in terms of the conflict between individual and society, but points out that it is more precisely the drama of women and the institutions and laws that repressed them; *Evolution*, pp. 255–6. The same observation applies to many of the dramas of individuality of the eighteenth century, including, to mention only the most obvious, *Pamela, Clarissa, La Religieuse, Julie, ou la nouvelle Héloïse*, and *Les Liaisons dangereuses*.

6 As Jean Rousset puts it: "la vérité est cachée ou déformée, elle se dérobe à des regards qui n'en peuvent voir qu'une partie, il faut donc parler pour la rétablir, et il faut que plusieurs parlent tour à tour en s'engageant personnellement" (the truth is hidden or disfigured, it conceals itself from the gaze, which can see only a part of it; it is therefore necessary to speak in order to re-establish it, and many people must speak in turn, involving themselves personally); *Narcisse romancier*, p. 99.

7 It is also possible to read Manon as a figure for personal narrative itself, which once placed in circulation within a society, tends to elude control by its creator and lend itself to multiple perversions in the hands of anyone *recounting* it. The promiscuity of the narrative makes it not only unreliable, but pernicious, since it can be appropriated into a variety of contexts and can destabilize the structures of authority that depend on the unitary meaning of those contexts. As we shall see in subsequent chapters, the use of the heroine to allegorize narrative, and specifically literary fictions, is hardly unique to Prévost: it will recur even more forcefully in the works of Richardson and Rousseau.

8 Cf. Spacks, *Imagining a Self*, p. 38.

9 M. M. Bakhtin, *Dialogical Imagination*, p. 343.

10 The notion of authoritative discourse is bound up with that of paternal discourse by virtue of its reliance on precedence: "the authoritative word is located in a distanced zone, organically connected with a past that is felt to be hierarchically higher. It is, so to speak, the word of the fathers. Its authority was already *acknowledged* in the past. It is a *prior* discourse"; Bakhtin, *Dialogic Imagination*, p. 342.

11 In fact, separation from the father forms the deep structure of virtually all of the plots, English and French, prior to the appearance of the meta-novels in the later part of this study. Those protagonists who are not orphans at the outset (Moll, Marianne, Tom Jones), abducted (Pamela, Clarissa), or ejected from the household (Tom Jones, Suzanne in *La Religieuse*), either leave home (Manon, des Grieux, Jacob, Clarissa, Joseph Andrews, Jacques le fataliste), or become alienated from their father (Clarissa, Julie).

6

The Seduction of the Self (*La Vie de Marianne* and *Le paysan parvenu*)

If *Robinson Crusoe, Moll Flanders*, and *Roxana* chart a hesitant transition from a private relationship with the higher order of divine authority towards a more social conception of self-determination, the works of the French author Marivaux provide a fully developed version of self-definition that recasts individualism in terms of communal discourse.[1] Typical of the French tradition, Marivaux defines selfhood as inseparable from the secular, collective voice of society. Where Defoe's characters undertake their projects of self-determination in opposition to a collective Other which remains, at least until the latter stages of *Roxana*, relatively malleable and faceless, Marivaux's Marianne, from *La Vie de Marianne* (1731–42) and Jacob, *Le Paysan parvenu* (1734–5), work out their identity within a tightly woven social community of stridently self-assertive individuals, all of whom are preoccupied with promoting their own social identity, and all of whom speak for themselves in the text. The totality of their competing stories forms a collective account which functions in the novels explicitly as a proto-history: a continually revised shared story which assigns rank to the members of the society and adjudicates "true" character and "real" events. While it is only at the end of *Roxana* that the rivalry for the right to speak becomes a serious issue in the novels of Defoe, contention over voices and version literally permeates *La Vie de Marianne* and *Le Paysan parvenu*. Holding the floor, as it were, determines one's ability to control the developing narrative of one's identity. In the later novels of Richardson, Diderot, and Sterne, an intensified model of such rivalry between speakers will become the fundamental paradigm of human social interaction.

Rather than creating fictional identities for themselves, Jacob and Marianne engineer their metamorphoses by repeatedly narrating their actual experience, but they subtly alter and embellish it as their self-image evolves and they become more firmly integrated into the shared narrative. Their strategy emphasizes the *interpersonal* dimension of selfhood, which we can conceptualize as the permanent play between *teller* and *listener*, self-representation and validating response, but Marivaux's works will demonstrate that this relationship has an *intrapersonal* counterpart as well. Like Chasles',

Defoe's, or Prévost's characters, Marianne and Jacob relate their own stories retrospectively as a form of autobiography, but they do so with a far more acute sensitivity to the difference between their current dispassionate narration and their emotional confusion at the time of the events. Their consciousness vacillates continually between a state of emotional immersion in the flow of events and one of analytic ordering, such that the distance separating the narrator from the other characters in the story is replicated within the narrating consciousness as the distance separating the moment of relation from that of emotional experience.[2] Marivaux's protagonists are at every moment caught up in the awareness of their own narrational gesture. They generalize on the basis of the events they recount, get carried away with their generalizations, apologize for the digressions, and become distracted again.[3] And they continually modulate their field of reference in response to the developing narrative and the supposed responses of its public. The autobiographical act of self-comprehension thus takes on a texture and constitutes a theme in its own right within the novel, prefiguring the more epistolary narratives of self-consciousness of the next generation.[4]

Within this structure of self-representation, the narrating self is always its own most loyal public, evaluating and reacting to its own creation in much the same way as the external listener or reader.[5] The characters fleshed out in their retrospective narrations fascinate the narrators as much as they do their contemporaries in the stories, stimulating and seducing with their display of coquettish naiveté. In fact, the behavior of the narrated character often seems as surprising to the narrator as to the emplotted characters, eliciting a mixture of moral reflection and nostalgic identification which determines the course of the plot as much as any preconceived plan. This pattern of intrapersonal determination complements the more obvious interpersonal paradigm which relates individual to collective. The delight which one derives from one's own experience is a pre-requisite for delighting others, and vice versa; the positive reactions of other people both validate and elicit the gesture of self-representation: Marianne's "ideal self must appear to others so that she can be at one with this ideal self."[6]

Finally, Marivaux's works are the first to combine the eighteenth-century's two predominant models of how the individual acquires an identity and destiny: they blend the mechanism of social authority, which I have identified with the French tradition and illustrated with *La Princesse de Clèves*, with the paradigm of interpersonal narrative negotiation and intrapersonal selfhood which Defoe's works establish. Individual versus collective; single instance of narration versus shared cumulative narrative; the authority of the author versus that of the reader(s) – these will be the fundamental relationships within which individuality, selfhood, authority, history, and the novel, will define themselves in the course of the century. *La Vie de Marianne* and *Le paysan parvenu* prefigure these complex models of reciprocal determination by insisting on the interplay not just between individual story and collective history, but also between narrational self and narrated self, between the two identities of narration/narrative as experienced ordering and the experiencing of an order. And Marivaux explicitly aligns this dialectic of identity with that of history: his characters' identity is not simply conditioned by their past, it is inextricably bound up with the relationship of past to present. The Marivaudian self thus draws its energy from the gap between the identity it is spinning out and its identity as fabricator, from simultaneously seeing its creations *realized* and realizing its own strange relationship of detachment, yet subordination, to the order of reality it posits.

In the opening paragraphs of *Le Paysan parvenu*, the narrator, a wealthy self-made man who has worked his way up from a peasant background, explains the advantage of telling one's own story when one has humble origins:

> C'est une erreur, au reste, que de penser qu'une obscure naissance vous avilisse, quand c'est vous-même qui l'avouez, et que c'est de vous qu'on la sait. La malignité des hommes vous laisse là; vous la frustrez de ses droits; elle ne voudrait que vous humilier, et vous faites sa charge; vous vous humiliez vous-même, elle ne sait plus que dire. (P. 25)[7]

> Besides it's an Error to imagine that an obscure Birth debases us, when we ourselves avow it, and are the first who proclaim it. The Malice of Mankind drops you there, you rob it of its Reward; its sole Aim was to humble you, you supplant its Pretensions; you humble yourself, it has nothing left to say.

Marivaux's characters talk – they do precious little else – and their favorite topic of conversation is themselves. Both Marianne and Jacob are fascinated with themselves – with their sentiments, situations, appearance, and effect on other people. And they both learn early on that in a world regulated by reputations the successful individual is the one who takes command of his or her own story. Only by anticipating society's naturally malicious account and appropriating the narration of one's origins and actions, can one effectively seize one's destiny.

The two works are frequently contrasted by critics on the basis of their opposing tones: the former deals with a young orphan girl's infiltration of aristocratic society on the basis of her virtuous behavior and disarming personality; the latter takes as its protagonist a robust peasant youth whose social climb depends more on his physical attributes and simple honesty than on refinement and virtue.[8] Yet both novels share a common formal and thematic structure. Each was published serially, each is unfinished, each presents the autobiographical account of an obscure individual's rise to wealth and status in Parisian society, and each intersperses its plot with numerous moral reflexions and digressions. Aside from differences of tone, the order of some episodes, and the sex of their protagonists, the plots are also remarkably similar: a young provincial comes to Paris; upon the loss of a benefactor finds her/himself cast adrift; arouses the interests of a wealthy member of the opposite sex on the basis of her/his physical charm; thereby gains prospective entry into the ranks of the respectable; meets with opposition from members of the new benefactor's family; confronts these opponents in a pseudo-judicial hearing and obtains the support of yet more powerful allies through a skillful performance of self-presentation; and is in the process of becoming self-reliant and restructuring her/his romantic involvement when the story is abandoned.

Published over eleven years, *La Vie de Marianne* is both the earlier and the later of the two works, and its lengthy plot presents a veritable apprenticeship of self-representation.[9] Like other works preoccupied with the relationship between birth, virtue, and social identity, it situates its protagonist at the limiting point of non-identity by making her an orphan, the only existing record of whose origins is a vague account of her parents' death at the hands of highwaymen. To gain acceptance in the society of the aristocrats, Marianne will repeatedly re-present this episode in the most favorable light possible – conjecturing the nobility of her parents, for example, on the basis of a report that there were servants with them during their voyage – and supplement the notion of identity based on *origins* with one based on intrinsic *qualities*, by effacing the character in her story under a narrational performance that demonstrates her noble soul. Jacob, in *Le Paysan parvenu*, will do much the same. He will initially embellish his origins – by portraying his peasant father in flattering terms, first as a "bon fermier de Champagne" (p. 127) (good farmer from Champagne) and then simply a man who "demeure à la campagne où est tout son bien" (p. 239) (who lives in the country, where all of his wealth is) – and then gradually displace that history with the record of his virtuous behavior in the present.

Marianne's task differs from Jacob's in that she has, as it were, less to work with. As her first sponsor bluntly puts it: "quelque conjecture avantageuse qu'on puisse faire de votre naissance, cela ne vous donne aucun état, et vous devez vous régler là-dessus" (p. 65) (Let the Conjectures of your being born of noble Parents be never so probable, yet do they fall short of Certainty; and this is what you are to build upon).[10] But instinctively recognizing that her lack of a past gives her more liberty to construe her origins favorably, she sets about establishing her identity as a person of quality on the basis of her current behavior, which she uses as a proof of probable noble blood and thus as a justification for consideration on a par with the best of society. Even more than Moll or Roxana, Marianne recognizes the importance of self-presentation, and particularly the fact that a well-wrought tale not only portrays her in a favorable light, but imparts an aura of its own to her destiny: "il y a de certaines infortunes qui embellissent la beauté même, qui lui prêtent de la majesté. Vous avez alors, avec vos grâces, celles que votre histoire, faite comme un roman, vous donne encore" (p. 105) (there are certain misfortunes that embellish even beauty itself, that endow it with majesty. In these cases you have, along with your charms, those which your story, made like a novel, gives you in addition). The emotional effect of her story hardly escapes her, and she is quick to capitalize on its aura of romantic tragedy when she meets Valville, the young nobleman with whom she will fall in love:

> j'avais mon infortune qui était unique; avec cette infortune, j'avais de la vertu, et elles allaient si bien ensemble! Et puis j'étais jeune, et puis j'étais belle; que voulez-vous de plus? Quand je me serais faite exprès pour être attendrissante, pour faire soupirer un amant généreux de m'avoir maltraitée, je n'aurais pu y mieux réussir (P. 143).

> I had my Misfortunes, which were singular in their Kind. Besides, I was virtuous, and these two Things went well together hand in hand. And then I was young, and perfectly handsome. What would you desire more? Had I proposed to make myself the most engaging and most affecting Woman in the World, so as to force a generous Lover, to torture himself to Death, for having offended me, I could never have succeeded better.

Through successive refinements of her performance, Marianne will meld the positive values of her story of Marianne the orphan with the spectacle of her beauty and selfless virtue, creating an identity that transforms both her past and her present.

However, if stories impart values to their characters, it is because society has extrapolated from its organizing narratives a repertory of stock roles, and once associated with a particular narrative, individuals are expected to conform to their roles. Thus, as the heroine of a tragedy, Marianne risks being narratively coerced into a tragic destiny. Her depiction as helpless orphan carries with it a prescription of subordination, passivity, and humility, and invites others to treat her accordingly – as she finds out when her first benefactor, the lecherous M. de Climal, offers her a place as a servant on the basis of her tale of woe. His behavior, as he later makes clear, is predicated directly by the story of her misfortune which Marianne has disseminated:

vous êtes une orpheline, et une orpheline inconnue à tout le monde, qui ne tient à qui que ce soit sur la terre, dont qui que ce soit ne s'inquiète et ne se soucie, ignorée pour jamais de votre famille, que vous ignorez de même, sans parents, sans bien, sans amis, moi seul excepté, que vous n'avez connu que par hasard, qui suis le seul qui s'intéresse à vous . . . (P. 128; cf. also 130–1)

You are an Orphan, and one who is a Stranger to all the World; who has no relation on Earth; whom no Body cares for, or is uneasy about; absolutely unknown to your own Family, which your self cannot give an Account of; destitute of either Parents or Fortune, or Friends, except me, whom you came acquainted with by meer Chance; who alone am concern'd for you . . .

M. de Climal's strategy is narrative and his logic historical: if Marianne accepts his representation of her plight, she will have to assume the role it reserves for her. Acquiescing to his depiction of her past and present, she will have to acquiescence to his plot for her future. This same tactic of narrative coercion appears in *Le Paysan parvenu* (pp. 43–4); it will be used repeatedly by Marianne's adversaries later in her story, and particularly when she is arraigned before a government official and given the option of marrying an underling or becoming a nun (pp. 273, 280, 284, 289, 296ff.). In each case, the orphan is confronted with a version of her situation which argues for her submission. Her interlocutors expect her to conform to their vision of her not as one responds to the coercion of one individual by another, but in the way one accepts that which *is*. They do not see their suggestions as personal volition, but as the logical expression of a state of affairs: Marianne's origins are history, her identity determined by that history; as a stock part in a common story, her fate is sealed.

On dit que vous n'avez ni père ni mère, et qu'on ne sait ni d'où vous venez, ni qui vous êtes; on ne vous en fait point un reproche, ce n'est pas votre faute; mais entre nous, qu'est-ce qu'on devient avec cela? On reste sur le pavé; on vous en montrera mille comme vous qui y sont; cependant il n'en est ni plus ni moins pour vous. (P. 280)

They say you have neither Father nor Mother, and no one knows, neither whence you came nor who you are. That is not charged upon you as a Reproach; for you cannot help it. But, between you and I, what can a Body come to with all that? Nothing but being a Beggar about the streets. There are thousands in your case who are so; and yet you are not a bit the worse for it.

The logic of such arguments is that identity is not a function of self-expression, but a static component of an immutable order. Marianne triumphs over such arguments because she recognizes early on that "history" is as much a present narration as it is a narrative of the past, and that through her own presence and narrational initiatives, she can color the way her own story is perceived and discredit the narratives of her opponents. To combat her image of a miserable orphan, she need only provide a narration-al performance which overlays her message of humility with a picture of pride and dignity. Thus she responds to Climal's offer of a maid's post:

> Hélas! monsieur, lui dis-je, quoique je n'aie rien, et que je ne sache à qui je suis, il me semble que j'aimerais mieux mourir que d'être chez quelqu'un en qualité de domestique ...
>
> Je lui répondis cela d'une manière fort triste; après quoi, versant quelques larmes: Puisque je suis obligée de travailler pour vivre, ajoutai-je en sanglo-tant, je préfère le plus petit métier qu'il y ait, et le plus pénible, pourvu que je sois libre, à l'état dont vous me parlez, quand j'y devrais faire ma fortune. (P. 65)

> Alas! Sir, said I, though I am destitute of every Thing, and quite ignorant of my Extraction, methinks, I would chuse to die, rather than live with any as a Servant.
>
> I made him this Reply with a very melancholy Air, and then shedding a few Tears, Since I am forced, said I, sighing and sobbing bitterly, to work for my Bread, I shall always prefer the meanest of Trades to that Condition, even though I were sure to make my Fortune by it.

Her narrational display carries its own message about the narrator's character and thus overlays the declaration of indignation with a marker of sensitivity. Marianne frequently relies on such techniques. Faced with the necessity of revealing her identity to Valville, the young nobleman who has fallen in love with her, she simply bursts into tears, noting that "cet abattement et ces pleurs me donnèrent, aux yeux de ce jeune homme, je ne sais quel air de dignité romanesque qui lui en imposa, qui corrigea d'avance la médiocrité de mon état, qui disposa Valville à l'apprendre sans en être scandalisé" (p. 104) (My Tears and Discouragement gave me in the Eyes of that young Gentleman a romantick kind of Dignity, which awed him, and which by making previous Amends for my indifferent Station, prepared *Valville* to hear of it without being shocked). To obtain the support of, and express her gratitude to, a woman of quality who, in response to one of her stories, offers to look after her, she engages in a delicate pantomime that reinforces her narration:

> je levai les yeux sur elle d'un air humble et reconnaissant, à quoi je joignis une très humble et très légère inclination de tête; je dis légère, parce que je compris dans mon cœur que je devais la remercier avec discrétion, et qu'il fallait bien paraître sensible à ses bontés, mais non pas faire penser qu'elles me consolassent, comme en effet elles ne me consolaient pas. J'accompagnai le tout d'un soupir. (P. 180)

> I cast my eyes upon her, with a modest and grateful Air, to which I added a very humble, but very slight Inclination of my Head. I say slight, because my

Heart very well understood, that I ought to thank her with Discretion; and that what I had to do, was merely to shew myself sensible of her extreme kindness, but not to give her to understand, that it was any Comfort to me; as indeed it was not. I accompanied the whole with a Sigh.

Although at the beginning of her adventure, Marianne relies primarily on such narrational affect to assert her identity, she soon learns that direct management of narrative content provides an even greater measure of control over one's fate. When the lecherous Climal attempts to sully her name, the young girl passes from a defensive posture to one of aggressive narration. Disputing the narrative authority that he enjoys as an aristocrat,[11] she challenges his version of things with a stunningly well-documented indictment that reconsiders each of his claims in the light of his own past actions. By systematically comparing M. de Climal's recent actions to his "historical" character of a man of charity and piety, she discredits his version of "Marianne la perfide" and replaces it with her own (pp. 150–4).

The episode marks a turning point in *La Vie de Marianne* – and in our story here – not only because it foregrounds the contingency of history on the motives of the historian by producing two versions of the same events by two different narrators, but because it extends the notion of narrative to include the stories of someone other than the protagonist and expands the range of those stories to include recent events in the narrator's experience as well as the remote past. It is, in short, a simplified version of the discursive activity that pervades everyday social interaction and binds a community of individuals together within a shared version of unfolding events. Almost immediately after breaking off her relationship with Climal, Marianne will refine her command of this new form of expression in her encounter with a new sponsor, Mme de Miran. Recounting her entire story in vivid detail, but with controlled emphasis, she skips rapidly over the uncertainty of her origins, implying that her parents were wealthy nobles ("ils ont été assassinés par des voleurs qui arrêtèrent un carrosse de voiture où ils étaient avec moi; leurs domestiques y périrent aussi" [they were assassinated by some Highwaymen, in a Stage-Coach, in which I was with them; their Servants were likewise killed]) and dwelling rather more on the quality of the woman who raised her ("une sainte personne" [a most pious Woman]) and her own selfless virtue ("je rachèterais sa vie de la mienne" [I would give my life to recall hers]). To this immaculate background, she adds the tale of the evil M. de Climal ("il a découvert ses mauvais desseins par de l'argent qu'il m'a forcée de prendre, et par des présents que je me suis bien doutée qui n'étaient pas honnêtes" [he shewed his bad Designs, by some Money and Presents that he gave me, which I very justly suspected, not to be out of any good Intention]), her own irreproachable refusal of his propositions ("j'ai répondu qu'il me faisait horreur d'être si hypocrite et si fourbe" [I answered, that I was struck with Horror, to see him so monstrous a Cheat and a Hypocrite]), and her current homeless state: "je ne sais plus de quel côté tourner, si le père Saint-Vincent, de chez qui je viens en ce moment pour lui conter tout, et qui m'avait bonnement menée à cet horrible homme, ne trouve pas demain à me placer en quelque endroit" (pp. 160–1) (I know not to whom to apply for Assistance, if Father St. *Vincent*, from whom I came this minute, who had, in the Simplicity of his Heart, directed me to this horrid Man, and to whom I have just told all, does not find a Place for me to Morrow).

If this little speech, as Marianne calls it, succeeds beyond her wildest dreams, inciting Mme de Miran to offer to support her henceforth as if she were her own daughter, it is because Marianne has tailored her performance to her public and, more importantly, integrated that public, and the present moment, into her adventure through a clever preamble. Not only does she arrange the emphasis in her account to elicit Mme de Miran's sympathy, she prefaces her performance with a few well-timed tears and a concise resumé of her misery, her flattering assessment of her interlocutor, and her (spur of the moment) (but dramatic!) desire to enter the convent:

Oui, madame, lui dis-je, pénétrée de ce discours et toute en pleurs, il est vrai que j'ai du chagrin: j'en ai beaucoup, il n'y a personne qui ait autant sujet d'en avoir que moi, personne de si à plaindre ni de si digne de compassion que je le suis; et vous me témoignez un cœur si généreux, que je ne ferai point difficulté de parler devant vous, madame. Il ne faut pas vous retirer, vous ne me gênerez point; au contraire, c'est un bonheur pour moi que vous soyez ici: vous m'aiderez à obtenir de madame la grâce que je viens lui demander à genoux (je m'y jetai en effet), et qui est de vouloir bien me recevoir chez elle. (P. 159)

Yes, Madam, said I to her, quite melted by her Words, and all in Tears, I own I am in Sorrow, and a very great Sorrow. Nobody has more Reason to be grieved: None is more to be pitied, and worthier of Compassion, than I am. And you shew me so generous an Heart, Madam, that I shall make no Difficulty of speaking before you. You must not go. You shall be no Constraint to me. On the contrary, it is a great Happiness to me that you are here. You will help me, to obtain the Favour, which I now beg on my knees of the Prioress, (and I really threw myself at her Feet,) which is, that she would be so kind, to receive me into her House.

Merging a description of Mme de Miran with her depiction of herself, Marianne offers her interlocutor a flattering role in her story as the generous consoler of a wronged virtue – and thereby encourages the aristocrat to take up the story as her own. To decline the charitable initiative which Marianne's account invites her to take, would be to give the lie to the flattering portrait of her as virtuous protector in that account. Moreover, identified by Marianne as a kindred spirit, Mme de Miran will necessarily tend to see the orphan in positive terms, and recount her story to other individuals, since any positive qualities she implies to the orphan will reflect on her as well. In other words, by aligning her interests and character with that of Mme de Miran, by suggesting that they are involved in a common endeavor, Marianne sets up a pattern of mutual implication. This pattern is more rigorously dialogical than those we have previously encountered, since it involves reciprocal narration and response; and it makes explicit the mechanism of dependency on an Other which Defoe's and Prévost's models of self-representation only start to explore: one's story can only function as a vehicle of self-determination to the extent that it both accommodates, and finds accommodation in, a validating Other, and thus receives circulation in the larger discursive economy defining social identity. This Other can be a single person, as here, or a larger community linked together by a sense of communality of interests or social roles.

It is such an integration of personal story into a larger system of narrative exchange which the subsequent sections of the novel depict. The first step in this process involves demonstrating the variability of history according to local requirements. After telling her story twice to Mme de Miran – once, cited above, when she wishes to gain admittance into the convent, and then a second time when she discovers that Miran is the mother of Valville, the young man with whom she is infatuated, and finds herself compelled to confess this other aspect of her identity to her protectoress – Marianne will retell it a final time to Valville, in accordance with a promise to his mother to try to dissuade him from his plan to marry her. In her longest self-narration yet, she covers not only her pathetic past and permanent handicap, but the charity of Mme de Miran, the story of the latter's telling of her story, and her subsequent attempted self-sacrifice. Following several dramatic suggestions of her own unworthiness should she marry Valville (Pourriez-vous sentir autre chose pour moi que de l'horreur, si j'en étais capable? Y aurait-il rien de si abominable que moi sur la terre ... (p. 193) (Could you have any other Sentiment but Horror for me, if I were capable of doing it? And should I not be the most detestable Creature on Earth), she again presents a scenario of self-sacrifice – this time in favor of Valville's interests. Predictably, this vision of tragic self-abnegation reduces both mother and son to tears and forecloses on the possibility that they could actually accept Marianne's proposal. Far from renouncing her, Valville can cite her as justification for his passion: "Ma mère, lui dit-il, vous voyez ce que c'est que Marianne; mettez-vous à ma place, jugez de mon cœur par le vôtre. Ai-je eu tort de l'aimer? me sera-t-il possible de ne l'aimer plus?" (p. 194) (Mother, said he, you see what a Woman *Marianne* is: Pray imagine yourself in my Place; judge of my Heart by your own: am I in the wrong to love her? And will it be in my Power to cease to do so?).

Marianne's successive relations of her origins and recent misfortunes differ in their emphasis and lead to three different effects, underscoring the malleability of "historical" events according to immediate needs and audience. The episodes dramatize the way private narration is taken up by the collective and transformed through repetition into social reality. Marianne promotes her identity as noble orphan into shared truth by reiterating it persistently, reinforcing the content of her narrative with her current behavior as a narrator, modulating her story so as to accommodate her interlocutor in a flattering role, and thus eliciting, in the form of her audience's sympathetic reaction, an implicit validation of her creation.[12] By stressing her filial obligations to Mme de Miran and making the latter the heroine of her self-presentations ("vous voulez que Marianne vous appelle sa mère, vous lui faites l'honneur de l'appeler votre fille, vous la traitez comme si elle l'était; cela n'est-il pas admirable? Y a-t-il jamais eu rien d'égal à ce que vous faites?" (p. 364) (You will have *Marianne* call you her Mother, you do her the Honour to call her Daughter: You use her, indeed, as such; and is not this admirable? Was ever any Behaviour so generous as yours towards me?)), she encourages her to appropriate the story for herself – which is precisely what happens when jealous family members attempt legal action to stop Marianne's marriage with Valville: it is Mme de Miran who provides the initial, extremely flattering recitation of Marianne's past (pp. 296–9).

Once people's interests have merged with Marianne's, they cannot help but reinforce her chosen identity as part of their own projects of self-assertion. In promoting themselves, they will promote her and counteract the presence of her detractors, or even those individuals who know her in another context and inadvertently or out of malice "replace" her in her proper role. For Marianne, this is finally the most valuable capacity of narration:

Mon aventure remuait donc les trois cœurs qui m'étaient les plus chers, auxquels le mien tenait le plus, et qu'il m'était le plus consolant d'inquiéter. Vous voyez que mon affaire devenait la leur, et ce n'était point là être si à plaindre: je n'étais donc pas sans secours sur la terre. (Pp. 367–8)

My Adventure, therefore, was working upon the three Hearts that were dearest to me, to which mine was most devoted, and which it was most comfortable for me to perplex. You see that my Affair was become theirs, and this was no indifferent Satisfaction. I was not then destitute of Help on the Earth.

Le Paysan parvenu illustrates this lesson more bluntly by literalizing it on the level of sexuality: Jacob merges his desire (for social advancement) with the (sexual) desire which older women express for him. As a male, he is not constrained by the rules of modesty and self-effacement that restrict Marianne, and he quickly learns that by offering amorous adventure to older, monied women loathe to be involved with a mere peasant, he can accelerate his social metamorphosis. To justify her incipient inclination for Jacob, his first mistress (in the literal sense of the word: he is a servant) procures him a post and the possibility of learning to read, write, and acquire some polish. Jacob's second protectress, a fifty-year old widow, abolishes the class distinction between herself and Jacob simply by marrying him. Recognizing that her interests make it imperative that he appear marriable, Jacob allows her to dictate his behavior, name, clothes, and future profession, transforming him from lumpkin to respectable bourgeois husband.

An even more striking example of merging interests occurs when the hero is called before a magistrate charged by the widow's sister with preventing the marriage. Present at the hearing is an older aristocratic widow whose immediate lascivious interest in Jacob makes it impossible for her to condemn the disproportion between his age and that of his fiancée. When Jacob's opponent clumsily remarks that her sister is the same age as the widow, she forces the latter to defend the marriage or accept the grotesqueness of her own interest in Jacob – an interest Jacob quickly acknowledges and encourages in order to gain her support (pp. 124–6).

But for these transactions to succeed, the protagonist, like Marianne, must first demonstrate that he shares the fundamental traits of the class he wishes to enter. And it is here that Jacob differs from Marianne. Rather than attempting to demonstrate his disinterested nobility through a narrational performance, as she does, he relies on a strategy of rational analysis that recasts identity as a purely local, historical category and demonstrates that his metamorphosis typifies bourgeois social mobility. His argument is that his story does not differ essentially from the history of his detractors when considered in the proper perspective. When his landlady compares him unfavorably to a neighbor, Jacob, who has changed his name to Monsieur de la Vallée, is quick to point out that status is a local phenomenon:

> Mais entre nous, monsieur de la Vallée, reprit-elle, a-t-il tant de tort? voyons, c'est un marchand, un bourgeois de Paris, un homme bien établi; de bonne foi, êtes-vous son pareil, un homme qui est marguillier de sa paroisse?
>
> Qu'appelez-vous, madame, marguillier de sa paroisse? lui dis-je; est-ce que mon père ne l'a pas été de la sienne? est-ce que je pouvais manquer à l'être aussi, moi, si j'avais resté dans notre village, au lieu de venir ici?
>
> Ah! oui, dit-elle, mais il y a paroisse et paroisse, monsieur de la Vallée. Eh!

pardi, lui dis-je, je pense que notre saint est autant que le vôtre, madame d'Alain, saint Jacques vaut bien saint Gervais. (P. 114)

But between you and I, Mr. *de la Vallée*, answer'd she, how was he so much in the wrong of it? Lookee, he is a great Shopkeeper, A Burgess of *Paris*, and a Man of good Business; truly how are you his equal? Why, he is Church-warden of the Parish!

What do you call him, Madam, said I, Churchwarden of the Parish? Do you think my Father has not been Churchwarden of his? Or do you think I should have miss'd being one my self, had I stay'd at our Village, instead of coming hither?

Well, well, said she, but this is a Parish, a great Parish, Mr. *de la Vallée*. Troth! said I, I fancy our Saints are as good as your's, Mrs. *d'Alain*; St. *James* is as good as St *Gervase*.

Later, when arraigned before a public official and charged with opportunism by his future sister-in-law, he relates personal identity to the position one happens to occupy at any given moment along a continuum of advancement from the country to the city which is shared by all members of the bourgeoisie, including his accuser:

Est-ce que M. Habert votre père . . . était un gredin, mademoiselle? Il était fils d'un bon fermier de Beauce, moi fils d'un bon fermier de Champagne; c'est déjà ferme pour ferme; nous voilà déjà, monsieur votre père et moi, aussi gredins l'un que l'autre; il se fit marchand, n'est-ce pas? Je le serai peut-être; ce sera encore boutique pour boutique. Vous autres demoiselles qui êtes ses filles, ce n'est donc que d'une boutique que vous valez mieux que moi; mais cette boutique, si je la prends, mon fils dira: Mon père l'avait; et par là mon fils sera au niveau de vous. Aujourd'hui vous allez de la boutique à la ferme, et moi j'irai de la ferme à la boutique; il n'y a pas là grande différence; ce n'est qu'un étage que vous avez de plus que moi. (P. 127)

Was Mr. *Habard* your Father . . . a Beggar then, Madam? No, he was the son of a good Farmer of *Beauce*, and I am the Son of a good Farmer of *Champagne*; there's Farm for Farm; you see your Father and I as much Beggars one as another; he was a Tradesman, was he not? perhaps I may be one; and then there will be Shop for Shop. As it is, you Ladies his Daughters, are but a Shop better than me; but if I take this Shop, my Son will be able to say, my Father kept one, and then my Son will be upon a Level with you. You are stepping from the Shop to the Farm, and I am stepping from the Farm to the Shop; the odds is'nt much; you are only a degree above me.

By this logic, personal identity or character is not a static attribute pertaining to one's situation at a given moment, but a pattern of change over time, the validity of which can only be assessed within the context of other such patterns of evolution sanctioned by society. As Jacob points out by citing the larger plot structures of the bourgeoisie, identity is not a static label of origin, but a sequence of events or stages of personal development graspable as history. One is identified by one's plot, as it were, rather than merely by the position one currently holds within that plot, and one justifies one's actions by citing other similar plots and thus inscribing one's individual experience within the collective experience. This is a lesson Jacob might have learned from his landlady, who uses stories of other disproportionate marriages in the neighborhood to justify Jacob's union with his protectress, Mlle Habert (pp. 103–4), and it pivots on the same logic that Marianne's detractors use, when they argue that certain stories or social itineraries impart certain qualities to the individuals engaged in them.

In sum, Marianne and Jacob each manage their story somewhat differently, but they both advance an implicitly narrative notion of personal identity. Possessed of precise origins, Jacob can directly compare his history to that of his detractors, dismissing apparent differences of rank as a mere chronological lag in their respective evolution from peasant to bourgeois. As he sees it, identity is inseparable from a process of continual social ascendance, in which he is one stage or generation behind his opponents but nonetheless their equal by virtue of the fact that he will eventually occupy their place. By thus enclosing their two destinies within a larger framework of necessary episodes, he merges his story with that of his superiors' history and posits their common destiny. He appropriates the *narrative* of his target class, that is, he aligns the events of his past with the history of the class to which he aspires.

Marianne cannot correlate her fate to that of her superiors in quite the same way: not only is her story less certain than Jacob's, but the class to which she aspires does not ground its identity in its rise from the country to the city, nor indeed even in its recent history. True aristocracy is not based on hard work, public service, commercial success, or administrative functions. Its hallmark is a heritage of authority and privilege based on intrinsic superiority, the original grounds of which are beyond dispute, being too remote to be examined. It cannot accrue over the short term, as can the petit bourgeois respectability to which Jacob aspires. In this sense, Marianne's obscure origins are actually advantageous, since it cannot be proven that she is not noble.[13] To prove that she is, she needs to demonstrate her intrinsic nobility of character, which she does through her *narration*: repeatedly stressing the immensity of the gulf that separates her story from that of Mme de Miran, she elaborates a commonality of character on the basis of a shared, current response to that story.[14] She proves she is of good blood by telling her story as would a person of refined sensibilities and honor, proposing that one react to her in the way a charitable aristocrat would. As narrative fact, her identity cannot be shown to be the same as that of the average member of the class to which she aspires, but as narrational act, it can.

While I have thus far focused on the interaction between individual and collective as the key to social identity, Marivaux's novels also depict an *intrapersonal* version of selfhood based on the relationship of the narrating self to its narrative product. This relationship is most accessible in the scenes of deliberate self-representation that recur within the plots of *Le paysan parvenu* and *La Vie de Marianne*, but it also informs the more general autobiographical gesture which governs the works as a whole. The tableau of ingenuous youth which Marianne and Jacob provide for the Parisians in the novel finds its replication in the more permanent spectacle which the narrated self – the self as character in the autobiography – provides for its reflective, narrating, authorial counterpart. While this narrating self is conscious of itself as an analytic awareness that assesses feelings and events in an attempt to grasp the structures of the self and society, the narrated self it recovers and reanimates through its recollections is frequently felt as a mere intuition of individuality – a spontaneous emotive response to the world that not only precedes and prepares the fall into self-consciousness, but delights the members of society and the narrating self with its candid reactions:

> Je ne saurais vous dire ce que je sentis en voyant cette grande ville, et son fracas, et son peuple, et ses rues. C'était pour moi l'empire de la lune: je n'étais plus à moi, je ne me ressouvenais plus de rien; j'allais, j'ouvrais les yeux, j'étais étonnée, et voilà tout. (*La Vie de Marianne*, p. 56)

> My Amazement at the Sight of that large, populous and noisy Town far exceeds all Description. It was the Empire of the Moon to me. I was perfectly out of my Wits. I had lost my Memory. All I could do was just to move my Body, and open my Eyes. I was, in short, a meer gaping Machine.

Such expressions of undifferentiated affect alternate with the narrator's reflections: "Voyez si ce n'était pas là un vrai instinct de femme, et même un pronostic de toutes les aventures qui devaient m'arriver" (ibid.) (How is that for a genuine feminine instinct and even a prefiguration of all the adventures that were to befall me.) But the relationship of these two modes of consciousness is not one of opposition, but rather that of complementarity. They correspond to the two senses of the concept of *experience*, that is, the "encountering, undergoing, or living through things," as opposed to the "practical wisdom resulting from what one has encountered, undergone, or lived through,"[15] and this complex notion of experience can in turn be thought of as the individual or personal correlative of the larger collective equation of history, understood as both the succession of human events in time and the reflective narrative of those events. Each mode of experience participates in its own way in the organization of reality. The self encounters and experiences the world, and in so doing converts undifferentiated reality into personal experience, but that experience is only *understood* after the fact by the reflective analysis of the self-conscious experienced self which situates it in a larger pattern. At the same time, the encounter between the experiencing self and the world is itself informed by the construals of reality which the reflective self has previously stipulated. In that sense, neither mode of experience can be posited in the absence of its converse; the narrating self is inseparable from, and dependent upon, its narrated counterpart, and vice versa.

Marivaux's novels reiterate this inseparability on several planes and through several different versions of the relationship between the "experienced" self and the experiencing self. Most striking, perhaps, is the alternation, within the autobiographical narrative, between dramatizations of personal experience and sentential generalizations about social behavior. Typically, the recollection of an episode in the narrator's personal experience as a newcomer to Parisian society flows directly into a generalization by the narrator about women, men, love, vanity, or some other such social notion:[16]

> Finissez donc, monsieur, dis-je à Valville en retirant ma main avec assez de force, et d'un ton qui marquait encore que je revenais de loin, supposé qu'il fût lui-même en état d'y voir si clair; car il avait eu des mouvements, aussi bien que moi. Mais je crois qu'il vit tout; il n'était pas si neuf en amour que je l'étais, et dans ces moments-là, jamais la tête ne tourne à ceux qui ont un peu d'expérience par devers eux; vous les remuez, mais vous ne les étourdissez point. (*La Vie de Marianne*, p. 99)

> Indeed, Sir, I don't understand this. Pray Sir, be quiet, said I to *Valville*, taking my Hand from him with a pretty deal of Strength, but in a Tone, which still might have informed him, that I was but just awakened from a Trance: But perhaps he was not able to discern this, being no less agitated than myself. Though I really believe he discovered all: For he was not so great a Novice in Point of Love as I was: And on Occasions like this, those who have a little Experience this Way, never lose their Presence of Mind. You may move them much, and raise great Emotions in their Minds, but cannot amaze them.

> je restai pleurant entre mes quatre murailles, mais avec plus de consternation que d'épouvante; ou, si j'avais peur, c'était par un effet de l'émotion que m'avait causée mon accident, car je ne songeai point à craindre pour ma vie.
> En de pareilles occasions, nous sommes d'abord saisi des mouvements que nous méritons d'avoir; notre âme, pour ainsi dire, se fait justice. Un innocent en est quitte pour soupirer, et un coupable tremble; l'un est affligé, l'autre est inquiet.
> Je n'étais donc qu'affligé, je méritais de n'être que cela. Quel désastre, disais-je en moi-même. Ah la maudite rue avec ses embarras! Qu'avais-je

affaire dans cette misérable allée? C'est bien le diable qui m'y a poussé quand j'y suis entré.

Et puis mes larmes coulaient: Eh mon Dieu! où en suis-je? Eh mon Dieu! tirez-moi d'ici, disais-je après. (*Le Paysan parvenu*, p. 141)

I remain'd weeping between my four Walls, rather out of Consternation than Fear; or if I had any Fear, it was entirely owing to the violent Shock which this Accident had given me, for I had no notion of being apprehensive for my Life.

Upon such occasions we are immediately seiz'd with those emotions which we deserve to feel; our Consciences, if I may use the Expression, do themselves Justice. An innocent Person sighs, and a Criminal trembles; the one is afflicted, and the other tormented.

Therefore I was only afflicted, I deserv'd to be no more; what a Disaster, cry'd I to my self! oh the cursed Street with its Throng of Coaches and Chairs! what Business had I in that miserable Alley? It was certainly by the Impulse of the Devil that I enter'd it.

And instantly the Tears trickled down: Oh my God! where am I? O my god! deliver me from hence, cry'd I.

As the latter citation makes clear, with its general moral observation sandwiched between two dramatic segments, it is difficult to say whether the recollection triggers the maxim, or whether the maxim predicates the recollection. Although it is possible to read the alternation between artless effusion and sentential organization as a reiteration of the genesis of self-consciousness out of a primordial state of confused existence,[17] one can also argue that the moral generalizations drive the plots of the novels, soliciting the various episodes of "spontaneous" experience as a rule solicits an example. From this point of view, the reflection would not be subordinate to the experience it explains, but the motor force behind the recounted reality.[18] In fact, more than once the narrator in *La Vie de Marianne* will be carried away by her own sentential discourse in much the same way as Marianne is swept along by her successive encounters. In the middle of a description of Marianne's coquettish behavior in church, for example, the narrator breaks in:

Les petites choses que je vous dis là, au reste, ne sont petites que dans le récit; car, à les rapporter, ce n'est rien: mais demandez-en la valeur aux hommes. Ce qui est de vrai, c'est que souvent dans de pareilles occasions, avec la plus jolie physionomie du monde, vous n'êtes encore qu'aimable, vous ne faites que plaire; ajoutez-y seulement une main de plus, comme je viens de le dire, on ne vous résiste plus, vous êtes charmante.

Combien ai-je vu de cœurs hésitants de se rendre à de beaux yeux, et qui seraient restés à moitié chemin sans le secours dont je parle!

Qu'une femme soit un peu laide, il n'y a pas grand malheur, si elle a la main belle: il y a une infinité d'hommes plus touchés de cette beauté-là que d'un visage aimable; et la raison de cela, vous la dirai-je? Je crois l'avoir sentie.

C'est que ce n'est point une nudité qu'un visage, quelque aimable qu'il soit; nos yeux ne l'entendent pas ainsi: mais une belle main commence à en devenir une; et pour fixer de certaines gens, il est bien aussi sûr de les tenter que de leur plaire. Le goût de ces gens-là, comme vous le voyez, n'est pas le plus honnête; c'est pourtant, en général, le goût le mieux servi de la part des femmes, celui à qui leur coquetterie fait le plus d'avances.

Mais m'écarterai-je toujours? Je crois qu'oui; je ne saurais m'en empêcher: les idées me gagnent, je suis femme, et je conte mon histoire; pesez ce que je vous dis là, et vous verrez qu'en vérité je n'use presque pas des privilèges que cela me donne.

Où en étais-je? A ma coiffe, que je raccommodais.... (P. 91)[19]

But the little Particulars I now mention are little in the Recital only. They dwindle almost to nothing in the Narration. But you are to inquire of the Men the real Worth of them. One thing is very true, *viz.* that often on the like Occasions, with the prettiest Looks in the World, you are no more than pretty, and do but barely please. But add to your Charms a fine Hand besides, as I told you just now, and no Man alive can withstand it, and you charm the whole Sex.

How many Hearts have I seen refusing a Surrender to the finest Eyes, who never had been subdued without the Help I am speaking of?

Let a Woman be even ugly, 'tis no great Matter if she has but a fine Hand. There are thousands of Men more affected by that Article of Beauty than by the handsomest Face. But shall I tell you the Reason? Indeed I believe I have hit on it.

It is because an handsome Face is no Nudity, but ordinarily discovered. Let it be ever so charming, our Eyes still desire something else. But a fine Hand is in some Sort an Advance towards Nakedness. And there is a Kind of Men, whom you fix at least as surely by tempting as by pleasing them. Their Taste, as you see, is none of the best; nevertheless it is generally the most encouraged by Women and in particular by Coquets.

But shall I always be making Digressions? I think I cannot forbear it. A Crowd of Ideas press upon me. I am besides a Woman, who is recounting her own History. Be pleased to weigh these Things and you will see that I lay not Claim to half the Privileges these give me.

Where did I leave off? Ay, about my Hood, which I was ordering . . .

Although it is easiest to see how reflection and experience drive each other mutually at the level of the autobiographical gesture, where recollected events trigger generalizations and generalizations lead to further narrational and narrative events, the same interplay can be found within the reactions of the inexperienced characters within the plot, where it makes itself felt as an oscillation between emotion and reflection. Marianne, for instance, experiences very little which she does not immediately convert into a calculation:

> A cette proposition, je rougis d'abord par un sentiment de pudeur; et puis, en rougissant pourtant, je songeai que j'avais le plus joli petit pied de monde; que Valville allait le voir; que ce ne serait point ma faute.... (*La Vie de Marianne*, p. 94)

> This Proposal put my Modesty to the Blush; but nevertheless I reflected that I had the prettiest Foot in the World; that *Valville* should presently have a sight of it, and that it would be none of my Fault.

And such calculations frequently lead to new experiences. This can occur in at least two ways. The character can be carried away by the calculation, much as the narrator is carried away by sentential digressions. This happens to Jacob, in the midst of a calculated performance of innocence:

> J'avoue pourtant que je tâchai d'avoir l'air et le ton touchants, le ton d'un homme que pleure, et que je voulus orner un peu la vérité; et ce qui est de singulier, c'est que mon intention me gagna tout le premier. Je fis si bien que j'en fus la dupe moi-même, et je n'eus plus qu'à me laisser aller sans m'embarrasser de rien ajouter à ce que je sentais; c'était alors l'affaire du sentiment qui m'avait pris, et qui en sait plus que tout l'art du monde. (P. 96)

> I acknowledge at the same time that I affected as moving an Air and Accent as possible; I assum'd the Tone of a Man who cries, and endeavour'd to adorn the Truth a little; but what is very singular, my Invention prevail'd upon me first. I acted my Part so well, that I deceived my self, and had nothing to do but to go on without adding any thing to my real Conceptions; it was the Sentiment which struck me, and that's more powerful than all the Art in the World.

Alternatively, the characters' reflections can generate new experiences by providing a delusive ground of certainty against which the surprise of the new encounter can erupt. It is at their moments of greatest calculation that Marianne and Jacob find themselves overthrown by a sudden emotion or carried away by their own discourse. Thus Marianne, completely absorbed in an elaborate display of coquetry for the local churchgoers, finds herself suddenly bowled over by the sight of Valville and unable to concentrate on her performance:

> Parmi les jeunes gens dont j'attirais les regards, il y en eut un que je distinguai moi-même, et sur qui mes yeux tombaient plus volontiers que sur les autres.
> J'aimais à le voir, sans me douter du plaisir que j'y trouvais; j'étais coquette pour les autres, et je ne l'étais pas pour lui; j'oubliais à lui plaire, et ne songeais qu'à le regarder. (P. 91)

> Among the young Gentlemen whom I thus obliged to fix their Eyes upon me, there was one whom I looked at myself with more Attention than the rest, and whom my Eyes seemed most inclined to behold. I was extremely pleased to see him, though hardly sensible of it myself. With regard to the others I was a perfect Coquet; with regard to him perfectly unaffected. So that I gave up the Care of pleasing him to indulge the Delight I took in looking at him.

Finally, the character's reflections can lead to calculations and explanations which merge with the narrator's sentential discourse, thus bringing together not only the two faces, but also the two phases, of experience: that of the young Marianne/Jacob and that of the older narrating Marianne/Jacob:

> Pour moi, je ne disais mot, et ne donnais aucun signe des observations clandestines que je faisais sur lui; il n'aurait pas été modeste de paraître soupçonner l'attrait qui l'attirait, et d'ailleurs j'aurais tout gâté si je lui avais laissé apercevoir que je comprenais ses petites façons: cela m'aurait obligé moi-même d'en faire davantage, et peut-être aurait-il rougi des siennes; car le cœur est bizarre, il y a des moments où il est confus et choqué d'être pris sur le fait quand il se cache; cela l'humilie. Et ce que je *dis* là, je le *sentais* par instinct. (*La Vie de Marianne* p. 95, my emphasis)

> For my part I was perfectly silent, and gave not the least sign that I privately observed him. For it would not have been decent, to seem to suspect the vast Attraction my Foot had on him. Besides, I should have spoiled all, had I let him know, that I understood the Meaning of his little Artifice. For I shou'd have been under the Necessity of using more Reserve with him. And I had perhaps made him blush at his Intentions. For the human heart is very odd and strange. There are Occasions in which it is confounded and ashamed to be discovered in the Fact, when it strives to be concealed. Such a Disappointment mortifies it extremely; and what I now *tell* you, I then *felt* by meer Instinct.

At such instants, when experience as living through things is grasped as knowledge by the experienced self, and when the certainty of experience is felt intuitively, the Marivaudian self attains its highest level of intensity. More typically, the tension of experience is articulated historically, as the difference between past and present identity. In these moments the past becomes present and the self is actualized both as feeling (or character) and as cognition (or narrator), in the play between former and current action and understanding. For example, when Jacob finds himself transformed into M. de la Vallée, he is caught up in a voluptuous self-satisfaction:

> Figurez-vous ce que c'est qu'un jeune rustre comme moi, qui, dans le seul espace de deux jours, est devenu le mari d'une fille riche, et l'amant de deux femmes de condition. Après cela mon changement de décoration dans mes habits . . . ce titre de monsieur dont je m'étais vu honoré, moi qu'on appelait Jacob dix ou douze jours auparavant . . . Aussi étais-je dans un tourbillon de

vanité si flatteuse, je me trouvais quelque chose de si rare, je n'avais point encore goûté si délicatement le plaisir de vivre...(*Le Paysan parvenu*, p. 174)

Imagine how it must be with a young Rustick, like me, who, in the space of only two Days, was become the Husband of a wealthy Woman, and the Gallant of two Ladies of Quality. Besides, there was the alteration of my dress, which wrought a strange effect. The Title of Sir, with which I found myself honoured, who, but about a dozen days before, was call'd plain *Jacob*;...For my part, I was wrapp'd in a Transport of Vanity, it was something so novel. Till then, I had never known the Delicacy of Living...

It is the suspension between two moments and two identities which generates the pleasure here. Once regularized, even the most intense pleasure wears off: "l'âme s'accoutume à tout, sa sensibilité s'use" (*La Vie de Marianne*, p. 202) (the soul accustoms itself to everything, its sensitivity decreases), and if a mere pair of slippers sends M. de la Vallée into ecstasy, it is because he has not yet settled into his new role:

c'était en me regardant comme Jacob que j'étais si délicieusement étonné de me voir dans cet équipage; c'était de Jacob que M. de la Vallée empruntait toute sa joie. Ce moment-là n'était si doux qu'à cause du petit paysan. (P. 226)

It was in considering myself as Jacob that I was so delightfully surprised to see myself in this get-up; it was from Jacob that M. de la Vallée derived all of his joy. That moment was so sweet only because of the little peasant.

In these two examples, the shock of two identities separated in time and not yet reconciled within the logic of reflection elicits a moment of delight – a "surprise" not unlike that of love, as depicted in Marivaux's dramas. In *La Vie de Marianne*, where the contriving of a sympathetic persona by the heroine is a more deliberate matter, a similar pleasure occurs when the reflective self becomes absorbed in its own creation. This is particularly evident in the later sections of *La Vie de Marianne*, where the protagonist's increasingly elaborate self-presentations become objects of contemplation in their own right:

Mon récit devint intéressant; je le fis, de la meilleure foi du monde, dans un goût aussi noble que tragique; je parlai en déplorable victime du sort, en héroïne du roman, qui ne disait pourtant rien que de vrai, mais qui ornait la vérité de tout ce qui pouvait la rendre touchante, et me rendre moi-même une infortunée respectable. (P. 320)

My recital became interesting; I most candidly made it in a noble, lofty and tragical Strain: I spoke as a deplorable Victim of Fatality might have done, as a romantic Heroine who said nothing but what was true; but who adorned the truth with every thing that could render it moving, and give me all the off-set of a respectable Unfortunate.

Through repeated recountings, "Marianne the Orphan" has evolved into a character of fictional extravagance, "Marianne the narrator's" detachment from which can be measured in the increasing use of the third person:

> je me proposai une conduite qui était fière, modeste, décente, digne de cette Marianne dont on faisait tant de cas. (Pp. 343–4)

> Avez-vous oublié à qui vous parlez? Ne suis-je pas cette Marianne, cette petite fille qui doit tout à votre famille, qui n'aurait su que devenir sans ses bontés... (P. 359)

> ce serait bien alors que vous auriez raison de détester le jour où vous avez connu cette malheureuse orpheline... (P. 360)

> I proposed to act with equal Spirit, Modesty, and Decency, and in a Manner worthy of that *Marianne* which was so highly esteemed.

> Have you forgot who you now speak to? Am I not still that *Marianne*, that little Girl who owes every Thing to your Family, who would have been at a Loss what to do with herself, had it not been for their Bounties?

> Then indeed you should have great Reason to curse the Day of your first Acquaintance with the unfortunate Orphan Girl...

As the first citation indicates, Marianne's persona is not only an object for her admiration, but a role she assumes, and when she succeeds in immersing herself in one of her roles, in being swept away by her own fiction, she experiences a doubling of self similar to Jacob's and finds the equivalent of his existential pleasure:

> je revenais toute émue de ma petite expédition, mais je dis agréablement émue: cette dignité de sentiments que je venais de montrer à mon infidèle, cette honte et cette humiliation que je laissais dans son cœur, cet étonnement où il devait être de la noblesse de mon procédé... tout cela me remuait intérieurement d'un sentiment doux et flatteur... (P. 361)

> I was coming with great Emotion from my little Expedition; but it was a pleasing Trouble, I assure you. That Dignity of Sentiments I had just shewed before my traitor; that Shame and Humiliation I had left in his Heart; that surprize he must have of the Nobleness of my Proceeding... all this worked upon me inwardly, by a soft, pleasing Sentiment.

The binary tension of identity can thus be conceptualized historically as the difference between former (naive) self and current (experienced) self, or narratively, as the play between the self as narrated object and narrating subject. But both of these oppositions break down over time, as the continual increment of experience (and the narrative) accumulates a contextual weight of its own that rivals the original pre-narrational experience of the autobiographer. In other words, as the characters Marianne and Jacob accumulate experience, they become increasingly sophisticated, reflective, and difficult to distinguish from their mature narrating counterparts.[20] When this occurs, the character begins to derive more pleasure from recollection and reflection than from the first-hand experiencing of reality, as in the continuation of the above citation:

> Voilà qui était fini. Il ne lui était plus possible, à mon avis, d'aimer Mlle Varthon d'aussi bon cœur qu'il aurait fait; je le défiais de m'oublier, d'avoir la paix avec lui-même; sans compter que j'avais dessein de ne le plus voir, ce qui serait encore une punition pour lui; de sorte que, tout bien examiné, je crois qu'en vérité je me le figurais encore plus à plaindre que moi; mais qu'au surplus c'était sa faute: pourquoi était-il infidèle?
>
> Et c'étaient-là les petites pensées qui m'occupaient en allant au-devant de Mme de Miran, et je ne saurais vous dire le charme qu'elles avaient pour moi, ni combien elles tempéraient ma douleur. (P. 361)

> He could no longer (as I thought) love Miss *Varthon* as comfortably as he would have done. No; that could not be. I could have defied him to forget me, and be in Peace with himself; not to reckon that I intended not to see him any more, which would be an additional Punishment inflicted on him: So that, every Thing well considered, I really believe that I fancied his Condition still more deplorable than mine, but that it was his own Fault indeed; for why should he be a false Man, and not suffer for it?
>
> These were the little pretty Thoughts I was taken up with, as I advanced towards Mrs. *De Miran*, and you cannot imagine how greatly I was delighted with them, nor how much they allayed my Grief.

The charm of recollection, the suspension between original experience and the knowledge derived from that experience, have become part of the internal structure of the character, rather than a function of the gap between the character and the autobiographer. Sapped of its original impetus, unable to maintain the contrast between the young and the mature Marianne, the autobiography falters and stops. Totally self-conscious, too experienced to experience anything naively, the Marivaudian character can no longer sustain the tension that animates the self. The novel ends, without ever really concluding.[21]

In their depiction of selfhood as co-determined by private self-representation and public account, Marivaux's works articulate a paradigm that will persist through most of the century. Although narcissistic self-fascination is inherent in the self as he depicts it, his protagonists elaborate their identity as individuals primarily within the relationships they entertain with others: their sense of self is indissociable from what others say about them, from the place they are assigned in the accounts of those they admire or respect. To alter their identity, they must not only adopt the behavior and discourse of the class to which they aspire, but graft their story onto the running record of that class by getting its members to sanction their account and further disseminate it. We remember a primitive version of this process in its most spartan anthropological terms from *Robinson Crusoe*, where Friday becomes a man (as opposed to a savage) by virtue of his apprenticeship in the discourse of Robinson's culture and his integration into Robinson's story. Richardson's works will confirm the pattern by making the narrative internalization of the collective values by the individual, and the assimilation of the individual's exemplary narrative by the community, complementary moments in the reconciliation of individualism and historical determinism.

Selfhood in this new framework is necessarily split between intense self-consciousness and an attunement to public norms. While *La Vie de Marianne* and *Le paysan parvenu* exploit the charming aspects of this split, and particularly the erotic fascination a calculated innocence holds for the averted spectator, self-consciousness will take a more sinister turn in the later works of Richardson, Fielding, Diderot, and especially Laclos. Caricaturing Richardson's distribution of humanity between straightforward honesty and calculated machination, Fielding's novels, and to some extent those of Diderot, will present a world permeated by deceit and hypocrisy in which only a *deus ex machina* can assure a just recompense for honest and spontaneous action. And Laclos will provide the limiting case of a consciousness so taken with artifice that the very notion of spontaneous action becomes untenable. Entirely taken up with the orchestration of its image, the self will have lost the ability of blind, dumb reaction, and with it the delight that comes with the surprise of sensation and the sudden confrontation with a new identity.

The relationship of individual to community constitutes only one axis of the equation of Marivaudian selfhood. The space separating the outsider from the insider, the distance and difference which one feels with respect to the Other, and which alternates with an ever stronger sense of being similar and close to that same Other, is only a spatial, interpersonal version of a tension and fascination which is felt temporally and intrapersonally as the oscillation between spontaneous experience and reflective understanding. This intrapersonal difference from the self is a function of narration, or more precisely of the autobiographical gesture which makes of the self an object of contemplation and attempts to *relate* that object both to its contemporaneous context, which is to say the past, and to the present writing consciousness.

The two axes of the self-Other relationship, the intrapersonal and the interpersonal, situate selfhood within the play between subject and object, and they can be separated only theoretically. In practice, the pressure of the collective gaze forces the subject to see him- or herself as an Other, or object, and to evaluate his/her spontaneous gestures with respect to their effect on the public. The interpersonal agenda of assimilation requires continual intrapersonal monitoring of one's expression, words, and general performance, which situates identity between calculation and action. Social behavior is always to some extent a performance, but in Marivaux's works it is a performance whose public is double: the fascination one exercises on the social Other is the complement of that which one holds *as* Other for the detached reflective self. And just as the self (as performer) finds validation in the positive responses of the collective Other who confirms its social metamorphosis, the self (as author) finds validation in the Other which it creates (or re-creates) as a narrated character from its own experience.

To the extent that the self as Other gains its objective consistency through the process of narrative self-representation, Marivaux's works explicitly correlate self-narration with self-*alter*ation: it is through recounting itself that the self becomes something other than what it was; narration is the vehicle of personal change, and not merely the servant of a pre-existing order. This notion will become the central theme of the novels of Samuel Richardson, but it finds initial expression in Marivaux's definition of consciousness as the relationship of a structuring narrational present to its structured, narrative past. The theme of his novels is, finally, the evolution of this relationship over time: the way the recounting consciousness alters its account in response to its perception of its past self, thereby altering the image to which it reacts and to which the community responds – which in turn triggers further responses and revisions.

Because it is this process that interests Marivaux, and not just his protagonists' ascendance in the class hierarchy, his tales of social metamorphosis are abandoned once the narrated self has attained a level of self-consciousness which makes it difficult to distinguish from the narrating self. The moment of fascination is that pleasurable ambivalence when the self perceives itself as at once one with, yet detached from, the community, at once swept along by the flow of experience, yet at the same time the articulator or author of that experience. The fundamental drama of his works is that of historical selfhood grasping itself as such, within the tension between two social situations, moments in time, and modes of consciousness. His characters attain their most powerful sense of identity when they are both on the inside and the outside of collective discourse, both present and detached, reacting to the moment and recollecting the past, both experiencing their destiny as the unpredictable flow of reality and structuring their experience as the pattern of their identity. And to the extent these two perspectives correlate to the two faces of history, as course of events and reflection on the past, the Marivaudian moment is that of identification of, and in, history.

NOTES

1　Although he is best known as the major French eighteenth-century dramatist, Marivaux's two major novels, *La Vie de Marianne* and *Le paysan parvenu* were highly successful and contributed to the development of the genre both in France and abroad. *La Vie de Marianne, ou les aventures de Madame la comtesse de **** which appeared in eleven installments from 1731 to 1742, was translated into English from 1736 to 1742 as *Life of Marianne: or Aventures of the Comtess of *** ...*, 3 vols (London: Charles Davis, vol. 1, 1736; vol. 2, 1741; vol. 3, 1742). A second edition in two volumes followed in 1743, and a new translation in 1747. *Le paysan parvenu*, published in five installments in 1734–5, came out almost immediately in English as *Le Paysan parvenu: or the Fortunate Peasant. Being the memoirs of the Life of Mr. ____* Translated from the French of M. de Marivaux (London: John Brindley, Charles Corbett, and Richard Wellington, 1735). Translations in the text will be taken from these two editions, with minor emendations. Marivaux's literary career spanned nearly half a century (his first published work, *Le père prudent et équitable* dates from 1712; *La Provinciale*, another comedy in one act, was published in 1761, two years before his death), and included not just comedies and novels, but short stories, parodies, moral essays, serial columns, humorous pieces, and an imitation of the influential British *Spectator*, which he entitled *Le Spectateur français* and published from 1721 to 1724. The eighteenth-century English author Clara Reeve ranks Marivaux among the best French novelists of the century, praising his works as being "of capital merit... pictures of real life and manners"; *Progress of Romance* vol. 2, p. 129.

2　Jean Rousset, *Narcisse romancier*; pp. 111–12; see also p. 135. Rousset first analyzed this narrative structure of the "double-registre" (double register), which splits the self into narrated experience and narrating observation, in "Marivaux ou la structure du double registre," in *Forme et signification*, pp. 45–64. See also my "Convergence et Equilibre dans *Le Paysan parvenu*," *French Forum*, 1, no. 2 (May 1976), pp. 139–52. Georges Poulet conceptualizes the oscillation as a repeated awakening to existence, triggered by an emotion (love), in which the self awakens to an inchoate sensation of undifferentiated existence, followed by a "prise de conscience" (sudden self-awareness) in which the existing self appears as such to itself: "A l'extrêmité de toute émotion il y a toujours chez Marivaux une fraîche apparition de soi-même à soi-même" (at the far end of every emotion in Marivaux there is always a fresh revelation of one's self to one's self); *La Distance intérieure* (*Etudes sur le temps humain*, II) (1952) (Paris: Editions du Rocher, 1976), p. 20.

3　Henri Coulet, *Le Roman jusqu'à la révolution*, vol. 1, pp. 348–50.

4　*La Vie de Marianne* in fact nominally adopts the conventions of epistolarity: the first-person narration addresses itself to a close friend, to whom it is supposedly being sent in installments. François Jost, "Le roman épistolaire et la technique narrative au XVIIIe siècle," *Comparative Literature Studies*, 3 (1966), pp. 397–427, cites this work as a prime example of one variation of the "static" epistolary genre, in which no real exchange of letters is involved, and where the epistolary account is not itself a mode of action within the plot, but which nonetheless retains the conventions of familiar address to the recipient and lively expression of personal emotions. For Marie-Paul Laden, *La Vie de Marianne* combines the advantages of the memoir novel and those of the epistolary novel, allowing a "writing to the moment" similar to that sought by Richardson; *Self-Imitation*, pp. 87–8.

5 Rousset, *Narcisse romancier*, pp. 103–13.

6 Laden, *Self-Imitation*, p. 98.

7 All citations are from *Le paysan parvenu*, ed. Michel Gilot (Paris: Garnier-Flammarion, 1965), which reproduces Frédéric Deloffre's edition of the original editions of 1734 and 1735 (Paris: Garnier, 1959).

8 See, for instance, Michel Gilot's introduction to his edition of *Le paysan parvenu*.

9 According to the chronology of Marivaux's work compiled by Frédéric Deloffre, *La Vie de Marianne* (Paris: Garnier, 1963), pp. lxxxvii–xcviii, Marivaux solicited a royal privilege for a work entitled *La Vie de Marianne* and submitted a manuscript to the censor in February of 1727, although the first volume did not appear until 1731. The five installments of *Le paysan parvenu* were published in 1734–5 between the second and third parts of the "earlier" novel.

10 All citations are from *La Vie de Marianne*, ed. Michel Gilot (Paris: Garnier-Flammarion, 1978), which reproduces Frédéric Deloffre's 1963 edition of the original installments, as emendated by Henri Coulet. During the course of Marianne's story, as her case is progressively adopted by other women, her parents' status will be inflated. At one point her benefactor, Mme de Miran, will qualify her unknown parents as "étrangers de la première distinction" (foreigners of the highest distinction) (p. 297).

11 The link between narrative authority and social rank and its displacement by a form of authority validated by formal conformity to a paradigm of reason is discussed by Terry Eagleton in *The Function of Criticism*, pp. 14–27.

12 See Laden, *Self-Imitation*, pp. 102–5, for a good analysis of this mechanism of self-creation.

13 Rosbottom, *Marivaux's Novels*, p. 95, notes that Marianne "soon learns the advantages that mysterious origins provide," and his reading similarly stresses her maturation as an active member of the social network.

14 What Patricia Meyer Spacks notes of Richardson's Pamela, namely that "the ability to play out an elaborate drama of 'honour' shows her to be a native aristocrat" (*Imagining a Self*, p. 209), applies to Marianne as well.

15 *Webster's International Dictionary*, third edition, s. v. "experience."

16 These moral analyses, with their preciosity and excessive refinement, are characteristic of Marivaux's writing in general and gave rise in the eighteenth century to the term *marivaudage*. According to Frédéric Deloffre, *Marivaux et le marivaudage* (Paris: Les Belles Lettres, 1955), marivaudage originally denoted "une forme trop raffinée d'analyse morale" (an overrefined form of moral analysis) (p. 6) but has since evolved, along with a reassessment of Marivaux's works, to designate "un badinage spirituel et galant" (a witty, gallant banter-

ing) (p. 7). In current usage, the term refers both to the type of writing typical of Marivaux and the form of social banter it represents – a "propos, manège de galanterie délicate et recherchée," (phrase or game of delicate, *recherché*, gallantry) as defined by *Le Petit Robert* – and it underlines the centrality of public flirtation and self-consciousness in his novels.

17   As noted above, Georges Poulet is the primary proponent of such a reading.

18   Such a reversal of the normal paradigm of representation forms the comic device of one of Marivaux's earlier novels, *Pharsamon ou les nouvelles folies romanesques* (1712) reprinted in Marivaux, *Œuvres de jeunesse*, ed. Frédéric Deloffre et Claude Rigault (Paris: Gallimard "Bibliothèque de la Pléiade," 1972), where, according to Jean Rousset, "les événements narrés, loin de préexister à la narration comme le croit la conscience naïve du lecteur, sont subordonnés à l'instance narrative qui leur confère l'existence" (the narrated events, far from pre-existing the narration, as the naive readerly conscience thinks, are subordinated to the instance of narration which grants them existence); *Narcisse romancier*, p. 87. Marie-Paul Laden, *Self-Imitation*, p. 103, also discusses the "subordination of the narrated event to the speech event," although in terms of the real effect which the narration has on the heroine's life.

19   See also pp. 60, 83, for other examples. Rousset, *Narcisse romancier*, pp. 89–90, discusses other instances in *La Vie de Marianne* where the narrating act takes on aspects of the flow of experience which it purports to describe.

20   As Henri Coulet notes, the element of chance, which plays a major role in the early stages of the protagonists' adventures, also gradually disappears, as psychological motivation takes its place as the motor behind their destiny; *Le Roman jusqu'à la révolution*, p. 350.

21   Actually *La Vie de Marianne* merges into an entirely new story, related autobiographically by one of the nuns at the convent where Marianne is living. Marianne thus fades into the background, taking over the role of the mute listener to whom the story is recounted. The adventures of the new protagonist–narrator are curiously complementary to Marianne's – she is of noble birth but abandoned by her mother and thus without family – and her story could be read as an attempt to breathe new life into the drama of identity. But even this attempt at a fresh start eventually grinds to a halt for much the same reason: as the protagonist becomes less gullible, more self-reliant, and more consistent in her self-management, she gradually loses her distinction from her narrator(s). The impulse to self-definition that inaugurates the autobiography falters and ceases when the difference between protagonist and author, source of the latter's own existential pleasure and sense of identity, becomes imperceptible. *Le Paysan parvenu* has a similar outcome: when Jacob's naive innocent side and his reflective side merge in a unified expression of conventional social grace, his story loses its motor force and is abandoned with no explanation. (Actually, *Le Paysan parvenu* has a continuation, written by another author some years later, but its wooden emulation of Marivaux's style retains little of the tension between naiveté and calculation which makes the original's portrayal of selfhood so compelling.)

7

From Private Narration to Public Narrative (*Pamela*)

In the novels of Samuel Richardson self-representation, particularly *written* self-narration, becomes the explicit keystone of individual identity and self-empowerment within a social community. Composed as a series of letters in which the protagonists recount their every move, belief, motive, and plan, Richardson's two masterpieces, *Pamela* and *Clarissa*, published in 1740 and 1747–8, respectively, link both selfhood and social identity with the deliberate textualization of the self – the production of a written history of the individual that records personal experience at the moment of occurrence and uses that record to structure the future. This more consciously historical notion of personal narrative assumes an interpretive activity and readership that goes beyond the person or persons immediately confronting the narrator. The written record of Pamela's or Clarissa's history, in the form of letters that are carefully transcribed and circulated to interested parties, continues to exert its influence long after the events it describes (and in *Clarissa* long after the demise of the heroine), creating a textual identity for the protagonists that ultimately overtakes or displaces their original social status: Pamela becomes Mrs B. rather than a mere servant, while Clarissa's martyrdom becomes the occasion for her near-canonization within the very society that scorned her.

As letters, the textual accounts which Richardson's protagonists devise about themselves are specifically tailored to a future, broader discursive economy, one in which their story and identity can circulate as a document of their behavior. Attentive not just to the immediate effect of their account, but also to its long-term effect on the community as a shared textual legend, Pamela and Clarissa structure themselves with an eye to the moment when they will be assimilated into the collective past as exemplary figures of model conduct. Their writing thus hovers between the prolepsis of fiction, written in view of a future effect on the reader, and the retrospection of history, born of an attempt to grasp and preserve the significance of the past. By focusing on this duality, and on the necessity of integrating private destiny with collective account, *Pamela* and *Clarissa* bring the personal narration we have seen associated with the rise of individualism closer to the shared narrative we call history.

This transformation of personal story into shared history mirrors the evolving function of the novel. Narratives like *Pamela* and *Clarissa* are not just stories of individuals who shape the collective conscience through their narration; the novels themselves are instances of such a shaping within their own culture: "Richardson's novels are not mere images of conflicts fought out on another terrain, representations of a history which happens elsewhere; they are themselves a material part of those struggles, pitched standards around which battle is joined, instruments which help to constitute social interests rather than lenses which reflect them."[1] Within the plots of his novels as in the extended debates surrounding their publication, Richardson demonstrates as no previous author the extent to which narration and narratives shape the world, constructing the historical order that defines and grounds them.

While *Pamela* and *Clarissa* correlate individual fabulation to the larger economy of history and thus suggest more ambitious narrational agendas, they also open the question of how much control narrators have over *narratives*, that is, over the textual artifacts which they produce and release into circulation. Beyond the obvious problem of competing narrators, which forms a thematic axis in both novels in the form of the reported disputes between characters, these works examine the authority which narratives exercise once they become shared public constructs, susceptible to reformulation and reinterpretation according to the whims of their public. They dramatize what occurs when even the most carefully constructed characterization or plot enters a larger economy within which its impact is determined not just on the basis of its author's intentions, but in accordance with the conventions of narrative logic prevalent in the society at the time. This larger order, like the local discursive networks surrounding Marivaux's characters, is bodied forth in the competing constructions of reality forwarded by different individuals, each of whom is driven by a particular personal agenda, but also speaks in the name of a larger encoded ideology. The discursive economy into which Richardson's protagonists release their stories unites, then, mechanisms and agencies representing various orders of meaning and authority, all of which influence the ability of the self's story to gain currency. Within the interplay between these various orders, even the most elaborately orchestrated representation can acquire new logic and meanings, culminating in unforeseen ways and putting into question the individual's control over destiny which it was fashioned to celebrate.

In other words, Richardson's characters grasp the events that envelope and define them as parts of a larger narrative pattern, the shape of which is determined by several distinct and possibly conflicting agencies. Naturally the individual character, to the extent she has control over the ongoing representation of her textual self, can claim a share in the shaping of her destiny: because of their explicit reliance on textual representation, Pamela and Clarissa are even more aware than Marianne and Jacob of their narrative persona and the importance of constructing it so as to elicit the proper response from the public. On the other hand, however, Richardson's characters also come to recognize the determining potential of the *reading* act which their story requires as narrative. In effect, it is possible to understand the dramas of Pamela and Clarissa as the struggle between conflicting, self-interested ways of reading and conferring meaning on the world and the heroine's acts. Critics have noted how *Clarissa* in particular dramatizes narration's contingency on the obverse side of the narrative circuit, namely reading and interpretation.[2] The validating or competitive Other is central to *Pamela* as well. In fact, Richardson only makes explicit a preoccupation implicit in earlier works: as far back as *La Princesse de Clèves*, the gesture of interpretation, the reading of various events, and the negotiation of conflicting versions of the same story play a central role in the construction of reality. Richardson's contribution to this tradition lies in his demonstration that reading is *inseparable* from writing, and vice versa, that the primal gesture of self-definition – "that act through which individuals constitute themselves and define their connections with the world of other people"[3] – cannot be confined to either reading or writing, interpretation or narration, alone. The one always implies the other; an interpretation of reality comes into being only at the moment of its articulation; there is no act of narration that does not imply an interpretation. Accordingly, there can be no agenda of selfhood based on self-representation that does not enlist and depend on Others.

In Richardson's works these Others form a larger discursive economy consisting of a continuous fabric of competing readings and narratives – or plots. Just as any construction of reality that is articulated necessarily entails and implies an interpretation of previous constructions, any single individual's narrative reflects his or her reading and rewriting of conflicting plots authored by social rivals. Conversely, schemes of self-narration can only find actualization as narratives enmeshed in the readings and writings of Others. This network of transactions generates reality collectively and continuously as a shared history which is enacted by separate acts of representation but grounded in the underlying cultural scripts which enable such acts and are modulated by them. Richardson's works make the role of these grounding scripts clear: the Other against which Defoe's characters developed their autonomy, or upon whom Marivaux's protagonists counted for their social advancement, is but a personal incarnation of an impersonal order of complete Otherness, that of the codes governing all action, narrative or otherwise, within a society. The individualist narrative must accord itself to at least two orders of authority, then: the personal and the impersonal; that of the instance, and that of the grammar.

For reading and writing to be universal – whether taken in the broader sense I am using those terms or the narrowest sense of basic literacy – there has to exist a shared set of rules about the structure of stories or texts: a grammar of sorts, that need not be explicit and conscious, any more than grammar in the narrow sense is conscious. Such grammars are not the result of collective decisions, they simply come into being as the result of an extended practice: for the economy to thrive, patterns must be standardized; the more widespread the practice, the more powerful the rules. Culture, in the broadest sense of a set of rules, conventions, and paradigms for social action, is such a grammar; and the influence it exerts on both reading and writing emerge in *Pamela* and *Clarissa* as a new constraint on programs of narrational coercion – one that is all the more powerful for the fact that, unlike the rivalry of competing plots, the logic of convention cannot be associated with any obvious agent – or even necessarily perceived. The arch-villain Lovelace appears on the surface to express his singularity through his schemes, but his script quickly falls into conventional patterns whose outcome he cannot alter. His piteous downfall suggests that even the most elaborate attempt to transcend the values of the collective is doomed to failure.

Taken together, *Pamela* and *Clarissa* set the stage for an ambivalence that will persist for the rest of the century. They propose models of self-narration which offer greater control over one's destiny than earlier strategies precisely to the extent that they are more attuned to the narrative, conventional underpinnings of culture; but at the same time, by engaging the question of narrational/interpretive competition within the social community, as well as the relationship of individual performance to collective grammar, they raise the possibility of enclosure within larger shared scripts and systems of figuring reality. Each novel reacts to the problem differently, and the difference in their reaction accounts in large part for their disparate length and levels of complexity.

Both works share certain plot similarities – a young heroine is pursued by a ruthless nobleman who, in his attempts to seduce her, resorts to abduction, deception, imprisonment in a house governed by amoral female cohorts, and rape – and in both the course of events is chronicled and ultimately altered by the ongoing accounts penned by the heroine (and, in *Clarissa*, other characters) to an absent interlocutor. However, *Pamela* seems to present a utopian vision of self-determination in which the heroine's virtuous account of herself overcomes all opposition and causes her tormentor to relinquish his planned rape, propose marriage, and reform his ways, while in *Clarissa* the heroine's projects of self-determination and her tormentor's agenda of seduction appear to lead to mutual ruin and death. This surface plot would appear to juxtapose two perspectives on self-determination: in *Pamela*, the heroine succeeds in relating herself (in)to a new identity, whereas in *Clarissa* the narrators and their narratives fall victim to a competing plot or become irretrievably entangled within the warp of a logic they cannot control.

However, the unsteady relationship of personal narration to conventional narrative finds thematization in the second-level plot of each novel, and it is here that their difference emerges in all its complexity. Each work in fact consists of two parts. A first section tentatively underwrites the individual's ability to structure reality, tracing the heroine's attempts to master her destiny (and the villain's efforts to master the heroine) up to the point where she either succeeds in imposing her will on her master (*Pamela*) or is overcome by a more masterful narrator and plotter (*Clarissa*). The second half of each novel then turns around and revises the model extended in the first half. *Pamela* depicts the willful relinquishment of personal authority in favor of a dialogical relationship that empowers the Other both personally, in the shape of the husband, and collectively, in the roles dictated by society: Pamela learns how to be a perfect obedient wife, Mr B. an ideal husband. *Clarissa* dramatizes the systematic annihilation of the protagonists' initial plans in accordance with plot lines that can no longer be obviated (Lovelace is entrapped in his own plots and loses Clarissa and his life; Clarissa fulfills the prophecy of her parents by gaining renown as a fallen woman), but redeems its heroine through a movement of sublation into literary exemplar. Even as she overcomes abusive authority through the internalization and re-presentation of the principles of acceptable authority, Pamela gradually relinquishes her claim to absolute individuality in favor of a program of mutual reality construal that defuses the potential antagonism between her and her erstwhile adversary. *Clarissa* illustrates what happens when one does not make such concessions and attempts to monopolize the power in an interpersonal relationship; but it follows up on this catastrophe with a new strategy of self-expression that relies on the *textualization* of the self to overcome the tensions of interpersonal rivalry.

Clarissa ultimately transcends her downfall not because she incarnates flawless virtue, but because she transforms the plot line her parents and Lovelace have devised for her into a textual incarnation of her experience that can survive her demise and carry her ideal vision of her self into the shared narrative of her culture. Even as she wastes away, she transfers the responsibility for relating her adventure, and even her narrative voice, to a number of surrogate narrators, each of whom will further comment on and interpret her adventure before passing it on, embellished, for others to read.

Clarissa the heroine is transformed into *Clarissa*, a shared collective narrative, the function of which is identical within the novel and without. Clarissa (*Clarissa*) thus points the way for future generations of narrators, who find their strongest mode of self-expression in the fictive discourse of the novel and the cultural authority of the Author.

In both novels, finally, the pattern of self-determination culminates in the renunciation of monological authority. But while *Pamela* stresses the need for such a move on the interpersonal level to overcome the antagonism between competing authorities, *Clarissa* casts it in terms of self-perpetuation as a literary artifact within the enduring historical process of collective self-representation. By abdicating absolute control over her story and displacing the burden of her identity from her own running accounts or actions to an evolving shared history elaborated *on her account* by others, Clarissa shifts the framework of self-expression and self-definition from private narration to conventionalized, public narrative. She thus prefigures the emergence of the institution we call the novel – and the conventional agents we call the Author or the Reader – as the principal paradigms of selfhood. Future novelists will increasingly associate the imposition of the self's order on the world with the gesture of the novelist, just as the dialogic pair of rival wills and rival versions of reality that structure Richardson's novels in the persons of the seducer and the seduced will merge into the textually mediated relationship of teller and listener, Author and Reader. Finally, *Clarissa* provides an alternative for the absorption of individual will by collective law which *Pamela* depicts, by sketching out a strategy of deferred volition: Clarissa imposes her identity and values on the text of her culture more powerfully than any previous protagonist, but she does so only through the mediation of a new order that is at once completely public and profoundly private, totally conventional, yet answering to personal configuration. This order is that of the literary work.

More explicitly than the novels of Defoe and Marivaux, Samuel Richardson's *Pamela* tells a tale of narration. The long series of letters from the maid-in-waiting Pamela to her parents not only describes in exquisite detail, but eventually comes to regulate, the events in her metamorphosis, including the initial advances of her master Mr B., her resistance, his orchestration of her abduction and sequestration with the evil Mrs Jewkes, Pamela's failed attempt to enlist the help of the young parson Williams, her botched suicide, Mr B.'s attempted rape, his repentance, the ensuing love between the two young people, and her ultimate marriage and transformation into a noblewoman. Even more than Marianne's repeated recitation of her origins, or Jacob's winning accounts of his behavior, Pamela's act of narration, and the narrative of innocent goodness that act produces, function to win the respect of the aristocrat for the commoner and ultimately procure her metamorphosis. By recounting her character, Pamela, like her predecessors, imposes it on her adversaries and eventually wins their support for her cause.

Almost every particular of the plot structures in Richardson's work contributes to this emphasis on narration and narrative. Isolated from society for the better part of her adventure, the heroine/narrator has few means of action available to her other than writing. The relating of her sentiments and behavior provides her only mode of self-enactment. Further, the location of the story in the present tends to align consciousness with narration: Pamela's account is not a retrospective autobiography but an ongoing reportage of present tribulations and convictions, from hour to hour, day to day. Unlike her predecessors, she does not wait until long after the conclusion of her adventures to write them down. She recounts herself (and others) at every instant, and her accounts include details of the current situation, the act of writing itself, and the future shape events might take. The telling of her story becomes Pamela's means of *fore*telling history: by defining events in her own terms, she hinders their easy assimilation into competing designs and forces her adversaries to devote their energies to countering her vision.

The redirection of narration and narrative from the reflection of the past to the expression of the present and the projection of the future finds a perfect formal embodiment in the novel's epistolary mode. Perhaps the most important contribution of *Pamela* to the eighteenth-century novel is its emphasis on *writing* as the instrument of self-realization – writing not just as the expression of the self-as-consciousness, but also as a structure of persuasion and authority. Pamela's account is ostensibly destined for a limited readership, her parents, but it becomes the vehicle of her transformation when, in the course of the novel, Mr B. obtains access to her journals and letters and upon reading them progressively metamorphoses from seducer into devoted husband. The pattern then expands to encompass larger segments of social reality: excerpts from Pamela's journals are circulated to a wider audience of her contemporaries and become exemplary scripts within that microculture. This sequence of events poses in concrete terms the question of how writing, as opposed to oral relations, shapes reality, and how its effects may exceed the control even of the writer.

Divorced from its act of enunciation, the written account benefits from an assumption of mimetic precision which the oral account cannot sustain. Because it is presumed to reflect merely Pamela's reactions to her story, and not Mr B.'s presence, her private journal functions as a reliable document of her character, a clear window into the soul of its author.[4] Because Mr B. is free to interpret it as he sees fit, in the privacy of the reading act, it lends itself to assimilation within his own version of things and thus facilitates his reconciliation with Pamela. More generally, once it is put into circulation as a text, a written narrative like Pamela's lives in the events of its readings and acquires in the process an authority that can no longer be reduced to that of a single individual's volition. Thus, as we shall see, Pamela's expressed agenda, which is merely to be allowed to return to her parents untarnished, is sidetracked by her story once it falls into Mr B.'s hands. Her determined attempt at self-definition, and her ruthless depiction of Mr B., far from obtaining her liberty, seduce him – and her – into a relationship neither had envisaged at the outset. This turnabout, which occurs roughly half-way through the novel, confirms the promotion of personal narrative to a mediating function in the negotiation of social reality and foreshadows future emphasis on the unpredictability of textual self-representation. Within the plot, it inaugurates a long process of realignment between Pamela's vision of the world and the conduct of Mr B. and his household. Once the virtuous exemplar's history has internalized and redefined the ground of conduct, and acceded to a position of authority in the community, Pamela and Mr B. can abandon their antagonistic stances and renounce their competing claims to sole authority in favor of a dialogical model of reciprocal determination based on the shared authority of author and reader, husband and wife.[5]

Immediately following the central rape scene, Pamela and Mr B. embark on a program of communal identification, elaborating a shared identity whose authority will be grounded in reciprocal self-definition and correlated to the sacrament of their vows and the social institution of marriage. *Pamela* thus dramatizes not only the overcoming of abusive authority by the narrative of selfhood, but the conversion of a monological practice of self-representation into a dialogical process of mutual reality construal between narrative partners, each of whom alternately functions as author(ity) and reader (assent). The empowerment of the private account is celebrated, and perhaps to some extent repressed, by its deliberate absorption into the collective institution, in what Ian Watt has aptly termed a "pondered contractual protocol,"[6] its threat of a self-sufficient history displaced by a more reassuring dialogical model of co-authorship that merges effortlessly with the prevalent collective discourse of the period.

The opening paragraphs of the book state writing's potential as a weapon almost immediately. Because the letters she writes involve parties other than herself, Pamela has the ability of maligning a person's name, and Mr B.'s admonition in the first letter of the novel makes clear that he sees her narrational bent both as a threat to his reputation and a potential form of insubordination: "I am not angry with you for writing such innocent matters as these; *though you ought to be wary what tales you send out of a family*. Be faithful and diligent; and do as you should do, and I like you the better for this" (p. 44).[7]

Pamela's repeated entreaty of "Pray your honour, forgive me" (p. 44) when she is found writing this letter about her master, testifies well enough to her own sense that servants do not normally enjoy the right to pen portraits of their masters. Still, her immediate rejoinder to herself, "Yet I know not for what: For he was not undutiful to *his* parents; and why should he be angry that I was dutiful to *mine*!" (p. 44), indicates her conviction that as far as corresponding with parents goes, she enjoys duties and privileges equal to those of her master. It is within the play between these two stances or attitudes – that of subordination to authority according to established class distinctions and that of a claim to equal rights as regards one's own words – that Pamela's struggle for self-determination occurs. Unlike her predecessors, she is possessed of a fully determined social identity at the outset of her adventure; the family that is so conspicuously absent for the female protagonists of Defoe and Marivaux plays a major role in Richardson's work precisely to the extent that Pamela's writing exploits class distinctions as a means of self-determination, rather than an obstacle to it. Although on one level of analysis – that of duty to God and one's parents – Pamela equates her behavior with that of Mr B., she is well aware that a competing structure of secular authority grants her master privileges she cannot hope to claim. Rather than denying the existence or propriety of this system of authority, she espouses its arguments to her advantage, using the idea of her master's superiority to create an unbridgeable gap between them. Whereas her predecessors are only too eager to take on new identities and transcend their station, Pamela stubbornly clings to a stereotype of her own lowliness to keep her master at bay. Even before Mr B. makes his first move, she articulates the distance that separates them, and indicates her conviction that his identity as an aristocrat will prevent him from devoting too much attention to her:

> I am sure my master would not demean himself so, as to think upon such a poor girl as I, for my harm. For such a thing would ruin his credit as well as mine, you know: who, to be sure, may expect one of the best ladies in the land. (P. 49)

It is with good reason that Pamela asserts "I *must* call him gentleman, though he has fallen from the merit of that title" (pp. 53–4), for that characterization will form one of the axes of her defense. Each time she confronts Mr B., she reiterates his great distinction, the better to emphasize the impropriety of his attentions for her:

> You . . . have lessened the distance that fortune has made between us, by demeaning yourself, to be so free to a poor servant. (P. 55)

do you do well to put yourself upon a foot, as I may say, with such a poor maiden as me? And let me ask you, sir, whether this becomes your fine clothes, and a master's station? (P. 102)

I must needs say, that, indeed, I think you ought to regard the world's opinion, and avoid doing any thing disgraceful to your birth and fortune . . . a little time, absence, and the conversation of worthier persons of my sex, will effectually enable you to overcome a regard so unworthy of your condition. (P. 252)

Pamela thus turns to her advantage the social constraints that would seem to render her helpless. By relentlessly asserting "I am not of consequence enough for my master to concern himself, and be angry" (p. 91), she blocks his approach and naturally makes him angry. As Mr B. himself concedes: "'My pride of birth and fortune (damn them both!' said he, 'since they cannot obtain credit with you, but must add to your suspicions) will not let me descend, all at once'" (p. 116).

By refusing to subscribe to Mr B.'s abrogation of the social code, she forces him to choose between accepting permanent separation or arguing against rigid class separation. Convinced that he cannot do without Pamela, and that his present course of behavior is incommensurate with his station, he is brought to redefine the foundations of his identity along the lines she dictates, which is to say those of mutual respect, rather than mere wealth and privilege. Isolated from the object of his desire by her rigorous interpretation of the principle of class difference he invokes to overwhelm her, he relinquishes his claim of privilege, adopts the standards of virtuous behavior which Pamela defines, and makes her literally his equal through marriage. Thus while Pamela succeeds in transforming her identity even more radically than Marianne or Jacob, she does so not by molding herself to her betters, but by dismantling their claim to power from the inside.

The success of this strategy demonstrates two things. On the one hand, it shows that social identity is based on narrative and is vulnerable to narration. Although Pamela maintains her behavior is dictated by notions of honor and virtue that transcend secular convention, the barrier she erects between herself and Mr B. does not express any divine scheme; it merely caricatures the reputation-based caste system. Following a model we can trace at least as far back as *La Princesse de Clèves*, individual identity and power within the world of *Pamela* are shown to hinge principally on one's public persona, as modulated by the stories about one that circulate in society. Richardson's work dramatizes the breakdown of an assumption characteristic of earlier periods, namely that within such a system, an account's weight necessarily varies with the rank of its author. In earlier works, accounts of events and characterizations of individuals were evaluated first and foremost on the basis of their author's rank: in *Manon Lescaut* or *Moll Flanders*, the deposition of any person of quality suffices to put a lower ranking individual in prison; in *La Vie de Marianne*, Marianne's revelations of misconduct on the part of M. de Climal are met with disbelief and then muffled by the ecclesiastic to whom she relates them, until M. de Climal's confession some time later confirms her honesty and virtue. In *Pamela any* written account, even one put into circulation by a lowly domestic, has the potential of affecting the fortunes of the person it describes.[8] This is why Mr B. is so concerned that Pamela not reveal his behavior: "I own I have undervalued myself; but it was only to try you. If you can keep this matter secret, you'll give me the better opinion of your prudence" (p. 56).

In political terms, Pamela can only hold the threat of humiliation up to Mr B. because she is carefully recording and transmitting to her parents – and later the local clergyman, Mr Williams – the account of his demeaning behavior. Narration, and most particularly *writing*, thus becomes an exercise in pure power. It is not surprising that Mr B.'s driving obsession in the first part of the novel concerns Pamela's constant writing:

> I am watched very narrowly; and he says to Mrs Jervis, "This girl is always scribbling; I think she may be better employed." (P. 54)

> he has ordered Mrs Jervis to bid me not pass so much time in writing; which is a poor matter for such a gentleman as he to take notice of, as I am not idle other-ways, if he was not apprehensive of the subject I wrote upon. (P. 58)

> "you may only advise her . . . not to give herself too much licence upon the favours she meets with; and if she stays here, that she will not write the affairs of my family purely for an exercise to her pen and her invention. I tell you, she is a subtle, artful little gypsey . . . " (P. 60)

> "I can't let her stay, I assure you; not only because of her pertness, but because of her writing out of my family all the secrets in it." (P. 105)

Mr B.'s fear is that Pamela's "scribbling" will gain a wider audience than just her parents and Mrs Jervis, and although he publicly maintains "my reputation is so well established . . . that I care not what any body writes or says of *me* . . . " (p. 105), he elsewhere confides to Mrs Jervis: "I find I am likely to suffer in my reputation by the perverseness and folly of this girl" (p. 67); "I raised a hornet's nest about my ears, that, as far as I know, may have stung to death my reputation" (p. 98).

On the other hand, Pamela's success demonstrates that even when it does not function as a threat to the reputation of the people it describes, written narrative can directly alter the perceptions of those parties through the version of history it promotes. The heroine senses the advantageous role she plays in her story and she remarks to her parents (in a letter divulging behavior her master requested she keep secret) "Oh how poor and mean must those actions be, and how little must they make the best of gentlemen look, when they offer such things as are unworthy of themselves, and put it into the power of their inferiors to be greater than they" (p. 56). To ensure that she will remain "greater" than her master in all accounts, she takes great care to construct a portrait of herself that will contrast with that of Mr B. As his conduct grows ever blacker in her letters, and he gains the epithets of "wicked," "base" (p. 93), "hardened wretch" (p. 107), "black-hearted wretch" (p. 120), she takes on an aura of angelic innocence and charity:

> wicked as he has been to me, I wish his prosperity with all my heart, for my good old lady's sake. . . . and I then spoke and said "O the difference between the minds of thy creatures, good God! how shall some be cast down in their innocence, while others can triumph in their guilt!" (P. 99)

> O the unparalelled wickedness of such men as these, who call themselves gentlemen! who pervert the bounty of Providence to them, to their everlasting perdition, and to the ruin of oppressed innocence! (P. 130)

> what must that wicked master deserve . . . who, not content to be corrupt himself, endeavors to corrupt others, who would have been innocent if left to themselves! and all to carry on a base plot against a poor creature, who never did him harm, nor withheld him any; and who can still pray for his happiness, and his repentance. (P. 158)

Mr B. correctly foresees this strategy – "representing herself as an angel of light, she makes her kind master and benefactor, a devil incarnate" (p. 68) – but he does not realize that to combat it, he must insulate himself, as well as third parties, from Pamela's narrative. His plan only addresses half of the problem: to prevent Pamela from relating his actions he isolates her from the outside world, imprisoning her in another of his estates under the watchful eye of his grotesque, amoral toady, Mrs Jewkes. This measure seems reasonable (although not entirely, because he can never be sure she is not entertaining a secret correspondence by means of another servant or Mr Williams) but it in fact backfires: in eliminating his maid's "public," he increases his own vulnerability to her version of things, not only because he can no longer discount her characterization of herself as a tactic designed to enlist the support of third parties, but also because, as her sole reader, he becomes an unwitting party to her account. When, just prior to the attempted rape, he takes the place of Pamela's public by disguising himself as a servant and listening to his victim's "little history" of herself (pp. 238–40), he becomes her narrative respondent and finds himself drawn into both the history of his adversary and the structure it imposes on reality. To listen to the entirety of Pamela's tale without disputing it (and this is what circumstances oblige Mr B. to do) is in a very real sense to sanction the version of reality it proposes. Unable to maintain his own conviction that his victim is a "specious hypocrite" (p. 203), he can no longer go through with the rape. As he himself acknowledges:

> Your pretty chit-chat to Mrs Jewkes the last Sunday night, so full of beautiful simplicity, half disarmed my resolution, before I approached your bed. And I see you on all occasions so watchful for your virtue, that though I hoped to find it otherwise, I cannot but confess, my passion for you is increased by it. (P. 251)

As principal respondent to an account of limitless pathos, Mr B. has become a party to her story, an accomplice to her valiant resistance. By the time this occurs, however, Pamela herself is in a similar position. Indeed, the singularly monologic structure of the first half of the novel, which moves from Pamela's correspondence with her increasingly disembodied parents and her lengthy discussions with Mrs Jervis to the lonely voice of a secret journal, gives way immediately following the rape scene to a decidedly dialogic paradigm in which Pamela and her master elaborate an understanding of the situation *together*. That both characters should abandon their claims to monological authority results, ironically, from their respective inability to foresee the effect of their own plots. Absorbed in their struggle for authority, they fall victim to the authority of their stories, which, whatever their surface claims – and those claims are by no means all self-assertive – attest by virtue of their duration and intensity to a passion for transacting with the Other.

Mr B. is the first to intimate the power of well-wrought prose. Early on he cautions Pamela's interlocutors against accepting unquestioningly her version of things (pp. 60, 68), and in one of his retorts to her use of a fable by Aesop to characterize their relationship, he points out how Pamela uses established texts and figures to bolster the moral authority of her own tale:

> "So, Mrs Jewkes," said he, "you are the wolf, I the vulture, and this the poor harmless lamb, on her trial before us. You don't know how well read this innocent is in reflection. Her memory always serves her, when she has a mind to display her own romantic innocence, at the price of other people's characters." (P. 224)

To combat her rhetoric, he puts into circulation a number of stories of his own, beginning with letters to her father and to one of Mr B.'s tenants that discredit Pamela's story of abduction by explaining her absence in terms of a charitable attempt on the part of Mr B. to prevent her elopement with Mr

Williams (pp. 123–5, 138–9). These stories are successful enough – Pamela's father is not convinced, but the tenant farmer is – to suggest that the effect of a narrative does not necessarily depend on its truthfulness, and Mr B. will capitalize on this discovery just prior to his attempt at ravishment when he uses a fake letter to fool Pamela into thinking he has departed (p. 236).[9]

As a narrator, however, Mr B. only comes into his own when he appropriates Pamela's story for himself, writing her a scathing account of *her* behavior from *his* perspective. This throws the heroine off balance by forcing her to react to his unflattering depictions of her personality (pp. 200–5). Confronted for the first time with another party's conception of her personal identity, she has much the same reaction as her adversary. Taking exceptions to each of his characterizations, she disputes his very right to consider her:

> *Mean-spirited*, and *low*, and *forward*: if I am *low*, I am not *mean-spirited*. I wish I could not say, It is he that, *high* as he thinks himself, is *mean-spirited*. It is *degree*, not *man*, he says, that gives me apprehension. What can he mean by it? *A mirror of bashful modesty and unspotted innocence, he thought me!* What business has he to think of me at all? (P. 204)

What has happened here is that portions of Pamela's own narrative ("a mirror of bashful modesty and unspotted innocence") come back to haunt her as the words of another. That Mr B. can add an ironic turn to her own characterization and use it to his own ends should alert Pamela to the slipperiness of her story, as should Mr B.'s subsequent use of it in defense of his reprehensible behavior: "'you have given me a character, Pamela, and blame me not if I act up to it'" (p. 248). Once inscribed as texts and divorced from the persuasive resources of the narrational gesture, the stories one spins cannot be guaranteed to produce the desired effects – nor can one even be certain of their effects on oneself. That is what Pamela learns when, falling victim to her own characterization of herself, she nearly commits suicide in a paroxysm of bathos. Thwarted in her attempt to escape and overcome by the tragic role she has created for herself, she loses contact with current reality and is carried away by her fantasies:

> these wicked wretches, who now have no remorse, no pity on me, will then be moved to lament their misdoings; and when they see the dead corpse of the miserable Pamela dragged out to these dewy banks, and lying breathless at their feet, they will find that remorse to soften their obdurate hearts, which, now, has no place in them! And my master, my angry master, will then forget his resentments, and say, "Alas!" and it may be, wring his hands. "This is the unhappy Pamela! whom I have so causelessly persecuted and destroyed! Now

I see she preferred her honesty to her life. She, poor girl! was no hypocrite, no deceiver; but really was the innocent creature she pretended to be!"

. . . and the young men and maidens in my father's neighbourhood will pity poor Pamela! But yet I hope I shall not be the subject of their ballads and their elegies, but that my memory, for the sake of my dear father and mother, may quickly slide into oblivion! (P. 212)

Pamela at first resists taking credit for this lapse of melodramatic rapture: "that thought was surely of the devil's instigation; for it was very soothing and powerful with me" (pp. 211–12). But it is entirely in keeping with the increasingly dramatic picture she paints of herself and which she invokes, typically in the third person, as here, to elicit the sympathy of Mrs Jewkes and particularly Mr B. In one of their last confrontations prior to Mr B.'s proposal of marriage, for example, she consistently requests his pity not for herself, but for "the poor Pamela" (p. 252). Significantly, what will bring her to her senses and persuade her not to drown herself is the realization that she is both trying to rival God in her plot – "Who gave thee, said I to myself, presumptuous as thou art, a power over thy life?" (p. 213) – and that she risks botching her work with a poor choice of episodes: "Hitherto, Pamela, thought I, thou art the innocent, the suffering Pamela; and wilt thou, to avoid thy sufferings, be the guilty aggressor?" (p. 213). When, at the close of the scene, she expresses gratitude at escaping with her life, she rectifies her earlier misconstrual of responsibility for the episode: "I have been delivered from a worse enemy – *Myself!*" (p. 214).

What Pamela learns is that once consigned to narrative, her story and character prove unpredictable not because of the narrative's ineffectiveness, but because it can generate an excess of meaning over which she cannot always maintain control. Indeed, her tale does not enact her intentions. She does not succeed in dissuading Mr B. and returning to her parents; the role she ultimately takes is not that of poor pathetic Pamela, the servant, but of the proud Mrs B. This is, as Pamela is careful to specify, a role she welcomes with joy, but it is not, and could not be, part of the narrative she had fashioned for herself (p. 252). Similarly, Mr B.'s narrative undertaking literally exceeds his wildest expectations: he never expected Pamela to give herself to him, nor that he would reciprocate by marrying her. Yet this is the conclusion which his own writing brings about, in large part due to its unpredicted effect on Pamela:

This letter, when I expected some new plot, has greatly affected me. For here plainly does he confess his great value for me; and accounts for his rigorous behaviour to me. . . . to find him capable of so much openness, so much affection, nay, and of so much *honour* too, I am quite over-come. . . . to be sure, I must own to you, that I shall never be able to think of any body in the world but him! (P. 283)

Having failed to subordinate Pamela with assertions of inherited privilege, Mr B. wins her complete submission with a letter reaffirming her freedom which he writes after her departure. If his adoption of Pamela's tactics can be read as the acknowledgment of narrational/narrative authority over the privileges of the aristocracy, that authority lies as much within the narrative-as-text, conceived as an economy in its own right, as it does within the individualist act of narration that purports to fashion history. The second half of the book will attempt to balance these two forms of authority within the circuit of narrator/narratee, and demonstrate how they can be assimilated into collective structures of authority.

The pivotal point for this transition is the "rape" scene, which dramatizes both the uselessness of coercion as an expression of personal authority – not to mention desire – and the realization by both protagonists that they have failed in their plots and lost control of their strategy. The episode, like those that immediately precede and follow it, is structured around the collapse of the antagonistic transaction between Pamela and Mr B., the recognition that monological assertion cannot sustain self-representation, and the systematic dismantling of the monological model in a series of dramatic turnabouts. Mr B. makes the first move, rejecting his primary tool of physical coercion. Pamela in turn relinquishes the arms that have served her so well: she agrees to allow Mr B. to read her writing, and even to transmit her account to others; and she ultimately accepts his authority over the future turns of her story. Each eventually achieves a variation on the destiny she or he desires – for Pamela the maintenance and recognition of her virtue, for Mr B. the possession of Pamela – by renouncing unique authority over the self in favor of a dialogue of mutual self-construal.

The first move in this sequence is the most striking: just when Mr B. has his servant where he wants her – in bed and helpless – he abandons his plans. This makes perfect sense in terms of the struggle for authority. When he fails to go through with Pamela's ravishment, it becomes clear that Mr B.'s objective is less physical consummation than an admission of complete subordination on the part of Pamela.[10] Rather more intent on making his point verbally than pressing it home physically, he ignores Mrs Jewkes' admonishments to get on with the deflowering and pauses to dissert on his absolute power:

> Said she [Jewkes], (O disgrace of womankind!) "Don't stand dilly-dallying, sir. She cannot exclaim worse than she has done; and will be quieter when she knows the worst."
>
> "Silence!" said he to her. "I must say one word to you Pamela: it is this;

you now see, that you are in my power! You cannot get from me nor help yourself: yet have I not offered any thing amiss to you. But if you resolve not to comply with my proposals, I will not lose this opportunity." (P. 242)

In fact, when Pamela faints, rendering herself incapable of reacting to Mr B.'s proposals, she short-circuits his program. He does not carry out his threat, for, as his insistence on verbal compliance indicates, his goal is not physical possession but a share in Pamela's voice and destiny. Unconscious, Pamela is indeed completely in his power, but for that very reason can no longer offer the response he seeks: she cannot *acknowledge* him, and his love. Because she is helpless, she offers no test of his authority and inadvertently defuses the contest of wills that opposed them. As she will later remark: "[I] have reason to be thankful that I was disabled in my intellects. Since it is but too probable, that all my resistance, and all my strength, otherwise would not have availed me" (p. 243). If she remains a virgin, it is not because of her resolution, but because Mr B. realizes he desires her conscious assent, not her submission. Conversely, the rape scene invalidates Pamela's claims to independence and puts into question the value of her sharp wit. What she cannot accomplish by resistance, she obtains by losing control and enlisting the support of her opponent.

To nurture this incipient dialogic relationship Mr B. and Pamela both relinquish their former designs. For the master, this means giving up his pretensions to dominion over his servant's destiny and person, and focusing more on his own behavior: "if I am master of myself, and my own resolution, I will not attempt to compel you to any thing" (p. 244). He initiates the new relationship by explicitly requesting Pamela's forgiveness (p. 243), granting her request not to see Mrs Jewkes, and then, in an unprecedented move, confessing his passion has made him helpless and requesting that Pamela advise him on a course of action:

> "Now, Pamela, judge for me; and, since I have told you thus candidly my mind, and I see yours is big with some important meaning, by your eyes, your blushes, and that sweet confusion which I behold struggling in your bosom, tell me with like openness and candour, what you think I ought to do, and what you would have me do." (Pp. 251–2)

Three times he reiterates his request, refusing to chart a course of action without the advice of the woman he formerly tried to coerce to his own desires.

Pamela responds to the new role Mr B. offers her by relinquishing *her* claim to authority in a series of symbolic gestures. The most blatant of these is a pantomime of feudal thraldom in which Pamela, having called Mr B. "Lucifer," flees from her master in the garden, then stops when he bids her to stop, returns when he demands it, and humbly begs his forgiveness: "'If, sir,' said I, 'I am not to go for good, I cannot quit your presence till you pardon me. On my knees I beg you will': and I kneeled to him. 'I am truly sorry for my boldness...'" (p. 249). Without abandoning her honor, Pamela nonetheless vows obedience to her master in all other things even at the expense of her life:

> "I will endeavor, sir," said I, "always to preserve that decency towards you, that veneration for you, which is due from me to the son of that ever-honoured lady, who taught me to prefer my honesty to my life. Command from me, sir, that life, and I will lay it down with pleasure, to shew my obedience to you." (P. 249)

In accordance with this new humility, she shies away from counseling her master directly, and, in a marked departure from her habitual practice, declines to specify her own status or verbalize the matrimonial scenario at the back of her – and his – mind. Faced with his persistent demand that she take authority over his fate, she for the first time elects *silence*:

> "O sir," said I, "take not advantage of my credulity, and of my free and open heart: but were I the first lady in the land, instead of the poor abject Pamela Andrews, I would, I *could* tell you. But I can say no more." (P. 252)

Following this capital scene in which the protagonists literally trade roles, there will be a whole series of similar reversals. Mr B. encourages Pamela to continue writing (p. 275), begs forgiveness for causing her such distress (p. 276), and accedes to her wish to return to her parents. Pamela in turn imagining a further plot against herself, is surprised to discover she actually is going home. And when she obtains and reads a letter she was not intended to receive until later, she finds herself moved by it just as her master was moved by her "little history."

The final, and most symbolically charged gesture in this rite of reciprocal subordination comes when she agrees to turn over to her former tormenter the writings she has been hiding from him, that he may obtain complete access to her character as well as a hand in her self-definition. This concession occurs progressively and coincides, not surprisingly, with Mr B.'s emerging decision to share his identity with Pamela by taking her as his wife.

From this point forward in the novel, the two characters will devote as much energy to defining themselves anew, each in the image of the other, as they devoted in the first part of the novel to asserting their individuality. In narrative terms, the love that grows between the two young people coincides with, and is the affective correlate of, their new-found willingness to be defined by and through the other's voice. Pamela and Mr B. alternately assume the roles of narrator and respondent in a mutually agreed-upon project of reciprocal identification, in which authority over the final shape of their destiny is distributed between both functions and both individuals.

In conjunction with this agenda of dialogical authority Mr and Mrs B. will also strive to locate their destiny within the larger text of social usages and customs. This double program is most evident in the lengthy scenes following the protagonists' decision to marry. Ian Watt notes the apparent disproportion of these discussions and attributes them to an intention on the part of Richardson to produce "a new model of conduct for the relations between men and women,"[11] but they also elaborate a new paradigm of individualism that melds the self's confidence in its ability to shape destiny with a sense of the constraints that must be placed on that confidence.

The novel conceptualizes these under two distinct guises, that of history, firmly associated with the existing codes and procedures of the collective, and that of the respondent or individual(s) who validate(s) one's project. In other words, the final sections of *Pamela* present a revised notion of self-determination as a dialectic between the self's sense of agency and the agency of an Other, with this Other construed either as the larger ongoing narrative of history which frames and shapes our story even while we modify it, or as the Reader of our story whose consideration of it from a point other than that of its production confirms its introduction into the larger discursive economy. The former relationship closely resembles a dialectic in the general historical sense of the term, since it involves the ongoing synthesis of reality on the basis of new versions of experience which are fashioned in response to current situations and melded with the dominant cultural narrative. The latter relationship I have termed dialogical, since it focuses more precisely on the exchange between two parties by which new versions of reality gain currency or become public. While it obviously participates in the larger dialectic, it receives particular stress in its own right in the eighteenth-century novel, as the locus for the relationship between writer and reader, author and public.

This revised version of self-determination as dialogue and dialectic retains at its center the gesture of self-construction, but redefines it as a communal project to be elaborated within a dialogue with the (marriage) partner, and according to the templates and guiding authority of inherited, shared conventions. Abandoning her personal vision of divinely ordained virtue, Pamela turns her attention to the fulfillment of the social obligations associated with her new station. Rather than single-mindedly pursuing her own interests – which up to the moment of Mr B.'s conversion were at complete odds with those of his society – she subordinates them to the interests of her master, reworking her identity to conform to that of his wife. Pamela becomes Mrs B. by articulating the specifics of that role, and she finds those specifics in her conversations with her husband and the tradition he articulates.

Perhaps nowhere is this process more obvious than in their repeated negotiations of each other's, and particularly Pamela's, future conduct. In addition to numerous small discussions concerning the way Pamela should treat the servants, the way she must address her husband, and the conduct that Mr B. assigns himself, there are several longer passages explicitly dealing with the negotiation of each partner's role: the careful agenda Pamela sets up for her daily existence as mistress of the house (pp. 298–301); the rules for family order that Mr B. lays out (pp. 393–6); Mr B.'s narration of his former aversion to marriage and the things he would expect of a wife (pp. 463–7); Pamela's interpretation of his story and extrapolation of rules governing the relationship of wife to husband (pp. 467–70). The last of these episodes is the longest and the most revelatory as regards the careful negotiation of each spouse's identity. In keeping with the novel's rather feudal view of the way women relate to men, Mr B. articulates his expectations as law; but Pamela promptly re-counts these demands and adds her interpretation, sanction, or commentary as she sees fit. A typical example, with Pamela's commentary in italics:

27. A man should desire nothing of his wife, but what is reasonable and just. *– To be sure, that is right. Yet who, all this time, is to be the judge?*
28. She must not shew reluctance, uneasiness, or doubt, in obliging him; and that too at half a word; and must not be bidden twice to do one thing. *– Very lordly! But may not there be some occasions, where this may be a little dispensed with? But he says afterwards, indeed.*
29. That this must be only while he took care to make her compliance reasonable, and consistent with her free agency, in points that ought to be allowed her. *– Come, this is pretty well, considering. Yet, again I ask – Who is to be the judge?* (P. 469)

To the extent that the laws set down by Mr B. reflect not just his personal views, but also those of his society, the commentary Pamela elaborates, and which marks her renunciation of individual self-definition, *takes into account* the customs and usages of her husband, herself, and their world. Her dialogue with "his" text prefigures the dialectic that will unite individual utterance to collective narrative in later works.

This "intertextualization" of individuality entails an obvious reduction of autonomy, and there is no guarantee that it will always function as expected. The risks are amply illustrated by the long episode concerning Mr B.'s sister, Lady Davers. In the two letters recounting that lady's arrival during Mr B.'s absence, her attacks on Pamela, her quarrels with her brother, and the subsequent reconciliation of all parties, the potential for rivalry or hostility between personal narration and the collective narrative is explored. These letters are the longest of the book, forming nearly a third of the second volume, and their length alone testifies to the importance of the problem. What happens when parties representing the collective account reject its assimilation of a personal project such as Pamela's? What happens when one member of the dialogue refuses to hear the other's account? This question comes up in earlier novels such as *La Vie de Marianne* in an attenuated form, but in Richardson's work, where the relationship of individual narration to collective narrative begins to receive detailed analysis, it emerges as an explicit theme. In *Clarissa* it will form the linchpin of the struggle between the protagonist and her adversaries, eventually culminating in the formulation of a more powerful strategy for imposing one's self on one's culture – a strategy that allows the heroine to retain her character even as she melts into her culture's discourse. *Pamela*, however, at least in the scene with Lady Davers, proposes no better solution than the subordination of personal voice to conventional expression. Significantly, the two long letters that chronicle the confrontation with Lady Davers almost totally abandon the epistolary conventions that characterize Pamela's private narration. The narrative merges into a dramatic series of arguments, invectives, and entreaties which are articulated as a dialogue of multiple voices and from several points of view. At the same time this collective discourse emerges in place of the self's private monologue, the heroine underwrites her assimilation into the manners of the aristocracy by refusing to accept any role other than that of mistress of the house, guiding her responses to Lady Davers' abusive treatment on the basis of her sense of what the wife of a Mr B. would do.

> "If," said I, "to attend your ladyship at table, or even kneel at your feet, were required of me, as a token of respect to Lady Davers; and not as an insult to her brother, who has done me an honour that requires me to act a part not unworthy of his goodness to me, I would do it. But, as things are, I must say, I cannot." (P. 411)

She no longer speaks in the voice of Pamela, poor maidservant, but in that of Mrs B. Her arguments and behavior no longer reflect the humble character Lady Davers last knew, but rather the more reserved, aloof persona Pamela and Mr B. have constructed together since their change of tactic two weeks earlier. When Mrs Worden, Lady Davers' maidservant and formerly Pamela's peer, invites Pamela to join her for dinner, the latter exhibits little of her former humility:

> "You are very kind, Mrs Worden," replied I; "but times, as you said, are much altered with me. I have been of late so much honoured by better company, that I can't stoop to your's." (P. 415)

Whether one interprets Pamela's metamorphosis as a loss of identity – the absorption of individual *discours* by the anonymous *langue* of the gentry[12] – or as the appropriation of collective discourse to an extravagant personal agenda, it is clear that identity cannot avoid the question of its cultural framework and narrational accomplice. Just as Marianne could not sustain her new persona in the presence of a hostile interlocutor, Pamela cannot "be" Mrs B. without a public willing to sanction her performance. When Lady Davers refuses to validate the heroine's "ladylike" behavior, and encourages her nephew and maidservant to do the same, Pamela is helpless to impose her new role on them. In fact, *Mr* B.'s "new" identity fares no better than his wife's within this miniature society. When Lady Davers gets hold of a letter Mr B. wrote to Pamela, she reinterprets his words cynically in light of *her* sense of her brother's identity:

> "'*It will be six miles difference to me.*' [Ah, wretched Pamela! Seest thou not that thy influence is already in the wane? Hadst thou kept thine innocence, and thy lover had been of thine own rank, sixty miles would have been no more than one to him. Thinkest thou that my brother's heart is to be held fast by that baby-face of thine? Poor wretch! How I pity thee! . . .]" (P. 417)

Unable to fill the role of Mrs B. in the absence of her husband, Pamela chooses the only logical course of action: she flees to the neighboring estate of friends, where, along with Mr B., she will find a sympathetic public already initiated into her new character.

Identity thus becomes conscious of itself as the product of a self-presentation that depends on the cooperation of a public for its dissemination within the social economy. And to the extent this forces Pamela to see herself as a character in a larger drama, she becomes more of an author in the conventional sense of the term: an individual finding her self-expression in the construction of a persona or character, the various traits of which are elaborated not in isolation, or as the expression of some intensely personal vision, but in conjunction with the discourse of society, and more particularly that subset of society that forms her immediate interlocutionary partner or reader. Like Diderot, Fielding, or Sterne, she acknowledges the contingency of her character on its reception by a public. The private account of an inner self elaborated in concert with her parents at the outset of the novel is no longer adequate to her new identity, which has a broader range of possibilities and correspondingly greater need for public approbation.

This wider "readership," with its complex expectations and conflicting demands, imposes on the self a careful formulation of words and deeds which can only lead to increased self-consciousness and, in extreme cases, a sense of separation between one's narrational self and one's narrative self similar to that we noted in Marivaux's works. Compelled to ever more exhaustive dramatizations of her thoughts and actions, Pamela gradually elaborates a persona for herself whose situation not only functions as a referent for her discussions – even after her metamorphosis – much as a literary character, but also as the cause of her writing. This double identity correlates well to the novel's narrative format: to write a letter about one's self is to become at once created and creator, and to the extent that the heroine's identity constitutes itself entirely within her narrative and narration, Richardson's novel defines a self that is, even more acutely than Marianne or Jacob, at all times both subject and object, aware of itself as the organizing activity that structures reality and as one of the constructs of that activity – one of the components of that reality. At once her own author and character, Pamela is both origin and effect of a reality that shapes her as she formulates it. As events in the "real" world, her adventures dictate the course of her narration and shape her character; as components of a narrative she is constantly and consciously formulating, these same events obey her authority and originate in her character. Because the self is both the motor force behind its accounts and the product of those accounts, it must henceforth be grasped in terms of a dialectic: neither an artificial façade erected to dissemble a "true" personality, nor a primordial template unchanging through time, but a narrative construct and narrational activity that evolves over time as the result of its own prior shape and current actions.

This notion will receive more extensive treatment in later works, such as Diderot's *Jacques le fataliste*, where the relationship between free will and the determination of history will be framed in terms of a dialectic between author and character, as well as between the great book of history and the smaller tale each of us spins out through his or her actions. While Richardson's work does not directly address abstractions of such magnitude, it does set the stage for a dialectical formulation of the self's dual identity as author (or creative authority) and character (or passive agent), by emphasizing the dual identity of personal history as event and account, and the two faces of experience as undergoing and understanding. Within *Pamela* this duality does not end in conflict. Just as Pamela's independence and self-definition is diluted by its merger with the language and categories of the collective, so too is the characteristic Marivaudian hesitation between a spontaneous self and a reflective self replaced in *Pamela* by a permanent state of "natural" self-consciousness, grounded in the inseparability of the (determining act of) narration and the (determined order of) narrative. Unlike Roxana or Moll, Pamela feels no tension between a "real" identity and the role she plays in the world; she does not revel, like Jacob or Marianne, in the ambiguity between craft and innocence. She is at all times confident in her identity, at one with her character, but that character is at all times subject to modification – and conscious of that contingency.

However, the equilibrium between these two faces of identity can be sustained only because neither is taken to its logical conclusion in *Pamela*. The potential tension between the self's capacity for invention and its claim of helplessness will only find full treatment in Richardson's far more ambitious *Clarissa*. When the *narrational* underpinnings of identity are forgotten or denied, when the self represses the consciousness of its own agency in the arrangement of reality, the individual will appear the pawn of history, a mere character in a plot authored at a higher level: this is the paradigm we have seen in Pamela's abortive suicide episode; it will reappear in the first part of *Clarissa* as a sustained attitude of the heroine; and it also subtends Jacques' persistent fatalism in *Jacques le fataliste*. Conversely, a repression of the self's *narrative* frame, a denial of the narrator's enclosure within a larger grounding set of conventions, will result in exaggerated claims of power and absolute free will: this is in a sense the stance of Mr B. in the beginning of the novel, when he resists the inscription of his identity within the code of his class; it is the stance of Lovelace, the villain of *Clarissa*; and it will characterize a host of later characters in the eighteenth century, all of whom are similarly intent on fashioning history to their own ends.

NOTES

1   Terry Eagleton, *The Rape of Clarissa* (Oxford: Basil Blackwell, 1982), p. 4.
2   In *Clarissa's Ciphers* (Ithaca: Cornell University Press, 1982), for instance, Terry Castle provides an elegant reading of *Clarissa* as a hermeneutic struggle between various parties, each of whom desires to impose his or her meaning on the world and suppress Clarissa's construction of events. William Warner, *Reading Clarissa* (New Haven and London: Yale University Press, 1979), pp. 143–258, argues, on the basis of the interpretive struggles attending *Clarissa's* publication and its critical reception in the eighteenth and twentieth centuries, that debates between the novel's author and his many correspondents replayed the tactics of its protagonists, while the novel's more general thematization of the struggle to control history is reiterated by subsequent generations of critics who have tried to reduce its complexity to a meaning that would reflect and promote their own ideologies.
3   Castle, *Clarissa's Ciphers*, p. 47.
4   See Watt, *Rise of the Novel*, pp. 217–20.
5   *Pamela's* relatively straightforward thematization of writing and discourse as modes of power and foundations for selfhood lends itself to many different readings which may overlap mine to various degrees. Marie-Paul Laden, *Self-Imitation*, compares the novel to *La Vie de Marianne* and is particularly attentive

to Pamela's objectification of herself, her strategy of grasping or realizing herself from the position of the spectator to her drama. Patricia Meyer Spacks, *Imagining a Self*, sees the key struggle in the book as one of "manipulation of language, involving the different import of words for various users and hearers of them" (p. 210), and correlates Pamela's triumph with her successful defense of her valuation of "honor." Michael McKeon's interpretation corresponds in its general lines to many of the patterns I explore here, but correlates the complex reversals and alterations in Pamela's and Mr B.'s postures to specific subsets of the larger socio-economic, epistemological, and ethical trends which he sees the eighteenth-century novel mediating more generally.

6 Watt, *Rise of the Novel*, p. 170.

7 All citations are taken from the Penguin Edition of *Pamela*, ed. Peter Sabor (London: Penguin, 1980), which reproduces the author's final revised version of the work published posthumously in 1801.

8 Just such a situation was decried by Defoe, in his fascinating tract *The Great Law of Subordination*, published anonymously in 1724. The work contains several accounts of domestics who, either in defense of their reputation or in retaliation for abuses received, use narratives to oppose their superiors. One such tale, introducing the theme of the perversion of authority by the empowered classes, tells of a servant who is insulted by a neighboring squire who then disputes the servant's account of the incident. The servant takes the squire before justice to get his reputation cleared, declaring "that he would not be call'd Dog, and Rogue, and Rascal, by ne'er a Gentleman in the Country; that he valued his Reputation as much as Esq; — at any time, and that his Livelyhood depended upon it" (p. 27). Another tale relates how a particularly malicious chamber-maid, intent on another's place, orchestrates and executes an entire program of slander which destroys a gentleman's household. Persuading a fellow servant into spreading the word that her master is sleeping with his housekeeper, she engineers his destruction by proxy, ruining the other servant, who is prosecuted for slander, in the bargain (pp. 227–56).

9 It is of course Fielding who takes this pattern the furthest, making dishonest narratives the core of his comic epics *Joseph Andrews* and *Tom Jones*, some years later.

10 As McKeon argues, *Origins*, p. 359, the need to dominate Pamela can be read as an extension of Mr B.'s basic aristocratic ideology of paternalistic domination. I would note, however, that to the extent Mr B. "takes power to consist in the ability to make others accept one's version of events as authoritative," he relies on a narrative conception of authority and power that is increasingly common to all classes and ideologies.

11 Watt, *Rise of the Novel*, p. 168.

12 For a Marxist interpretation of Pamela's absorption into the class of the gentry and her consequent loss of personal voice see the introductory chapter of Eagleton's *Rape of Clarissa*. For Eagleton, the heroine, who is in part the "bearer of Richardson's ideological project of integration with the gentry," is not a "free agent but the function of an historical *plot* which the bourgeoisie have been long hatching" (p. 35).

8

Textualizing the Self (*Clarissa*)

Richardson's enormous novel *Clarissa, or, the History of a Young Lady* differs from *Pamela* most obviously in that while the latter concludes idyllically, *Clarissa* culminates in the death of its protagonist, her self-confidence and esteem shattered by her estrangement from her family and her ruthless rape at the hands of a calculating rake, Lovelace. Such radically opposed dénouements force a reassessment of the practice and consequences of self-determination, particularly since there are substantial overlaps in the plot structure. A bright, handsome, verbally adroit daughter of a well-to-do bourgeois family, Clarissa Harlowe rebels against a perversion of authority as does her predecessor. But the abusive agent in this case is her father, a pig-headed arrogant tyrant who is determined she should marry a revolting but financially attractive suitor, rather than remain unmarried or follow her own inclinations. Imprisoned in her home as punishment for disobedience, Clarissa resists all of her family's threats and gradually establishes an epistolary relationship with Lovelace, a dashing young rake despised by her family, but to whom she feels inclined, in spite of his reputation. Faced with her father's threat of a forced marriage, she is tricked into fleeing her home by Lovelace, who subsequently sequesters her in a house of his own, attended by a bevy of fallen women – former conquests. After a protracted campaign of deception, designed to wear down Clarissa's defenses progressively and terrify her into submission by convincing her that her family is pursuing her and contemplating force, Lovelace grows impatient, and with the aid of a potion and his female helpers, ravishes his prisoner. Contrary to his expectations, this only strengthens Clarissa's resistance to him; after various other trials, she succeeds in escaping and finds aid and comfort in Lovelace's former accomplice, Belford. Refusing any reconciliation to the now miserable Lovelace, and having been repudiated by her family, she undertakes to set the record straight on her account by relating her story to all those she feels may have been affected by it; after which she takes leave of this world, but only following elaborate preparations, which include commissioning her own coffin, composing her funeral inscription, and bidding adieu to the rapidly growing group of admirers who have been won over to her cause by her writings.

Although it emphasizes verbal virtuosity, linguistic invention, narration, and the construction of personal history more blatantly than any of its predecessors, Clarissa lacks any significant dimension of social climbing. Unlike Pamela and virtually all of the previous eighteenth-century protagonists we have studied, Clarissa does not use self-presentation to change her identity or advance to a higher social class. She is already a member of the wealthy bourgeoisie that elicits so much envy in the novels of Defoe and Marivaux, and neither her copious writing nor that of her principal rival in the novel, the rake Lovelace, serves the end of upward mobility. Nor could it, really, since *all* the characters of *Clarissa* work at configuring identity and reality through narration; Clarissa is not the only narrator in her story, which is composed of letters from an extensive cast of individuals. Far from being a special gift of the protagonist, relating one's self and one's version of social reality appears the fundamental gesture of selfhood, and to this extent the novel must be read as an exploration of what occurs when a practice that was previously limited to a small subset of individuals is extended to society in general. For individualism as Defoe or Marivaux depict it, the results appear disastrous. Both the heroine and her adversaries, each of which can be thought of as embodying a particular brand of self-determination or self-promotion, meet with apparent ruin. On the one hand, this collapse stems from the degeneration of Pamela's happy paradigm of dialogical negotiation into a circus of competition, deceit, and manipulation. On the other, it occurs because the characters' various plots are overwhelmed by a conventional script which swallows up individual authority in the warp of its own inexorable development.

There are many similarities linking Pamela and Clarissa: a fierce spirit of self-determination, a passion for "scribbling," a keen sense of honor, and a refusal to relinquish control over one's destiny. Similarly, the two novels share a common nucleus of episodes leading up to their dramatic turning point: abduction, sequestration, attempted seduction and rape. But around this shared armature the novels elaborate opposed perspectives on self-definition. *Pamela* resolves the tension between its protagonist's constructed identity and the role society assigns her by chronicling the merger of her personal narration and the broader script of social custom. It thus specifies the utopic ideal of individualism as the representation of collective value within free self-realization. *Clarissa* portrays a darker world in which such efforts of structuring run up against both the rival scripts of enemies and an impersonal narrative economy that regulates all of the characters' attempts to shape history and propels their stories towards an outcome unforeseen by their original narrational gesture. The emergence of this double obstacle of a hostile dialogical framework and an overriding impersonal economy puts into question the ability of individuals to structure their identity and destiny through straightforward self-narration and marks a revision of the confident individualism of *Robinson Crusoe, Moll Flanders, La Vie de Marianne, Le paysan parvenu,* or even *Pamela.* The collapse of such individualism is the theme of the first part of *Clarissa* in particular, although it informs the stories of the heroine's antagonists up to their demise. In the second half of the novel, however, following Clarissa's rape, a new paradigm of self-expression will emerge in conjunction with the heroine's story – a paradigm which will turn the dialogical and collective constraints on self-expression into a positive strategy for imposing one's story on history.

The inadequacy of a simple, individualistic notion of narration, and hence a unified concept of the self, is figured from the outset by *Clarissa*'s narrative format. Framing his story in what he calls "a double yet separate correspondence: between two young ladies of virtue and honour, . . . and between two gentlemen of free lives" (p. 35),[1] Richardson encloses self-construction within an ongoing dialogical exchange with an indispensable interlocutor. This grounding of the story in a system of reciprocal correspondence emphasizes the narrating self's contingency on the active, co-authoring or interpretive gesture of an interlocutor or narratee.[2] At the same time, Richardson's novel distributes the central narrational function between several characters, rather than a single protagonist, thus departing from the unified vision of earlier novelists that underwrote, consciously or not, the association of narrational fluency and self-definition with a single moral stance. While the central figure of the novel is undoubtedly Clarissa, the craft of narration as a means of constructing reality and altering history finds clearer exemplification in her antagonist Robert Lovelace. His tirelessly ingenious contrivances to spirit Clarissa away from her family, convince her of impending danger from her brother, placate her with false news, encourage her with staged conversations performed by hired impostors, and terrify her into helplessness with faked disasters, quite literally construct an alternate, fictional history to ensnare his victim. He thus realizes a possibility that has hovered in the background since Robinson Crusoe's use of fiction to deceive visitors or Roxana's elaborate lies, but which receives explicit articulation for the first time in Richardson's writing: his goal is not to construct an identity for himself which he will then assume, but, like Mr B. (prior to his reform), to elaborate a destiny for *another* person, the consequences of which will be born by that victim and not by himself.

Lovelace's gesture of detached manipulation incarnates the extreme claims of narrational power to which an exaggerated confidence in one's ability to shape not just one's own history but that of others can lead. Similar excessive agendas of historical mastery will persist for the remainder of the century in the works of Diderot, Fielding, and Laclos, finding their culmination and clearest philosophical enunciation in the works of de Sade. Characters such as Mme de la Pommeraye, Blifil, Valmont or Merteuil all share the delusion that one can master the narrative transaction, and they all repress the increasingly evident dialogical and dialectical underpinnings of story and history. Their compulsion seems at once progressive, in that it seeks to push the use of narration as a form of power to its logical limit, and reactionary, in that they attempt to retain the advantages of a refined grasp of narrative logic while repressing the limitations implicit in their own model. Their persistence in the later novels as a negative impulse that is emphatically quashed functions within the genre's strategy of self-defense as a demonstration that one-sided authority, narrative tyranny, and mastery of the cultural grammar are practical impossibilities. Richardson inaugurates this tradition with the subplot of Lovelace's self-destruction, which dramatizes the mitigation of personal initiative by the informing matrix of cultural scripts and the collective practice of competing narration within which it occurs.

If the excess personified by Lovelace is that of the fabulating self as detached coercion, Clarissa prefigures the inverse relationship of individual to history – at least in the first half of the novel. The vision of historical passivity she espouses prior to her rape gestures nostalgically toward the tradition of spiritual autobiography by stubbornly denying the self's responsibility for the ordering of the world. Although she is willing to admit that the machinations of Lovelace and her siblings may alter the perception others have of her motives, she declines to read this as evidence that history and reality itself may hinge on careful arrangement or self-interested interpretation. More specifically, she rejects the agency of her own narrational/ interpretive mediation in the production of her story.

Critics are divided on whether Clarissa is an inept narrator, clinging to an obsolete notion of a natural world in which language reflects reality, or a crafty narrator wielding the subtle arm of a narrative that passes itself off as "neutral, objective, and truthful,"[3] but there seems to be general agreement that whatever one's judgment of her awareness and mastery of language, she is loath to acknowledge the very mediation or agency in which Lovelace glories. The latter revels in thinking himself the sole author of reality, the God-like "name-father": "Preferments I bestow, both military and civil. I give estates, and take them away at my pleasure. Quality too I create. And by a still more valuable prerogative, I *degrade* by virtue of my own imperial will, without any other act of forfeiture than my own convenience. What a poor thing is a monarch to me!" (p. 569, L174.2). Clarissa, by contrast, though just as desirous of seeing her own version of the story triumph, adheres to the doctrine of a world order without a mortal author, a narrative, in the terms of my argument, with no narration – a state of nature bearing no trace of the ego's intervention. She desires vindication and inscription on her own terms within the larger collective narrative, but she does not want that story to be merely the result of narrational "art." One might say that prior to her rape, Clarissa does not grasp – or, depending on one's reading, cunningly represses, for strategic purposes – the mechanisms of history; she wants the place of honor in the collective account but is both unwilling to accept that account as the product of mere narration and, consequently, unable to assume her share of responsibility for shaping it in a way that would benefit her case.

Thus the episodes leading up to the rape scene – which pit her first against her family and then Lovelace, who abducts and sequesters her under the guise of saving her from marriage to an avaricious dolt – oppose the rake's and the family's ferocious manipulation of reality to Clarissa's persistent belief in an unmediated world. On the one side, monsters of *narration* promote themselves through the invention of history; on the other, their victim clings to the chimera of a selfless *narrative*, an agentless history that reflects immutable truths. The novel's most dramatic sections pivot on this juxtaposition of two extremes of the narrative equation. At one extreme, the superior individual exalts in his fabrication of reality and appropriates for selfish narration the authority of history. At the other extreme, selfless virtue declines any responsibility for the shape of the world that encloses her, promoting instead a vision of history as that which simply *is*. Each of these perspectives inverts the other's excess in a similar attempt to maintain a one-sided notion of the individual story's relationship to the community's history. Yet the disastrous outcome to which they lead argues persuasively for an alternate approach that would incorporate both individual scheme and impersonal design in a productive dialectical relationship: Clarissa succumbs to Lovelace because she does not recognize – in both the literal and diplomatic senses of the word – the essential place of individual art in collective reality; Lovelace loses control of his art when he fails to recognize the extent to which "his" plot is being dictated by a larger agentless text – that of his culture, with its conventions of seduction, its grammars of contrivance. The debacle of the rape, which marks the failure of each to win over the other, as well as the undoing of the Harlowe family ambitions, confirms the inadequacy of their respective programs.

The collapse of the various plots and non-plots in the first half of the book will usher in a new strategy in the second half, where the heroine, eschewing both exaggerated self-promotion or contrivance *and* total self-effacement, devises a new means of constituting the self within and through history. Assigning to her new friend, Belford, the major burden of narrating her story, Clarissa retreats to the position of a formal author, ultimately being displaced in the world of her readers by the text of her misfortunes. As Lovelace, Clarissa's family, and her friends are gradually apprenticed to the tasks and functions of the reader, the project of self-identification slides from the arena of interpersonal relationship to that of cultural institution, in the guise of the literary work. This shift builds on, and requires for its comprehension, a prior demonstration of the flaws inherent in Clarissa's and Lovelace's "one-sided" approaches to narration and narrative. Such is the function of the first half of *Clarissa*, which is distributed evenly between Clarissa's voice, dominating the initial sections of the novel, and Lovelace's, which progressively stifles hers as his plots close in around her. Like a play in two acts separated by a central scene of violence, the novel first poses a dilemma and dramatizes its insolubility, by showing how each character's attitude towards language, truth, authority, and the individual's relationship to society is pitted against and eventually undone by that of the other. Then, out of this debacle of reciprocal disaster, on the far side of desperation, the heroine fashions a solution and effects a transcendence.

To Outwit and Impel[4]

Lovelace provides a test case of individual fabulation, an exploration of the extent to which an inventive individual can shape history through his story. To seduce Clarissa, he orchestrates a fictional version of outside reality, complete with invented places, characters, and events. Some of his elaborate fictions, such as Mrs Fretchville, the landlady he creates, then has fall victim to small-pox, require only a bit of fraudulent correspondence, while others, such as the illness he brings on by taking some ipecacuanha, involve elaborate staging and preparation. His most extravagant contrivances, such as the extended negotiations with "Captain Tomlinson," purported to represent the interests of Clarissa's uncle, call for in-the-flesh appearances by fictitious characters, and Lovelace accordingly hires actors and provides them with a script. Others, such as the "fire" he stages, require the services of an entire cast and even some rehearsals – as when he coaches his two female accomplices on how best to play the roles of the ladies of quality (Lovelace's own relatives) they are to impersonate.

The superficial end of all of these contrivances is to entrap Clarissa: to discourage her attempts to escape by convincing her of lurking danger, while at the same time entangling her in a meticulously plotted sequence of postponed marriage and new hopes for reconciliation with her family, all of which is designed to wear down her resistance to Lovelace's advances. At the same time, Lovelace makes abundantly clear that the physical possession of Clarissa is of little interest to him in comparison to the thrill of plotting:

– *Preparation* and *expectation* are, in a manner, everything: *reflection*, indeed, may be something, if the mind be hardened above feeling the guilt of a past *trespass*: but the *fruition*, what is there in that? (P. 163, L34)

– More truly delightful to me the seduction progress than the crowning act – for that's a vapour, a bubble! (P. 616, L193)

Not only is the process of fabulation a source of pleasure in and of itself – "so much delight do I take in my contrivances, that I shall be half sorry when the occasion for them is over; for never, never shall I again have such charming exercise for my invention" (p. 674, L209) – it constitutes Lovelace's very identity, his superiority over other people and his sense of self: "there is nothing on which I value myself so much as upon my *inventions*" (p. 447, L117). As he laments to Belford, "if I give up my contrivances, my joy in stratagem, and plot, and invention, I shall be but a common man" (p. 907, L264). Plotting for him is the natural activity of an aristocratic mind accustomed to having a say in the destiny of its social inferiors; it is the medium of his control and the confirmation of his privilege.

Lovelace goes to great pains to make clear for Belford to what extent not only Clarissa, but her entire family, are his pawns. Long before he succeeds in tricking Clarissa to flee her home, he already boasts of his manipulation of the Harlowes (pp. 144–5, L31), and subsequent to Clarissa's abduction, he will reiterate his claim:

I knew that the whole stupid family were in a combination to do my business for me. I told thee that they were all working for me, like so many underground moles; and still more blind than the moles are said to be, unknowing that they did so. I myself, the director of their principal motions; which falling in with the malice of their little hearts, they took to be all their own. (P. 387, L97)

The import of this claim only becomes clear in a subsequent passage where Lovelace combines his boast with a passage characterizing his own activity in similar subterranean terms:

Here have I been at work, dig, dig, dig, like a cunning miner at one time, and spreading my snares like an artful fowler at another, and exulting in my contrivances to get this inimitable creature absolutely into my power. Everything made for me – Her brother and uncle were but my pioneers: her father stormed as I directed him to storm. Mrs Howe was acted by the springs I set at work: her daughter was moving for me, and yet imagined herself plumb against me: and the dear creature herself had already run her stubborn neck into my gin, and knew not that she was caught (P. 517, L152)

As the images of the mole and miner reveal, Lovelace's activity and that of his adversaries are but one: he undermines their plans through their own actions. Because he orchestrates their responses through the stories he spreads – such as the rumor that he is going to storm Harlowe Place – he literally expresses his will in the person of the Other.[5] While he clearly takes pride in the dashing bravado of his own person, his individuality finds its most elegant expression and fulfillment in the gestures of other individuals he manipulates. Like an author of realist fiction, he delights in producing a world that answers his will while maintaining the illusion of being an autonomous order.

Along the same lines, it is worth noting the adjectives Lovelace uses to describe himself in the passage cited above. Unlike his "stupid," "blind" opponents, he relies on cunning and *art*. One of Clarissa's repeated criticisms of Lovelace, and the trait she inevitably chooses to distinguish her own sincere discourse from his deceit, is that of artfulness. Yet for Lovelace, this is no reproach at all; for *all* people, even those most sincere, are so in his view only out of artfulness. Reality, like character and event, are for Lovelace purely linguistic constructs. Quoting a seventeenth-century drama, he quips: "He who seems virtuous does but act a part, / And shows not his own nature, but his art" (p. 143, L31). Lovelace's art differs from that of other people only in its refinement and its self-awareness. He does not hesitate to pursue his beliefs to their logical conclusion, as in the passage cited, and subordinate the characters and acts of "real" individuals to the same premises of artful invention that underlie his "fictional" creations – indeed, his manner of referring to both is nearly identical, the actions of characters like "Mrs Fretchville" and "Captain Tomlinson" being related as though they actually existed.

To assume that all behavior is cunning is to make of human interaction a game, and that is precisely what Lovelace does, especially in his exchanges with Clarissa.[6] Just as games imply rules, when Lovelace recounts his moves to his confidant, he has a tendency to present them as the product of principles or maxims, ranging from the outrageous, oft-repeated "once subdued always subdued," or personal rules of procedure ("In all *doubtable* matters the *minutiae* closely attended to and provided for are of more service than a thousand oaths, vows and protestations made to supply the neglect of them" p. 473, L131), to broader generalizations about human behavior upon which the rake can fine-tune his strategy: "– Now women, Jack, like not novices. They are pleased with a love of the sex that is founded in the knowledge of it. Reason good. Novices expect more than they can possibly find in the commerce with them" (p. 802, L236). The latter type of observation reiterates a tendency toward moral generalizations that can be found as well in the novels of Defoe and Marivaux, but in *Clarissa* they surface in a program of unabashed manipulation. With the normalization of narrative deceit and "artful" personalities, such maxims fill the function of a general grammar of social behavior, the explicit mastery of which will be advanced as the means to power.[7]

One of Lovelace's other principles – "never to ruin a poor girl whose simplicity and innocence was all she had to trust to" (p. 162, L34) – indicates another aspect of the game of narration: glory is proportionate to the stature and skill of the opponent. If Lovelace is so drawn to Clarissa it is because she appears to him a worthy opponent, whose defeat will assure him prestige:

> my triumph, when completed, will be so glorious a one, that I shall never be able to keep up to it. All my future attempts must be poor to this. I shall be as unhappy after a while, from my reflections upon this conquest, as Don John of Austria was, in his, on the renowned victory of Lepanto, when he found that none of his future achievements could keep pace with his early glory. (P. 559, L171)

Obviously, such a vision of epic grandeur assumes an opponent worthy of Lovelace's attentions. Thus he justifies his own progressively ruthless tactics on the assumption that Clarissa is just as artful: "– Well do *thy* arts justify *mine*; and encourage me to let loose my plotting genius upon thee" (p. 425, L109). However, his overblown expression of conquest reveals a vulnerability peculiar to the notion of self-as-competitor. Critics have stressed the freedoms Lovelace takes with conventions of language and social interaction, but his postulation of reality-constructing as a game between equally artful opponents encloses him in a structure of dialogic dependency that compromises this independence: he needs an adversary to express his individuality; his selfhood is bound up in a structure of competition. And like a master chess player faced with an anarchic child who moves the pieces randomly, he finds himself locked in competition with an opponent he cannot beat. For Clarissa does not understand the game – or even acknowledge that it is a game. She cannot sanction Lovelace's expertise because she is not privy to the complexity of his virtuoso manipulation, and *were* she privy to it, she would not applaud it.

From the outset, then, Lovelace is imprisoned in a contest he cannot really win. For victory, like seduction, occurs by way of a conventionalized plot, an essential component of which is that moment when the vanquished adversary acknowledges the superiority of his or her opponent – the end of the match when the competitors shake hands and thus commit to history the record of their triumph or defeat. Such a moment is essential to Lovelace's endeavor, and it is hopefully prefigured in his optimistic cant "once subdued, always subdued." The rake counts on his victim's cheerful acknowledgement of defeat, as well as her future submission to his whims – and preference for his company – in deference to his demonstrated prowess in the game of love. Thus Lovelace's former conquests, the girls at "Mrs Sinclair's," eagerly serve him in his assault on Clarissa in the hopes of both garnering his favor and extending the glory of the man they have acknowledged as their master.

Of course such ultimate compensation comes only once the game is over, and Lovelace, like any competitor, depends on an intermediate, provisional accolade during the course of his struggle, in the person of the applauding spectator. This is the function of Belford, who is not simply a blank slate upon which the rake can record his deeds, but the public whose acclaim he requires for his sense of accomplishment. However, Belford's growing reticence to praise his friend consigns Lovelace to an increasingly isolated, monological plight. Belford senses almost from the outset that where the two contestants are not playing by the same rules, there can be no triumph in winning – "what glory, what cause of triumph wilt thou have, if she should be overcome?" (p. 501, L143) – and he stresses that his forewarnings are for Lovelace's sake, not just Clarissa's: "all that I have written is more in thy behalf than in hers – since she may make *thee* happy – But it is next to impossible . . . that thou canst make *her* so" (p. 502).

Even discounting moral compunction, Lovelace has good reason for caution. His companion's final admonition in the same letter is not simply an expression of disapproval; it resonates with a familiarity that should alarm the rake: "consider well what thou art about, before thou goest a step farther in the path which thou hast chalked out for thyself to tread, and art just going to enter into" (p. 503). Were Lovelace the perceptive genius he thinks himself to be, he would realize that Belford can only speak with such certainty about what his friend "is about" because he knows the end of the story. He recognizes in Lovelace's clever scenario a familiar plot line that is already inscribed in their culture, which has, in that sense, already *taken into account* the rake's moves and digested its patterns. Within this larger matrix, Lovelace's tale of seduction is but one thread in a vaster narrative; its meaning is not fixed but variable, according to the context of analysis; but its sequence is stereotyped. As Belford brutally puts it: "thou that vainly imaginest that the whole family of the Harlowes, and that of the Howes too, are but thy machines . . . what art thou more or better than the instrument even of her implacable brother and envious sister, to perpetuate the disgrace of the most excellent of sisters, which they are moved to by vilely low and sordid motives?" (p. 604, L189).

Like any individual Lovelace only has limited purchase on the larger text of culture within which his quest is encoded; he cannot hold final authority over his game. Like all players or tellers of tales, he is regulated by rules he does not write; his goals and character are inscribed within the collective narrative of his period. What he takes for original stratagems are merely variations upon conventional possibilities, refinements of plots made possible by the deeper logic of seduction resident in his culture – a logic Lovelace invoked at the very instant he inscribed his behavior within the paradigm of "the rake" and tailored it according to the social and sexual commonplaces of his epoch.

In short, Lovelace's plot is one whose turns are well worn and whose characters leave little room for improvization. He cannot renounce his project without relinquishing his title of champion rake: "if I should [marry Clarissa], Jack ... what a figure shall I make in rakish annals?" (p. 846, L246). Having qualified himself as greatest of the "mad fellows as are above all law, and scorn to skulk behind the hypocritical screen of reputation" (p. 419, L106), he finds himself bound by the laws of libertinage. Gradually it dawns on him that his plot is directing him: "Oh Belford, Belford, how have I puzzled myself as well as her! – This cursed aversion to wedlock how has it entangled me!" (p. 734, L227); "What will be the issue of all my plots and contrivances, devil take me if I am able to divine!" (p. 820, L243). As his frustration and regret grow, he increasingly frames his conduct in terms of the very social commonplaces he formerly purported to transcend, acknowledging that he is the agent of his narrative and his culture as well as its author, its subject in the political and thematic senses of the word as well as the phenomenological:[8]

> As to the manner of endeavouring to obtain her, by falsification of oaths, vows, and the like – do not the poets of two thousand years and upwards tell us that Jupiter laughs at the perjuries of lovers? And let me add to what I have heretofore mentioned on that head a question or two.
>
> Do not the mothers, the aunts, the grandmothers, the governesses of the pretty innocents, always, from their very cradles to riper years, preach to them the deceitfulness of men? – That they are not to regard their oaths, vows, promises? – What a parcel of fibbers would all these reverend matrons be, if there were not now and then a pretty credulous rogue taken in for a justification of their preachments, and to serve as a beacon lighted up for the benefit of the rest? (P. 847, L246)

From writer of history, Lovelace has become its pawn; his story is no longer his, but that of many men; the narrator has been ensnared in his narrative; its thrust and direction, answering to the logic of the social categories he has invoked, do not merely represent him, they manipulate him as well. In other words, the nominal author has become a character in his own fiction, a fiction that reflects, beyond its maker's will, the logic of a fantasy intrinsic to his culture: that of the male as absolute master.[9]

This loss of self to a narrative that even its author cannot reign in finds striking dramatization in Lovelace's allegory of his conscience who, seizing his pen in the course of the above meditation, expresses herself in these words:

"But let me reflect, before it be too late. On the manifold perfections of this ever-admirable creature, let me reflect. The hand yet is only held up. The blow is not struck....

"Yet already have I not gone too far? Like a repentant thief, afraid of his gang and obliged to go on in fear of hanging till he comes to be hanged, I am afraid of the gang of my cursed contrivances.

"As I hope to live, I am sorry at the present writing, that I have been such a foolish plotter as to put it, as I fear I have done, out of my *own power* to be honest. I hate compulsion in all forms; and cannot bear, even to be *compelled* to be the wretch my choice has made me! – So now, Belford, as thou hast said, I am a machine at last, and no free agent.

"Upon my soul, Jack, it is a very foolish thing for a man of spirit to have brought himself to such a height of iniquity, that he must proceed, and cannot help himself; and yet to be next to certain that his very victory will undo him. (P. 848, L246)

Of course Lovelace *does* proceed, and his "victory" does undo him, by the very laws of his own game. Censored by his only audience, unable to get his adversary to acknowledge his expertise and accept his rules, driven on solely by the lock-step progression of a scenario he cannot elude, he moves joylessly toward rape, aware that by this single move of brute stupidity he will not only disqualify himself from the game but undercut its claims, demonstrating that mastery has less to do with cunning than with simple bestial force: "*Abhorred be force! – be the thoughts of force! There's no triumph over the will in force!*" (p. 879, L256).[10] Thus ends his campaign of narrational mastery, and subsequent to the rape his voice will progressively fade and disappear. To understand why he never succeeded in recruiting Clarissa to his contest of manipulation, we must backtrack and consider *her* program during this period and the versions of reality, identity, and narrational art it predicates.

A Person out of her Own Direction[11]

Clarissa's notion of the relationship between reality and her narrative is considerably more difficult to grasp than that of Lovelace, not only because her "'representational' model of truth, which abstracts truth from its strategic contexts,"[12] is closer to the way we assume language works and thus less glaringly evident than Lovelace's contrivances, but also because her relationship to her identity and story evolve during the course of the novel. Abandoning her intransigent belief in natural language once she has been raped and her reputation and destiny sullied, she will develop out of the story of her ruin a positive means of managing her eventual history. The two pre-rape conflicts, which pit her against two different adversaries and tactics, serve only as preliminary contests that underscore the two sides of the story/history equation and the excesses to which they can lead. The first contest between these two divergent and equally deficient stances centers on the demand of Clarissa's family that she marry Solmes, the repulsive suitor, and her subsequent isolation and sequestration. Aside from a few letters and a surprise interview in the garden, Lovelace exists during this part of the book primarily as a topic of conversation – the subject of the stories recounted by Clarissa, her family, and Anna Howe, her best friend and primary correspondent. The second struggle, which commences once she is tricked into fleeing her home, reverses this situation: Lovelace, rather than her father, becomes her prison keeper, and her family persists only through rare correspondence or second-hand reports.

Because these two subplots display an inverted symmetry, it is tempting to think of them as opposed to one another – contrastive or complementary perspectives within a common framework. Indeed, each party, the family on the one hand and Lovelace on the other, seems prone to a different bias as regards the issue of individualism and collective values. Clarissa's family aligns itself with institutional authority and the community; Lovelace professes contempt for that authority. On the one side, collective interest pre-empts the individual's right to participate in her destiny; on the other, individual fabulation asserts its manipulation of collective interest. Yet a number of structural similarities, and most especially Clarissa's own consistently aversive reactions, undermine this neat dichotomy and show the extent to which both attitudes rely on a similar distortion of the complex relationship of individual narration to collective narrative.

Although Clarissa's argument with her family does not at first glance resemble her relationship with Lovelace, her adversaries in both cases rely on a similar strategy: they subordinate reality, history, and authority to self-interest, fashioning a world and law that serves their personal ends. Within this perspective, there is little room for any negotiation; the text of reality either conforms to the individual's ambitions or not. It is at this point that Lovelace diverges from Clarissa's family; for while he readily admits his pretention to historical authority and revels in the glory that his manipulation of reality procures, Clarissa's family hides behind the screen of shared beliefs and pleads the righteous defense of commonly held convictions. In their actions, both of the heroine's opponents deny the notion of reality as a shared story that individuals inherit with their culture and redefine in negotiation with their peers over time; they demonstrate through their deeds the belief that narration is everything, history is but a naive name for story. However, only Lovelace will have the courage to articulate and defend this position openly. Clarissa, on the other hand, promotes an equally extreme vision of the world as impersonal, unchanging order, predicated by divine ordinance and immune to personal reconfiguration. For her, reality is not the product of individual schemes but the enduring frame of reference against which individuals can measure themselves. As that which is beyond dispute, history is not collectively negotiated story, much less the residue of personal ambition, but the record of the unchangeable.

While Lovelace glorifies personal invention, Clarissa's relatives take the opposed stance, exalting the collective values of honor, family name, and the authority of the father over the individual initiative of the daughter. Refusing to concede the agency of their own personal ambition or spite behind such categories, they foist on Clarissa a notion of selfhood entirely bound up within the vested power structure, a scenario dictated by the larger story of the Harlowes' rise to prominence – and, further back, the ascendance of the bourgeoisie in general. However, much in the same way that Lovelace's highly vaunted practice of unbridled invention must answer to a restrictive grammar he cannot subvert, the Harlowes' exaltation of collective interest conceals an agenda of self-glorification and narrational manipulation. The heroine understands this, and since she *also* claims to represent the collective account, she does not hesitate to point out that, as regards her problems, "all was owing to the instigations of a brother and sister, wholly actuated by selfish and envious views" (p. 110, L20). The schemes of her siblings not only foreshadow Lovelace's invention of history by redefining Solmes as an honorable man but, in their ensnarement of Mr Harlowe, prefigure the rake's strategy of "execution through the other." By convincing their father that Clarissa's resistance to their plans is in fact a challenge to parental authority, they make him the agent of their plot – a move Clarissa is quick to point out: "and now my brother has engaged my father, his fine scheme will *walk alone* without needing his leading-strings; and it is become my father's will that I oppose, not my brother's grasping views" (p. 96, L17).

Unlike Lovelace, Clarissa's siblings promote their interests with a minimum of personal intervention, under the guise of collective law. Yet Clarissa does not bow before this law, because she knows it is cited fraudulently by her opponents: her father's pig-headed rage, like the cowering avarice of Solmes or the rabid envy of her brother, has little in common with the code of family authority *she* respects, and she will not sacrifice her own happiness to this travesty. As she remarks to her epistolary Other, Anna, "surely, my dear, I should not give up to my brother's ambition the happiness of my future life – Surely I ought not to be the instrument to deprive Mr Solmes's relations of their natural rights and reversionary prospects, for the sake of further aggrandizing a family . . . which already lives in great affluence and splendour" (p. 105, L19).

The refusal to sanction her family's decision confirms a pattern we have seen developing from *La Vie de Marianne* and *Le paysan parvenu* through *Pamela*, where the protagonists successfully contest the authority of their adversaries by rejecting the latter's "authoritative" interpretation of events. In *Clarissa* the views of an entire collective are thwarted by a single determined rebel, demonstrating the degree to which an articulate, independent narratee can discredit even the most widely underwritten fictions. This increased emphasis on the interdependence of collective account and personal interpretation is in line with the emerging evidence of both the dialogical structure of narration and the less obvious *dialectical* relationship of individual narrational act to shared narrative text. The first of these notions most visibly informs the struggle between Clarissa, Lovelace, and the family in the first half of the novel, while the latter emerges subsequent to the rape in Clarissa's translation of her self into a quasi-literary cultural text.

That the heroine succeeds in stalling her family's agenda and resisting Lovelace's plots confirms first and foremost the emerging dialogical conceptualization of stories – whether oral or written, "fictional" or "historical." Reality, like any account, is always fashioned within a system of exchange and reciprocal validation that links narrator to narratee – or more precisely, lest we associate the active role of structuring with only one member of the dialogue, the *functions* of narrator and narratee. The narrative or structure of reality that results from the constant articulation and acknowledgment of experience forms a middle ground which is stable, to the extent that both parties are satisfied with its shape, and textual, to the extent that it is stable and available to both parties as the product of their activity. When the reader or narratee of an account sanctions the activity of its writer or narrator by acknowledging and understanding the account, he or she promotes it to the status of accepted fact. Even if it is only a *literary* fact, that is, recognized as a valid member of the class of texts we call fiction, it nonetheless enters history and is assimilated to the text of reality informing further reading and writing: the text is henceforth assumed to represent an existing cultural category, and its author is promoted to the rank of author.

The reciprocal aspect of narration is present in earlier novels, but not problematized. The narrating protagonists of Chasles, Defoe, Marivaux, or even Prévost, seldom encounter significant resistance to their accounts, and they are the sole authors of their narratives. *Clarissa's* extension of narration to society in general complicates this pattern by insisting on the suspension of identity and reality between the two poles of transmission and reception. In *Clarissa* even more than in *Pamela*, construals of fact depend on a reading act; one can only be assured of getting one's point across to the extent that one is assured of a reader or interlocutor at least minimally willing to cooperate. And every author or narrator is also a reader, divided between the gesture of proposing and that of validating proposals. Clarissa observes that "were we perfect, which no one can be, we could not be happy in this life, unless those with whom we have to deal (those, more especially, who have any control on us) were governed by the same principles" (p. 106, L19). That is why the family's endeavor to compel Clarissa is no more successful than hers to persuade them. The same can be said of her attempt to reform Lovelace, or his to possess her: in a world where narration is commonplace and its mechanisms widely known, the prerogatives of the narratee or reader become cultural reflex. To disable a story, one need only refuse to listen to it – or better still, one can oppose or confuse it with a conflicting account more in accord with the narrative norms of society and thus more likely to elicit belief. Of course, in so doing, one also deprives oneself of a potential narrative partner, which in turn weakens the transactional circuit grounding one's own identity. Thus even though the scope and import of narration expand with its redefinition as dialogical exchange, that same paradigm precludes any "singlehanded" manipulation of history. It is possible to read the entire sequence of events up to the rape in this light.

Clarissa's brother and sister, for example, specifically tailor their strategy to disrupt the normal dialogical circuit uniting Clarissa and her family. To deprive their rival of any public, they succeed in getting her locked in her room, forbidden to speak to her parents and prevented from corresponding with anyone. This effectively allows them to discredit her intentions and, as she puts it, "put what interpretation they please on my conduct" (p. 106, L19). Unable to speak or write to her parents, Clarissa cannot contest her siblings' versions of events; they can structure her story as they wish, functioning simultaneously, in her words, as "the authors of my disgrace within doors, the talkers of my prepossession without, and the reporters of it from abroad" (p. 108, L20). She will later accuse her brother directly: "you may congratulate yourself on having *so far* succeeded in all your views, that you may report what you please of me, and I can no more defend myself, than if I were dead" (p. 121, L24.2). Deprived of a public for her version of things, she is powerless to structure her destiny. But by the same token, her family's exclusion of her deprives *them* of her complicity: because they will not speak with her, they have no chance of *realizing* their project. She writes to her uncle John "if deaf-eared anger will neither grant *me* a hearing, nor *what I write* a perusal, some time hence the hard-heartedness may be regretted" (p. 252, L59), and it is clear that her decision to flee with Lovelace is to a large degree motivated by the latter's receptive attitude: he not only listens to Clarissa when no one else will, he exalts her "*free* choice" and "*unbiased* favour" in selecting a husband (p. 170, L36) and "promises compliance in every article with my will: approves of all I propose" (p. 356, L88). By refusing to enter into narrative negotiation with Clarissa, her parents foreclose on their own version of reality; by making her dependent entirely on their enemy for the answering voice that grounds her sense of self, they unwittingly advance Lovelace's case. As her identity becomes more heavily invested in the exchange with the rake, she becomes less their daughter and more his lover.

Needless to say, once in Lovelace's clutches, Clarissa finds herself facing an even more devious opponent. Like her brother and sister, Lovelace attempts to block his adversary's activity of self-definition by short-circuiting the dialogical exchanges necessary for that work. Secure in his own relationship with Belford, he disables Clarissa not simply by suppressing her voice but by appropriating and confusing it. Where her family tries to subdue her through simple isolation, Lovelace also dissipates her energy through art, engaging her in an endless dialogue that exhausts without advancing, because her partner continually misleads her. His hope is that by incorporating the objections of his victim into his own agenda and stealing her plot line, as it were, he can blur her sense of the distinction between their two visions. By appropriating her story into his own, he hopes to maintain his supremacy as sole arbiter of reality.

Of course, Clarissa has intimations of this tactic: from her initial encounter with him and throughout their co-habitation, she expresses repeated misgivings about his sincerity. But lacking any context for comparison – any alternative audience – she must rely on him. As she becomes increasingly dependent on him as the sounding board for her own self-expression, she falls ever more certainly, as she frequently says, "in his power."[13] The dialogical nature of narration necessarily inscribes the schemer – even the most virtuous and unwilling schemer – within a structure of mutual dependence *vis-à-vis* her public. Dependent on an interlocutor determined to misconstrue everything she says, Clarissa can never get her narrative on firm ground, so to speak. By the same logic, however, Clarissa's wariness, which increases with Lovelace's growing arrogance, forecloses on *his* victory: having raised her suspicions, he has alienated her cooperation and lessened his own influence. His ultimate recourse to brute force – which mirrors the Harlowes' imprisonment of Clarissa – marks the failure of his own narrational agenda.

It remains to explain why, given that (1) Clarissa and Lovelace are attracted to each other, (2) Clarissa has ample time, once abducted, to engage Lovelace in dialogue, and (3) she is reputed to be particularly gifted in the art of persuading, she nevertheless cannot mollify Lovelace and dissuade him from his plans.[14] If her wariness *vis-à-vis* his constructions of reality explains her refusal to yield to him, his belief in her virtue and confidence in his own narrational superiority should lead him to a sense of victory and a relinquishment of his plans. If this never occurs, it is because of the peculiar incompatibility of Clarissa's attitude toward language and his own. Lovelace's program of manipulation and staging obviously leaves little room for sharing authority, but Clarissa's approach to narration is less tolerant still, if only because it denies the possibility of any narrational agency in the production of history.

Much has been made of the heroine's pretention to neutral narration in the second letter of the novel: "I will recite facts only, and leave you to judge of the truth of the report raised that the younger sister has robbed the elder" (p. 41, L2).[15] Whether or not one assumes her treatment of her siblings to be impartial – and even *she* owns that it is not[16] – her self-presentation presupposes a factual historical record that can speak for itself. "Facts" enjoy their special status because they are undisputed, and if they are facts about people or events, they are recorded as History – which is but the compendium of the stories everyone agrees on. Accordingly, part of Clarissa's strategy, when taxed with disobedience and commanded to marry Solmes, is to cite past history as proof of her merit (and evidence that her parents are behaving aberrantly):

> I did not know, I said, that I had given occasion for this harshness; I hoped I should always have a just sense of their favour to me, superadded to the duty I owed as a daughter and a niece; but that I was so much surprised at a reception so unusual and unexpected that I hoped my papa and mamma would give me leave to retire in order to recollect myself. (P. 60, L7)

In her subsequent exchanges with her mother, this will be a theme to which she returns:

> I have not, I hope, made myself so *very* unuseful in my papa's family, as – (P. 94, L17)

> I said, I hoped I had so behaved myself hitherto that there was no need of such a trial of my obedience as this. (P. 95, L17)

> I told her, I was sorry that I had had so little merit as to have made no deeper impressions of favour for me in their hearts; but that I would love and honour them as long as I lived. (P. 108, L20)

> I ever valued myself upon my sincerity: and once, indeed, had the happiness to be valued for it. (P. 314, L78)

Clarissa's plea to her mother, "But let *my* actions, not *their* misrepresentations . . . speak for me," (p. 93, L16) concisely sums up her attitude. In her mind, identity and virtue cannot, *must* not, derive from mere chatter; they find their guarantee in a higher scripture of facts that is not merely the narrative residue of another person's schemes or the interpretive squabbles of the community, but rather the simple, unalterable transcription of that which is.

In conjunction with this vision of historic immutability, the heroine portrays herself as a pawn in a larger design, a player neither responsible for her plight nor empowered to alter it:

> whatever course I shall be *permitted* or be *forced* to steer, I must be considered as a person out of her own direction. Tossed to and fro by the high winds of passionate control, and, as I think, unreasonable severity ... (Pp. 280–1, L69)

> How I am driven to and fro, like a feather in the wind, at the pleasure of the rash, the selfish and the headstrong! ... and between them, I have not an option ... What a perverse fate is mine! (Pp. 328–9, L80)

Such images of historical impotence reiterate Clarissa's assumption that her behavior is a simple consequence of other people's initiatives, rather than a freely chosen path of action: "this vehemence on my side is but the natural consequence of the usage I have met with" (p. 307, L78). This argument not only exonerates the heroine of responsibility for her predicament and actions, but allows her to maintain her alignment with the discourse of virtue: after all, if she deviates from the path, it is only in natural reaction to her vicious opponent's unnatural treatment of her. Increasingly, she will take refuge in the role of "a young creature, who by her evil destiny is thrown into his [Lovelace's] power" (p. 589, L184). The moral advantages that go with such a stance are double: Clarissa is not only better than her opponents because her conduct mirrors the script of virtue, she is better because she does not engage in the despicable practice of narrational art.

Unfortunately, such righteousness does not wash well with her partners in dialogue, since all of their endeavors to defend themselves only make them appear more artful and more despicable. Not surprisingly, they regard Clarissa's stance as just another, particularly devious, narrational strategy. True innocence, as embodied, for instance, in little Rosebud, the poor peasant virgin that Lovelace takes under his protection, neither voices its difference nor excites rivalry, whereas Clarissa's insufferable contention that she is above artifice conflicts only too obviously with the efficacity of her discourse, simultaneously aggravating her enemies' jealousy and pride.

More important though, is the way Clarissa's attitude disables the whole process of mutual history-making. Truthfulness, purity, and virtue are useful at the level of fiction or literature, where their perfection can function as an ideal to be emulated, rather than a pose to be exposed, but when such absolutes are claimed by one member of the narrational circuit, they paralyze the system of reciprocal determination by denying narrative agency in the fashioning of truth and history. This explains both Lovelace's and Clarissa's inability, prior to the rape, to gain the upper hand. Lovelace can never win Clarissa's respect because her world view precludes admiring his cleverness or accepting his mastery. At the same time, Clarissa's allegiance to the script of passive virtue prevents her from mastering her own fate – taking any of the steps that would insulate her from Lovelace's schemes or hasten their marriage.[17] Only after the brutality of the rape, which irrevocably severs her plot line from that of the "virtuous daughter" and thereby simultaneously asserts the susceptibility of history to human intervention, will Clarissa take her fate into her own hands. Permanently excluded from the story she once thought was her own, she will reassess the structure of history in general and take over the active management of her history in particular.

The fragmentary, only partially coherent ramblings of Clarissa following her violation testify to this profound realignment of her relationship to her own story and reality. Recognizing that her reliance on artless virtue laid the groundwork for her fall ("I was too secure in the knowledge I thought I had of my own heart./My supposed advantages became a snare to me" (p. 891, L261); "My fortunes, my rank, my character, I thought a further security" (p. 892, L261)), she attenuates her aversion to contrivance and opens her own narration and dialogue to *art*. Thus, in the famous penknife scene when Lovelace stages the "discovery" of Dorcas' treachery to lure Clarissa out of her room, he finds himself foiled by his opponent's carefully dramatized suicide threat (L281). This scene, like Clarissa's escape from the brothel, her attempted corruption of Dorcas, or the "allegorical" letter she writes about her visit to her "father," show that once apprised of the nature of the game and obliged by circumstances to accept rules she previously scorned, Clarissa is more than a match for her opponent. She is as capable as Lovelace or her siblings of exploiting the dialogical structure of narration to her own ends. However, Clarissa will not make the same mistake as her adversaries: she will not attempt to suppress the authority of the Other in the narrative circuit, much less delude herself with dreams of self-sufficiency by embellishing on Lovelace's practice of invention in order to fool a single "reader." Rather, she will rely upon the communal process of narration and narrative to elaborate a textual version of herself that will embody and perpetuate as shared legend the identity she could not attain in the flesh.

"There is a shame which bringeth sin, and there is a shame which bringeth glory and grace" writes Clarissa in one of her many meditations (p. 1207, L413), and it may well be in reference to her story before and after the rape. For after her fall, she will use the story of her misfortune to gain the sympathy – indeed, in the public's eyes, the *grace* – that she could not obtain when still untarnished. Immediately following her escape from Lovelace's clutches, she undertakes a systematic investigation of the people and events she has dealt with since fleeing her family. This investigation reveals for her the extent to which the components of her past were mere inventions of a clever narrator, but it also marks her entry into a larger network of correspondence, the many members of which – Lovelace's uncle, Lady Betty Lawrence, Miss Rawlins, Mrs Hodges, Mrs Norton, Mrs Howe – will become agents for her cause in the future. Rather than hiding her story as she did in the pre-rape episodes, Clarissa sets about publicizing it, which not only procures allies for her against Lovelace but, more importantly, distributes the burden of her identity among a large segment of the population. As a fallen woman, she no longer elicits the resentment or jealousy of her interlocutors; as someone desirous of managing her history, she can no longer pretend disinvolvement with art. Her moral loss thus opens the way to an active and fruitful negotiation of her story with a broad spectrum of agents, for whom her misfortune becomes a legend, or piece of history in which they can participate.

That Clarissa expects vindication once her story is circulated is scarcely in doubt. In her opening sequence of letters, she alludes consistently to her victimization and the benefits she will gain from the publication of her account. Thus she writes to Mrs Howe,

My story is a dismal story. It has circumstances in it that would engage pity, and possibly a judgement not altogether unfavourable, were those circumstances known. (P. 976, L297)

To Mrs Norton,

that I may not make you think me more guilty than I am, give me leave briefly to assure you, that when my story is known, I shall be entitled to more compassion than blame, even on the score of going away with Mr Lovelace. (P. 986, L307)

And to her sister,

I am not half so culpable as I am imagined to be; as would be allowed if all the circumstances of my unhappy story were known. (P. 1165, L380)

It is in her letter to Lady Betty Lawrence, however, that she sketches out the rudiments of the history she will promote:

I will not offer to clear myself entirely of blame: but, as to *him*, I have no fault to accuse myself of. My crime was the corresponding with him at first, when prohibited so to do by those who had a right to my obedience; made still more inexcusable by giving him a clandestine meeting, which put me into the power of his arts. And for this, I am content to be punished: thankful that at last I have escaped from him; and have it in my power to reject so wicked a man for my husband: and glad if I may be a warning, since I cannot be an example:

which once (very vain, and very conceited as I was!) I proposed myself to be!
(P. 985, L306)

This simple narrative, at once confession and expiation, will form the basis
for an increasingly powerful affective account of her misfortune, which
Clarissa will not only write in installments to Anna Howe, but present in
a dramatic narration to Mrs Lovick and Mr and Mrs Smith (L349), and
ultimately conceptualize as a textual record: "Oh that my words were now
written! Oh that they were printed in a book! that they were graven with
an iron pen and lead in the book for ever!" (p. 1125, L364). Not only will
Clarissa's sufferings serve as an admonition for future generations and
substitute for the legal proceedings to which her friends urge her (cf. L428,
L456), but Clarissa herself is, in the words of Mrs Norton, "brightened"
and "purified" by them (p. 1328, L459).

Were Clarissa to strive for complete control of her history, however,
attempting to monitor and manipulate the responses of her public, she
could not attain the apotheosis she envisions. Only by giving herself over
to the process of shared narration that Lovelace, her family, and even she
herself tried to suppress in the first half of the book, can she ensure her
entry into history under her own terms. To escape the pitfalls associated
with monological narration, she will relinquish authority to her reader(s),
and most notably Belford, who, after patiently reading in the wings for over
one thousand pages, finally comes into his own in the last quarter of the
novel as Clarissa's primary reader – and writer.

Having formulated her objectives, the heroine gradually withdraws from
the scene, writing fewer and fewer letters as she slips away towards immor-
tality. It is Belford who, becoming Clarissa's agent in a literary and legal as
well as figurative sense, takes over responsibility for the promulgation of
her virtue and the castigation of Lovelace. As the heroine withdraws from
history as lived time, Belford diligently transcribes her into history as
shared cultural text, where she will survive long beyond her physical death
and continue to exercise on people the beneficent influence she never
achieved as mere mortal. Even as his exchanges with Lovelace and Morden
displace the heroine's transactions with her family and seducer as the center
of the novel, Belford's voice progressively displaces Clarissa's as the author
and authority of her life. As if to mirror and confirm the inseparability of
reading from writing, the primary reader of Clarissa's downfall becomes by
the end of the novel her voice and author – quite literally her executor.
Clarissa in turn merges into a text, a tragedy circulated indefinitely –
indeed, up to the present day.

This image is not mine, but that of the diligent Belford, who correctly
perceives the literary quality of the story he has been entrusted to circulate.
In a long passage, which I cite in full because it so neatly lays out the legend

of Clarissa as he (and no doubt Richardson) envisions it, the dying martyr's executor casts his ward's life in the formal terms of a great work of tragic drama:

> But here is MISS [CLARISSA] HARLOWE, virtuous, noble, wise, pious, unhappily ensnared by the vows and oaths of a vile rake, whom she believes to be a man of honour: and being ill used by her friends for *his sake* is in a manner *forced* to throw herself upon his protection; who, in order to obtain her confidence, never scruples the deepest and most solemn protestation of honour. After a series of plots and contrivances, all baffled by her virtue and vigilance, he basely has recourse to the vilest of arts, and to rob her of her honour is forced first to rob her of her senses. Unable to bring her notwithstanding to his ungenerous views of cohabitation, she awes him in the very entrance of a fresh act of premeditated guilt, in presence of the most abandoned of women assembled to assist his cursed purpose; triumphs over them all by virtue only of her innocence; and escapes from the vile hands he had put her into: nobly, not franticly, resents: refuses to see, or to marry the wretch; who, repenting his usage of so divine a creature, would fain move her to forgive his baseness and make him her husband: and, though persecuted by all her friends and abandoned to the deepest distress, obliged from ample fortunes to make away with her apparel for subsistance, surrounded by strangers, and forced (in want of others) to make a friend of the friend of her seducer. Though longing for death, and making all the proper preparatives for it, convinced that grief and ill usage have broken her noble heart, she abhors the impious thought of shortening her allotted period; and, as much a stranger to revenge as despair, is able to forgive the author of her ruin; wishes his repentance, and that she may be the last victim to his barbarous perfidy: and is solicitous for nothing so much in this life as to prevent vindictive mischief *to* and *from* the man who has used her so basely.
>
> This is penitence! This is piety! And hence a distress naturally arises that must *worthily* affect every heart. (P. 1206, L413)

To the extent this plot summary replicates the plot of Richardson's novel, it underlines a conclusion one can no longer avoid: what is chronicled in the protracted decline of the heroine is nothing less than the metamorphosis of Clarissa into *Clarissa*, the systematic textualization of the protagonist's identity, and the transposition of identity from the battleground of dialogical rivalry to the dialectical field of culture, historically conceived. Withdrawing from the confrontational rivalry of social intercourse, with its conflicting agendas and interests, Clarissa reinvests her identity in a literary artifact, a written account in which she plays the role of central character, not author, and in which she will live even after her death. Abandoning her private dreams of perfection, she accedes to the public sphere of martyrdom; relinquishing the notion of simple representational language, she finds in the literary text's suspension between narration and narrative a depersonalized, and hence less volatile, version of the dialogical structure of the self, one which can assure her of indefinite circulation within society and history.[18] To elude the destructive rivalry that has engulfed simple dialogue, she transposes her identity into a text, where it will be negotiated and perpetuated by a new pair of agents, author and reader. These new terms are functions, not flesh and blood individuals; they inhere in the text and can be occupied by any individual wishing to make it part of his or her own experience, through reading and (re)writing. The transaction they embody is more properly dialogical than the struggles that Clarissa will leave behind her, as it involves two parties of equal authority, bound together in a relationship of perfect reciprocity. Only by dying and being reborn as a text – a "character" necessarily and always both "here and now," both the reader's and the author's, can the heroine attain this level of interaction between self and Other. As text, Clarissa (*Clarissa*) will live through an Other: a reader for whom she poses no menace, and who can realize her- or himself through the Other of Clarissa (*Clarissa*) – the literary character or narrative in dialogue with which identity elaborates itself.

As the textually motivated play between author and reader emerges as a paradigm for the dialogically conceived self, literature displaces self-construction to become the mediating order through which the individual can inscribe him or herself on history. In place of the direct, contemporaneous structuring of reality which Lovelace carried to its highest art, and which not only places one in competition with other individuals but confines one's gesture to a severely limited public and future, literature permits a deferred yet perpetually reborn actualization of individuality. It repeatedly imposes the self *on* history *through* the history of its readings, with, it is true, a reduced measure of control over the shape of one's destiny, but, for that very reason, an endlessly permutable rebirth of individuality. By explicitly casting identity in the form of a text that is from the outset and will always remain "other" or "novel," the literarization of the self provides a less competitive, more persistent format for personal history. It allows the self to find its actualization within the narrational gesture of the Other, thus penetrating the cultural economy from the "inside" and defusing the play of antagonism which has come to grip the social dialogue of selfhood.

Because this process of self-actualization can occur over and over, among many readers of the same generation as well as successive generations of readers, the textualization of identity also predicates a dialectical conception of selfhood. Reappropriated by successive generations according to their dominant ideologies, which will in turn be modified by the meaning *Clarissa* brings to them, Clarissa finds her full realization in the ongoing dialectic of individual interpretation and collective truth. Unable to negotiate a reconciliation between her own self-determination and the exigencies of her society while living, she becomes the vehicle for such a reconciliation as literary exemplar.

The episodes of Clarissa's apotheosis and Belford's conversion are the most striking example of this transaction, though by no means the only one: the members of her family, as well as those of Lovelace's, and Colonel Morden, and her landlord and his wife, all of these become part of an expanding system. To translate her self into cultural text, Clarissa needs readers who, by interpreting her story, contribute to its production, make it theirs in a sense, and therefore gain a stake in its perpetuation. Such readers in turn require readers of their own, who will assimilate *their* stories, and so forth. This is exactly the paradigm of the latter portions of *Clarissa*, in which the heroine recounts her story to Belford, who literally appropriates it to his own identity by recasting its lesson in the form of a persistent sermon addressed to *his* reader, Lovelace. Reading Clarissa's story as a tale of virtue, Belford himself becomes virtuous; the fallen girl's accounts and pleas become his own as they are embellished and further transmitted to the rake, for whom they are *Belford's* accounts, as well as Clarissa's, as much a relation in the present as of the past. Gradually, Belford's (Clarissa's) story will spread through society, appropriated by successive readers and narrators, each of whom will further promulgate his or her version of the exemplary tale.

That the heroine deliberately elects this policy of perpetuation through the Other finds confirmation in her willingness to let Lovelace's writing (and other people's reading of his accounts) serve as record of her behavior during their relationship (L391). She trades the role and authority of the writer in favor of the more potent existence she will have as textual dialectic. The text cannot provide absolute stability for her identity – witness the divergent readings to which the novel has given rise – but it guarantees her access to, and permanence within, the larger text of her culture: in a very real sense, Clarissa becomes history when *Clarissa* becomes history.

Indeed, Clarissa's metamorphosis perfectly replicates the structure of history as a relationship between a present gesture of comprehension and past, textualized experience.[19] Once the episodes of her life have been put in a textual form (the collection of letters) and released into the economy of reading and interpretation, "Clarissa" no longer can be thought of as a mere person, or even a fictional character, since she does not exist entirely within the text or within the reading act, but rather in the relationship of the one to the other, the relationship of a present (narrational) act – that of the reader/writer Belford (Lovelace, Morden, the critic, etc.) – to a past (narrative) fact, the episode of her fall (or of its description, genesis, or reception). No flesh and blood individual need intercede in this transaction to disrupt or efface with her presence (and present narration) the reader's narrational reconstitution of him- or herself as (through) Clarissa/*Clarissa*. Nor should one trivialize the importance of this transaction. The continual dialectic of reading, relating, and self-expression does not just restructure history, but, to the extent such restructuring is the basis for our perception of reality, it *is* history: the constant unfolding of empirical reality cannot be extricated from the perceptual and conceptual matrix within which it occurs and which it continually realigns.

Finally, to the extent that *Clarissa* makes its heroine's apotheosis a function of this dialectic rather than of her initial strategy of "sliding through life to the end of it unnoted" (p. 40, L1), the novel locates the crucial relationship of selfhood between narration and narrative. Clarissa attains the identity she desires by committing the history of her dishonor to the dialectic of history – within which it appears for each new party a narrative susceptible to appropriation and retransmission. Thus Belford, Colonel Morden, Lovelace's family, Mrs Norton, and even Clarissa's own family will each in turn read her story and redistribute it as his or her own narration. At the origin of this chain of narrative "realities" and narrational constructs lies not simple fact, but more *historical* reality: another story – the destiny contrived by Lovelace and his accomplices for their unwitting victim Clarissa. At its end, there is no conclusion, merely another narration/narrative such as my reading – and yours. By giving herself over to the dialectic of (received)(public) narrative and (personal)(private) narration, Clarissa "writes" her history in a way she never could in life. As the heroine in a story of violation and death collectively embellished as it is passed from one individual to another, her identity merges with the text of her culture and attains the exemplarity to which she aspires.

If Clarissa's sublation into history implicitly valorizes literature as a means of expressing individualism in a world driven by narration, it does not preclude the recurrent delusion of narrative mastery. The manipulation of collective opinion and the coercion of the Other which Lovelace undertakes will continue to resonate in successive novels as a generalized strategy of self-promotion, doomed to replay the same scenario of self-defeat and thereby reassert the dialogical and dialectical foundations of narrative representation. Similarly, the compulsion to reduce social interaction to a set of rules or strategies will persist as an inevitability of averted self-representation: in a world where everyone promotes their own version of events, standard frameworks of reference or conventions of persuasion necessarily emerge, the mastery of which is a temptation few individuals seem able to resist. While the codification of reality equips the rake with a means of dominating his peers, it also ultimately assures his defeat, by relocating authority for his actions in a collective protocol he cannot suspend.

Clarissa provides an alternative mode of self-representation, one that relinquishes understanding the *langue* of conventions grounding it, or controlling the history of its reception, in favor of an act of self-textualization that commits the self to history. In effect, Richardson's heroine argues against attempting to grasp the codes that regulate self-expression at the same time that she implicitly elevates literary expression to a function of beneficial social and historical mediation. In its selection of a communal practice of textual narration, reception, appropriation, and retransmission as the mode of its heroine's redemption, *Clarissa* promotes and makes to appear innocuous the institution of which it is an instance, while at the same time, through the negative example of Lovelace, discouraging its reader from attempting the task of cultural definition it performs.

Future novelists will make this gesture, which remains rather covert in Richardson, the centerpiece of their plots. The struggle for domination which Clarissa disavows will remain the paradigm for social interaction *within* the plots of Fielding, Diderot, Sterne, and Laclos, where the dialogical exigencies of narration will take the shape of a unstable master/slave relationship; but *outside* of this plot, or more accurately above it, emerges a meta-plot involving the Author's gesture of self-representation, and that of the Reader to whom it is addressed and in whose hands the Author's identity and future lie. As the characters dramatize the futility of trying to master history through the successive failures of their enterprises and the reversals in their relationships of dominance, the Author and Reader exemplify, through their bantering negotiation of the meaning of the stories, the culturally beneficial dialogue of textually mediated selfhood. The understanding of social relationships that is implicitly censured as a practical endeavor in everyday relationships with one's contemporaries finds encouragement within the "innocent" domain of formalized literary representation.

This institutionalization of the narrative phenomenon carries predictable risks. As the novel gains an identity of its own as a serious cultural institution, the rules governing its production and reception become more explicit – and invite abuse. Conventions of writing and reading emerge to compete with individual intention as the arbiters of meaning and the authority over narrative. Unlike Lovelace, though, the authors (and Authors) who derive their authority from these conventions do not conceal them from their readers; rather they make the reciprocal determination of Author and convention a central theme in their writing, synchronizing their increasing claim to cultural authority (implicit in the privileged negotiation of meaning which they carry on with the Reader) with the negation of their autonomy. As if to compensate for the recognition that authoring is a fundamental – perhaps *the* fundamental – form of power, since it posits the structures

around which further debates must turn, the metanovels consistently ironize the Author's claims of power and underscore the primacy of a grounding, agentless grammar of determining conventions – one which is by
definition immune to appropriation or subversion. A strange ambivalence
thus informs the later novels of the century: on the one hand, they make
increasingly ambitious claims for the superior perspective of the professional author – the individual who goes Lovelace one better by grounding his
identity in the *explicit, public* invention of reality; on the other hand, such
omnipotence increasingly parades its reliance on social and literary conventions – a larger systematic order that does not just put into question the
author's control over his production, but relieves him of responsibility for
its meaning and ethical impact.

NOTES

1 Citations are from the most accessible unabridged version of *Clarissa*, which
   reproduces the novel's first edition: ed. Angus Ross (Penguin Books, 1985). I
   include letter numbers for the convenience of readers using the Shakespeare
   Head edition.
2 The epistolary form is generally associated with Richardson's avowed goal of
   "writing to the moment" or, in Ian Watt's words, providing a "short-cut . . . to
   the heart" (*The Rise of the Novel*, p. 222), but as critics have shown, it can also
   be read as thematizing the self's isolation from the world or the abortiveness of
   indirect communication (Janet Altman, *Epistolarity: Approaches to a Form* (Columbus: Ohio State University Press, 1982), p. 27) or even the estrangement
   of the literary reader (Preston, *Created Self*, pp. 38–93. It is in any case clear
   that correspondence is itself a highly conventionalized genre and hardly spontaneous. If, as Watt argues, the rise of the middle class brought about a shift
   towards a more "suburban" ideal of privacy and made daily correspondence the
   forum for the expression of one's more intimate sentiments (pp. 212–15), then
   the conventions governing such formal, scheduled transcription of personal
   experience have displaced the aleatory give-and-take of personal conversation as
   the dominant mode of expressing the "minute-by-minute content of consciousness which constitutes what the individual's personality really is" (p. 217). Such
   obsessive transcription in turn implies a desire to control not just the self, but
   the world that encloses it: "the prolific 'scribbling' of Clarissa, Lovelace, and
   the others reflects a will to define experience, to transform the elusive moment
   into discourse" (Castle, *Clarissa's Ciphers*, pp. 19–20). This is the historiographical gesture par excellence.
3 Warner, *Reading Clarissa*, p. 5. For Warner Clarissa's narration is simply one
   more weapon in a generalized narrative struggle: "we shall find nothing in this
   novel that we can call neutral, objective, or true. Instead we shall uncover
   ingenious and elaborate pieces of artifice, inventions designed for warfare. And

none is more powerful than Clarissa's – the idea of narrative, a narrative which is neutral, objective, and truthful" (p. 5). Terry Castle rejects this assessment, seeing "Clarissa's basic linguistic assumption . . . that words embody, absolutely and transparently, the inner life of the speaker" (*Clarissa's Ciphers*, p. 67) as the condition of her brutalization by Lovelace, who "knows that the text one writes has no obligation to any objective realm of things" (p. 84).

4   "To outwit and impel, as one pleases, two such girls as these, who think they know everything; and by taking advantage of the pride and ill-nature of the old ones of both families, to play them off likewise at the very time that they think they are doing me spiteful displeasure; what charming revenge!" (p. 464, L127).

5   The mole is Lovelace's favorite metaphor for the surreptitious schemer, and he will later apply it to Anna Howe and Clarissa as well; see p. 851, L248.

6   Warner, *Reading Clarissa*, p. 29.

7   For an extensive analysis of the role of sententiousness in the French tradition, see Bennington, *Sententiousness*. Bennington's theoretical analysis of the genre of sententious discourse is valuable for an understanding of the phenomenon in English literature as well as French.

8   Warner, *Reading Clarissa*, pp. 87–92, uses the figure of the "subject," with its simultaneous implications of philosophical control and political subservience, to describe the way Clarissa orchestrates her ultimate triumph (of which more later), but it is equally applicable to Lovelace's inversely charged decline.

9   Terry Eagleton casts Lovelace's compulsion in the even more universal terms of oedipal angst (*The Rape of Clarissa*, pp. 52–63). I would suggest his neurosis, in whatever metalanguage one wishes to frame it, is as much cultural as psychological to the extent that *none* of the male characters in the first half of the book escape the obsession with appropriating Clarissa to their own projects. They all manifest a near pathological fear of her independence and a rabid jealousy of her attraction to Lovelace.

10 In the more freudian terms of Terry Eagleton's reading, Lovelace's loss is equally dramatic: "once Lovelace is reduced to the humiliating gesture of having to drug his victim in order to rape her, he has lost the war even before he has performed the act. A forced victory is no victory at all: Lovelace can hardly demonstrate that all women are secretly lecherous if Clarissa is unconscious at the crucial moment" (*The Rape of Clarissa*, p. 83).

11 *Clarissa*, p. 280, L69.

12 Eagleton, *The Rape of Clarissa*, p. 83.

13 See, for instance, pp. 380, L94; 394, L98; 398, L98.

14 Clarissa's family frequently refer to her persuasiveness, which they see as a means for her to undermine their own vision of the world, as well as proof of her hypocrisy; see pp. 154 (L32.4), 194–5 (L42), 253 (L60), 1322–3 (L459), and 1366 (L485); also Castle, *Clarissa's Ciphers*, pp. 61–2.

15 See especially Warner, *Reading Clarissa*, pp. 3–27; even Watt views Clarissa's correspondence with skepticism: "we can never assume that any statement should be taken as the complete and final truth" (p. 260).

16 "The poor Bella has, you know, a plump, high-fed face, if I may be allowed the expression – you, I know, will forgive me for this liberty of speech sooner than I can myself; yet how can one be such a reptile as not to turn when trampled upon! – " (p. 60, L7).

17 Ian Watt's framing of the relationship between Clarissa and Lovelace as "brought about by two codes which doom their holders to a psychological attitude which makes human love impossible" (*Rise of the Novel*, p. 270), draws on the notion of a cultural imperative that I associate with Lovelace's inability to dissociate himself from his plot; but where I envision the dilemma of the two "lovers" to reside in their incompatible attitudes towards self-creation and the manipulation of reality, Watt explains their clash in terms of Clarissa's puritan repression of the flesh and the rake's suppression of his sensibility and "the gentler elements in his personality" (ibid.).

18 Eagleton, *The Rape of Clarissa*, p. 74, notes Clarissa's elevation into martyrdom and the public sphere, but on the following page inexplicably maintains that "she refuses incorporation into social discourse and transforms herself instead into a pure self-referential sign". Martyrdom may be many things, but it is never purely self-referential. Moreover, as Belford's plot résumé abundantly illustrates, Clarissa is firmly enmeshed in the public discourse even before her death; her martyrdom culminates the process of integration that she herself initiated.

19 The definition is Henri-Irénée Marrou's. Speaking of the notion of historical reality, he writes, "le réel ici, la seule réalité qu'ait jamais désignée le langage, c'est la prise de conscience du passé humaine, obtenue dans la pensée par l'effort de l'historien; elle ne se situe ni à l'un, ni à l'autre des deux pôles mais dans le rapport, la synthèse qu'établit, entre présent et passé, l'intervention active, l'initiative du sujet connaissant" (the real here, the only reality which language has ever designated, is the consciousness of the human past which is obtained in the mind by the historian's effort; it is found at neither one nor the other of the two poles, but rather in the relationship, the synthesis established between past and present by the active intervention, the initiative of the knowing subject); *De la connaissance historique* (Paris: Seuil, 1954), p. 37.

9

The Necessary Other: the Dialogical Structure of the Self

A structural characteristic of eighteenth-century concepts of selfhood and authority that informs all of the works covered to this point and emerges as a central theme in the plots of Richardson is that of dialogical reciprocity. The self, and to a less obvious degree the systems of authority framing its endeavors, are grounded in a dialogical relationship to an Other, or reflective presence, whose reactions confirm or contest the viability of personal representations.[1] This Other can take a variety of forms, many of which we have already seen: the omnipresent recording eye of the collective, an intuition of divine intention with which the solitary individual converses, a fetishized object of carnal love such as Manon Lescaut, a double that reflects and seconds one's repressed impulses, such as Amy in *Roxana*, or, as in *Pamela* and *Clarissa*, the sexual Other whose attempts to inscribe the self within its own agenda function simultaneously as a stimulus to resistance and a force of attraction. Many of these different modalities of the Other occur concomitantly within a single novel, presenting the narrator-protagonist with conflicting modes and avenues of self-realization. All such variations, though, are subtended by the dialogical structure of narration, which in the early novels manifests itself on two planes: the interpersonal or social, and the intrapersonal or historical. On the one hand, the party to whom one addresses one's versions of events reacts to those accounts, either sanctioning or denying their validity; on the other, the narrated projection of the self in the past, as character in the narrative, provides the narrator with an ongoing image of her or his experience, according to which the current state can be assessed. Both of these exercise pressure on the self by presenting an image of its developing public identity, by providing an ongoing resonance and reflection of its creation.

In its most rudimentary and least effective manifestation, the dialogic relationship occurs as a private conversation or narrative transaction that develops in isolation from, and in opposition to, the social collective. The order of institutionalized authority can also be thought of as "other" to the extent that the protagonist elaborates his or her agenda of individualism in contradistinction to it, but insofar as this order refuses to listen to the individualist's projects and is in turn excluded by them, the relationship is not dialogical. It is precisely because they do not converse normally with the institutions and values of their culture that Defoe's heroes initially seek their identity in a more private transaction with divine Other, sexual partner, or sidekick, and that Chasles' heros and the chevalier des Grieux elaborate alternate private relationships within the intimate dialogue of love. Similarly, Pamela's correspondence with her parents compensates for her initial inability to make herself heard by Mr B., the justice of the peace and embodiment of the law. The gradual conversion of the latter into a viable dialogic partner for the young woman marks her social redefinition into a lady and the realignment of the law with virtuous individualistic conduct.

This compensatory private dialogue has no equivalent public counterpart in the earliest novels: the protagonists of Mme de Lafayette never disseminate their stories deliberately to a general public, and those of Defoe do so only retroactively, to a reading public chronologically remote from the events recounted, and of whom no response is required. In the works of Richardson, however, the private dialogues of the characters lead directly to a relationship of individual to public, through the intermediate stage of an extended, multiple dialogical exchange – the multiple correspondences and dialogues into which the protagonists enter. As a consequence of this multiplication and generalization of the narrative transaction, the most averted characters shift their attention to the consistent patterns or systematic tendencies that underlie all such exchanges, reformulating their own identity in terms of its command of such codes. The dialogical ground thus acquires a third dimension: that of the relationship between personal expression and encoded norms. While such a relationship is implicit in all individualistic agendas, from Mme de Lafayette on, it only attains explicit formulation as the ground of selfhood in the character of Lovelace. Later works will pursue this abstract formulation primarily as it applies to formalized literary narrative and the manipulation of conventions; and like Lovelace, the Authors in the works of Fielding, Sterne, Diderot, and Laclos will equate their awareness of this intertextual version of the dialogical compact with an epistemological advantage.

At its simplest level, the dialogical need for an Other involves social and cultural *validation*, or the assent of an outside party to one's construals of reality, values, and identity. This is most obvious in Richardson's novels, but what one critic remarks of *Pamela*, namely that it "testifies the power of public opinion. The heroine knows that her chastity represents a viable resource only inasmuch as its value is externally affirmed,"[2] applies to a greater or lesser degree to all of the self-representations we have seen. Marianne's or Jacob's elaborate self-presentations, des Grieux's tragic posturing, Roxana's contractual negotiations, Robinson's internalization of providential and social order, all hinge on the ratification of an Other, as does, in a more tragic mode, Clarissa's apotheosis and martyrdom. The internalization of authority dramatized by these novels, whether Christian or secular in nature, is inseparable from the idea of accreditation by an authoritative order of discourse whose reception and acknowledgement of "my" construals of myself signals their assimilation into the design of reality. The ideal individualist represents consensual authority through private expression, and it is the approbation or resistance of the Other that determines whether or not this self-representation will gain currency in the economy into which it is released. Pamela's elevation is made possible by the successive accreditation of her virtue, character, and intrinsic "quality," by Mr B., his servants and neighbors, his sister, and their micro-society in general, just as Clarissa's redemption occurs through the ever-expanding acclamation of her story by a reformed public.

The validating Other may be a single person, a group of people, a specific social class, or even, as in *Robinson Crusoe*, the personification of a principle, and may be construed as either representing or opposed to some higher order(s) of authority – it is in this sense that the eighteenth-century novel comes closest to the notion of dialogical exchange as a global principle similar to that enunciated by M. M. Bakhtin.[3] In the early novels especially, but also in the later plots of manipulation such as Lovelace's, the function of validation is frequently distributed between a knowing accomplice and unknowing pawns, whose norms the hero emulates and whose responses validate his or her fictions in spite of their fundamental antagonism. Des Grieux succeeds in prolonging his fantasy precisely because he can get authority figures of his class to sanction the tragic story he tells them and excuse his behavior as the standard sexual apprenticeship of an aristocrat; Moll's success as a thief depends on her victims' credulity and willingness to take her stories at face value; Lovelace's ability to insinuate himself into Clarissa's confidence hinges on his calculation of the effect of various accounts on the young woman.

However, this inadvertent validation by a dupe is never sufficient in and of itself, because the victim remains unaware of the deception and cannot confirm the extraordinary accomplishment of the dissembler. Therefore, the individual who grounds his or her identity in the mastery of other individuals and the collective always requires a complicitous Other external to the deception, one to whom it can be related as a work of art, and who can appreciate its contrivance. To the extent this appreciating Other shares the self's values and strategies, however, it also necessarily holds the potential for rivalry. The pressure of opposing versions of reality elicits refinements and growth in the self's grasp of its position in the world precisely to the extent that it presents a rival version of that world. The Other is necessarily both resistant and receptive, both a rival and an accomplice, and the self must be the same. However, in the earliest novels this paradoxical mixed function does not really find expression. Rather, the world is dichotomized into two stable sets of Others: the accomplices and the antagonists, the latter being associated with the various forms of authority against whose constraints the individual asserts his or her autonomy, such as the legal order which Moll subverts in the streets of London, or the social order which Robinson flees by going to sea.[4] This collective Other provides a baffle for the self's articulation of its *difference*, a means of assessing the exceptional behavior that confirms its individualism. However, this difference seems unable to sustain itself as such. Even in the earlier novels where it is not muddled by emotional attraction as it is in Richardson's works, the individualist's attitude towards the authoritative Other is marked with ambiguity. In spite of their rebellion, Robinson, Moll, Roxana, des Grieux, all eventually abandon their stance of antagonism in favor of complicity and come to embrace the Other which they initially spurned. This conversion is mediated by the narratee of the confession, and its motivation is to be found in the inadequacy of the validation which an antagonistic or marginal Other can provide. Marginal accomplices, like Roxana's Amy, Moll's various partners, the lovers in *Les Illustres Françoises*, or Manon Lescaut, provide only a provisional, ultimately unsatisfactory, resonance for the self, precisely because they cannot represent the order whose approbation the protagonist seeks. Manon's approval of the chevalier, for instance, cannot confirm his internalization of the order of authority, nor inaugurate a relationship of complicity between the prodigal son and the institutions he has flouted, since she does not speak in society's voice. Likewise, Amy cannot reconcile Roxana to virtue, since she is alien to its principles.

Individualism requires for its confirmation the certainty that the individual account has internalized and entered the collective record, and such certainty can only come from a party or parties representing that collective. That is why virtually all of the early "histories" of rebellion are told to a third party, whose reception and acknowledgement of the narration functions as its ultimate validation and confirms the assimilation of the personal story into the collective history. This narratee can be either specific, as in *Les Illustres Françoises* or *La Vie de Marianne*; general, yet known to the narrator, as in *Le paysan parvenu*, which is recounted to a familiar, restricted public; or anonymous, as in Defoe's autobiographical works. But the narratee always functions similarly, performing a double mediation: on the one hand, between the rebellious protagonist, or character in the account, and the repentant protagonist, or narrator of the account, and, on the other, between the protagonist and the orders of authority or collective norms he or she resists. Straddling the temporal gap between the reformed narrator, whose acquaintance is made prior to the commencement of the tale, and the narrated character, whose extraordinary behavior will unfold over time, the narratee can validate almost any conduct before the fact, certain that it leads to an edifying conclusion. And in some stories, the narratee mediates the conversion of specific figures of authority in the plot from an antagonistic to a complicitous function. This pattern occurs in *Les Illustres Françoises* and in *Manon Lescaut*, where the chevalier tells his story to an older nobleman of his class who, touched by Manon, yet possessed of the principles of virtue which the chevalier has transgressed, can, through listening to his story, perform his reintegration into the order of society. Through his confession to this figure, des Grieux expresses his repentance to his father and acknowledges the latter's authority, by turning his personal experience over to the gentleman for judgment, approbation, or condemnation, much as does Pamela, when she turns her journals and letters over to Mr B. The story of resistance to the collective order is assimilated into the order as an exemplar by dint of its reception and internalization by a member of that order.

The novels of Richardson refine and intensify the dialogical transaction in several important ways that will inform the next generation of fiction. First, by textualizing the protagonist's account, in the form of letters which can be circulated beyond their original receiver and even beyond the life span of their writer, they merge the private compensatory dialogue within the plot with the overarching validating dialogue with the narratee that frames the plot. To the extent that Pamela's and Clarissa's accounts are read by several different parties, there can be, and are, several narratees for the same narrative, and they are all situated within the plot, as it is happening, rather than standing on the outside and evaluating it retrospectively. The protagonist's story is told to characters of her own ontological and historical status, and receives its sanction immediately, by a member of her society, as well as prospectively and tentatively at the hands of a future "reader."

Richardson's works do not merely allow for the perpetuation of selfhood through an extended dialogical economy, they specify its imperative. The conversion of antagonism into alliance, itself a prerequisite for the furtherance of the individualist agenda and the individual's social maturation, is linked to the willingness of each party to the dialogue to relinquish the claim to absolute authority – to let the Other be the author. A productive dialogue requires that each party alternately propose and sanction, accepting the initiatives of the Other which come with the Other's accord. There is always an undercurrent of rivalry in the dialogical equation, as well as one of complicity, but that rivalry only degenerates into antagonism when one party or the other insists on being sole author(ity) and dictating the order of things singlehandedly. It is Lovelace's inability to negotiate this equilibrium between authoring and validating in *Clarissa* – his obsession with being sole arbiter of a relationship distributed across the narrative transaction – that seals his doom. As *Jacques le fataliste* and *Les Liaisons dangereuses* will reiterate in equally dramatic terms, such attempts to transcend the reciprocity of dialogical selfhood and found one's identity on the coercion and control of the Other always fail.

By contrast, Mr B. and Pamela – and *a fortiori* Clarissa – realize their potential by virtue of their acceptance of the dialogical compact and the relinquishment of monological authority which it entails. Mr B.'s endorsement of his servant's script is not only itself a narration requiring *her* corroboration as narratee, but the sign of his own accession to a posture of self-definition. Having finally acknowledged the validity of her construals of their situation and her sense of herself, he graduates from the position of an abusive authority figure unable to procure his own happiness to that of a self-defining individual capable of setting his own course and, literally, perpetuating himself. Conversely, Pamela ceases regarding him as a mere antagonist, all of whose initiatives are to be resisted. Clarissa's deliberate orchestration of her sublation into shared text, following her ravishment, signals a still more complete relinquishment of mastery (or, in her case, of mastery's passive correlate, immunity to collective discourse). Fielding's *Tom Jones* will figure this double movement of relinquishment of personal authority and self-textualization even more completely, by doubling the protagonist's apprenticeship into shared discourse with the story of the Author's inauguration of a dialogue with future readers that will endure for centuries to come.

The commonest eighteenth-century metaphor for the productive relationship of rivalry/complicity which Lovelace and Clarissa cannot sustain, but which Pamela and Mr B. succeed in establishing, is of course love – which is in some respects the master trope of the dialogical conception of selfhood in general. "In" love, the self realizes itself through the reactions of the Other, and vice versa; it attempts to appropriate the Other self in the same gesture as its expropriates its self, internalizing the world of the loved one through the externalization of personal sentiment. In its most grandiose manifestation, *Julie, ou la nouvelle Héloïse*, the dialogue of love will ground not simply a model household but a model society. In its failed or compromised incarnations, where the equilibrium of reciprocity and mutual determination cedes to outright antagonism or complete abdication of authority, as in *Clarissa*, with the relationships of the heroine to Lovelace and Belford, respectively, love degenerates into *seduction* or *friendship*. The novels of Rousseau and Laclos will pursue the intricacies of such transformations, as well as the feasibility of sustaining either love or one of its incomplete faces over time. Each of these novels concludes differently as to the possibility of sustaining love, but both demonstrate that the degraded relationships of simple friendship and pure antagonism are both inadequate and unsustainable.

If none of the novels we will be covering, including the comic metanovels of Fielding, Sterne, and Diderot, present a model of successful narrational mastery, of a permanent, stable subordination of the Other to one's personal schemes, it is in part because antagonistic dialogues tend to self-destruct, but also in part because of the increasing association of the Other with a conventional order which cannot be transcended. As mentioned above, Richardson's novels show that all such two-party dialogues mediate a further relationship between individual instance and collective practice. In both *Pamela* and *Clarissa*, characters speak in the name of larger cultural values, such as honor, virtue, or paternal authority, and implement scenarios and modes of self-expression that are prescribed by their culture. It is his knowledge of such larger patterns of practice that allows Lovelace to predict the behavior and reaction of Clarissa's family at every step of his plot, and will permit Blifil to orchestrate the expulsion of Tom Jones from Paradise Hall. Even broader trans-historical patterns of social behavior will be cited by the Author in Fielding's works as the basis for his typification of social roles; and in Rousseau's work a similar notion of cultural determination finds explicit theoretical formulation: the model community outlined in *Julie, ou la nouvelle Héloïse* derives its coherence from the script of conduct its members maintain in the form of codified usages and grammars of self-expression.

It becomes increasingly clear with successive novels that the interpersonal dialogue between speaker and listener, or author and reader, mediates the more abstract relationship of personal expression to shared rules. To the extent that such rules are maintained and transmitted as texts, not only literary, but historical, legal, statistical, artistic, and economic – for all social endeavor in any field is regulated by narratives of past usage, protocols of traditional procedure, and scripts of behavior – the relationship of personal expression to collective convention implies a transaction between private narrational instance and public historical narrative. In the deliberately intertextual allusions of Fielding, Sterne, and Diderot – who construct their novels, and especially the figures of authority within those novels, out of citations and rereadings of other texts in other traditions – the configuration of usage and convention which grounds authority will increasingly be linked to the narratives which sustain it. Those narratives in turn are in a continual state of revision under the impact of the accumulating instances of their enactment: even as they are reread, cited, invoked, or merely alluded to, the scripts of shared usage are being written. This process of (re)articulation exemplifies the dialogical process in its broadest sense of (evolving) historical knowledge; and if it is most obvious in theoretical writing, it also inheres in the fictional re-presentation of human behavior which continually redefines the social reality it claims to express. In Sterne's and Diderot's more fully developed models of history as narrative economy, the dialogic relationship of interpersonal rivalry/complicity merges with a dialectic paradigm of history and reality as orders of representation that shape, and are shaped by, the individual instances of expression they determine. It is here that the clearest treatment of the relationship of story to history can be found, as well as the foundation for the future claims of the novel to a position of cultural authority.

Even as fictional narrative comes to be understood as instantiating the cultural tradition it revises – as an ongoing intertextual rearticulation of a larger story to which it belongs – so too do the author and reader, and the textual transaction in which they are realized, acquire a paradigmatic function as regards the dialogical relationship. Again, Richardson's novels prefigure this development in their insistence on writing as a mode of power and on the text's simultaneous empowerment of writer and reader. Just as Mr B.'s reading of Pamela's letters gives him an advantage over her only, by empowering her voice,[5] so too do readers simultaneously empower and determine the identity of authors – and vice versa. The reading self enacts its identity and exercises its autonomy in an act of construal that is modulated by a text produced by the authorial Other, but at the same time, it is the act of reading that concretizes, albeit very locally, the identity of that Other/author. Conversely, the authorial self realizes itself in the response of the reading Other which it nevertheless modulates through its narrative. And to the extent that both author and reader enact their identities through a text that presents itself as re-presenting some past state of events, selfhood is suspended not only between "myself" and the Other, current act and previous (or future) act, but also between retrospection and prospection: the author looks forward to the reading while re-articulating the past; the reader determines the past in reading forward to the narrative's end. The literary transaction of writing/reading thus mediates the dialogical expression of selfhood and the dialectical reformulation of shared history: the Other in (and against) whose words and categories the self constitutes itself is "realized" as a previous (future) intention empowered by previous (future) conventions, which the reading (writing) "I" represents and revises in a single gesture.

In the metanovels of the second half of the century, the less complex relationship of "naive" narrator and narratee is retained as a component of the plot – which will be structured as a universal field of continual narration suspended between rivalry and alliance – but the framing agents of that plot, the reader and author, will themselves be thematized along the same line, taking the form of a "Reader" and "Author," whose discussions and bickering replay in literary terms the social and amorous interactions of the recounted characters. This literary dialogue retains the reciprocal dependency of its social counterpart, and is subjected to similar perversions, mostly comic, when the Author attempts to coerce the Reader and usurp all of their shared authority, but it also explicitly foregrounds the relationship of instance to system, and narration to history, to the extent that it is mediated, more explicitly than conversation, by formal conventions and literary tradition. Eventually, this straightforward and extremely self-conscious thematization of the "dialogic" of selfhood and history will fade away, rendered superfluous by the conventionalization of its message and the resultant conviction that the Other against which the self elaborates itself is first and foremost an impersonal system. As the faith in the self's ability to comprehend and revise this system declines – and it declines in part because the later novels argue against it – the plots of self-representation of the eighteenth century transmute into the nineteenth century's chronicles of social order.

NOTES

1 The function of the "other" has been most frequently noted with respect to Defoe's work; cf. Homer Brown, "Displaced Self," John Richetti, *Defoe's Narratives*, and McKeon, *Origins*, p. 361.

2 Spacks, *Imagining a Self*, p. 210.

3 See ch. 1, n.31, above, p. 21.

4 Brown, "The Displaced Self," conceptualizes the ambivalent attitude of Defoe's protagonists with respect to the order of the undifferentiated Other, which they both fear and need, in terms of a pattern of self-concealment and self-exposure.

5 See McKeon, *Origins*, p. 361.

10

Self-ish Narration and the
Authorial Self (*Joseph Andrews*)

With the exception of *Clarissa*, all of the works we have considered thus far chart the rise in prosperity of their protagonists, from a relatively humble beginning to a position of reputation and influence. The ease with which they attain their new identity, like their ultimate rank and moral status, may vary greatly, Roxana and Moll Flanders by no means being the equivalent of Marianne, Jacob, or Pamela. Yet each ultimately relies on narration as a means of securing social identity or modifying his or her station. Henry Fielding's two great comic novels, *Joseph Andrews* and *Tom Jones*, published in 1742 and 1749, parody the pattern of social advancement through discourse even as they substantially refine the concept of narration and its relationship to identity and social organization.[1] The male heroes of the novels have much in common: both are of low birth – Joseph Andrews is the supposed brother of Pamela Andrews, Richardson's heroine, while Tom Jones is a bastard; each finds himself hampered by his low station in the pursuit of his beloved; each undertakes a lengthy peregrination, meets an older companion, and undergoes a series of ordeals and mishaps, before being reunited with his love; and each is metamorphosed at the end of the novel into a man of quality, when a new account of his origins turns up and reveals him to be of superior birth. Joseph turns out to be the son of a respectable retired country gentleman, Tom that of the eminent Squire Allworthy's sister.

These rather contrived transformations occur solely on the basis of oral reports, and they confirm the importance of collective accounts in determining individual identity. Yet in comparison to the painstaking narrative strategies of Marianne or Pamela such metamorphoses seem nearly parodic. As one critic aptly puts it, "Pamela is a strategist, Tom the happy-go-lucky beneficiary of his creator's benevolence."[2] Indeed, much of Fielding's comic effect derives from his tendency to exaggerate to the point of absurdity themes and plot devices used more seriously by his predecessors. His plots parody not only problems of class difference, social identity, marriage, and the protagonist's accession to the gentry, but also the mechanisms of authority, rivalry, self-interest, and plotting which structure the world. The device of dialogue or debate, which plays such an important role in Richardson's works, degenerates here into outright combat, social discourse into insult and slander. The main thing separating *Joseph Andrews* and *Tom Jones* from the works of Fielding's predecessors, though, is their ironic, omniscient point of view. For the first time, the characters do not relate their own stories. Rather, they are recounted by a sardonic, learned Author, whose comments on both the antics of his cast of social buffoons and his own literary and moral pretentions rival the actions of the protagonists as the focal point of the narrative. Critics in Fielding's time and in our own have lambasted the superficiality of his characters and the offhanded way in which their behavior is presented by the narrator.[3] There is no question that it is difficult to reconcile such an apparently frivolous work as *Joseph Andrews* with the seriousness of Pamela which it parodies. Yet I would propose reading the comic simplicity of Fielding's characters as a consequence of the narrator's desire to emphasize the distance that separates him – and his reader – from the world he relates, and that this desire in turn derives from his very serious concern about the uses and abuses of narration.

The practice of invention and contrivance which I have been associating with narrational behavior has not disappeared from these novels; rather it has been generalized to permeate the entire fabric of society. Fielding's protagonists wander through a world rife with hypocrisy, deceit, infidelity, dishonesty, and selfishness, a world in which identity and character fluctuate with the collective account prevailing at the moment. And that account, more often than not, reflects not facts, but the selfish motivations of its authors. Significantly, however, the protagonists themselves stand above this selfishness: they exhibit little interest or skill in manipulating public opinion and systematically subordinate their own interest to the Christian principles they espouse. As personifications of selflessness in a world where narrational craft is systematically associated with self-promotion, they cannot recount their own story: a disinterested professional narrator, the Author,[4] constructs their history for them.[5] This Authorial voice, whose running commentary on the protagonists' behavior and the Reader's supposed reactions gradually coheres into a distinctive personality and moral presence, unifies the novels and provides the central consciousness and selfhood around which they are organized. We have seen how *Clarissa* discredits its protagonists' attempts at mastering or negating the collective negotiation of truth, promoting instead a strategy of public self-expression in which the individual commits her identity to a shared dialectical process of collective interpretation and rewriting. *Tom Jones* and *Joseph Andrews* go a step further by making the embodiment of that commitment, the literary Author, the most substantial character in his own fiction.[6]

One function of the Author is to clarify the moral questions posed by the characters he oversees. Fielding structures his epics around three different modes of behavior and levels of narrative awareness, each of which may be associated with a different degree of self-awareness and a different mode of self-expression. At the bottom level, his works present an antagonistic perversion of selfhood dialogically conceived: the fictional world abounds with characters embroiled in dispute, rivalry, and the narrational manipulation of identity, all of which practices bear the brunt of the Author's relentless irony. One level above this morass of hypocrisy, the protagonists of Fielding's work enjoy a moral superiority based on their disinterest in monitoring their stories. Particularly in *Joseph Andrews*, whose structural affinities with *Don Quixote* are heralded by its full title,[7] the hero and his sidekick, Adams, ignore the narrative economy of their society, emblematizing values of selfless charity and virtue in a world regulated by selfish vanity and greed.

This structure of juxtaposition requires for its moral elucidation a higher plane of understanding, one that grasps the contrast between the virtuous and the vain as a general commentary on human nature rather than a reportage of specific instances. This third level is the domain of the Author who glosses the local dramas of the plot in terms of the universal patterns of human behavior they typify. If the characters in Fielding's novels seem caricatural and trivial in comparison to the psychological complexity of Clarissa and Lovelace, it is because the burden of self-expression, with all its attendant conflicts and ambiguities, has been shifted to this higher metanarrative plane, where the subject of the self's discourse is its own public narrational activity.

Overlaying with ironic commentary the narration of the fictional characters it invents, the Authorial self tells its story indirectly, finding expression through the tales it relates about – and to – surrogate selves inhabiting the ontologically distinct realms of fiction and the community of future readers. What is remarkable in this complex equation is that whether the Author is relating the "history" of his characters, commenting on their moral shortcomings and virtues, discussing the goal of his own narrational gesture, or contemplating the ultimate effect of the public narrative it produces, he is always talking about an aspect or projection of his self – he is always consolidating his own identity. Constituted through narration, linked in a dialogue with the recipient of that narration, identified by the textual narrative it creates, and preoccupied with the reception and revision of that narrative over time, the self is more than ever at the center of the novel, but it has taken on a new identity: it has merged with the cultural spokesman called the "Author." The detachment of narrational consciousness from the products of its art, which can be traced back to characters like Roxana and Moll, but which has been increasing steadily as the narrators become more sophisticated and self-conscious, is promoted by Fielding to a theme in its own right.[8]

The Author's stress on this detachment, his insistence on the fictionality of his creations, goes hand in hand with a larger strategy designed to enhance the image of "art" and to clear the way for realistic fiction to assume a role of cultural authority. His plots, like Richardson's, focus on the vicious behavior to which narrational hubris leads. But by emphasizing the fictional status of his own narrational production and underlining the discrepancy between the behavior he portrays and his own purely inventive, selfless narration – which has as its pendant the complementary activity of the Reader – he procures for literature an exemption from the general condemnation of narrative artfulness. Literary contrivance cannot be likened to the vice-ridden practices the Author describes since it does not advance any specific individual's immediate self-interest. Indeed, it flaunts its lack of historical referentiality. Although the Author's inventions and his attitude towards his characters are every bit as arrogant and cruel as, say, Lovelace's designs, they do not represent a particular historical individual or purport to modify the "here and now":

> I describe not men, but manners; not an individual, but a species. Perhaps it will be answered, Are not the characters then taken from life? To which I answer in the affirmative; nay, I believe I might aver, that I have writ little more than I have seen. (P. 185, 3:1)[9]

The curious double status of these creations, taken from life but not from history, provides a key to the complex mediation between personal experience and cultural order which the Author's narration occasions. To maintain that his characters are at once the synthesis of his personal experience and the expression of a recognizable species is to promote himself to the role of spokesman for human nature, organizer and articulator of shared perception. In other words, the Author assigns himself the function of cultural authority. To reduce the pluralism of society into a coded repertoire of behavior is to identify cultural types, to take on the responsibility of unraveling and systematizing the chaos of social reality for one's reader. Readers that chuckle with the Author, and thus sanction his classifications, necessarily assimilate them into their own sense of reality and will wittingly or unwittingly perpetuate them in their own further narrations and narratives – whether those be formal literary criticism or merely conversations with other parties. In this sense the Author's narration or self-expression becomes a locus of authority within that evolving, shared text of reality we call culture; in the shape of an enduring, shared *narrative*, his story, and the identity it conveys, become the vehicles for further transactions between individuals, and between individual members of a culture and that culture as a shared system.

Of course to elicit our belief, the Author's "species" must reflect at least minimally *our* experience and invite interpretation according to that experience. They must function as the extension of the reader's *and* the author's personal experience, expressing a self that is never entirely its own, never localizable in space or time, but bound up in a further (or former) gesture of ordering or relating. The narrating self that announces itself as literary, whether taken as an author's gesture, a reader's interpretive response, or even the imprint of a larger cultural or historical community, by definition realizes itself in some other time through the intervention of some other party. And it does so through the mediation of a perpetually reenacted fictional narrative that functions analogously to culture in that it links each individual narrating (reading) act not only to the Other of the reader (author), but to the community and its traditions.

This recasting of identity in dialogical and dialectical terms is not unique to Fielding. In their own way, Pamela's merger with the collective order and Clarissa's conversion of her private story into a public history dramatize the tension between self as narration and self as narrative, self as writer and self as written – personal authorship and cultural authority. But Richardson's novels do not explicitly invoke the institution of literature. Fielding's do, and they associate the dialectic of meaning within which literary works live, with that which conditions the development and sustenance of the self, by superimposing on the model of primitive individuality – his characters' attempts to manipulate social identity, and his protagonists' attempts to steer clear of, and survive, such behavior – the plot of the Author's enterprise of self-representation. Fielding's thematization of the Author's and Reader's relationship to the fictional world and to the broader dialectic of history will not attain the extremes of a Sterne or a Diderot, but his novels clearly mark a shift toward self-consciously narrative conceptions of the self from which there will be no return.[10]

In his preface to *Joseph Andrews*, the Author identifies the mainspring of his art as the exposure of affectation, "from the discovery of [which] arises the ridiculous – which always strikes the reader with surprize and pleasure" (p. 29). Affectation, in turn, has but two sources: "as vanity puts us on affecting false characters, in order to purchase applause; so hypocrisy sets us on an endeavor to avoid censure by concealing our vices under an appearance of their opposite virtues" (p. 28).[11] Almost all of the characters in *Joseph Andrews*, with the exception of Joseph, Adams, and Fanny, exhibit at least one of these vices, the caricaturing of which furnishes the novel its comic texture.

In *Joseph Andrews*'s world of negotiated merit, vanity and hypocrisy involve not only the management of one's identity but the depreciation of the character of others as well. It is not surprising that nearly all the characters are involved in the fabrication of their peers' identity, and the plot of the novel finds its complications in the continual definition and redefinition of the protagonists at the hands of their opponents. The identity of the main players and the general armature of the plot underscore Fielding's desire to parody the logic of *Pamela*: not only is Joseph Andrews the brother of the illustrious Pamela; his nemesis, the hot-blooded Lady Booby, is the sister of Mr B. – here, Squire Booby. Pursued by Lady Booby, in whose service he works as a domestic, Joseph resists on the same grounds as his sister, and is consequently dismissed. Setting out to rejoin his beloved Fanny in the country, he meets the naive Parson Adams, and the two travelers undergo a series of misfortunes, humiliations, and strange encounters, their status changing with each new person they meet, before rejoining Fanny, rescuing her from an attempted rape, and reaching the country seat of the Boobys. There they are joined by the Squire and Pamela (now a pretentious, snotty parvenue), and, after various attempts on the part of the Boobys to block Joseph's marriage with Fanny, a pedlar arrives, revealing Joseph to be of noble blood, and not Pamela's brother after all, thus freeing him to marry.

From the opening scenes, in which the disparity between Joseph's birth and that of Lady Booby poses the problem of social rank, to the final dénouement, where a series of personal accounts bring about a literal re-identification of the protagonist, the relationship of an individual's identity to the public and personal accounts that embrace it furnishes the thematic underpinnings of the plot. Fielding's fictional world is *historical* in the dialectical and narrative senses of the word: it is a world where the worth and character of individuals is under constant negotiation, where their treatment and identity hinge not on any permanent virtues they may possess, but on the version of themselves (and others) currently in force in a given environment.

The episodes illustrating this paradigm in *Joseph Andrews* are too numerous to mention in full. Among the most obvious within the first two books alone: the rapid swings in Joseph's fortune at the hands of Lady Booby and Slipslop (1:7, 1:9); the turnabout in the first innkeeper's treatment of Joseph, when she determines him to be of more consequence than she originally believed (1:15); the judgment of the prisoner accused of robbing Joseph (1:14, 1:15); the story of Lenora's fluctuating treatment of Horatio, with respect to his rival Bellarmine (2:4, 2:6); the arrest of Adams and Fanny on the word of her would-be rapist, and their subsequent hearing and release (2:10, 2:11); the change of attitude of the hostess, when she discovers Adams to be, and then not to be, the brother of Trulliber (2:15). The most concentrated example of how identity fluctuates with the accounts of one's peers is provided by the debate in chapter 3 of the third book, in which the same gentleman is defined in radically different terms by three successive people; a sustained instance of a similar ambivalence can be found in Lady Booby's endlessly vacillating judgments of Joseph, whom she alternately praises and vilifies according to her control of her passion.

The accounts which the cast of *Joseph Andrews* deliver have little to do with any notion of truth or fundamental character; rather, they are dictated by self-interest, which most often alternates between the pecuniary and the sexual. The limiting case is that of a criminal's false testimony, which Fielding uses as a dramatic catalyst in his plots. The would-be rapist who accuses Adams and Fanny of trying to rob him (2:10, 2:11), the abductors of Fanny who claim she is an adulterous wife (3:12), or even Lawyer Scout, who fabricates a charge against Fanny and Joseph (4:5), all attribute their own moral shortcomings to another party. Such cases of lying differ slightly from the deceit involved in vanity, in that the lying person is most certainly more aware of distorting the truth than the vain or hypocritical person would admit to be, but they have effects similar to other cases of narrational shenanigans and they pertain to the same narrative promotion of self-interest.

It is not simply the little people of the novel who suffer continual reidentification. An important aspect of the paradigm in question is its universality: people of all classes continually negotiate the characters of their peers, inferiors, and superiors. This is something Lady Booby knows well. When she initially contemplates opening her heart to Joseph, she ponders, "then, say you, the world will never know any thing of the matter, yet would not that be trusting to your secrecy? Must not my reputation be then in your power? Would you not then be my master?" (p. 49, 1:5). In a world where everyone has a say in the formation of reputations, even the humblest are to be feared. This is why Lady Booby dare not dismiss her impertinent chambermaid Slipslop once the latter has learned of her infatuation with Andrews:

> But the dismissing Mrs Slipslop was a point not so easily to be resolved upon; she [Lady Booby] had the utmost tenderness for her reputation, as she knew on that depended many of the most valuable blessings of life; particularly cards, making court'sies in public places, and above all, the pleasure of demolishing the reputations of others, in which innocent amusement she had an extraordinary delight. She therefore determined to submit to any insult

from a servant, rather than run a risque of losing the title to so many great privileges. (P. 61, 1:9)

Besides confirming the growing link between narration and social mastery, Lady Booby's plight parodies the dialogical mechanism of selfhood. To be what she wants to be, the Lady requires an accomplice, someone who will not only defend her reputation, but sanction her own "demolitions." This partner is generally Slipslop, but near the end of the work the lawyer Scout, Squire Booby, and even Pamela, provide support when it comes time to slander Fanny – whose beauty naturally excites the envy of her rivals. Thus Lady Booby and Scout will portray Fanny as an "ugly slut" and beggar (p. 269, 4:3), in order to enhance the Lady's own image and justify the lawyer's legal mischief. A similar pattern is apparent when it comes time to disparage Pamela. The trusty Slipslop wastes no time in seconding her mistress:

> "what do you think of the dowdy, my niece I think I am to call her?" Slipslop, wanting no further hint, began to pull her to pieces, and so miserably defaced her, that it would have been impossible for any one to have known the person. The lady gave her all the assistance she could, and ended with saying – "I think, Slipslop, you have done her justice; but yet, bad as she is, she is an angel compared to this Fanny." (P. 277–8, 4:6)

Here Slipslop and Lady Booby are momentarily united by their common interest in Joseph. But the dialogic accord can easily break down into rivalry in such cases. When that occurs, each member of the dialogue turns his or her attention on the other's affectation, attempting to ridicule or discredit his or her authority. For every Lady Booby pretending to disdain her footman, there is a Mrs Slipslop confronting her with a contrary vision of herself; for every posturing barman, there is a barman's wife, ridiculing his judgment.

A more ridiculous scenario occurs when one is confronted with an entirely uncooperative partner – one who cedes neither to rivalry nor shared envy. In this case the whole narrational project risks breaking down, and one is left with no options other than to discredit the other party's qualifications to speak. Thus, when Adams naively blurts out that Fanny "is the handsomest woman, gentle or simple, that ever appeared in the parish," Lady Booby explodes:

> "You are very impertinent," says she, "to talk such fulsome stuff to me. It is mighty becoming truly in a clergyman to trouble himself about handsome women, and you are a delicate judge of beauty, no doubt. A man who hath lived all his life in such a parish as this, is a rare judge of beauty. Ridiculous! Beauty indeed, – a country wench a beauty. – I shall be sick whenever I hear beauty mentioned again." (Pp. 265–6, 4:2)

Finally, Lady Booby's rabid slander of rival females proposes a further subversion of the dialogical compact in a world driven by vanity: since vanity compels us to claim qualities we do not have, and since the presence of those qualities in others is likely to put our paltry affectation into perspective, it is always in our interest to calumniate virtuous rivals whenever the opportunity presents itself. As the paragon of perfect purity and beauty, Fanny is an obstacle to anyone aspiring to those qualities. To the extent that virtue is relative, the self's relationship to others – at least among the legions of vain hypocrites peopling Fielding's work – is always one of either rivalry, should the other party possess virtues we are desirous of appearing to have, or complicity, should we perceive in the other person an ally in our disparagement of some third, envied party.

The narrative underpinnings of identity extend far beyond the local arena of personal accounts, however. The most pervasive and influential account is the impersonal narrative of culture which underwrites the social hierarchy. One marker of that hierarchy is the idea of fashion, as analyzed by the Author in a long digression on the relativity of social rank in chapter 13 of his second book:

> Now this word *fashion*, hath by long use lost its original meaning, from which at present it gives us a very different idea: for I am deceived, if by persons of fashion, we do not generally include a conception of birth and accomplishments superior to the herd of mankind; whereas in reality, nothing more was originally meant by a person of fashion, than a person who drest himself in the fashion of the times. (P. 158, 2:13)

If fashion has come to be equated with superior "birth and accomplishments" it is because conformity to the cultural text – the current conventions of dress, speech, and behavior which constitute fashionability – has displaced intrinsic character or merit as the basis of identity and authority. This is the negative side of identity based on self-representation: generalized to society at large, the practice of devising a public persona, and appraising others on the basis of the persona they put forth, results in a collective frenzy of emulation and performance. Rather than expressing one's self, as does the true individualist, the degenerate pseudo-individualist tries to perform the identity of the envied Other. The long interpolated story of Mr Wilson illustrates this most vividly. His odyssey from one fashion to another commences with his program of acquiring the *reputation* of a gentleman, and to do so he merely assimilates the superficial vocabulary and dress of the class. Successive calamities reveal to him the extent to which all of society is grounded in fictions, from the "beaus of the Temple" who "drank with lords they did not know, and intrigued with women they never saw" (p. 199, 3:3), to the coquette whose "life is one constant lye" (p. 203), to the philosophers, or *"rule of right-men"* (p. 205) who take the notion of relativity to its logical extreme by declaring there is "nothing absolutely good or evil in itself" (p. 206).[12]

Mr Wilson's story serves a moralizing purpose; he accordingly learns from his misfortunes and ultimately repudiates society to retire in the country with his wife. But his habit of associating identity with fashions is shared by most of the other minor characters in the novel. Indeed, lest the use of the term "fashion" should suggest that the confusion of character and convention applies only to the upper classes, the Author is quick to observe the relativity of rank: "the lowest of the high, and the highest of the low, often change their parties according to place and time; for those who are people of fashion in one place, are often people of no fashion in another" (p. 159, 2:13). He explains how each individual, from the lowly postillion, who cleans the footman's clothes in the morning, to the footman who dresses the squire's gentleman, or the squire himself who attends his lord in the afternoon, relates to those below him as a figure of authority and greatness, while appearing to those above him a low person. Further, he adds, "Nor is there perhaps, in this whole ladder of dependance, any one step at a greater distance from the other, than the first from the second: so that to a philosopher the question might only seem whether you would chuse to be a great man at six in the morning, or at two in the afternoon" (p. 159, 2:13).[13]

The social universe of *Joseph Andrews*, then, is structured by the script of culture and the engine of collective discourse, as embodied at the most particular level in the everyday gossip, calumnies, and reports circulated among people of a given locale, and at the most general level by the conventions and fashions that subtend class distinction. And the conclusion of the novel, which depicts the assignment of new identities and positions of authority to the protagonists, illustrates how the transcript of social rank accumulates from the repetition and dissemination of individual tales – in this case, those of the pedlar, Mr and Mrs Andrews, and Mr Wilson, whose accounts, sanctioned by Squire Booby and his entourage, become common knowledge and hence part of local history. Once in circulation within a significant community, individual story is automatically promoted to shared history, and it is the necessary reiteration of such history as a framing plot to individual accounts, present and future, that constitutes the presence of culture in personal narration.

There are, though, in *Joseph Andrews*, characters who have withdrawn from this economy, such as Mr Wilson, or who refuse to take part in it.[14] The hero and his companion Abraham Adams are the most obvious examples of the latter kind. In marked contrast to their fellow mortals, they eschew the narrative management of the world. The apparent moral simplicity of Fielding's work, which sets virtuous characters adrift in a world corrupted by fictions of self-interest, reflects a pattern we have seen in Marivaux and Richardson, where moral protagonists are pitted against unscrupulous opponents.[15] What sets Fielding's work apart from his predecessors' is his apparent association of superior morality with narrative naïveté or non-participation. In an environment of constant fabulation, deception, and hypocrisy, where destinies are made or broken on hearsay and gossip, his heroes say little; their sidekicks speak willingly, but with no understanding of the rules governing social discourse.

The most glaring example of this social innocence is Adams. "Designed a character of perfect simplicity" as the Author says in his preface, the Parson is "as entirely ignorant of the ways of this world, as an infant just entered into it could possibly be. As he had never any intention to deceive, so he never suspected such a design in others" (p. 43, 1:3). The Author later specifies that Adams "never saw farther into people than they desired to let him" (p. 148, 2:10), and indeed, he presents a combination of bookish erudition and practical dysfunction. His lack of memory and foresight, which accounts for many of the predicaments confronting the three protagonists, is matched by a boundless naïveté regarding the character of others. The assumption that governs his behavior to his fellow man is that "nature generally imprints such a portraiture of the mind in the countenance, that a skilful physiognomist will rarely be deceived" (p. 181, 2:17), and he feels himself to be just such a "skilful physiognomist." Accordingly, when he attempts to borrow money from the miserly Trulliber (2:14), or takes up a pipe-smoking stranger's impromptu offer of lodging and horses (2:16), or suffers the practical jokes of a prankster gentleman and his entourage (3:7), he perceives no deceit, vanity, greed, or cruelty.

Nor can Adams conceive of calumny: "'God forbid! (said Adams,) that men should arrive at such a pitch of wickedness, to be-lye the character of their neighbour from a little private affection, or what is infinitely worse, a private spite'" (p. 107, 2:3). More generally, he seems unaware of the role that cultural codes play in the assignment of rank and character. Lady Booby's constant changes of character or the innkeepers' rapid turnabouts in their treatment of Joseph and his friend, are as incomprehensible to him as Wilson's behavior as a youth, or Slipslop's refusal to acknowledge Fanny (2:12, 2:13). Because it implies a subservience to social opinion and a management of identity alien to the Christianity Adams preaches, the entire mechanism of social identification depicted in *Joseph Andrews* remains beyond his ken.

Adams is generally considered to function as a moral paragon. I would suggest, though, that while his inability to read the world implies a refusal of the very notion of the consensus negotiation of truth, he does not himself provide a positive model for emulation. His dogmatic fidelity to scriptural law and the classical tradition is superficially admirable, but his inability to furnish any solutions to the dilemmas of everyday reality, or even to live up to his own principles of stoicism, disqualifies him as a functional exemplar. His character expresses perhaps the Author's nostalgia for a simpler age, but his buffoonish social dysfunctionality signals the same Author's acknowledgement that the historical machinery of social reality can no longer simply be denied. Like Clarissa prior to her abduction by Lovelace, his is a virtue out of step with social reality.

If Adams lacks self-consciousness, it is because he denies the very possibility of self-fashioning which that concept implies. To structure one's self according to the fashions of the times is to subscribe to a notion of reality as an evolving story dictated by cultural authority, a shared text subject to revision by its readers and writers in conjunction with their shifting interests. Adams cannot accept this, if only because he envisions a world regulated by an unvarying script transcendent of historical change. Naturally, one form this script takes is that of divine authority: "it was his maxim, that he was a servant of the Highest, and could not, without departing from his duty, give up the least article of his honour, or of his cause, to the greatest earthly potentate" (p. 321, 4:16). Fashion cannot serve as a basis for action because it reflects the unbridled textuality of culture – its constant re-evaluation, reinterpretation, and recounting of reality – and thus provides no basis for moral decision. In place of this narrational flux, Adams proposes the stable narrative of scripture. He spurns textuality as historical process, while espousing canonical text as the origin of history. From his perspective, the plots and fictions of man count for little; they are but insignificant digressions in a grander pattern beyond our surmise. As he tells Joseph, in manner of consolation, when the latter thinks he has lost Fanny:

> We did not make ourselves; but the same power which made us, rules over us, and we are absolutely at his disposal; . . . as we know not future events, so neither can we tell to what purpose any accident tends. . . . whom do we resist? or against whom do we complain, but a power from whose shafts no armour can guard us, no speed can fly? A power which leaves us no hope but submission. (P. 250, 3:11)

This subordination of human actions to a higher scheme or authority not only echoes Robinson Crusoe's use of providence to console himself for his shipwreck, it also foreshadows Jacques' brand of fatalism and his notion of the great scroll in *Jacques le fataliste*. Unlike Jacques, however, the parson will advance no explicitly secular version of his argument capable of accounting for historical progress; nor will he emulate Crusoe and align the will of providence with all of his earthly deeds. Nonetheless, he will advance other forms of textual authority to supplement dogma as the master plot of history. The divine order he preaches is seconded by the almost equally canonical order of classical texts he continually cites. For however unwilling he is to read the current world, he has no such hesitation as regards accounts of worlds past. Literature, at least literature sanctioned by the tradition he represents, is a source of knowledge second only to the Scriptures.

The importance of book learning is apparent from the first scene of the novel where Adams appears. His opening scene in the novel juxtaposes him against the local doctor, whose experience he contests on the basis of his theoretical knowledge gleaned from books (1:14). This valorization of textual authority over practical experience recurs in Adams' praise of the Greek classics (3:2), but finds its strongest expression in the argument with the sailor, regarding experience (2:17), where Adams berates his interlocutor:

> "I will inform thee; the travelling I mean is in books, the only way of travelling by which any knowledge is to be acquired.... if a man would sail round the world, and anchor in every harbour of it, without learning, he would return home as ignorant as he went out." (P. 181)

Such statements elucidate Adams' social dysfunction as they reveal his own vanity, suggesting that he may not be as valid an exemplar as he might like to think. He cannot learn from his interactions with other men, because he discounts the value of personal experience. His reality is a rigid system of principles that does not yield to momentary expediency or change over time, an ideal script immune to the vicissitudes of local interest. Like his model in Cervantes, he applies a textual tradition literally to the world and maintains the ideals of that tradition against the economy of selfishness that regulates the course of history. Indeed, one might say that Adams embodies the struggle of History, conceived as a canon of authoritative texts, to impose its values and patterns on history, conceived as an ongoing social and textual transaction. He articulates the text that will brook no textuality. And just as the text of History cannot react to its reception in the course of history, neither can Adams alter his conduct in deference to the ignoble practices that surround him. He is doomed to replay endlessly the same scenario of selfless charity, whether surrounded by innocence or rapacious self-interest.

In contrast to his garrulous mentor, Joseph seldom speaks and almost never discourses on abstract subjects or enters into debates. Indeed, he exhibits so little of the behavior we normally associate with realistic characters that one critic has dubbed him "little more than an unconscious lump."[16] Paradoxically, the rare instances when he does speak his mind, such as his discussion of public schools with Adams (3:5) or his subsequent discourse on the absence of charity in the world (3:6), indicate a keen sense of observation and an ability to arrive at reasoned judgments on the basis of experience. Unlike his dysfunctional mentor, Joseph sees through affectation easily, and he can defend his position effectively when he needs to. When Adams berates him for being too attached to Fanny and counsels, typically, that "we must submit in all things to the will of Providence, and not set our affections so much on any thing here, as not to be able to quit it without reluctance" (p. 290, 4:8), only to fall into despair himself upon learning of the death of his son, Joseph does not hesitate to point out his friend's hypocrisy and turn the Parson's example to his own advantage: "'well, sir,' cries Joseph, 'and if I love a mistress as well as you your child, surely her loss would grieve me equally'" (p. 292, 4:8).

Joseph tempers his book-knowledge with the lessons of first-hand experience, and his inability to find a scriptural accounting for certain patterns of behavior does not blind him to their mechanism: "all rail at wickedness, and all are as eager to be what they abuse. This I know not the reason of, but it is as plain as daylight to those who converse in the world, as I have done these three years" (p. 224, 3:6). "Converse in the world" is precisely what Adams does not do, at least in the sense of learning that is here implied; and this difference between the two friends not only defines their respective attitudes *vis-à-vis* experience, history, and morality, but outlines the role they play as mediate categories between the corrupt fictional world and the enlightened plane of the Author.

If Adams embodies a textual erudition and authority entangled yet unheeded in the din of social discourse, Joseph gives tentative form to an analytic wisdom that transcends that discourse by reflecting on its own experience. He does not actively implement that wisdom in the way Tom Jones will – and this is a point to which I shall return – but he at least signals an alternative to the authoritarian dysfunction of Adams. Finally, each of these postures dramatizes one aspect of the grander literary enterprise which encircles hero and character alike, and which involves the higher order of consciousness exemplified by the Author.

In the prefatory chapter of the fifth book of *Tom Jones*, the Author claims "to open a new vein of knowledge, which, if it hath been discovered, hath not, to our remembrance, been wrought on by any antient or modern writer. This vein is no other than that of contrast, which runs through all the works of the creation, and may, probably, have a large share in constituting in us the idea of all beauty, as well natural as artificial: for what demonstrates the beauty and excellence of anything, but its reverse?".[17] Taken literally, this assertion not only explains the strong contrast between the heros of Fielding's novels and their less virtuous counterparts, but invites a favorable judgment of the narrator himself. If the two heros of

Joseph Andrews benefit by comparison with their peers, how much more so must the author, whose erudition, authority, and analytic detachment dwarf by comparison both Adams' learning and Joseph's penetrating reflections on human nature. To the extent that one grants Joseph and Adams moral superiority on the basis of their distance from the economy of affectation, one also cedes it to the Author. Whether one chooses or not to identify that narrator with Fielding, the moralizing force of *Joseph Andrews* ultimately accrues to the creator of the fiction, and, by extension to fiction itself.

There is no need to rehearse here the breadth of erudition which the Author displays, by manner of digressive instruction, while relating his story. Citations from classical authors abound, both Greek and Roman, as do long discussions of Homer, history, the epic, satire, and the stage. Mock battles and self-conscious lyrical exordia punctuate the vulgar rompings of the characters, while frequent moral digressions – such as that on fashion, cited above – are interspersed among the more active scenes. Obviously, once the Author has acquired a voice of his own within the narrative and claimed paternity of its characters and episodes, he can take credit for the characters' erudition without accepting responsibility for their pretensions. In a highly moralizing book like *Joseph Andrews* this is no trivial point, for it is precisely the critical remove separating Authorial voice and protagonist's voice that immunizes the Author from the fate of his creations.

Further, by expressing his knowledge of the Ancients through Adams, the Author transcends the dilemma his own plot poses. Where Adams fails to impose his textual authority on contemporary culture, the Author succeeds, if only by investing the otherwise down-to-earth personage of the parson with an exaggerated respect for such authority. He insinuates textual authority into eighteenth-century English society simply by making it one animating force in that society as he portrays it. And by insisting on the stupidity of those individuals who do not grasp and respect Adams' erudition, the Author forestalls a like response on the part of his Reader. Accommodating within his own narration the scenario of its failure, he prevents that failure by associating it with an ignorant public with which the Reader dares not identify. To the extent we play along and nod knowledgeably at the Author's learning, we confirm his superiority, which shines all the more brightly in contrast to Adams's; with a few notable exceptions such as Mr Wilson, no one responds to Adams with more than snorts of contempt or ridicule.

If the Author goes to great lengths to fortify his narration with erudite textual references, he also, like Joseph, extolls the truth value of his own experience, and his reader's. In *his* work, he maintains, "every thing is copied from the book of nature, and scarce a character or action produced which I have not taken from my own observations and experience" (p. 30,

Preface) – a claim he will reiterate in the prefatory chapter to Book Three: "I have writ little more than I have seen" (p. 185). Unlike the writers of history, however, the "romance-writers" whom the Author prefers to call "topographers or chorographers," their business being "chiefly to describe countries and cities, which, with the assistance of maps, they do pretty well," the class of writer to which the Author belongs focuses rather on "the actions and characters of men" (p. 183, 3:1). It is this attention to the behavior of men, rather than to their chronological or topographical situation, which grounds the claim that "truth is only to be found in the works of those who celebrate the lives of great men" (p. 183, 3:1).[18] Such a celebrant is our Author, whose representation of universal patterns of conduct and the laws of human nature, rather than particular individuals, provides a transhistorical vision that rivals Adams' divine truth.

The "types" the Author portrays persist through history in a variety of particular incarnations:

> The lawyer is not only alive, but hath been so these 4000 years, and I hope G—— will indulge his life as many yet to come. He hath not indeed confined himself to one profession, one religion, or one country; but when the first mean selfish creature appeared on the human stage, who made self the centre of the whole creation; would give himself no pain, incur no danger, advance no money to assist, or preserve his fellow-creatures; then was our lawyer born; and whilst such a person as I have described, exists on earth, so long shall he remain upon it. (P. 185, 3:1)

It is this persistence of his creation that underwrites the Author's claim to superiority with respect to his characters as well as his fellow writers. By portraying self-ishness in its most generalized form, as the behavior of "types" that recur in various guises throughout history, he at once reveals the mechanism underlying history and transcends that mechanism. Calculated "not to expose one pitiful wretch, to the small and contemptible circle of his acquaintances; but to hold the glass to thousands in their closets, that they may contemplate their deformity, and endeavour to reduce it" (p. 185, 3:1), his portrayal of the lawyer can function beyond the historical moment of its composition, serving not merely to advance the interests of its Author but to improve generations of readers to come.

This is the assertion that is made in the first paragraph of the novel, where the Author in effect promotes literature to a position of primacy over life, on the grounds of its greater extension:

> But as it often happens that the best men are but little known, and consequently cannot extend the usefulness of their examples a great way; the writer may be called in aid to spread their history farther, and to present the amiable pictures to those who have not the happiness of knowing the originals; and so,

by communicating such valuable patterns to the world, he may perhaps do a more extensive service to mankind than the person whose life originally afforded the pattern. (P. 39, 1:1)

Martin Battestin has identified a possible source for this justification of writing in the sermons of Isaac Barrow, who similarly felt that accounts of exemplary actions could promote morality.[19] Whether or not Fielding was conscious of the parallel – it was a commonplace of the century that exemplary narratives could emendate moral norms – it is clear that he is claiming for literary narratives the authority of both history and the pulpit. Considered in the light of the Author's statements about his characters, this is a remarkable move indeed, for there are no "originals" in his narrative, only generalized types. The valuable patterns he offers mankind, and which put the activity of the professional narrator in a class by itself, are themselves already the product of personal fabulation – indeed of a professional, i.e., artful, narrator; the great men we are to emulate are already filtered by the perspective of one individual's selfhood and personal experience. The "book of nature" from which "everything is copied" turns out to be inaccessible to the majority of mankind. Only the intercession of a benevolent, and henceforth essential, mediator affords us the opportunity of learning from our betters. The experience of reading provides surer access to truth than first-hand experience.

Again, Sterne and Diderot will go further with the obvious analogies between Creation and literary creation, divine authority and literary or cultural authority, story and history. Fielding's shift of attention from the local practice of self-narration we have seen in Defoe, Marivaux, and Richardson, to the more ambitious enterprise of literary narration prefigures the more fiamboyant gestures of his successors: by foregrounding his own endeavor, making it one of the themes of his fiction, and expanding its scope to include all manner of characters, actions, and historical periods, the Author makes himself the indispensable agent of truth and the authority over his culture. This operation requires that the narrative appear to reflect at one and the same time the Author's agency and his public's world, and it will be perfected in *Tom Jones*, where the mimetic illusion of the story is constantly doubled by signs of its brilliant artifice. In *Joseph Andrews* the formlessness of the plot provides only minimal proof of the Author's virtuosity, and the woodenness of the protagonist(s) prevents their full assimilation to public experience. Yet this is not an agenda that can do without a partner. Just as Christianity depends for its effectiveness on a believing subject – one who, against the overwhelming evidence of universal impiety and hypocrisy, will ceaselessly affirm the authority of God – so too the omnipotent narrator needs a "good-natur'd reader to apply my piece to my observations" (p. 30, Preface).[20] In spite of its apparent simplicity, this formulation poses something of a dilemma. In order to apply the Author's "piece" to his "observations", the Reader must keep both in view at all times, grasping each feature of the fiction as both a component of a natural world, echoed in his or her own experience, *and* as a confirmation of the Author's thesis. Conversely, if it is to underwrite this bifocal perspective, the narrative must reflect nature and exemplify the behavior of mankind at the same time that it reinforces its creator's argument by displaying his hand in its configuration. It must at all moments appear drawn from nature, yet the product of art, alloying the authority of history with the story of its authorship and inviting the reader who is to be improved by its reading to emulate the judgments of its maker.[21]

Moreover, to the extent he takes his moral mission seriously, the Author must not only approximate the content of history in his fiction, creating a world that appears to reflect nature as his Reader has experienced it, but also enact and elicit the process of history he claims to represent. He must embody in his own discourse the very revision of experience at the hands of reading which his agenda proposes as its moral justification. For how can the Reader take seriously the correlation between literary narration and a better moral universe if the narrative that reflects that universe divorces moral conduct from narrational and interpretive activity, or if the world portrayed by the privileged literary narrator itself resists improvement in the course of its narration?

Yet this is precisely what *Joseph Andrews* does, and therein, I would contend, lies its fundamental shortcoming. It has been argued that the structure and characters of *Joseph Andrews* embody the beliefs of latitudinarian Christianity to which its author subscribed.[22] The work is less successful in demonstrating the efficacy of the *literary* enterprise it advances. For there is no evidence anywhere in the novel that an enlightened narrational or interpretive practice brings about moral emendation. Indeed, there is precious little moral development at all in the work. The type characters such as Lady Booby, Slipslop, the innkeepers, or Trulliber remain unmoved by their encounters with the heroes, who in turn remain unswervingly loyal to their principles from beginning to end. Joseph and Fanny neither degenerate nor get better with experience, they merely complete their appointed rounds. In fact, as critics have noted, many of the central episodes of *Joseph Andrews* could be rearranged with no appreciable effect on the plot.[23] Lacking any particular order or necessary link to one another, these episodes neither constitute a moral argument nor foreground the craft of their maker.

Similarly, it is difficult to see how the selfless simplicity of the protagonists can function either as analogue to nature or exemplar for the reader;

Adams' social dysfunction is hardly more desirable, finally, than his opponents' cruel hypocrisy. Wolfgang Iser, who concedes that "there is no indication whatsoever as to how people really *should* behave,"[24] sees in the absence of a distinct moral recipe the opening of a "virtual dimension," a space within the text in which the reader can elaborate a virtual morality.[25] While this is a clever way to reconcile the Author's moral agenda with a piece that does not seem to fulfill it, it reveals, in its very contrivance – the logic of which would lead one to conclude that the most masterful moral work is one which simply juxtaposes static, irreconcilable antinomies – an awareness of the novel's crudeness.

Ultimately, it seems to me, *Joseph Andrews* adumbrates a theoretical alternative to the morally degenerate narrative self-ishness it portrays, but it does not successfully implement that model. The world it depicts is decidedly more historical than those we have previously seen, in the sense that shared stories regulate virtually every plane of society, every domain of personal endeavor; but the privileged literary representation of human nature which the novel proposes as a mode of knowledge transcendent of such "history" does not itself provide sufficient indication of how one ought to survive in a world driven by narrative. Only in *Tom Jones* will Fielding address this question directly.

NOTES

1 The relationship of Fielding to Richardson is an issue beyond the scope of this study. *Shamela*, the biting parody of *Pamela* that was published in 1741 and is attributed to Fielding, leaves little doubt as to his judgment of Richardson's moral stance and art. Similarly, *Joseph Andrews* commences with a barb directed at *Pamela*, and announces itself as the adventures of her equally chaste brother, Joseph, although the prevalent critical view, following Martin Battestin, *The Moral Basis of Fielding's Art* (Wesleyan, Conn.: Wesleyan University Press, 1959), is that Fielding's work "was written, not in negation of *Pamela*, but in affirmation of a fresh and antithetic theory of the art of the novel" (p. 10). On the other hand, Frederick Bissell, in his cursory résumé of Fielding's novels, *Fielding's Theory of the Novel* (New York: Cooper Square, 1933), mentions the similarities between *Le paysan parvenu* and *Joseph Andrews*, p. 5; while Robert Alter, in *Fielding and the Nature of the Novel* (Cambridge, Massachusetts: Harvard University Press, 1968), p. 108, notes the formal affinities between Fielding and authors such as Marivaux in their use of interpolated stories.

2 Patrick Reilly, "Fielding's Magisterial Art," in *Henry Fielding: Justice Observed*, ed. K. G. Simpson (London: Vision Press Ltd., 1985), pp. 75–100; p. 94.

3　Alter, *Fielding and the Nature of the Novel*, pp. 3–25, 65, provides an interest-
　ing résumé of critical antagonism to Fielding. He theorizes that the hostility to
　Fielding's simplistic treatment of human behavior, and in particular sex, is
　rooted in the Puritan tendency to attach extreme importance to sexual matters
　and a corresponding reluctance to see them trivialized.

4　In keeping with the convention established in earlier chapters, I shall reserve
　the uppercase "Author" or "Reader" to designate the thematized author that
　appears as a meta-character in the novels, and the reader he addresses.

5　Fielding's works include substantial framed narratives and depict extensive
　dialogical self-exposition, and his last novel, *Amelia*, uses the familiar device
　of lengthy first-person narrations; but the major brunt of the story-telling in
　Joseph Andrews and *Tom Jones* falls to the Author.

6　Cf. Reilly, "Fielding's Magisterial Art," p. 76.

7　*The History of the Adventures of Joseph Andrews, and of his Friend Mr. Abraham
　Adams. Written in Imitation of the Manner of Cervantes, Author of Don Quixote.*

8　Patricia Meyer Spacks, *Imagining a Self*, p. 6.

9　Citations are from the Penguin edition by R. F. Brissenden (Penguin Books,
　1977), which follows Martin Battestin's Wesleyan Edition, with minor spelling
　emendations; book and chapter numbers are included for use with other edi-
　tions.

10　As these remarks suggest, I attribute the relative failure of *Amelia* to its impli-
　cit retraction of Fielding's bold new innovation. Once the Author has made
　himself the center of attention, and the characters demoted to the rank of
　mere vehicle, he cannot regress to the outmoded convention of the historical
　narrator–character.

11　Samuel Johnson proposes a similar distinction: "Affectation is to be always
　distinguished from hypocrisy, as being the art of counterfeiting those qualities
　which we might, with innocence and safety, be known to want"; *The Rambler*,
　no. 20 (May 26, 1750), p. 119.

12　An even more biting indictment of mindless emulation can be found in Saint-
　Preux's commentaries on Paris, in *Julie, ou la nouvelle Héloïse*.

13　This hierarchy of relative rank, which Diderot will reiterate in *Jacques le
　fataliste* in the guise of Jacques' theory that every person has a "dog," or
　someone lower by whom they can measure their superiority, is also reminiscent
　of Jacob's argument in *Le paysan parvenu* that differences of rank are essentially
　differences of moment in one's itinerary of social advancement.

14　In distinguishing only between two major classes of character, I am obviously
　glossing over further distinctions that might be made in the context of different
　critical approaches. Sheldon Sacks, for instance, manages to distinguish for his
　purposes no less than "seven classes of agents, each class defined according to
　the similarity of its members' roles in controlling our reactions to represented
　acts, thoughts, and characters"; *Fiction and the Shape of Belief* (Berkeley:
　University of California Press, 1966), p. 232.

15　Martin Price, *Forms of Life* (New Haven: Yale University Press, 1983), p. 9, is
　sensitive to this same structure in *Tom Jones*: "Fielding constructed a novel in

which an artlessly imprudent hero could not hope to acquit himself with success in a world of self-interest."

16 Sacks, *Fiction*, p. 96.

17 *The History of Tom Jones, a Foundling*, ed. R.P.C. Mutter (Penguin Books, 1985), p. 201.

18 Johnson similarly extolls the value of biography; *Rambler*, no. 136 (July 6, 1751).

19 Battestin, *Moral Basis*, pp. 33–4.

20 Both Alter, *Fielding and the Nature of the Novel*, p. 18, and Wayne Booth, *The Rhetoric of Fiction* (Chicago: University of Chicago Press, 1961), p. 217, note the analogy between the agency of the narrator in Fielding and that of providence.

21 Bryan Burns is also sensitive to the tension in *Joseph Andrews*, but he interprets it in terms of conflicting desires, rather than of contradictory exigencies: "Throughout *Joseph Andrews*, in fact, there is a conflict, never entirely resolved, between the desire to open the reader to a rich, free narrative of the often wayward doings of a life on the road and the desire to produce a highly patterned novel with a didactic core. This is the dilemma at the root of the book: . . . its urgent intimacy with experience, but at the same time its attempt to transcend this naturalistic attentiveness in the interest of symmetry of structure and thematic (in the end, ethical) control"; "The Story-telling in *Joseph Andrews*," in *Henry Fielding: Justice Observed*, ed. K. G. Simpson (London: Vision Press Ltd., 1985), pp. 119–36; pp. 120–1.

22 Battestin, *Moral Basis*.

23 See, for example, Sacks, *Fiction*, pp. 209–13.

24 Wolfgang Iser, *The Implied Reader* (Baltimore: Johns Hopkins University Press, 1974), p. 41.

25 "The worldly wise are lacking in morality, the moralist in self-awareness, and these two negative poles carry with them a virtual ideality against which the reader must measure himself; this ideality is the configurative meaning of the text, the product of the reader's own insight, creating standards below which he must not fall"; Iser, *Implied Reader*, p. 44.

11

The Emergence of Literary Authority
(*Tom Jones*)

Fielding's own sense of *Joseph Andrews*'s inadequacy finds confirmation in the manifold refinements he brings to *Tom Jones*. Critics are divided as to whether this second comic epic merely expands upon, or completely revises, the techniques and devices of its predecessor,[1] but all seem to agree that it is better wrought. For our purposes, the significant alterations are of two orders. On the one hand, modifications to the plot structure and the character development create a fictional world consonant with the Author's concept of progressive moral improvement. Among such changes I would count the introduction of complex motivation; the replacement of an episodic plot by one of progressive linear development; and the substitution of a morally complex, highly social, self-conscious protagonist (and his equally complex sweetheart, Sophia) for the static Joseph (and the nearly inert Fanny). On the other hand, a number of modifications make more evident the agency of the Author in the articulation of the fictional world: a labyrinthine, interconnected plot; an exaggerated formal symmetry in the disposition of events and characters; a precision with respect to chronology and duration; an increase in the number and range of Authorial interventions; and most important of all, an attention to the Reader's reactions and function in the fulfillment of the book's purpose.

While the presence of an ironic, detached Author signals the emergence of a new self-conscious metanovel, the plot of *Tom Jones* continues, and in fact caricatures, the tradition established by Defoe, Marivaux, and Richardson. Tom is in many senses the archetypal – at this point in history perhaps the stereotypical – eighteenth-century hero: an orphan of unknown birth; gifted with above average looks, intelligence, integrity, and spirit; in love with a person above his station; taken under the protection of a person of means and influence; and ultimately rewarded with a social metamorphosis and re-identification. Even more than was the case with his predecessors, however, Tom's metamorphosis is regulated by narrative: from the moment of his birth, his identity is the subject of public speculation, and the various stages of his maturation, expulsion from Paradise Hall, wanderings, and eventual reunification with his sweetheart Sophia Western, are all modulated by the stories people contrive on his account.

Early on, the Author remarks that "mankind have always taken great delight in knowing and descanting on the actions of others" (p. 95, 2:4),[2] and indeed, the driving force behind his hero's adventures will be the fictions people devise about Tom and his conduct. There are actually two distinct plot lines, both of which involve narration and its relationship to identity and the public narrative. On the one hand, Tom Jones, a bastard of unknown paternity, is expelled from the household of his foster father, the good Squire Allworthy, on the basis of a series of misrepresentations of Jones' character and behavior by Blifil, Allworthy's conniving nephew, and Blifil's two mentors, Square and Thwackum. Reconciliation with Allworthy through the revelation of Jones' true character forms one major thread of the plot, which will wend its way through a series of intermediate adventures that befall Tom on his way from Paradise Hall to London, each of which in turn relates the vicissitudes of fortune that result from varying reports of Tom's identity. The second plot line concerns Jones' love for Sophia Western, daughter of the neighboring squire – a passion that is initially thwarted by Jones' presumed low birth, and subsequently by his loose tongue. After Jones' expulsion from Allworthy's home, and faced with the prospect of a forced marriage with Blifil, Sophia leaves home and makes her separate way to London, several times crossing Jones' path en route and discovering, to her distaste, his adventures and his public discoursing on her subject. Ultimately, Jones learns narrational discretion through his experiences on the road and in London, and a sequence of revelations concerning his birth reveal him to be the eldest son of Bridget Allworthy and heir to the Squire's estate; upon receiving this news, he and Sophia are united in wedlock.

The interaction of personal and public account is at the heart of this structure. Not only is Tom's identity based on a carefully constructed fable from the outset – his true mother and supposed mother have contracted to deceive both Allworthy and the entire village until the time of the former's death – but his education, expulsion, adventures on the road, alienation from Sophia, and eventual re-identification and marriage, all involve judgments of character on the basis of received reports. Revisions of his "true" identity saturate the plot, from the continual fabulations of Partridge – the man accused of being his father, who, knowing better and imagining Tom to be the mad runaway heir to the Allworthy estate, attaches himself to the foundling during his wanderings – or the rantings of Squire Western, who sees in him the illegitimate usurper of the family fortune, to the less grandiose but more numerous assessments of his character by the innkeepers, travelers, chambermaids, and soldiers whom he encounters, all of whom reverse their treatment of Jones at the drop of a phrase, as it were. Stories inform virtually every aspect of identity, affect virtuous as well as mischievous people, and can alter the most profound friendships. Even Jones' "parents" are selected on hearsay and driven from the village, in spite of the vigorous denials of the "father" and the lack of any evidence to incriminate the "mother." Allworthy himself, although virtuous, is almost entirely motivated by received reports, on the basis of which he commits a series of judgmental blunders, in spite of his efforts to uncover the truth. Not even the strongest relationship between individuals can go against received opinion: Squire Western passes from extravagant affection for Jones, his beloved hunting partner and comrade, to that of rabid hatred, then back to affection, as the young man's identity evolves from that of mere neighbor, to uppity bastard seeking to dilute the Western name, and finally to that of wealthy nobleman, whose marriage will further consolidate Western's holdings.

Like *Joseph Andrews, Tom Jones* generalizes the practice of self-interested narration: virtually every level and type of social being participates in the construction of the shared text of reality, from the vitriolic housekeeper, Mrs Wilkins, who terrorizes the local villagers, or the blundering, garrulous Partridge, whose incessant boasting is at the heart of Tom's problems on the road to London, to the hypocritical Lady Bellaston, who is intent on seducing Tom without compromising her reputation. In contrast to Joseph, however, Tom also participates in this process and is defined in terms of it; and his story of maturation as an individual involves not a withdrawal from the collective story of his society, but rather an apprenticeship in the intricacies of social interaction and virtuous behavior in a world regulated by circulated accounts. The concept of social identity, and *a fortiori* the shared experience we call history, towards which the novel evolves is neither monological nor unitary, neither simply personal contrivance nor autonomous stable truth, but an evolving record of transactions between individual and collective, narrational instance and narrative context. As the story's outcome suggests, truth in such an environment is a function of duration and consensuality, and thus ultimately resistant to major tampering. From a caricature of the perversion of history on a local scale, which dramatizes how a self-interested version of a person's character and behavior can be constructed out of slanted testimony and muddled judgment, the plot of *Tom Jones* progresses to a revision of that person's identity within a larger arena, and at a later point in time, on the basis of a growing plurality of testimony in his favor and a steady accumulation of positive reports of his conduct.

The two extremes of behavior, the two ethical stances around which this progression is articulated correspond to two opposed narrational practices, two contrary attitudes with respect to the authoritative narrative of the collective. The negatively valued model, that of detached mastery and manipulation for personal profit, is epitomized by Blifil, whose negative accounts of Tom's character during their childhood and youth cause the latter to be expelled from Allworthy's home. The rhetoric of calumny used by Blifil, and the communal practice of fabricating the "truth" about people on the basis of circulating reports, receive thorough analysis in *Tom Jones*, one of the consequences of which is to expose the vulnerability of human judgment to collective narrative. Incarnated by Jones' benefactor, Allworthy, the credibility of formal judgment – its ability to get at the truth – is steadily undermined by the latter's successive misguided verdicts, which alter the fate of Jones, his presumed mother and father, and his friend, Black George, the gamekeeper.

In each case, Allworthy's judgment is influenced by the accounts of others, for he seldom has any direct access to the events in question. These accounts are in turn accredited or discounted on the basis of the "accountant's" reputation. Thus when Jenny Jones cannot be found to confirm the innocence of Partridge, Allworthy accepts the general allegation of her waywardness and roundly concludes "that the evidence of such a slut as she appeared to be, would have deserved no credit" (p. 107, 2:6). Conversely, when the self-righteous Blifil reports that Black George has been taking hares illegally, the gamekeeper is summarily punished on the basis of his accuser's status (3:10). There is no judgment that does not depend upon an account, nor is there any such account that does not harken back to a further account that validates its articulation. Late in the novel, Mrs Miller's repeated protestations of Tom's innocence will start to sway Allworthy only once they are backed up by the narratives of Mr Nightingale and the now-repentant Square. Even a mother's testimony as to the identity of her offspring is put into question and requires a further report to substantiate it: Jenny Jones' insistence that Tom is not her son will not be accepted until substantiated by the law, in the form of Dowling's report of Bridget Allworthy's legacy.

Tom Jones differs markedly from *Joseph Andrews* in its formalization of the narrative basis of legal judgment, but also in that the most important accounts in the later novel are careful strategies in a long-term plan of self-advancement, and not spontaneous, obvious responses to perceived immediate self-interest. True, the overall plot is set against a backdrop of spontaneously vicious gossip, epitomized by the villagers and servants, some of whom, like Mrs Wilkins the housekeeper, endeavor ceaselessly to ingratiate themselves with their masters by castigating their inferiors. But the mainsprings of the plot – the revelations by Captain Blifil of Mrs Partridge's suspicion that her husband is Tom's father, or the younger

Blifil's conniving misrepresentation of his actions and those of Tom, or the compact between Bridget Allworthy and her accomplice Jenny Jones, or the intrigue on the part of Lady Bellaston to have Jones pressed into the navy – all result from conscious, elaborately orchestrated, sustained projects of narrational treachery.

Blifil's tactics exemplify such treachery and illustrate in what respects it differs from previous models. Most striking is the fact that this new, ignoble variety of narrational manipulation focuses less on self-representation and the subordination of the addressee than on the destruction of a third party through slander. Blifil avoids dialogical confrontation with Jones, preferring to address himself directly to the crucial elements of their common "public" – Allworthy, Thwackum, and Square. However it is also noteworthy that Blifil manages this microcosmic public sphere by blending elements of truth with self-interested distortion, thus underlining the extent to which "facts" are contingent on their narrational context.

The simplest of these techniques consists in omitting or adding components to the story. To condemn Black George, Blifil "by the hasty addition of the single letter S, . . . considerably altered the story; for he said that George had wired hares" (p. 148, 3:10), when in fact the gamekeeper had taken only one, many months past. Conversely, when the child Blifil relates Tom's assault on him, he omits mentioning that he provoked the other by calling him a "beggarly bastard" (p. 131, 3:4), but he adds another, apparently unrelated, fact to his account, which devastates Tom's counter-argument. When Tom contests his story, Blifil counters by denying the insult and accusing his rival of lying – and he backs up his accusation with reference to an episode when Tom concealed the name of his accomplice in a case of minor poaching:

> Upon which Master Blifil said, "It is no wonder. Those who will tell one fib, will hardly stick at another. If I had told my master such a wicked fib as you have done, I should be ashamed to shew my face"
>
> "What fib, child?" cries Thwackum pretty eagerly.
>
> "Why, he told you that nobody was with him a shooting when he killed the partridge; but he knows . . . yes he knows; for he confessed it to me, that Black George the gamekeeper was there. Nay, he said, – yes you did, – deny it if you can, that you would not have confest the truth, though master had cut you to pieces." (P. 132, 3:4)

Blifil's strategy here is to use a bit of truth about Tom – just a bit, for he mentions nothing of Tom's motives for lying – in order to discredit his adversary's true account and shift attention from his own lie. Since Tom is honest he cannot deny the truth, nor dare he attempt to bring the discussion back to the matter at hand. Ironically, Blifil counts on Tom's honesty to prove him a liar; focusing on a detail in the past, he distorts the present and plants a seed of suspicion for the future.

As the explicit personification of self-interest – one of those "minds whose affections ... are solely placed on one single person, whose interest and indulgence alone they consider on every occasion" (p. 170, 4:6)[3] – Blifil must go to great lengths to mask his motives, manipulating his interlocutor into making a favorable judgment on him by feigning a reluctance to promote his own cause or condemn others. In the famous scene where he releases Sophia's pet bird and provokes Tom's fall into the canal, he immediately declares himself guilty, alleging a Christian desire to give the bird freedom (4:3). Naturally he is forgiven for having yielded to this laudable impulse, his malice concealed by his ready admission of his act. Similarly, when interrogated by Allworthy concerning Tom's behavior on the night of the Squire's illness, Blifil will perform an even more remarkable tour de force, feigning an unwillingness to inform on the rival whose ruin he has premeditated:

> "How," said Allworthy, "hath he done anything worse than I already know? Tell me, I beseech you." "No," replied Blifil, "it is now past, and perhaps he may have repented of it." "I command you, on your duty," said Allworthy, "to tell me what you mean," "You know, sir," says Blifil, "I never disobeyed you; but I am sorry I mentioned it, since it may now look like revenge, whereas, I thank Heaven, no such motive ever entered my heart; and if you oblige me to discover it, I must be his petitioner to you for your forgiveness."
> (P. 284, 6:10)

By feigning reluctance to speak uncharitably of his rival, Blifil makes Allworthy extract from him the story of Tom's behavior, and he makes that behavior appear all the more culpable with respect to his own, by refusing to condemn it.[4] Having lured Allworthy into commanding him to recount what he knows, he produces an artful resumé of all of Tom's questionable behavior during the period when Allworthy was ill. Focusing only on the negative aspects of his rival's conduct, which he contrasts to his own actions and those of his cronies, Blifil carefully adheres to the facts of Tom's behavior, but skews his uncle's perception of those events by avoiding any mention of Tom's motives.

The full extent of Blifil's calculation emerges only in the Author's commentary, where we learn that he had not only carefully nurtured the whole account for several weeks, but gone to considerable trouble to prevent the premature revelation of Tom's sins:

> In reality, Blifil had taken some pains to prevail with the parson, and to prevent the discovery [of Tom's behavior] at that time [when Allworthy was

still ill]; for which he had many reasons. He knew that the minds of men are apt to be softened and relaxed from their usual severity by sickness. Besides, he imagined that if the story was told when the fact was so recent, and the physician about the house, who might have unravelled the real truth, he should never be able to give it the malicious turn which he intended. Again, he resolved to hoard up this business, till the indiscretion of Jones should afford some additional complaints; for he thought the joint weight of many facts falling upon him together, would be the most likely to crush him; and he watched therefore some such opportunity as that with which Fortune had now kindly presented him. Lastly, by prevailing with Thwackum to conceal the matter for a time, he knew he should confirm an opinion of his friendship to Jones, which he had greatly laboured to establish in Mr Allworthy. (Pp. 285–6, 6:10)

Like Lovelace, Blifil is a man who plans history, calculating the effect his accounts will have; however, the brunt of that effect falls not on the addressee, but on the referent. Moreover, he is no extraordinary individual, no supernarrator, but merely a particularly strong incarnation of a practice rampant in his society and of which the novel furnishes many other examples – such as his father Captain Blifil, Thwackum, Square, Lady Bellaston, and Lady Western, to name just a few. And just as the effect of the narrative is displaced to a third party who is generally not present to defend himself, the agency of the narration is dissembled under the guise of simple fact. The hypocrites' management of their reputations occurs through their slander of others and involves a covert, permanent deceit that shuns acknowledgement and attempts to foist its art off as the simple emergence of truth. Unlike Lovelace, who craves dialogical struggles, seduces Clarissa in spite of his bad reputation, and actually relishes the challenge this presents – and the prestige that comes to his persona of a rake as a result – Blifil founds his selfhood on a lie which he nurtures from infancy on, concealing his smallness of mind and malice from all those around him – even from his supporters in the household who, perhaps from a sense of discretion common to the selfish, never explicitly discuss his motives or true interests. His is a sense of self grounded in permanent duplicity, but having no dialogic accomplice, a consciousness quite literally constituted by the need to project a character other than its own, and consumed with the double goal of promoting and concealing its self-interest.

For Blifil and those like him, identity is a construct or permanent mask, self-expression a continual mis-representation of the acts and characters of others, the dialogical Other a rival to be duped. This is the negative vision of narrative selfhood which arises from the generalization of the process of self-representation to all members of society – not just the extraordinary – and which will persist to the end of the century: "some have considered the larger part of mankind in the light of actors, as personating characters no more their own, and to which, in fact, they have no better title, than the player hath to be in earnest thought the king or emperor whom he represents" (pp. 299–300, 7:1). If in the work of Defoe, Prévost, Marivaux, and Richardson the construction of a public persona is associated primarily with the protagonists, all of whom are for that very reason exceptional, by the time of *Tom Jones* it has become a paradigm for identity in general, embracing the majority of mankind and problematizing in the process any notion of simple unitary truth or facts. All social identity is founded in representation; all representation is in the final analysis self-representation, even if its apparent referent is always another person; and all self-representation is necessarily colored by self-interest:

> let a man be never so honest, the account of his own conduct will, in spite of himself, be so very favourable, that his vices will come purified through his lips, and, like foul liquors well strained, will leave all their foulness behind. For tho' the facts themselves may appear, yet so different will be the motives, circumstances, and consequences, when a man tells his own story, and when his enemy tells it, that we scarce can recognize the facts to be one and the same. (P. 379, 8:5)

This observation by the Author is elicited by a biased report of his misfortune which Tom Jones addresses to Partridge, and it underlines that while Tom's selflessness would seem to put him at the opposite pole from Blifil, even he cannot avoid construing past events to his advantage when he recounts his story. Once personal accounts have become the standard currency for social transactions, every individual must continually represent him- or herself – or rather *mis*represent, since no self-accounting can ever be impartial, whatever the character of the individual delivering it, and regardless of whether it represents the self directly or by inference. Partridge and Mrs Honour consistently inflate the fortunes and rank of their respective masters, and deflate those of their peers, so that more prestige might accrue to themselves. In like manner, the various innkeepers boast of the quality of their clientele in an effort to enhance their own standing.

The same naturally holds true for the process of interpretation which is an integral part of the narrative reordering of the world. People read the actions of others and the consequences befalling them in accordance with their own personal goals and character – an axiom that we have already noted in the works of Marivaux and Richardson, but which is more vigorously illustrated by the works of Fielding. Thus, the Author assures us, a single story, such as his relation of Jones' misfortunes with regard to Sophia, will produce different, if equally satisfying conclusions in diverse characters for wise and good men may consider what happened to Jones at Upton as a just punishment for his wickedness, with regard to women, of which it was indeed the immediate consequence; and silly and bad persons may comfort themselves in their vices, by flattering their own hearts that the characters of men are rather owing to accident than to virtue. (P. 579, 12:8)

Drawing a comparison between theater audiences and the public in the greater drama of life, the Author maintains that any given event will be greeted with as many different reactions and interpretations as there are social species (pp. 300–1, 7:1).[5]

However, to say that events and individuals gain their specificity in the telling and the listening is not necessarily to open the field of truth to tampering by calculating individuals. For one thing, the very multiplicity of "identities" which a single individual or act acquires – and sheds – over time makes it difficult for any single construal to dominate. Every event exists in multiple versions and evolves over time according to the character and motives of the person reporting it: this is the pattern that *Tom Jones* drives home with such episodes as Tom's lying to spare Black George, his drunkenness on the day of Allworthy's sickness, his apparent indiscretion regarding Sophia's name, or his proposal of marriage to Lady Bellaston, to name just the most egregious examples. At the same time, the sum record of any given individual's actions and statements over time accumulates into a narrative trend which has the force to withstand rival (mis)representations by virtue of its consistency and the number of its agents. Individuality in *Tom Jones*, if indeed it may still be called such, is realized only as a social, historical collaboration, worked out like any other fact within a process of self-representation, reportage, and construal; it is never the product of an isolated event or person, nor merely a collective plot, but rather at all times the evolving relationship between the two. There is thus a social imperative, a need to enter the enterprise of collective (hi)story-making, which explains both Tom's complex moral status and his difference from Joseph Andrews.

It is Tom who comes to represent the inverse social attitude to Blifil, but only after an extended apprenticeship into the world of collective discourse. If Tom seems given to excess and decidedly less virtuous than Joseph Andrews, it is because he plunges headfirst into what the Author refers to as "conversation . . . with all ranks and degrees of men" (p. 439, 9:1). We remember this notion from *Joseph Andrews* as the principle upon which Joseph based his knowledge, and the Author reintroduces it in *Tom Jones* as part of his prescription for authors wishing to write similar histories. His admonition that "a true knowledge of the world is gained only by conversation, and the manners of every rank must be seen in order to be known" (p. 656, 14:1) clearly implies that the wise man can only become so through social intercourse,[6] and, indeed, the plot of *Tom Jones* confirms that one cannot become much of anything at all in the absence of such intercourse. The revision of Tom's character and origins occurs gradually, as his own actions and statements are woven into the accounts of those with whom he interacts. When, near the end of the novel, the increasing testimony of his supporters tips the scales of probability against Blifil's solitary lie, Tom's character emerges as an accepted fact; so too does the story of his origins, once corroborated by the testimony of multiple parties.

Tom grows into a worthy successor to Allworthy (whose renown explicitly results from his frequent and consistent intervention in the affairs of others), by extending his goodness to all he meets, while Blifil fades into insignificance in the greater world beyond Paradise Hall. The manipulator of history is ultimately overwhelmed by it, while the character who gives himself over to it eventually acquires an identity in excess of his aspirations. The outcome of the plot thus not only recalls that of *Clarissa*, but allegorizes the gesture of the Authorial self who similarly commits himself to history.

From a sheerly mechanical point of view, Tom's willingness to become involved in the stories of others facilitates the eventual discovery of his origins by expanding the points of contact between his story and those of others. It is his entanglement with Mrs Waters (alias Jenny Jones – his supposed mother), Partridge (his supposed father), Mrs Miller, his landlady, and Nightingale, his friend, to mention just the most obvious, that disseminates the record of his good acts and brings his whereabouts to the attention of those familiar with his origins. He demonstrates that even if one cannot foresee what outcome is likely to result from becoming involved in the problems of others, for anything at all to occur one must be enmeshed within the collective account, since although the larger movements of the discursive economy are unpredictable and irreducible to any single act, they nonetheless depend on individual instances for their sustenance. As the Author aptly puts it, "the world may indeed be considered as a vast machine, in which the great wheels are originally set in motion by those which are very minute, and almost imperceptible to any but the strongest eyes" (p. 212, 5:4).[7]

Of course Tom's reidentification entails more than the willingness to interact with others. There are many characters in the book only too eager to append their destiny to that of other parties in the hopes of advancement – Square, Thwackum, Mrs Honour, and the unshakable Partridge, to name just the most obvious. Tom's reconciliation with Sophia and Allworthy occurs only after a social apprenticeship in which the hero learns to temper his social intercourse with judgment, discretion, and an awareness of its possible consequences. With respect to the three variables which the Author cites as coloring facts – motives, circumstances, and consequences[8] – Jones, whose motives are almost always above reproach, has to learn to weigh his proposed action in terms of current circumstances and possible consequences. His drunkenness, for instance, is motivated by his joy at the news of Allworthy's recovery and his irrepressible desire to celebrate, but he scarcely contemplates the circumstances (his benefactor is still sick) nor the consequences (it will be held against him and lead him to engage in other unmentionable behavior with Molly Seagrim). Later, when he toasts Sophia with soldiers he meets on his journey, he again acts out of a reasonable motive (to do honor to the woman he loves), but neglects the circumstances or possible results of his act. The same could obviously be said of his ceding to the advances of Mrs Waters in an inn filled with gossips and busybodies, or his involvement with Lady Bellaston.

If Tom is all motive, with little attention to circumstance and consequence, his protector, and the figure of judgment in the novel, Squire Allworthy, is inversely deficient. His unjust condemnation of Jones and his tenacity in maintaining his good opinion of Blifil both result from a blindness to motive. He knows only the circumstances, and consequences of Tom's behavior: that he lied about Black George, that he hit Blifil, got Molly Seagrim pregnant, became inebriated during the Squire's illness, and so forth. Tom's motives mitigate if not excuse all of these actions; but Allworthy has little discernment for motives, which is why he accepts Blifil's accounts even near the end of the novel, when evidence of a massive lie is mounting. Critics tend to locate the moral impact of the novel in Tom's apprenticeship of prudence, but the plot lays nearly equivalent stress on Allworthy's discovery of his own interpretive shortcomings. I would suggest that both the hero and his benefactor have to acquire a sophistication in the handling of stories and history before the novel can reach its happy conclusion.

Allworthy needs to weigh motives, and particularly self-interest of the type that drives Blifil, Thwackum, and Square, if he is to mete out justice on the basis of received accounts; and this is precisely what he does, in discounting Thwackum's letter, sorting out the story of the lawyer who interceded in Tom's case, and accepting Mrs Waters' and Dowling's accounts of Tom's birth. Tom needs to temper his passion with a calculation of possible consequences and an eye to the circumstances of his actions. This is precisely what he does in his long harangue to Nightingale, whom he urges to think of the consequences, before abandoning Nancy Miller (14:7). Later, when he turns down Mrs Hunt's proposal of marriage it will be on the grounds of his situation (he is already engaged elsewhere), an idea that did not occur to him in his earlier encounters with women (15:11). He confirms his reform, and his sensitivity to motives, once again, when he sees through the plot of Mrs Fitzpatrick and declines all of her proposals to gain access to Sophia illicitly (16:9).

It is on the basis of this incipient reform, and her longstanding conviction of the goodness of Tom's motives, that Sophia will forgive and accept Tom. She is, finally, the novel's only mature character in the narrative sense, able both to discern the motives behind Tom's and Blifil's contrasting behavior, and to balance the disparate versions of Tom's past and her future that assail her in the persons of her father, Mrs Honour, Lady Bellaston, and her Aunt Western. And the union of Tom and Sophia, Allworthy and Western will mark the reconciliation of passion and wisdom, virtue and energy.

Finally, the positive models of social behavior in *Tom Jones* try neither to coerce nor to elude history – and here again, I mean by that term the economy of personal and shared accounts that underlies the world and plot of the novel – they learn to understand and work within it. They do not attempt to gain control over their fate and that of others in the way that Lovelace sought to, through fabrication of mendacious worlds, but neither do they withdraw from the practice of collective accounting that envelops them. This is what sets them apart from the passivity of Joseph Andrews or the dysfunctional idiosyncrasies of Adams: they actively participate in the negotiation of reality characteristic of their society and culture, while eschewing nevertheless the illusion that any individual can master the communal narrative. It would be an exaggeration to argue that through a revision of his behavior Tom graduates to a position of control over his destiny. For unlike Lovelace, or even Roxana, Moll, or Marianne, he understands that he is part of an evolving system, the larger patterns of which exceed his vision. He cannot foresee the coincidences that will eventually restore his fortune; he cannot know that when he aids Mrs Waters, or the highwayman, or takes on Partridge as a companion, he is actually preparing a reconciliation with Allworthy and the revelation of his heritage. Yet he pursues his course, confident in the correctness of his attitude towards his fellow man.

To the extent that he functions as the exemplary counterpart to the paradigm of hypocritical self-contrivance epitomized by Blifil, Tom's confident engagement in history proposes an ideal of individualism which is in some respects reactionary with respect to the tradition we have been charting. The notion of an intrinsic tendency or consistency of behavior that has nothing to do with conscious planning, reflection on self-image, or the management of others, stands in sharp contrast to the calculation that underlies in varying degrees Defoe's, Marivaux's, and Richardson's heroes, and which reappears in a vulgarized form in Fielding's work as the self-interested manipulation characteristic of the majority of people. Tom is not driven by schemes of glory, self-advancement, or seduction, nor even by principle like Clarissa, who consistently refuses expedients that might alleviate her suffering but require some compromise of her beliefs; nor does a particular self-image influence his behavior, as in the case of Marianne, Jacob, or Pamela. No reflections on his public persona hinder his impulses, no questions of strategy interfere with his desires; he simply follows his heart:

> Mr Jones had somewhat about him, which, though I think writers are not thoroughly agreed in its name, doth certainly inhabit some human breasts; whose use is not so properly to *distinguish* right from wrong, as to *prompt* and *incite* them to the former, and to restrain and with-hold them from the latter. (P. 167, 4:6; my italics)

This renunciation of understanding in favor of simple action seems at first glance consistent with Fielding's vision of the social equation. In a world of individualism run rampant, where virtually everyone is promoting different versions of reality, and where virtually all perceptions of reality are colored by personal motive, it is unrealistic to aspire to absolute certainty and, indeed, self-knowledge. One can but follow one's inclinations and trust that the economy is such that good actions will ultimately work to one's benefit. Such a conclusion might find a precedent in the work of Richardson, where even the Herculean efforts of an intellect such as Lovelace's ultimately succumb to the plural narration instigated by Clarissa; and we could justify Tom's lack of a desire to control history as merely the logical pendant to the generalization of narration – as a prefiguration of a new breed of protagonists aware of, and at ease with, their enclosure in a grander design to which they can contribute, but never master. Such characters will not displace the manipulative individualists but co-exist with them, as representatives of an antithetical understanding of the relationship of individual to collective.

This reading, with its invitation to nostalgia for a pre-historical mode of action that would gravitate towards that which was right without the unstable mediation of an account of prior events, not only clashes with the plot, where Jones' initiation to prudence explicitly involves organizing events in a causal scheme and weighing possible consequences, it also conflicts with the posture of the Author who proposes it. For while the hero makes no move to master the historical equation, his creator exhibits no similar restraint. Fielding does not simply relate the tale of a man at peace with the discursive flux that defines and empowers him; he accompanies his story with an analysis of the mechanisms driving that discourse: even as Tom asserts by example a proper *faith* in history, the Author foregrounds his own compulsion to *understand* it.

If, as the Author tells us, motives, circumstances, and consequences constitute truth, then the Author himself is the source of all truth, for it is he who consistently reveals all three to us – although not always at the same time. In fact, the style of narration in *Tom Jones* blatantly calls attention to all three components of its formula by systematically withholding one or more. Thus, when Blifil delivers the report that condemns Tom, we learn only after the fact of his motives for having waited so long (6:10). Nor, when Mrs Fitzpatrick relates her story, does the Author reveal until later the precise circumstances of her liberation from her husband, and Sophia's motives for suspecting those circumstances (11:7, 11:8, 11:10). The Author attributes his delay in telling the whole story in such cases to his desire not to outpace his characters: "as the lady did not think it material enough to relate to her friend, we would not at that time impart it to the reader" (p. 541, 11:8), but the net effect of such a practice is to underline his agency in the articulation of the story and his ahistorical perspective: "Fielding makes us continually aware that he holds the strings and that he will make his puppets hop about exactly as he pleases until he chooses to set them down."[9] By consistently inverting the order of events and presenting, for example, first the appearance of Squire Western at Lady Bellaston's, and then only subsequently an explanation of how he came to be there, the Author displays the fact that he, unlike his reader or the characters he portrays, stands outside of the flow of time and the chronological reversals it holds. By returning only later – sometimes hundreds of pages later, as in the case of the episode at Upton[10] – to elucidate the reasons for certain acts or the circumstances leading up to particular occurrences, he draws attention to the truth of his thesis about the importance of circumstances, but he also foregrounds his own pre-knowledge of all that history holds.

Thus although *Tom Jones* espouses the course and mechanism of history, it also displays its maker's control of that mechanism; and it drives home that point with a variety of formal and thematic devices. The realistic temporal development of the plot contrasts sharply with the asynchronous perfection of its underlying scheme, which is based most obviously on contrast and symmetry. The story is structured around the symmetrically constituted households of two wealthy, widowed Squires and their sisters, clergymen, and two offspring.[11] Every major character has at least one pendent, sometimes more, representing opposing moral or philosophical stances – Tom versus Blifil, Square versus Thwackum – or countervailing social groups or mores – Squire Western versus his urbane and urban sister, Allworthy versus Western, Molly Seagrim versus Sophia.

The action itself unfolds in three sections, composed of six books each, and covering, respectively, the hero's childhood in the country, apprenticeship on the road, and maturation in London. This tight architecture is seconded by a systematic use of symmetry, parallel constructions, and contrasts on both the level of the individual episodes and in the disposition and personality of the characters.[12] This systematization of the world goes beyond mere opposition. In his elegant analysis of *Tom Jones*, Robert Alter points out that all of the major characters can be arranged along vertical axes of relative energy or vitality, running from impetuous libidinal spontaneity – Western – to the moral prudence and restraint of Allworthy. Variations in sexual behavior are organized similarly – from the repressed artifice of Aunt Western, through the middle ground of Lady Bellaston and Mrs Waters, to the raw sexuality of Molly Seagrim – as are the philosophical markers of the Allworthy household and their pupil, from "Blifil, whose flow of energy is a thin, mean trickle," to "Square, who hypocritically conceals his very real lust," to Thwackum who "channels his vigorous energy into the hard-clenched violence of a schoolmaster's sadism."[13] These schematic arrangements are seconded by the expressive names given the characters, and which reveal their function in the author's plan.

Was such formal contrivance not sufficient to attract the reader's notice, the more straightforward Authorial interventions would surely drive home the point that this history, though it be taken from history, is also his story – or, as he puts it, "the author's offspring, ... the child of his brain" (p. 506, 11:1). And some of the Author's harangues leave little doubt as to the subordinate role of the Reader with respect to those stories:

> First, then, we warn thee not too hastily to condemn any of the incidents in this our history, as impertinent and foreign to our main design, because thou dost not immediately conceive in what manner such incident may conduce to that design. This work may, indeed, be considered as a great creation of our own; and for a little reptile of a critic to presume to find fault with any of its parts, without knowing the manner in which the whole is connected, and before he comes to the final catastrophe, is a most presumptuous absurdity. (P. 467, 10:1)

Suspended in the current of the narrative, the reader can neither perceive in its totality the Author's scheme, nor ignore its presence as a structuring force: we are, in a word, in much the same position as the book's hero. Conversely, from his vantage point outside of his history, which he can contemplate both as a process of unfolding and a pre-existent order, the Author enjoys a depth of understanding which no reader can equal – and, in fact, which no participant in history such as he describes it could ever experience:

> the reader is greatly mistaken, if he conceives that Thwackum appeared to Mr Allworthy in the same light as he doth to him in this history; and he is as much deceived, if he imagines, that the most intimate acquaintance which he himself could have had with that divine, would have informed him of those things which we, from our inspiration, are enabled to open and discover. (P. 136, 3:5)

There are at least two ways to understand or justify this claim of superior wisdom. On the one hand, familiarity from the outset with *all* of the events that "will" transpire gives the Author a transhistorical grasp of his history which neither character nor reader can possess. Running through the various reactions which he supposes his account of Black George's villainy will elicit among the different strata of society, he remarks

> Now we, who are admitted behind the scenes of this great theatre of nature (and no author ought to write anything besides dictionaries and spelling books who hath not this privilege) can censure the action, without conceiving any absolute detestation of the person, whom perhaps nature may not have designed to act an ill part in all her dramas: for in this instance, life most exactly resembles the stage, since it is often the same person who represents the villain and the heroe; and he who engages your admiration to-day, will probably attract your contempt to-morrow. (P. 301, 7:1)

In contrast to the spectators of his history, and, if we are to believe his analogy, to most spectators in the theatre of life, the Author understands that what we take for a person's identity is often merely a temporary role, the consequence of a set of circumstances that may in time be altered: "a single bad act no more constitutes a villain in life, than a single bad part on the stage" (p. 302, 7:1).

On the other hand, although the Author's history purports to represent human nature in general and, by extension, how history works, it does not relate *his* story, nor indeed that of any individual *in* history, but rather that of mankind in *general*. He can thus claim exemption from the myopia that self-definition entails. If the average person's accounts of reality are distorted by self-interest, the Author's are not. He can resist the rush to judgment which self-interest and a limited historical perspective involve, thus eluding the process of revision he describes. In short, by foregrounding his command of motive, circumstance, and consequence, and stressing his position on a plane superior to that of the characters he describes, the Author underlines the fact of his exemption from the world he details. By writing a history over which he alone has authority, he gains a command of history unavailable through other modes of social discourse.

This emergence of a privileged grasp of history can be read in terms of two traditions already alluded to in this study. On the one hand, it can be understood as the latest metamorphosis of selfhood, which, confronted with the inevitability of its ground in the collective account, now casts itself as purely public discourse in an attempt to claim its situation as its own free choice. On the other, it can be correlated to the emergence of a particular form of public discourse, the novel, and the agents of that discourse, the novelist and reader, as the repositories of cultural authority.

From the first of these perspectives, *Tom Jones* can be read as the story of its author's own coming to terms with history as the order that defines him. "In the beginning of *Tom Jones* was the author. By the end of the first sentence both his relation to the story and our attitude toward him were already well on the way to being established: the story was his perform- ance."[14] No longer convinced of the efficacy of direct intervention in the manner of Lovelace, Fielding borrows from Clarissa the strategy of sub- lation into literature. In the persona of the Author – a device whose indirect or mediated self-expression gets around the pitfalls of self-interest – he simultaneously relates his understanding of history as a dialectic of social discourse and orchestrates his own emergence in that dialectic as a literary figure.

The Author's presence as a character rivals his own creations in *Tom Jones*. The work's opening paragraphs focus not on the hero, who will begin to take shape as a character only several chapters later, nor on the setting of the action, but on the enterprise of the professional author and the nature of the public narrative he proposes. The subject of the latter, we are informed, is quite simply "Human nature," in which there is "such prodigious vari- ety, that a cook will have sooner gone through all the several species of animal and vegetable food in the world, than an author will be able to exhaust so extensive a subject" (p. 52, 1:1). As if the selection of such a subject were not in itself testimony enough to his mastery, the Author further informs us that the "excellence of the mental entertainment consists less in the subject, than in the author's skill in well dressing it up" (p. 52, 1:1), and to prove his point, and give us a preview of his absolute control over the narrated world, he reveals his plan to commence the action in the country, proceeding thence by degrees to "all the high French and Italian seasoning of affectation and vice which courts and cities afford" (p. 53, 1:1).

The precedent established by the first chapter will carry throughout the book, each successive section or book being prefaced by a dialogue between Author and Reader or a discussion of the Author's principles and beliefs. These eighteen chapters are full of admonitions on how to read, how to write, and what constitutes the comic-epic genre; they reflect an obvious concern with how the Author and his work will be perceived by future generations. Whatever his purported objectivity and distance with regard to the social machines he describes, the Author is clearly very much interested in securing an identity in the future text of his culture. The purpose of his narrative is quite explicitly to express his art, beliefs, wisdom, and senti- ments for generations to come, reanimating in the experience of others the selfhood he cannot be certain of imposing directly:

> Come, bright love of fame, inspire my glowing breast: ... fill my ravished
> fancy with the hopes of charming ages yet to come. Fortel me that some
> tender maid, whose grandmother is yet unborn, hereafter, when, under the
> fictitious name of Sophia, she reads the real worth which once existed in my

Charlotte, shall, from her sympathetic breast, send forth the heaving sigh. (P. 607, 13:1)

In the place of immediate fortune, the Author elects permanent existence as part of his culture's text; he abandons the delusion of individualism and of knowing who he is, for the dream of endless re-identification and re-presentation in future readings and writings:

> Do thou teach me not only to foresee, but to enjoy, nay even to feed on future praise. Comfort me by a solemn assurance, that when the little parlour in which I sit at this instant, shall be reduced to a worse furnished box, I shall be read, with honour, by those who never knew nor saw me, and whom I shall neither know nor see. (P. 607, 13:1)[15]

Fielding's version of what is by now a familiar dialogical concept of selfhood envisions a Reader who, like the Author, is not a single, static entity, but the embodiment of a recurrent transaction over time, re-presented in as many different incarnations as there are readings of the text. As one of his contemporaries puts it, "he that writes is a Sort of Actor in the World as long as his Works continue to be read: He entertains, he informs, he advises; and at once perpetuates the Fame of his Abilities, and the Use of them."[16] The Author's repeated prescriptions indicate that while he recognizes his inability to coerce future readers into specific interpretations, he nonetheless wishes to impose limits on their activity. At the same time, however, he acknowledges that although he is the law-giver, he has value only as part of the hypothetical Reader's agenda:

> as I am, in reality, the founder of a new province of writing, so I am at liberty to make what laws I please therein. And these laws, my readers, whom I consider as my subjects, are bound to believe in and to obey; with which that they may readily and chearfully comply, I do hereby assure them, that I shall principally regard their ease and advantage in all such institutions: for I do not, like a *jure divino* tyrant, imagine that they are my slaves, or my commodity. I am, indeed, set over them for their own good only, and was created for their use, and not they for mine. (P. 88, 2:1)

A compact thus bonds the Author – who, incidentally, here confirms that he is but a construct created for the purpose of a literary transaction – to the Reader. Each functions as one pole in an ongoing dialogue of selfhood; together, they embody the dialectic of narration and narrative. The Author bodies himself forth in an act of narration, a progressive unfolding in time of a personalized vision of reality. Yet, as he himself intimates in the citations above, the world he reveals progressively, already exists in the form of a complete scheme; from the personal point of view, it is his grand plan, but from the literary point of view it is a text or narrative, stable in its configuration and fixed in its totality prior to the intervention of the reader.

In other words, if the Author expresses himself generally as an ongoing narration, he also exists for the Reader as a finished narrative, one of the texts of our culture which is available to all and subject to endless reinterpretation. The same can be said for the Reader, who exists for the Author both as a stable thematic component of the narrative he bequeaths to history (the Reader) and as a future narrational moment of re-articulation according to personal vision (the reader). When the Author writes "if the reader's imagination doth not assist me, I shall never be able to describe the situation of these two persons" (p. 708, 15:5), he both acknowledges his reliance on a future interpretive gesture and incorporates that gesture, and his acknowledgement, into the thematic matter of his work. This is the hallmark of a metanovel.

Reading and writing, finally, emerge in *Tom Jones* as mutually implicating gestures of narration the locus of whose transaction we call a narrative. The formal difference between the Author and the Reader boils down to what one might call a difference of precedence or origin, which is, finally, the difference between reading and writing, nostalgia and prolepsis, a sense of the narrative – and the Other associated with it – as preceding one's narration or following it. Fielding, in other words, makes explicit the model I previously extrapolated from earlier works: a reader interprets a text which is already there, narrating his or her identity within the pre-existing narrative of some Other. Readers find themselves in the words of the Other; authors envision themselves in the Other of their words, creating a narrative which is never there, will only be completed (upon reading) by the Other it enables at some point in the future. As the Author of *Tom Jones* remarks, on the subject of one of his more spectacular figures of speech, "the great beauty of the simile may possibly sleep these hundred years, till some future commentator shall take this work in hand" (p. 62, 1:6).

Self-interest, then, has not disappeared from the novel as a positive force; it has merely attained the logical form towards which the tradition had been moving it. Over and above the interaction with contemporary, collective discourse which Tom Jones epitomizes, the Author and his Reader elaborate a more active dialectical exchange between personal gesture and extant order which recuperates for its agents the sense of control which has disappeared from the plot.

Thus as a privileged form of the narration and narrative which subsists only as hypocrisy and vanity in the fictional world, literature, and specifically the comic-epic novel, assumes a position of primacy over its culture. By telling the story of a world specified to be *like* his, yet not specific to any place or time, and by showing exactly why and how this story is exempt from the limitations of other narration and narrative, the Author makes good on the intimation of literature's role that we saw in *Clarissa*. He formulates a literary self and thus escapes the equation of self-interest even as he establishes that equation as the paradigm for social man. In a world driven by "self-ish" accounts that advance only particular interest, the literary narrative, with its transhistorical types and universal human paradigms, and with its explicit invitation to completion or realization by an Other, engineers for each of its agents a confrontation with the Other of his or her particular realization. Unlike history, such a narrative gains its referential thrust in the process of its actualization: as an exemplary paradigm to be invested with, and related to, the experience of its reader (who in that gesture determines the intention of its author), fiction is always "about" the process, moment, place, and agent of its articulation. In this respect, the novel defines the culture that adopts and validates it, becoming in the process a form of law unto itself: a cultural authority. With *Tom Jones*, fiction comes into its own explicitly as master narrative, as the story of history and the history of its own ascendancy.

NOTES

1 To cite but two instances: while Robert Alter maintains that "virtually everything realized in the art of *Tom Jones* is at least implicit in *Joseph Andrews*" (*Fielding and the Nature of the Novel*, p. ix), Sheldon Sacks maintains categorically that "it is an error to assume that in *Tom Jones* Fielding extended the principles underlying the form of *Joseph Andrews*, but did it better" (p.102).

2 Citations are from the Penguin edition, edited by R. P. C. Mutter (London, 1985), which is based on the so-called "third" edition of 1749. Book and chapter references are included for use with other editions.

3 See also 4:5; 6:4.

4 Blifil uses a similar tactic in 18:5, when, confronted by Allworthy with evidence that he tried to tamper with the witnesses to Tom's duel, he pleads guilty of the crime of "compassion for those who do not deserve it" (p. 828), maintaining that his intervention was on Tom's behalf.

5 The same applies, of course to the Author's history. See, for instance, p. 605, 12:14: "our readers will probably be divided in their opinions concerning this action; some may applaud it perhaps as an act of extraordinary humanity, while those of a more saturnine temper will consider it as a want of regard to that justice which every man owes his country."

6 See also p. 438, 9:1: "there is another sort of knowledge beyond the power of learning to bestow, and this is to be had by conversation .... for however exquisitely human nature may have been described by writers, the true practical system can only be learnt in the world." The most extended and explicit justification of broad social intercourse can be found in the Author's invocation of Experience in 13:1 (p. 609). Ironically, Dr Johnson, who thought very little of *Tom Jones*, expresses much the same idea in his prescription for contempor-

ary writers: "The task of the present writers ... requires, together with that learning which is to be gained from books, that experience which can never be attained by solitary diligence, but must arise from general converse and accurate observation of the living world"; *Rambler*, no. 4 (March 31, 1750).

7　See also pp. 815, 18:2: "Instances of this kind we may frequently observe in life, where the greatest events are produced by a nice train of little circumstances." Numerous episodes come to mind of "coincidences" that secure Jones' ultimate happiness and which consistently result from his willingness to communicate his story and become involved in those of others. Three obvious examples: his indiscretion with Mrs Honour, in the muff incident, which advances his relationship with Sophia; his involvement with the would-be highwayman, who turns out to be Mrs Miller's cousin and inaugurates that lady's good opinion of Jones (14:3); and his intervention in the affair between Nancy Miller and Nightingale, which wins over Mrs Miller definitively (14:4–7), and opens the way to reconciliation with Allworthy.

8　See citation above: "so different will be the motives, circumstances, and consequences, when a man tells his own story, and when his enemy tells it, that we scarce can recognize the facts to be one and the same" (p. 379, 8:5)

9　Robert Alter, *Rogue's Progress*, p. 85.

10　See p. 815, 18:2.

11　Robert Alter, *Fielding and the Nature of the Novel*, pp. 94–5.

12　In the first book already, the scene of Allworthy's sermon to Jenny is juxtaposed to its satiric counterpart, which pits the housekeeper Mrs Wilkins, who has an entirely different notion of charity than Allworthy, against her master's sister, Bridget Allworthy. Lest we fail to note the comic scene's function as a counterpart to its serious equivalent, the Author appends a signal: "A Dialogue between Mesdames Bridget, and Deborah; containing more Amusement, but less Instruction than the former" (p. 70, 1:8). This is a pattern that extends throughout the novel. Alter explores the variety and function of these various symmetries in some depth; *Fielding and the Nature of the Novel*, pp. 87–97.

13　Ibid., p. 90.

14　John S. Coolidge, "Fielding and the 'Conservation of Character,'" *Modern Philology*, 57 (1960), pp. 245–59; p. 249. This is an assessment shared by Mark Kinkead–Weekes: "The Author's appearance on the Stage has shown that the narrative voice is to be regarded as a performance, like all the other characters"; "Out of the Thicket in *Tom Jones*," in Simpson, *Henry Fielding: Justice Observed*, pp. 137–57; p. 141.

15　The pre-eminence of literature over other avenues of self-expression is echoed by D'Argens, *Lettres juives*, no. 48, vol. 2, pp. 165–6: "L'habile Historien, le Poëte célebre, le grand Philosophe conserve un avantage sur le Conquérant & le Géneral. La mémoire des uns ne présente à l'imagination que le souvenir de quelques actions passées; mais les ouvrages des Savans transmettent, font revivre d'âge en âge leur génie & les connoissances de leurs Auteurs. Vingt siècles après leur mort, ils parlent encore avec autant d'éloquence & de vivacité que de leur vivant; & leur esprit se communique à tous ceux qui lisent leurs Ecrits" (The skillful historian, the celebrated poet, the great philosopher enjoy an advantage over the conqueror and the general. The memory of the latter presents the imagination only with the recollection of a few past actions; but the works of the learned transmit and revive from one age to another their genius and the knowledge of their authors. Twenty centuries after their death they still speak with as much eloquence and vivacity as when they were alive; and their mind expresses itself to all those who read their writings). Samuel Johnson expresses similar convictions: "The regard which they whose abilities are cm ployed in the works of imagination claim from the rest of mankind, arises in a great measure from their influence on futurity. Rank may be conferred by princes, and wealth bequeathed by misers or by robbers; but the honours of a lasting name, and the veneration of distant ages, only the sons of learning have the power of bestowing"; *Rambler*, no. 136 (July 6, 1751).

16 James Ralph, *The Case of Authors*, p. 50.

12

Exemplification and the Authoring of Utopia (*Julie, ou la nouvelle Héloïse*)

For the blind Force or Weight of an ungoverned multitude can have no steady nor rational Effect, unless some leading Mind *rouse it into Action, and* point *it to it's proper* End.... *It depends on some superior* Intelligence, *to give it both* Impulse *and* Direction.

John Brown, *An Estimate of the Manners and Principles of the Times*

The critic ("N.") in the dialogue, *Entretien sur les romans*, which Rousseau wrote as a preface to *Julie, ou la nouvelle Héloïse* (1761), remarks to the character of the editor–author ("R.") at one point that the novel seems almost to contain two separate books, an initial story of youthful passion, and a subsequent moral lesson which effaces the example of that story and appears to put its value in question (p. 576).[1] This pattern of revision goes beyond the "before/after" plot structure of earlier works such as *Pamela* in that it affects all levels of the novel's narrative organization – plot, character, subject matter, narrational mode, and point of view. While the first half of *Julie* presents an epistolary tale of passion, dominated by the first-person narrations of two young lovers seeking to express their ideals at the same time they satisfy their passion, its second half, which relates the lovers' reunion as virtuous friends many years later, is punctuated by long descriptions of an ideal political and social economy. These latter passages constitute a veritable political allegory: while they rather superficially retain the conventions of the personal letter, they are for the most part concerned with the depiction of how an exemplary social community ought to be organized, rather than with the intricacies of overwrought selfhood.[2]

Thus two kinds of narration and two types of narrative compete in *Julie*, and each invites a different operation on the part of the reader. The personal narration of the first half foregrounds the self; it is the narcissistic discourse of an ego fascinated with its own difference, intent on stressing those aspects of its identity which set it off from society and consequently exempt it from society's laws. The textual correlate of such narration is an equally exclusive narrative: a letter destined for a single individual, whose delayed reading not only emphasizes the distinction between narrational gesture and narrative product, but involves the correspondent in a dialogical circuit of mutual obligation.[3] As the lovers respond to each other's entreaties, they become ever more entangled in a profoundly egocentric discourse intent on reconciling moral propriety and sensual desire. Their struggle privileges sentiment as the basis of natural order and morality, and offers an image of the way readers themselves react to certain novels, constructing a world on the basis of a private transaction with a text addressed to their passions.

Such narration/narrative of the ego gives way in the second half of *Julie* to a far cooler discourse, in which the impassioned pleas of the self cede to the dispassionate account of how individuals and society should relate. Distributed among the various parties to a utopian social compact and addressed more often than not to a correspondent of whom little reaction is required, this account employs theoretical argument rather than sentiment, and it seeks to convince its reader that the social order it depicts is both logical and natural. The ideal society of the political allegory rejects the self-enclosed dialogue of sexual love as a basis for identity, stressing instead how individualized function within a communal economy can assure each member of the community a sense of worth and happiness. The individual in such an ideal society derives satisfaction by fulfilling an essential role in a collective mechanism of production and mutual service, rather than by cultivating a sense of exclusivity within a private erotic relationship. To mark this shift, nature, which in the first part of *Julie* is systematically correlated to the urges of individual sentiment, realigns itself with reason, order, and symmetry in the second half.

To the extent the reader of *Julie* internalizes these formal and thematic revisions, he or she confirms the ascendancy of conventional order and collectively regulated narrative over the free-flowing narration of sentiment. Communal order and social law displace rampant individualism as the foundation of identity within the novel's plot, just as a textual structure that indulges its reader's private fantasy gives way to one that demands a response grounded in the logic of analysis and the authority of theory.

In this sense, *Julie, ou la nouvelle Héloïse* does more than simply revise the concept of selfhood prevalent in earlier novels. Doubling the story of its protagonists' socialization with the drama of its own textual metamorphosis from sentimental description to political *prescription*, it implicitly redefines the function of novelistic discourse within its culture. Directed as much against the novels of worldliness as against the world they depict, Rousseau's work shifts the locus of novelistic attention from description to prescription.[4] It does not merely represent the world, it proposes a utopia and an ideal form of fictional discourse. But in outlining the laws that should govern society, as well as the strategies individuals should adopt to realize their selfhood within society, the novel necessarily enlarges the claims of its genre. Thus one can read the displacement of ego narration by didactic allegory in the second half of the novel as a second-level allegory which addresses the promotion of literature – and by extension the literary author – to a new position of authority over culture.

We have seen how, a decade earlier, Fielding's works lay the groundwork for the authority of the literary author over the laws of human behavior. In a sense Rousseau seems to backtrack by reintroducing the device of the found collection of letters and masking his hand in the formulation of his utopia. Yet, the presence of the professional author is everywhere in the novel, not only in the two prefaces, which dwell at great length on the possibility that the whole story is the invention of Rousseau, or in the numerous notes, commentaries, and clarifications with which he punctuates the text, but also in the character of the enlightened lawgiver, Julie's husband Wolmar, who, like the author, gives flesh to his theories by fashioning an ideal world. The sections of the novel that focus on Wolmar's utopian community, Clarens, seem all to insist on the subordination of individual passion to collective order, but beneath this message, *Julie* tells another story of how a privileged few, those who know how to observe the world and abstract from its chaos the laws of human nature, can author a culture and modify their own society. Rousseau's narrative repudiates individualism as a *general* strategy for happiness and morality, and thus rejects the vision of collective individualistic narration exemplified by the plot of *Tom Jones*, but it reiterates and elaborates the gesture of recuperating authority for the privileged few which we saw adumbrated in Fielding's Author. The authority of the lawgiver/author Wolmar is transhistorical like that of the Author, in the sense that it implements a general theory of social organization; but it also finds concrete implementation in the structuring of public morality which it initiates. Through the deliberate structuring of collective belief and habit, the author of the exemplary text attains a power more radical than even Lovelace could have envisioned – the power of the enlightened individual to influence the flow of collective history.

This is not a gesture that is easily admitted, however. The novel insists repeatedly that the vehicle of empowerment is a rule-bound economy – a self-sustaining system of changes and exchanges regulated by a set of laws the strength of which grows through repeated usage and assimilation into collective practice. Like any narrative system, whose effect within the social economy hinges on the way it intersects historical conventions of reading, the ideal political and social system prescribed by the lawgiver-cum-novelist in *Julie* ultimately exceeds the grasp of its author. Once a textual or political system is assimilated into collective practice, it resists management by any individual, even its originator.

The emblem of this resistance in *Julie* is Julie herself. As the embodiment of perfect virtue, she is the keystone to the ideal community of Clarens, all of whose members look to her as the exemplification of the community's laws. Since Clarens itself is founded as a demonstration of generalized reciprocal exemplification, Julie functions within the political theory as the exemplification of exemplification. She is the incarnation of Wolmar's theories, the first product of his enlightened reforms, and the vehicle of his most ambitious project, the reformation of Saint-Preux. Yet as Julie's story advances, it becomes increasing clear that while she mediates between all the parts and parties of the novel, she is ultimately beholden to none. Her story is that of a mediational power that goes beyond self-interested discourse as well as the laws of theory, ultimately putting into question even the authority of the man to whom she attributes her current mode of existence; and to the extent that she eventually transcends the individuals and theories she sustains, one might surmise that her textual counterpart, *Julie*, also exceeds its author's (and reader's) intentions, asserting the autonomy of the literary work and the economy it nurtures, even as it seems to empower the author.

Like many of the novels we have considered, *Julie* articulates its plot around a conflict between self-definition and social authority, expressed in the time-honored themes of rebellion against parental law and the class disparity separating two lovers. A young tutor, referred to as Saint-Preux, falls in love with his student, Julie, but the two can never marry because of the difference in their birth. A series of letters between these two lovers and their friends traces the story of their developing love, the social barriers that thwart it, and the eventual conversion of their illicit passion into a friendship based on a mutual love of virtue. The first half of the novel relates Saint-Preux's initial declaration, the consummation of their love, his self-imposed exile, the discovery of the lovers' clandestine correspondence by Julie's mother, the death of the latter, and Julie's subsequent marriage to her father's friend Wolmar. Simultaneously, it explores the limits of a truly radical individuality that maintains the primacy of personal conscience or the dictates of the heart over social custom. The second half of the work outlines a way to go beyond this opposition and unify collective will with individual happiness within a community based on collective, reciprocal emulation and adherence to a specified set of usages.

To a far greater degree than in earlier novels, which articulate the relationship of self to Other on the individual level, identity here is bound up with the larger contract that links individuals to surrounding social, cultural, and even theological orders. Unlike Lovelace and Clarissa, or Pamela and Mr B., or even Marivaux's or Defoe's characters, the hero and heroine of *Julie* are from the outset in nearly perfect accord; theirs is not a story of rivalry, seduction, manipulation, or trickery, but rather of a flaw-less reciprocity struggling to mesh its desires with those of society. For Julie and her lover Saint-Preux, in fact for all of the characters of this novel, the dialogical foundations of selfhood are given from the outset, but the mood of the dialogue is not that of a contest, in which the self affirms its autonomy against an adversary. The tone is rather one of spiritual commun-ion, sharing a single being. This is most graphically emblematized in the love which unites Saint-Preux and Julie:

> Nos âmes se sont pour ainsi dire touchées par tous les points, et nous avons partout senti la même cohérence.... Nous n'aurons plus que les mêmes plaisirs et les mêmes peines; et comme ces aimants dont vous me parliez, qui ont, dit-on, les mêmes mouvements en différents lieux, nous sentirions les mêmes choses aux deux extrémités du monde. (P. 27, 1:11)

> Nos âmes trop bien confondues ne sauraient plus se séparer; et nous ne pouvons plus vivre éloignés l'un de l'autre, que comme deux parties d'un même tout. (P. 148, 2:7)

> deux amants s'aiment-ils l'un l'autre? Non; *vous* et *moi* sont des mots proscrits de leur langue: ils ne sont plus deux, ils sont un. (P. 514, 6:7)[5]

> Our souls, if I may use the expression, touch in all points, and we feel an entire coherence... Henceforward our pains and pleasures must be mutual; and, like the magnets, of which I have heard you speak, that have the same motion though in different places, we should have the same sensations at the two extremities of the world.

> Our souls are too intimately blended ever to be separated; nor can we live apart from each other, but as two parts of one being.

> But have lovers a *regard* for each other? No, *you*, and *I* are two words prohibited in the lover's language. Two lovers are not two persons, but one.

The same intermingling of identity informs Julie's relationship to her cousin Claire. Affectionately referred to as "les inséparables," the two friends share nearly everything, from Saint-Preux's love (Claire mediates his relationship to Julie, transmits their letters, arranges their first kiss, inadvertently paves the way for Julie's deflowering, later falls in love with Saint-Preux herself, and is urged by Julie to marry him) to their children, all of whom are raised together, and of whom Claire remarks, "en voyant tous nos petits bambins jouer ensemble, nos cœurs unis les confondent, et nous ne savons plus à laquelle appartient chacun des trois" (p. 298, 4:1) (on seeing our little cherubs at play together... the union of our affections has so united them that we have not been able to distinguish to which of us they severally belonged). Even the cold and impassible Wolmar, a man who has never cried in his life and prides himself on his indifference to all things human, admits that his fulfillment depended on a compact with Julie: "je sentis que de vous seule dépendait tout le bonheur dont je pouvais jouir" (p. 370, 4:12) (I perceived that all my prospect of happiness depended on you alone).

As we shall see later, this merging of souls and destinies is fundamental to the way in which Julie and *Julie* affect those who enter into contact with them. The relevant point to note at this juncture is simply that in Rousseau's novel, self-definition has little difficulty accommodating its operations to a partnership. For the characters of *Julie* it is a given that the self finds its identity in its relation to an Other. Far more problematic is the relationship between this dyadic self and the social community that surrounds it, particularly as regards questions of morality.

Fortified by their reciprocal love, Saint-Preux and, to a lesser degree, Julie devise in the first half of the novel a private morality fashioned on the intuitions of the heart and the conviction that nature speaks through their emotions. They assume that "sitôt qu'on veut rentrer en soi-même, chacun sent ce qui est bien, chacun discerne ce qui est beau; nous n'avons pas besoin qu'on nous apprenne à connaître ni l'un ni l'autre" (p. 30, 1:12) (If we would but consult our own feelings, we should easily distinguish *virtue* and *beauty*: we do not want to be taught either of these); or, more simply, "les règles de la morale ne dépendent point des usages des peuples" (p. 172, 2:16) (moral principles do not depend on the customs of a people). This is a convenient formula, particularly when it is seconded by Saint-Preux's idea that true love functions as the catalyst for the entire range of virtuous action: "l'amour véritable est un feu dévorant qui porte son ardeur dans les autres sentiments, et les anime d'une vigueur nouvelle" (pp. 31–2, 1:12) (real love influences all our sentiments, and animates them with new vigor). This theory is echoed by Julie after their separation:

> Où est maintenant cet amour sublime qui sait élever tous les sentiments et faire éclater la vertu? (P. 147, 2:7)

> Tu reçus du ciel cet heureux penchant à tout ce qui est bon et honnête: n'écoute que tes propres désirs, ne suis que tes inclinations naturelles; songe surtout à nos premières amours: tant que ces moments purs et délicieux reviendront à ta mémoire, il n'est pas possible que tu cesses d'aimer ce qui te les rendit si doux, que le charme du beau moral s'efface dans ton âme. (P. 159, 2:11)

> Where is now that sublime passion which could elevate your sentiments, and display your virtues?

> Heaven hath bestowed on you an happy inclination for what is virtuous and good: listen then only to your own desires, follow only your own inclinations, and think above all on the growth of our infant affections. So long as the

remembrance of those delightful moments of innocence shall remain, it will be impossible that you should cease to love that which rendered them so endearing; it will be impossible the charms of moral excellence should ever be effaced from your mind.

In Saint-Preux's eyes, perfect natural love opens the heart to an awareness of beauty and truth that, because it reflects natural inclination, rather than mere social usage, carries its own moral certainty and exempts the lover from the laws of the collective: "si l'amour règne, la nature a déjà choisi; .... Telle est la loi sacrée de la nature, qu'il n'est pas permis à l'homme d'enfreindre" (p. 135, 2:2) (if passion prevails nature has already made the choice .... So sacred also is the law of nature, that no human being is permitted to transgress it).[6] Throughout the initial stages of their relationship, both lovers will invoke nature to justify their transgression. Thus Julie, in describing a rustic hideaway where they can tryst: "l'art ni la main des hommes n'y montrent nulle part leurs soins inquiétants; on n'y voit partout que les tendres soins de la mère commune. C'est là, mon ami, qu'on n'est que sous ses auspices, et qu'on peut n'écouter que ses lois" (p. 71, 1:36) (In this delightful place, no vestiges are seen of human toil, no appearance of studied and laborious art; every object around presents only a view of the tender care of nature, our common mother. Here then, my dear friend, we shall be only under nature's directions, and know no other laws but hers). Later, after her conversion to virtue, she will single out this correlation of passionate desire with virtue and a natural order above that of society as the logical flaw that led her astray:

> Il me sembla que mes sens ne servaient que d'organe à des sentiments plus nobles; et j'aimai dans vous moins ce que j'y voyais que ce que je croyais sentir en moi-même. Il n'y a pas deux mois que je pensais encore ne m'être pas trompée; l'aveugle amour, me disais-je, avait raison; nous étions faits l'un pour l'autre; je serais à lui si l'ordre humain n'eût troublé les rapports de la nature. (P. 250, 3:18)

> I thought that my senses only served as organs to more refined sentiments; and I loved in you, not so much what I saw, as what I imagined, I felt within myself. It is not two months since, that I still flattered myself I was not mistaken: blind love, said I, was in the right; we were made for each other, if human events do not interrupt the affinity of nature.

Ultimately, though, Julie rejects the opposition of nature to social order. Citing allegiance to a larger "natural" order according to which children do not betray their parents, she refuses to elope with Saint-Preux. Electing the law of the family and society over that of the heart, she finally accedes to her father's wishes, weds Wolmar, his old friend, and ceases all correspondence with Saint-Preux.

Saint-Preux's failure to win Julie stands as an indictment of his logic in the first part of the novel, and indeed, the second half of *Julie, ou la nouvelle Héloïse* develops a contrary notion of selfhood and virtue. In direct opposition to the egocentric discourse of clandestine love, a collectively produced narrative of political order explicitly links personal happiness and virtue to the individual's insertion within a carefully constructed social hierarchy. Returning from self-imposed exile of many years to take up residence with Julie and Wolmar at the latter's invitation, Saint-Preux discovers a new measure of fulfillment and self-realization when he finds his place within the idyllic community which Wolmar has founded at the country estate of Clarens. As the narrative advances, the story of the protagonists' passion loses ground steadily to an ongoing, systematic discussion of how individuals can find happiness in society, an ideal version of which is laid out in the lengthy descriptions of the utopic Clarens. The rhapsodies of "natural" morality and uncompromising individuality that dominated Saint-Preux's earlier letters now give way to lengthy accounts, penned to a distant friend, Edouard Bomston, of how Wolmar and Julie handle their servants, raise their children, manage their finances, cultivate their land, manufacture their beverages, decorate their home, arrange their gardens, entertain their guests, and generally ingratiate themselves with their neighbors and employees. The discourse of self-contained dialogic identity thus gives way to an extended political allegory of the ideal relationship between individual and community.

Underlying this utopia is the assumption that order is natural and that happiness comes with the acceptance of one's place in a larger order. As principle architect of Clarens, Wolmar's "seul principe actif est le goût naturel de l'ordre" (p. 368, 4:12) (only active principle is a natural love of order), and he believes that "le caractère général de l'homme est un amour-propre indifférent par lui-même, bon ou mauvais par les accidents qui le modifient, et qui dépendent des coutumes, des lois, des rangs, de la fortune, et de toute notre police humaine" (p. 369, 4:12) (the general character of mankind is founded on a kind of self-love indifferent in itself, and either good or bad according to the accidents which modify it, and which depend on customs, laws, rank, fortune, and every circumstance relative to human policy). To create a self-sustaining social order requires, then, that with the help of Julie, Wolmar inculcate in his subjects a set of rules, laws, and customs which, over time, will nurture their virtue along the lines he desires. The underlying principle of this agenda is the identification of personal interest with the interest of the social economy at large. Wolmar promotes such an identification morally and financially. On the one hand, he relies on a variety of financial inducements to ingratiate himself with his employees – an expense which, he is careful to point out, he more than recoups in increased loyalty and productivity.[7] On the other hand, he links obedience and self-restraint to self-satisfaction, promoting a vigorous smugness which Saint-Preux best expresses: "il y a dans la méditation des pensées honnêtes une sorte de bien-être que les méchants n'ont jamais connu; c'est celui de se plaire avec soi-même. . . . la jouissance de la vertu est tout intérieure, et ne s'aperçoit que par celui qui la sent" (p. 366, 4:11) (there is a kind of felicity in meditating on honest reflections, which the wicked never know, and which consists in being pleased with one's self. . . . the enjoyment of virtue is all internal, and is only perceived by him who feels it). In economic terms, the same principle dictates that one persuade all members of the community to be happy with their lot: "la grande maxime de Mme de Wolmar est donc de ne point favoriser les changements de condition, mais de contribuer à rendre heureux chacun dans la sienne" (p. 405, 5:2) (Mme de Wolmar's great maxim is therefore never to favor changes of status, but to contribute to making each content with his own).

But Wolmar's major ally in establishing the desired attitude in his underlings is quite clearly the pressure which collective discourse exercises on the individual. Arguing against education at one point, Wolmar remarks that in a rural economy such as his "on n'a d'égard qu'à l'espèce, chacun fait ce que font tous les autres; l'exemple est la seule règle, l'habitude est le seul talent, et nul n'exerce de son âme que la partie commune à tous" (p. 429, 5:3) (the good of the species only is consulted; every one acts in the same manner; example is their only rule of action; habit their only talent; and no one exerts any other genius than that which is common to all). Like his land, which he is convinced "produit à proportion du nombre des bras qui la cultivent" (p. 331, 4:10) (produces in proportion to the number of hands employed), the strength of his rules depends on the number of individuals that adhere to them. The greater the number of individuals that act virtuously within the community, the more likely that all will behave virtuously: once virtue takes root as the custom, it will naturally propagate itself.

To initiate the process of culture requires defining the role of each of its members. Each individual in the household is assigned precise duties, a specific space of operation, and a rate of pay that corresponds to his or her length and quality of service. Even Saint-Preux, when he arrives, is given specific guidelines for his behavior *vis-à-vis* Julie; Wolmar gives him a choice: "vivez dans le tête-à-tête comme si j'étais présent, ou devant moi comme si je n'y étais pas" (p. 317, 4:6) (behave when tête-à-tête, as if I was present; or in my presence, as if I was absent). Once the community is formed and functioning, however, the rules upon which it is founded tend to disappear under custom. Repeated patterns of behavior become a law unto themselves, as in the measures which Wolmar and Julie take to discourage commerce between the sexes:

Pour prévenir entre les deux sexes une familiarité dangereuse, on ne les gêne point ici par des lois positives qu'ils seraient tentés d'enfreindre en secret; mais, sans paraître y songer, on établit des usages plus puissants que l'autorité même. (P. 336, 4:10)

They do not, to prevent any dangerous intimacy between the two sexes, restrain them by positive rules which they might be tempted to violate in secret, but without any seeming intention, they establish good customs, which are more powerful than authority itself.

Over time, laws are assimilated into the values of those who adhere to them. Conditioned by their behavior, Wolmar's subjects develop a natural indifference for the glitter of the outside world and a bent toward virtue, most obviously embodied by Saint-Preux's conversion to platonic love and friendship.[8] But this "natural" indifference is the product of a carefully monitored process of historical reinforcement that functions suspiciously like culture, rather than a pre-existent order.

Two points must be retained here. On the one hand, Wolmar relies on the mechanism of culture to combat the authority of culture. By instigating and then nurturing a series of customs and conventions that dominate every aspect of his subjects' lives, from working week to holiday, apprenticeship to retirement, celibacy to marriage, Wolmar creates an alternative to the pluralistic cultural text of urban society; he engenders a carefully monitored counter-order designed to offset the evil influence of unbounded fashion and usage. On the other hand, he conceals his own authority in the process by identifying his contrived order with that of natural law.

In fact, the social economy of Paris, the Gomorrah of this allegory, functions almost exactly like that of Clarens, with one important difference: the Parisian play of constantly evolving fashion and "unnatural" convention is aleatory and pluralistic, whereas the order of Clarens is static, overseen by a single enlightened lawgiver. The urban French provide a tableau, as it were, of history gone berserk, of culture redefining itself randomly against its past, of individuals seeking to distinguish themselves from their peers through continual innovation and singularity.[9] The most striking emblem for this economy out of control is of course the Parisian noblewoman, whose need to outpace the bourgeoises who are constantly appropriating her costume and habits drives her to indecent dress and licentious language (p. 191, 2:21).

If Parisian society is in such sad shape, it is because the mechanism of collective example or emulation which underwrites cultural continuity is no longer subject to any constraining authority. Julie, Wolmar, and Saint-Preux frequently associate culture, and particularly urban culture, with moral debilitation,[10] which is the inevitable result when all parties feel free to "fashion" culture, limited only by their ability to master the collective discourse.

By contrast, Clarens evolves from a carefully controlled set of original precepts, and any individuals prone to redefine custom or introduce a discourse that runs counter to that sanctioned by Wolmar are promptly expelled from the community:

> Que s'il se trouve parmi nos gens quelqu'un, soit homme, soit femme, qui ne s'accommode pas de nos règles et leur préfère la liberté d'aller sous divers prétextes courir où bon lui semble, on ne lui en refuse jamais la permission; mais nous regardons ce goût de licence comme un indice très suspect, et nous ne tardons pas à nous défaire de ceux qui l'ont. (P. 341, 4:10)

> If there are any among them either man or woman, who do not care to conform to our regulations, but prefer the liberty of going where they please on various pretences, we never refuse to give them leave; but we consider this licentious turn as a very suspicious symptom, and we waste no time in ridding ourselves of those who have it.

To insure that his servants do not develop a set of customs on their own, Wolmar discourages them from innovating among themselves the very practice of social discourse that forms the basis of this study. At once compelled to engage in the social recreations their masters have carefully planned (weekly dances, contests, achievement awards, etc.), prohibited from discussing each other's performance behind each other's back, and encouraged to report to their master any deviant behavior on the part of their peers, the household servants at Clarens find their entire range of verbal and social intercourse mediated by their master (cf. pp. 329–52, 4:10).

Clarens functions as a counter-history, a world exempt from the nefarious influence of unbridled cultural narration and narrative. It shares the same deep structure of a self-perpetuating economy as its nemesis Paris, but its individual subjects do not enjoy the discursive freedom of their French counterparts: they are not permitted to innovate social custom and thus effectively write their own laws; they must remain content to re-enact those written by Wolmar. If they are willing to do so, it is because they identify those laws with natural order. On a very fundamental level, of course, cultural usage merges history and nature: the longer a community adheres to a given practice, the more natural that practice appears.[11] This is something that Wolmar and his accomplices acknowledge in their citations of social usage as proof of how natural their own laws are.[12] But it is essential to Wolmar's agenda that his common *subjects* not recognize the degree to which their customs are grounded in history, lest they be tempted to change them. For the people of Clarens, the rules and practices that regulate their lives must appear natural from the outset, even if they are the product of authorial artifice. Wolmar's abstract theory is the foundation of all usage, but it must conceal its workings, lest his inferiors be tempted to emulate him. Even on the material plane, nature must appear to be everywhere in collusion with Wolmar's elaborately contrived program. This complicity surfaces most blatantly in the description of Julie's garden, in the eleventh letter of the fourth book.

The garden is a veritable Eden which Julie has created with the simple native plants of the region, and it underscores her tenet that paradise – even natural paradise – is to be found in one's own back yard:

> Que fera donc l'homme de goût qui vit pour vivre, qui sait jouir de lui-même... ?... quand il est bien où il est, il ne se soucie point d'être ailleurs. Ici, par exemple, on n'a pas de vue hors du lieu, et l'on est très content de n'en pas avoir. On penserait volontiers que tous les charmes de la nature y sont renfermés... (P. 362, 4:11)

> How will a man of taste act, who lives to relish life, who knows how to enjoy himself... ?... when he is agreeably fixed, he does not desire to be elsewhere. Here, for example, we have no prospect, and we are very well satisfied without any. We are willing to think that all the charms of nature are inclosed here...

It is Saint-Preux who narrates the convergence of nature and human contrivance which the garden reveals. He is initially struck by its verdant exoticism – "je crus voir le lieu le plus sauvage, le plus solitaire de la nature, et il me semblait d'être le premier mortel qui eût jamais pénétré dans ce désert" (p. 353) (I thought myself in the most wild and solitary place in nature, and it seemed as if I were the first mortal who had penetrated into this desert spot) – and by the fact that nature alone seems to have done all the work. Julie quickly disabuses him, however, insisting that *she* in fact is behind the entire scheme: "Il est vrai, dit-elle, que la nature a tout fait, mais sous ma direction, et il n'y a rien là que je n'ai ordonné" (p. 354) (it is true, said she, that nature has done everything, but under my direction, and you see nothing but what has been done under my orders). Once apprised of this fact, Saint-Preux changes the object of his effusion to the artfulness with which Julie has created an exotic realm out of ordinary native plants. As the young man continues his promenade, each successive aspect of the garden – its junglelike profusion, the abundant water everywhere, the lack of contact with the outside world, the absence of obvious symmetry or human intervention – is revealed by Julie or Wolmar to be part of a global scheme, the implementation of which requires only time and patience. Like the staff at Clarens, who over time grow into the regime that Wolmar has legislated for them, the plants in the garden are simple robust natives that need only to be encouraged to develop in the right direction for them to take on a new identity as delightful and thriving components in an overarching harmonious order.[13] Properly supervised, the natural tendency of growth patterns to perpetuate themselves becomes the ally rather than the enemy of the enlightened ruler. Nature finds its highest expression not in the idiosyncratic twists of the individual (plant), but in the elegant design to which it contributes, and this design is the product of a privileged discursive agent. The emblem of nature is order and individual impulses can be called natural only to the extent that they reflect order, but in the final analysis the order is given by a master.[14]

Wolmar and Julie take great pains to hide their own hand in this transaction. In the garden they efface their presence behind the "natural" order by randomizing their plantings, eschewing symmetry, straight lines, and level planes, and encouraging certain plants and discouraging others through a regular program of seeding, fertilization, cultivation (p. 359, 4:11). In like manner, when they discuss their local regulations, they are careful to attribute them to nature. Not only does Wolmar see his obsessive love of order as a natural sentiment[15] (a prejudice Saint-Preux will extend to include symmetry (p. 413, 5:2)), but Julie uses nature as the authority for her pre-school program (pp. 425, 438, 5:3), her separation of the sexes (p. 337, 4:10), and her reticence to help those wishing to leave their agricultural serfdom:

> mais pour ceux que l'inquiétude ou l'ambition porte à vouloir s'élever et quitter un état où ils sont bien, rarement peuvent-ils l'engager à se mêler de leurs affaires. La condition naturelle à l'homme est de cultiver la terre et de vivre de ses fruits. Le paisible habitant des champs n'a besoin pour sentir son bonheur que de le connaître. (P. 404, 5:2)

> but for those who desire to raise themselves through fickleness or ambition only, she can very seldom be prevailed upon to give herself any trouble. The natural business of man is to cultivate the earth, and subsist on its produce. The peaceful inhabitant of the country needs only know in what happiness consists, to be happy.

Nature, finally, is the pretext for the Wolmars' remarkable resistance to change; it is the transcendent order to which they appeal for justification when expelling from their utopia individuals deluded enough to take their own destiny in hand; it is the antidote for history, narratively conceived – the law that immediately demotes alternative constructions of reality to the status of mere prejudice and fashion.

Wolmar's identification with the laws of nature is part of an overall strategy to make his subjects feel their customs reflect an eternal truth, not the experimental hypotheses of an individual, lest they be tempted to engage in some cultural innovation of their own. To achieve his goal of shaping history narratively without promoting such activity in others, he articulates a scenario for social interaction which is enacted into natural usage historically – that is, through continual reiteration within the collective discourse and behavior of the community – but which excludes from its scenario the theme of history as collective narration. The subjects of Clarens make history without knowing it: they retell and promote to the status of natural tradition a story of communal interdependence which is not originally theirs and which they dare not modify. And since Wolmar promotes his scheme under the aegis of nature, they do not even know that they are disenfranchised: Wolmar never communicates to them the theory that underlies his rule. To do so would be to raise the possibility of a communal narration in which every individual could intervene. Such a generalized practice of history would be indistinguishable from that of Parisian fashion, and it would undermine the privilege which Wolmar enjoys as sole author of his social order.

What is fascinating about this discrimination is that it also extends to the reader of *Julie, ou la nouvelle Héloïse*. The novel advances a model of cultural authority that would logically seem to apply to the effect of fiction itself. Like Wolmar's design, the patterns of behavior advanced by novels gain currency through a process of ongoing collective rearticulation, even though they originate in the design of a single enlightened author. Yet the author backs away from making this parallel explicit, just as Wolmar backs away from admitting that the environmental determination he cultivates might be responsible for shaping the minds and characters of his subjects (pp. 426–8, 5:3). The larger structure of the novel adumbrates a generalized model which it must simultaneously withdraw, lest the empowerment of the reader put into question the authority of the author and hence the stability of the moral lesson.

This ambivalence is perceptible both within the narrative proper, where Wolmar allegorically figures the literary author and Julie the literary work, and, more strikingly, in the prefaces, where the refusal to grant either fictional status or historical status to *Julie* underlines the author's bind with respect to his work: he can neither acknowledge his art nor give his creation over to the reader; he wants his story to function like history, indeed become history, while remaining his. The figure of Julie is the key to this delicate agenda, and it is a figure which, in the plot, eventually gets out of control and thus alludes to the slipperiness of the fictive narrative.

That Wolmar's relationship to Clarens roughly parallels that of the novelist to his work seems obvious. Like a novel, his utopia is essentially the articulation of a narrative plan. Wolmar adds or subtracts from his cast as he sees fit, assigns roles to his subjects, organizes their lives, forms their psychology, delimits their geographical mobility, and plays them off against each other, all the while maintaining the detached contemplative stance of a spectator or cinematic director. And the insistence on his atheism makes clear that the community derives its coherence not from divine scheme, but from the rigorous logic of an individual who uses collective discursive practices to institutionalize his own version of the social compact. Godlike himself, although unable to believe in God, Wolmar draws his power from an unswerving application of principles which he acquires by observing and reflecting upon human behavior:

> Si j'ai quelque passion dominante, c'est celle de l'observation. J'aime à lire dans les cœurs des hommes; comme le mien me fait peu d'illusion, que j'observe de sang-froid et sans intérêt, et qu'une longue expérience m'a donné de la sagacité, je ne me trompe guère dans mes jugements; aussi c'est là toute la récompense de l'amour-propre dans mes études continuelles; car je n'aime point à faire un rôle, mais seulement à voir jouer les autres: la société m'est agréable pour la contempler, non pour en faire partie. (P. 368, 4:12)

> If I have any ruling passion, it is that of observation: I love to read the hearts of mankind. As my own seldom misleads me, as I make my observations with a disinterested and dispassionate temper, and as I have acquired some sagacity by long experience, I am seldom deceived in my judgments; this advantage therefore is the only recompense which self-love receives from my constant studies: for I am not fond of acting a part, but only of observing others play theirs. Society is agreeable to me for the sake of contemplation, and not as a member of it.

Wolmar seems incapable of emotional involvement at the same level as his subordinates, in part because his understanding of the mechanisms he has devised for regulating individual behavior and collective morality places him outside of the economy they regulate. Like the author of a fiction, he defines a system in which others find their identity, but he himself stands at a certain analytic distance from his creation.

This disinclination to sentiment has but one exception: Julie. Wolmar is quite specific about the effect she has upon him when he first encounters her and witnesses her effusive pleasure at greeting her father: "vos transports, vos larmes de joie en l'embrassant, me donnèrent la première ou plutôt la seule émotion que j'aie éprouvée de ma vie. Si cette impression fut légère, elle était unique . . ." (p. 370, 4:12) (your transports, the tears of joy you shed when you embraced him, gave me the first, or rather the only emotion I ever experienced in my life. If the impression was slight, it was unique). Julie, as it turns out, affects everyone in a similar way: the spectacle of her perfect selflessness inspires in even the most venal hearts an irresistible urge to virtue. Claire tells her friend "on ne peut ni te voir ni penser à toi de sang-froid" (p. 326, 4:9) (it is impossible to see you, or think of you with indifference) and provides an elaborate analysis of how Julie converts other people to virtue:

> toutes les âmes d'une certaine trempe... transforment, pour ainsi dire, les autres en elles-mêmes; elles ont une sphère d'activité dans laquelle rien ne leur résiste: on ne peut les connaître sans les vouloir imiter, et de leur sublime élévation elles attirent à elles tout ce qui les environne. C'est pour cela, ma chère, que ni toi ni ton ami ne connaîtrez peut-être jamais les hommes; car vous les verrez bien plus comme vous les ferez, que comme ils seront d'eux-mêmes. (P. 142, 2:5)

> all minds of a certain temper transform, in a manner, every other into their own likeness; having a sphere of activity wherein nothing can resist their power. It is impossible to know without imitating them, while from their own sublime elevation they attract all that are about them. It is for this reason, my dear, that neither you nor your friend will perhaps ever know mankind; for you will rather see them such as you model them, than such as they are in themselves.

This assessment finds confirmation later in the novel, when Julie inspires the entire community of Clarens to replicate her conduct:

> Tout se fait par attachment: l'on dirait que ces âmes vénales [the servants] se purifient en entrant dans ce séjour de sagesse et d'union. L'on dirait qu'une partie des lumières du maître et des sentiments de la maîtresse ont passé dans chacun de leurs gens... (P. 352, 4:10)

> Le bonheur qu'elle goûte se multiplie et s'étend autour d'elle. Toutes les maisons où elle entre, offrent bientôt un tableau de la sienne (Pp. 402–3, 5:2)

> Everything occurs from a principle of attachment, and one would think that those venal souls were purified as soon as they entered into this dwelling of wisdom and union. He would imagine that part of the master's intelligence, and of the mistress's sensibility, was conveyed to each of their servants.

> The happiness she herself feels, multiplies and extends itself all around her. Every house she enters soon becomes a copy of her own.

We might well conclude, like the critic in the preface, that "cette Julie, telle qu'elle est, doit être une créature enchanteresse; tout ce qui l'approche doit lui ressembler; tout doit devenir Julie autour d'elle" (p. 585). (This Eloisa, as she is represented, must be an absolute enchantress; everything that approaches her must immediately resemble her; everything around her must turn into Eloisa.)

In this respect, Julie functions precisely in the same way as the moral novel expounded by the author figure, R., in the *Entretien sur les romans* –

and in particular as the kind of fictional narrative he calls a *tableau d'ima-gination*. Tableaux differ from portraits as poetry does to history, in Aristotle's classic definition: "poetry is chiefly conversant about general truth, history about particular."[16] As the character N. puts it, "dans un tableau d'imagination, toute figure humaine doit avoir les traits communs à l'hom-me" (p. 571) (in a picture which is the produce of imagination, every human figure should resemble human nature). The tableau, by presenting typical characteristics common to all readers rather than particular traits, allows a greater measure of identification – allows the reader to see her interests or experiences reflected in the conduct of the characters, and appropriate that experience for her self. Julie exemplifies just such an identification. She possesses all of the qualities common to her peers, but to a superior degree. At the same time, no particular trait distinguishes her – or limits potential identifications on the part of others who enter into contact with her. It is her friend Bomston who most lucidly analyzes this strange phenomenon:

> ce n'est pas que vous ayez ni l'un ni l'autre un caractère marqué dont on puisse au premier coup d'œil assigner les différences, et il se pourrait bien que cet embarras de vous définir vous fît prendre pour des âmes communes par un observateur superficiel. Mais c'est cela même qui vous distingue, qu'il est impossible de vous distinguer, et que les traits du modèle commun, dont quelqu'un manque toujours à chaque individu, brillent tous également dans les vôtres. (P. 137, 2:3)

> It is not that either the one or the other has any peculiar characteristic, whereby you might at first be known and distinguished, and through the want of which yours might well enough be mistaken, by a superficial observer, for minds of a common and ordinary cast. You are eminently distinguished, however, by this very difficulty of distinguishing you, and in that the features of a common model, some one of which is wanting in every individual, are all equally perfect in you.

While Bomston also extends this analysis to the character of Saint-Preux, only Julie seems to have a powerful effect on others. Even in the first book, she modifies by example the conduct of her lover, whom she convinces to renounce a longed-awaited tryst in order to succor an impoverished couple. Later she persuades Bomston himself to swallow his honor in order to prevent a duel between himself and Saint-Preux.

If the vision of Julie's goodness always strikes a sympathetic chord in the hearts of those who frequent her, it is because, like a novel, she melds her identity with theirs, even when she is dealing with social inferiors: "elle prend part à leurs plaisirs, à leurs chagrins, à leur sort; elle s'informe de leurs affaires, leurs intérêts sont les siens" (p. 332, 4:10) (she takes part in their pleasures, their cares, and their fortune; she inquires into their affairs, and makes their interests her own). Novels, like any form of representation, affect us in proportion to the familiarly of the situations they portray: "our passions are . . . more strongly moved, in proportion as we can more readily adopt the pains or pleasure proposed to our minds, by recognising them as once our own, or considering them as naturally incident to our state of life."[17] Identifying with those around her, Julie invites them to identify with the virtue she incarnates. She thus opens their hearts to their own latent goodness: "ton cœur vivifie tous ceux qui l'environnent, et leur donne pour ainsi dire un nouvel être dont ils sont forcés de lui faire hommage, puisqu'ils ne l'auraient point eu sans lui" (p. 306, 4:2) (your disposition enlivens every one round you, and gives them a kind of new existence, for which they are bound to adore you, since they derive it entirely from you).

Julie herself envisions the process of conversion to virtue in terms of an inner ideal, which is hidden in one's heart, and animated by passion:

> Laisse, mon ami, ces vains moralistes et rentre au fond de ton âme: c'est là que tu retrouveras toujours la source de ce feu sacré qui nous embrasa tant de fois de l'amour des sublimes vertus; c'est là que tu verras ce simulacre éternel du vrai beau dont la contemplation nous anime d'un saint enthousiasme . . . Ce divin modèle que chacun de nous porte avec lui nous enchante malgré que nous en ayons; sitôt que la passion nous permet de le voir, nous lui voulons ressembler. (P. 157, 2:11)

> leave, my friend, those idle moralists, and consult your own breast. It is there you will always find a spark of that sacred fire, which hath so often inflamed us with love for the sublimest virtue. It is there you will trace the lasting image of true beauty, the contemplation of which inspires us with a sacred enthusiasm. . . . That divine image of virtue, imprinted universally on the mind, displays irresistible charms even to the least virtuous. No sooner doth passion permit us to contemplate its beauty, but we wish to resemble it.

Julie attributes this inner model to the "Etre éternel": "c'est sa substance inaltérable qui est le vrai modèle des perfections dont nous portons tous une image en nous-mêmes" (p. 264, 3:18) (it is his unalterable substance, that is the true model of those perfections, of which we all bear the image within us), and she downplays her own role as an active agent of virtue.[18] Yet it is clear from the structure of the plot that the inner ideal requires for its manifestation an external analog or exemplar, and that the heroine of the novel embodies just such exemplification. Saint-Preux's conversion to virtue, Bomston's renunciation of a shameful marriage, and the ideal community at Clarens all depend on her example and realize their inner potential for happiness and goodness only once she has shown the way. Julie herself has no doubts about the necessity of external exemplification:

Enfin, que le caractère et l'amour du beau soit empreint par la nature au fond de mon âme, j'aurai ma règle aussi longtemps qu'il ne sera point défiguré. Mais comment m'assurer de conserver toujours dans sa pureté cette effigie intérieure qui n'a point, parmi les êtres sensibles, de modèle auquel on puisse la comparer? Ne sait-on pas que . . . la conscience s'altère et se modifie insensiblement dans chaque siècle, dans chaque peuple, dans chaque individu, selon l'inconstance et la variété des préjugés? (Pp. 263–4, 3:18).

In short, admitting the character and the love of virtue to be imprinted in my heart by nature it will serve me as a rule of conduct till its impressions are defaced; but how shall I be sure always to preserve this inward effigy in its original purity, which has no model, among sublunary beings, to which it can be referred? Is it not evident that irregular affections corrupt the judgment as well as the will, and that conscience changes, and in every age, in every people, in every individual, accommodates itself to inconstancy of opinion and diversity of prejudice.

Julie functions as precisely such a "model among sublunary beings," and her effect on those who frequent her can be likened to that of the literary text which, in the act of reading, embraces the reader and is fleshed out or endowed with qualities which are necessarily drawn from the reader's personal experience and inner ideals. Conceived in terms of the intimate relationship of one reader reading a text in solitude, this transaction finds its most obvious analog in the erotic relation that binds Saint-Preux to Julie in the early sections of the novel. Conceived in social terms, as the way a given novel informs and is read by the culture that appropriates it, the same transaction recalls the relationship of Julie to the community of Clarens, which she slowly transforms through her exemplification of domestic bliss. In both cases, the example/novel works against history, or what Julie calls "inconstancy of opinion and diversity of prejudice," by providing a structure with reference to which the "internal effigy" can reiterate and actualize itself. Julie functions as an antidote to the unbounded historical economy which is attacked in *Julie, ou la nouvelle Héloïse*. And to the extent that the *Entretien sur les romans* suggests a third way of looking at exemplification/fiction – namely as a contrivance of the author who wishes to impose his fictions on reality, one might well ask if fiction does not function for the author of *Julie* as an attempted repression of history, much in the same way that Wolmar's use of Julie to found an ideal community can be read as an attempt to negate historical change and return to a pre-historical idyll.

I am suggesting, in short, that we understand Julie as an emblem of three different economies, functioning on three different levels. She is the centerpiece of the novel's plot of individual social relationships, the crucial element in the enactment of the utopia, and the emblem of the novelist's resistance to history. However, it is important to note that she does not play a merely passive role at any of these levels of analysis; rather she consistently deploys a double function or identity, as both the product of the binary relationship in which she is involved, and its origin or impetus. Like a narrative, which both structures and is structured by its reader/author, she is a medium which defines and enables projects of individuality at all levels, even as she is shaped by them. As young girl, she is the catalyst of Saint-Preux's dialogical passion as well as of Claire's passionate friendship, but she also evolves under the pressure of their relationships; in her guise as the moral exemplar, Mme de Wolmar, she does not simply enact Wolmar's moral agenda and provide a fulcrum for the reordering of society, she also inspires and informs his entire project; similarly, as literary device, she figures both the author's overcoming of history and, as we shall see, his vulnerability to history: she expresses simultaneously his authority over culture and the narrative mechanism which grounds and exceeds that authority.[19]

Novels exert their influence on the culture of their public through a process of exemplification similar to that outlined by Julie. As Montesquieu puts it, referring to his own highly successful *Lettres persanes*, "ces sortes de romans réussissent ordinairement, parce que l'on rend compte soi-même de sa situation actuelle; ce qui fait plus sentir les passions que tous les récits qu'on en pourroit faire" (this type of novel ordinarily succeeds because one becomes conscious of one's own current situation; which elicits a stronger feeling of the passions than all the accounts of them one could make).[20] To the extent that *Julie* is specifically cited in the preface as a novel that functions this way, the heroine can be thought of as a trope for the work that carries her name and the moral novel more generally. Her docility and tractability with respect to the programs of Wolmar can thus be read allegorically as an oblique comment on the relationship *Julie*'s author entertains with his "work."

In the preface, or *Entretien sur les romans*, the same transaction between self and ideal that is associated with the character Julie, is attributed to the novel *Julie*, suggesting that the heroine's strange power to enrapture all who come to know her is a figure for the transaction between social individual and inner self that occurs in the reading of fiction. Unlike other *romans*, which typically present "les gens du bel air, les femmes à la mode... le raffinement du goût des villes, les maximes de la cour, l'appareil du luxe, la morale épicurienne" (p. 578) (people of rank and fashion... the refined taste of great cities, court maxims, the splendour of luxury, and Epicurean morality), *Julie* dwells on the routine of rural existence. Like its heroine, it espouses the condition of its public and provides them with an ideal vision of their existence. The author envisions how his work might effect its readers the way Julie does "hers":

Pourquoi n'oserais-je supposer que, par quelque heureux hasard, ce livre, comme tant d'autres plus mauvais encore pourra tomber dans les mains de ces habitants des champs, et que l'image des plaisirs d'un état tout semblable au leur le leur rendra plus supportable? . . . Comment pourraient-ils contempler le tableau d'un ménage heureux, sans vouloir imiter un si doux modèle? (P. 580)

Why may I not suppose that, by some fortunate accident, this book, like many others of still less merit, will fall into the hands of those inhabitants of the fields, and that the pleasing picture of a life exactly resembling theirs will render it more tolerable? . . . How can they possibly contemplate the representation of a happy family, without attempting to imitate the pleasing model? How can they be affected with the charms of conjugal union, even where love is wanting, without encreasing and confirming their own attachment?

As in the case of Julie's more personal form of exemplification, the ideal portrayed is already part and parcel of the beneficiary's conscience; the task of the example is to bring the subject to acknowledge and sustain that ideal. Julie, we have seen, molds her interests around those of her interlocutors; similarly, the fictional world is carefully modeled on the world of its intended reader:[21]

si les romans n'offraient à leurs lecteurs que des tableaux d'objets qui les environnent, que des devoirs qu'ils peuvent remplir, que des plaisirs de leur condition, les romans ne les rendraient point fous, ils les rendraient sages. Il faut que les écrits faits pour les solitaires parlent la langue des solitaires: pour les instruire, il faut qu'ils leur plaisent, qu'ils les intéressent; il faut qu'ils les attachent à leur état en le leur rendant agréable. (P. 579)

If, on the contrary, romances were only to exhibit the pictures of real objects, of virtues and pleasures within our reach, they would then make us wiser and better. Books which are designed to be read in solitude, should be written in the language of retirement: if they are meant to instruct, they should make us in love with our situation; they should combat and destroy the maxims of the great world, by shewing them to be false and despicable, as they really are.

Like Julie, the fictional exemplar works from "within" the identity of its reader, molding itself to the concerns of the individual it affects. And we remember that, like the fiction, Julie also works to render each of her subjects content with his or her lot (p. 405, 5:2).

From one point of view, we could say that in their shared mechanism of exemplification, Julie and *Julie* provide an antidote to the vagaries of culture, a way out of the historical economy that imprisons the Parisians, for whom "le bon, le mauvais, le beau, le laid, la vérité, la vertu, n'ont qu'une existence locale et circonscrite" (p. 165, 2:14) (the good, the bad, the beautiful, the ugly, truth, and even virtue itself, have all only a limited and local existence). Julie envisions just such a function for the moral example in her analysis of its mechanism cited above (pp. 263–4, 3:18). Since "conscience changes, and in every age, in every people, in every individual, accommodates itself to inconstancy of opinion and diversity of prejudice," only a sustained narrative of moral conduct, such as that presented by Julie (and *Julie*) can be counted on to provide a guide for individual comportment. This is the logic that underlies Wolmar's plan to reform Saint-Preux:

> Il est ardent, mais faible et facile à subjuguer. Je profite de cet avantage en donnant le change à son imagination. A la place de sa maîtresse, je le force de voir toujours l'épouse d'un honnête homme et la mère de mes enfants: j'efface un tableau par un autre, et couvre le passé du présent. (Pp. 383–4, 4:14)

> He is impetuous, but tractable and easily managed. I avail myself of this advantage to give a turn to his imagination. In the place of his mistress, I compel him always to look at the wife of his friend, and the mother of my children; I efface one picture by another, and hide the past with the present.

In the *Entretien sur les romans*, Rousseau envisions a similar function for his book *vis-à-vis* the reading public, and his explanations of its structure not only confirm the affinities between his project and Wolmar's, but clarify the parallel between the reader and Saint-Preux. When the critic in the *Entretien* complains about the disparity between the first and second halves of *Julie*, he notes that "les détails de la vie domestique effacent les fautes du premier âge; la chaste épouse, la femme sensée, la digne mère de famille, font oublier la coupable amante" (p. 576) (The detail of domestic occurrences effaces the faults of their younger years: the chaste and sensible wife, the worthy matron, obliterates the remembrance of former weakness). This is precisely the strategy of Wolmar, and Rousseau acknowledges its role in his work. Like Wolmar, who sees in Saint-Preux's attachment to Julie an assurance that he will pay careful attention to the example she now presents, the author explains that his project of moral improvement is aimed especially at those who would not have attended to the later parts of the novel, had they not first been seduced by the story of Julie and Saint-Preux's affair (p. 576). Moreover, the reader's involvement in the love story makes his conversion to virtue all the more poignant: "mes jeunes gens sont aimables; mais pour les aimer à trente ans, il faut les avoir connus à vingt. Il faut avoir vécu longtemps avec eux pour s'y plaire; et ce n'est qu'après avoir déploré leurs fautes qu'on vient à goûter leurs vertus" (p. 576) (My young folks are amiable; but to love them at thirty it is necessary to have known them when they were ten years younger. One must have lived with them a long time to be pleased with their company; and to taste their virtues, it is necessary we should first have deplored their failings).

Wolmar's plan is not just to convert Saint-Preux to virtue through the example of Julie, but to make of him a disciple of sorts, charging him with the education of his and Julie's children and thus the responsibility for carrying on the culture he has founded. In much the same way that Wolmar gradually indoctrinates Saint-Preux into the life of virtue, the endless didactic passages of the novel's latter sections secure Rousseau's ideal reader to his cause. Those who persevere through the hundreds of pages of moral discussion and assimilate its arguments will eventually suffer conversion to *Julie*'s way of thinking, just as those who frequent Julie ultimately emulate her. Like a book, Julie transforms others into herself through her selflessness. In the tableau, as in Clarens, in *Julie*, and in novels in general, "everything occurs through attachment" (p. 352, 4:10).[22] To have read *Julie* (known Julie) is already to some extent to have made oneself in its (her) image. Claire's observation of her friend, "Vous donnerez le ton à tous ceux qui vivront avec vous; ils vous fuiront ou vous deviendront semblables" (p. 142, 2:5) (You will lead the way for all those among whom you live; others will either imitate, or leave you) restates in personal terms the author's conviction that his book will elicit indignation from those readers for whom it has no utility ("tous les sentiments seront hors de la nature pour ceux qui ne croient pas à la vertu" [p. 3]) (all the sentiments will seem unnatural to those who know not what is meant by the word VIRTUE) while proving useful for the rest. Like Julie, "il ne plaira médiocrement à personne" (p. 3) (it will not meet with *moderate* approbation from any one). To the extent *Julie*'s reader comprehends and accepts the extraordinary effect of Julie on those around her, that reader also inadvertently validates the book's agenda for moral emendation and confirms its effect on at least one individual. Conversely, readers that find Julie preposterous will necessarily find the novel's moral program incomprehensible and the narrative unreadable – they will be expulsed like the recalcitrant servants of Clarens.

In other words, to the extent that its plot replicates exactly the objectives of its author and the transaction with its reader, *Julie* can be said to allegorize its own writing and reading and to locate the question of how, precisely, one might use the literary enterprise to regulate collective naturalization and monitor the course of social history – and this in spite of the pejorative comments in the two prefaces concerning the negative effect of novels. The insistence within the *Entretien sur les romans* on the affinities between Wolmar's plan and the author's, between Julie's function and *Julie*'s, reveals a self-consciousness about literary authority we have not seen prior to this moment. However, that self-consciousness is anything but unambiguous. For one thing, the strange dialogued form of the *Entretien* suspends the question of who, exactly, will ultimately determine the role that *Julie* plays in culture between two symmetrical agencies, that of the reader, N., and that of the author R., each of whom seems to have a penchant for expressing the ideas of the other. Even more striking is the author's refusal to declare his work either fiction or history (*tableau* or *portrait*) – a refusal which has the effect of both admitting yet limiting the author's authority (and responsibility) and the reader's interpretive activity. Such ambivalences suggest, I think, a wariness concerning the mechanisms of cultural coercion that the author formulates. R. is cognizant of the degree to which his authority hinges on the reader's perception of *Julie* and the degree to which that perception hinges on literary categories and conventions, such as the *tableau* and the *portrait*: that is why he refuses to pronounce one way or the other on the historicity of the characters.[23] Even if, like Wolmar, he tries to banish from his novel readers whose penchants or backgrounds conflict with its objectives, he always runs the risk of seeing his work take a course he did not envision, within a private interpretive transaction beyond his control. On the other hand, it is not entirely clear that he would not welcome such an eventuality – that his pleasure at limiting the assimilation of *Julie* into social discourse is not counterbalanced by the knowledge that for it to assume a position of influence in the larger cultural economy, it must be available to a variety of readings, enter into a variety of compacts with successive generations of readers, over which he has little control.

Both of these possibilities are figured in the plot by Julie's remarkable final letter to Saint-Preux, in which she puts into question Wolmar's entire agenda of virtue by professing that she is still passionately in love with Saint-Preux, and that the conversion of their relationship to one of Platonic friendship was a mere illusion:

> Je me suis longtemps fait illusion. Cette illusion me fut salutaire; elle se détruit au moment que je n'en ai plus besoin. Vous m'avez crue guérie, et j'ai cru l'être. Rendons grâces à celui qui fit durer cette erreur autant qu'elle était utile: qui sait si, me voyant si près de l'abîme, la tête ne m'eût point tourné? (P. 564, 6:12)

> Long have I indulged myself in the salutary delusion, that my passion was extinguished; the delusion is now vanished, when it can be no longer useful. You believed me to be cured and I believed it also. Let us give thanks to him who perpetuated that error as long as it was useful: who knows if, seeing myself so close to the abyss, my head would not have turned?

Although this confession seems to undermine Wolmar's theories, Julie goes on to explain how, having conformed to the program of virtue during her life with Wolmar at Clarens, she now feels free to express her absolute love for Saint-Preux: "J'ai fait ce que j'ai dû faire; la vertu me reste sans tache, et l'amour m'est resté sans remords" (p. 564, 6:12) (I have done what I had to do; my virtue remains unblemished, and my love without remorse). Freed by death from the series of trials which continual exposure to Saint-Preux represented for her, she enjoys the satisfaction of having fulfilled her duty and being able, finally, to reaffirm her compact with Saint-Preux:

> Mais mon âme existerait-elle sans toi? sans toi quelle félicité goûterais-je? Non, je ne te quitte pas, je vais t'attendre. La vertu qui nous sépara sur la terre nous unira dans le séjour éternel. Je meurs dans cette douce attente: trop heureuse d'acheter au prix de ma vie le droit de t'aimer toujours sans crime, et de te le dire encore une fois! (P. 566, 6:12)

> But can my soul exist without you? without you, what happiness can I enjoy? No, we will not part — I go but to expect you. That virtue, which separated us on earth, will unite us for ever in the mansions of the blessed. I die in that peaceful hope; too happy to purchase, at the expence of my life, the privilege of loving you without a crime, and of telling you so once more.

Given that Saint-Preux's relationship with Julie evolves under the direction of Wolmar from one of private passion to one of public discussion, and that this changing transaction with the character who figures fictional mediation makes of Saint-Preux an obvious figure for the reader, it is tempting to read this final turnabout as a reassertion of readerly authority and textual autonomy against the dominion of the author. Saint-Preux's analysis of his change of life under Wolmar makes clear that the latter's program of moral improvement has functioned exactly as the author in the *Entretien* envisions *Julie* working on its reader.[24] More important though, is the way in which he appropriates Wolmar's ideas and innovates a system of his own, which he intends to put to the test in educating Wolmar's children: "il m'est venu de nouvelles réflexions sur le même sujet, et j'ai réduit le tout en une espèce de système" (p. 463, 5:8) (some new reflections have suggested themselves on the same subject: I have reduced the whole into a kind of system). Emulating and transmitting to future generations his reading of the lessons and procedures of the author-figure, the young man becomes in turn the author. This transmission of authority is figured by the radical turn of the plot following Saint-Preux's acknowledgement of Wolmar's decision to charge him with the education of the latter's children (and thus to replace him, Wolmar, as author(ity) figure in the community). Saint-Preux dreams of Julie's death. Although his own fears are momentarily dispelled by a quick visit to Clarens, where he assures himself that she is safe and sound, when he relates the incident to Claire, she becomes convinced of its ill portent:

> vous m'avez transmis la frayeur que vous n'avez plus . . . Depuis votre fatale lettre un serrement de cœur ne m'a pas quittée; je n'approche point de Julie

sans trembler de la perdre; à chaque instant je crois voir sur son visage la pâleur de la mort. (Pp. 469–70, 5:10)

> You have infected me with a terror which you no longer feel... Since the receipt of your fatal letter, my heart is constantly oppressed. I cannot approach Eloisa, without trembling at the thought of losing her. I think every now and then I see a deadly paleness overspread her countenance.

Julie's death has no place in Wolmar's program. It is first articulated as a possibility by Saint-Preux; and as if to confirm the transfer of authority from the original law-giver to his most important reader, Julie indeed dies in the next book, much as predicted. Since Saint-Preux has already been converted, her function as exemplary text is fulfilled – the book has been read. As Julie and *Julie* both conclude, Wolmar's direct control ceases, but his project will live on and evolve in Saint-Preux's educational schemes, just as will the Author's. However, as Julie's final letter indicates, those schemes, like all traditions of narrative authority, depend on a radically private dialogical transaction of self and exemplary Other. Julie will remain with Saint-Preux, and available for re-membering in the future, just as *Julie* will remain with her reader.

From this perspective, *Julie, ou la nouvelle Héloïse* offers a prescription for reading and an allegory of exemplary fiction, as well as a plan for the organization of social communities. The author's implicit claim of authority over his culture is tempered by an acknowledgement that such authority depends on an informed, complicitous readership. And Saint-Preux's education, from a passionate egocentric reader who finds in the fictional transaction a grounds for refuting social compacts, to a discipline-bound reader who finds his identity in espousing the conventions of the collective, and finally, to a mature reader, who having mastered the rules can set forth his "own" readings and carry on the tradition, marks the author's attempt to reconcile his will to authority and sense of privilege with the mechanism of cultural negotiation he must acknowledge but cannot master.

Julie thus refigures in the broader cultural-historical terms of literary exemplars and their effects on readers and authors the same dialectic which Richardson first adumbrated in the interpersonal terms of individual and community. While the novel seems to claim for the author the right to dictate culture, this privilege finds a counterweight in the explicit figuring of the lawgiver's reliance on the exemplary individual who inspires him and on the epigones who will implement his vision over time. At the most private and the most public levels of analysis – that of the private reading act and that of his exemplar's enduring identity through history – the author's *Julie*, at once his creation and the Other that enables him, eludes his control just as Julie eludes Wolmar's. Like Wolmar, R. can modulate access to his Other through formal strictures, but he must relinquish control over it if he wishes it to play a formative role in the text of his culture and persist for the benefit of future generations. Like Wolmar, he is obliged to educate at least some individuals into the mechanisms underlying his manipulation of collective discourse, so that they can carry on the tradition. That he chooses to dissemble his method under an allegory of its own procedures shows only to what extent he shares the reticence of Wolmar to open the process of history to all members of society. His work is metaliterary, but only begrudgingly and for a select and persistent readership.

Perhaps the most interesting aspect of this whole process is R.'s double reticence to claim or relinquish authority. Having formulated the possibility of a fictional lawgiver – in fact the necessity for one, since without the social text prescribed by Wolmar, Julie's exemplary potential would go unrealized – he shies away from associating that function explicitly with himself (he refuses to qualify Julie as fictional or real, tableau or portrait) and from depicting it as authoritative (Julie finally does not relinquish her love for Saint-Preux or persist in her duties as first lady of Clarens). In this ambiguity, Rousseau foreshadows the more blatantly metanarrative ironies of Sterne, Diderot, and Laclos, all of whom either ironize their power over the reader as they flaunt it, or simultaneously glorify and undercut their characters' – and eventually their readers' – agendas of mastery over the narrative. These later writers bring the question of the fictional author's power out in the open, only to trivialize it; they produce far more thorough analyses of the narrative mechanisms of culture and history, only to discredit the attempt to master culture and history; alongside their compelling models of how the individual relates to the collective, they elaborate stories that dramatize the impossibility of really understanding that relationship. All such tactics pertain to a general trend to consolidate the novel's position as a mode of knowledge about its contemporary world, and particularly its culture, while simultaneously dissociating the genre from explicit claims of authority and hence from responsibility for the effects of its models.

NOTES

1 All quotations are from the Michel Launay edition (Paris: Garnier Flammarion, 1967); book and letter numbers are included for use with other editions. Translations are from *Eloisa, or a Series of Original Letters Collected and published by J. J. Rousseau*, 4 vols (Dublin: James Hunter, 1761), with occasional corrections of my own.
2 See for instance Paul de Man, *Allegories of Reading* (New Haven: Yale University Press, 1979), pp. 188–220.

3　Letters are the one form of narration/narrative practiced by all literate individuals in which the distinction between narration and narrative is both chronologically and textually perceptible: we all intuit, and indeed too often experience in the frustration of a clumsy epistolary relationship, the difference between the "original" narrational gesture that produces the letter and the letter or narrative itself, which is reconstituted some time later through another, distinct, narrational or readerly gesture.

4　As the author, R., explains in the *Entretien*, his work is designed in part as an antidote to the "torrent of poisonous maxims" which emanate from other forms of fiction and the discourse of worldliness, drawing people away from the simple life toward the glitter and debauchery of the urban world (p. 578). For a fuller treatment of the complex relationship of *Julie* to the novels it claimed to combat, see Geoffrey Bennington, *Sententiousness and the Novel*, pp. 137–75.

5　See also p. 41, 1:21; p. 49, 1:23; p. 56, 1:26; p. 74, 1:38; p. 120, 1:63.

6　See also p. 148, 2:7: "on gêne en vain nos inclinations; le cœur ne reçoit de lois que de lui-même" (In vain, however would men lay a restraint on the inclinations; the heart gives law to itself).

7　Pp. 332, 340–1, 4:10.

8　A more concise example of this process can be found in the description of how the domestics gain a sense of honor from the weekly staff competitions (p. 340, 4:10).

9　In his novel *Les Egarements du cœur et de l'esprit* (1735–8), Crébillon fils depicts with cynical amusement this obsession with constant innovation, and analyses the mechanism of continually evolving collective values on which it is based; cf. ed. Jean Dagen (Paris: Garnier-Flammarion, 1985), pp. 208–23.

10　See for instance Claire's assessment: "Ainsi, tout dépérit avec les mœurs. Le meilleur goût tient à la vertu même; il disparaît avec elle, et fait place à un goût factice et guindé, qui n'est plus que l'ouvrage de la mode" (p. 503, 6:5) (Thus every thing goes to ruin, when manners grow corrupted. Even taste depends on morals, and disappears with them; giving way to affect and pompous pretensions, that have no other foundation than fashion).

11　The tendency of every culture to think its own conventions "natural" appears as a consistent topic in eighteenth-century discussions of history. See, for instance, Bolingbroke, *Letters*, pp. 25–6, "there is scarce any folly or vice more epidemical among the sons of men, than that ridiculous and hurtful vanity, by which the people of each country are apt to prefer themselves to those of every other; and to make their own customs, and manners, and opinions, the standards of right and wrong, of true and false." Jean Baptiste du Boyer d'Argens, *La Philosophie du bon sens*, 3 vols (The Hague: Pierre Paupie, 1747), 1:54, expresses much the same idea: "chaque Province, chaque ville a ses erreurs particulières, & les peuples qui les habitent, en sont généralement imbus. Ils se communiquent les impressions qu'ils prennent dès leur jeunesse, & se fortifient mutuellement dans leur croiance, par le consentement unanime de tous ceux avec qui ils ont le plus de liaison" (every province, every town has its particular delusions, with which its inhabits are generally imbued. They communicate to one another their impressions from childhood on, and reinforce each other's belief mutually through the unanimous consent of all those with whom they have the most conversation). See also Edward Gibbon, *Essai sur l'étude de la littérature* (London: T. Becket and P. A. de Hondt, 1762), pp. 60–4.

12 For instance, Saint-Preux justifies the "natural" division of the sexes on the basis of its historical prevalence among different cultures, baldly asserting "tel est l'ordre que son universalité montre être le plus naturel" (p. 337, 4:10) (This is the order, which, from its universality, appears to be most natural).

13 "Tout ce que vous voyez sont de plantes sauvages ou robustes qu'il suffit de mettre en terre, et qui viennent ensuite d'elles-mêmes" (p. 359, 4:11) (All that you see are wild and vigourous plants, which need only to be put into the earth, and which afterwards spring up of themselves).

14 Peggy Kamuf, *Fictions*, pp. 97–122, reads the garden in a convincing feminist optic as not merely the spatial representation of Julie's transformation into Mme Wolmar, but also as her symbolic place of refuge from the law of patronymy that has subsumed her other identity as Julie.

15 See p. 369, 4:12: "cet amour de l'ordre que j'ai reçu de la nature" (this love of order which I received from nature).

16 Aristotle, *Poetics*, trans. Thomas Twining (reprinted London: J. M. Dent and Sons, Ltd., 1947), 2:6 p. 20. The distinction also was pertinent to theoretical essays; cf. Charles Pinot Duclos, *Considerations sur les mœurs de ce siècle*, nouvelle edition (Paris: Prault fils, 1751), p. 10: "cet examen doit se faire sur les mœurs générales, sur les différentes classes qui composent la société, & non pas sur les mœurs des particuliers: il faut des tableaux & non pas des portraits" (this investigation must be directed at general manners, at the different classes making up society, and not at the moral comportment of individuals: we need *tableaux* and not *portraits*).

17 Samuel Johnson, *Rambler*, no. 60 (October 13, 1750), 2:28; see also no. 4 (March 31, 1750), 1:18–20. Interestingly, Johnson disagrees with Aristotle on the value of history versus poetry, noting, one page later in the same essay, that "those parallel circumstances, and kindred images, to which we readily conform our minds, are, above all other writings, to be found in narratives of the lives of particular persons; and therefore no species of writing seems more worthy of cultivation than biography." Johnson's implication that affective adhesion comes primarily from belief in the historicity of the lives portrayed is not only reactionary with respect to his age, which, as the example of Rousseau shows us, tended increasingly to focus on verisimilitude, but inconsistent with respect to his own moralizing enterprise in the Rambler, which in later issues relies increasingly on imaginative stories to make its points.

18 Naturally, Julie can also be read as the embodiment of divine love among mortals, just as her infinite capacity for love logically finds its own inspiration in the example of divine love: "On dirait que rien de terrestre ne pouvant suffire au besoin d'aimer dont elle est dévorée, cet excès de sensibilité soit forcé de remonter à sa source" (p. 446, 5:5) (It might be said, no terrestrial object being equal to her tenderness, her excess of sensibility is reduced to ascend to its source).

19 One can also understand Julie's different function on three levels from the viewpoint of the reader, who, during reading, enjoys an intimate dialogical relationship with her which she informs and from which she evolves; who, as a collective readership, finds in her a countermodel to the ephemeral trends of fashion; and who, as critic, understands her as the expression of her author's project.

20 Montesquieu, *Pensées, Oeuvres complètes*, ed. André Masson, 3 vols (Paris: Nagel, 1950), vol. 2, p. 627. For a good eighteenth-century discussion of the mechanics of exemplification in fiction, see Kames, *Elements of Criticism*, pp. 4–40.

21 Like Julie, R. avoids the company of those who are beyond salvation. His readers are not urban sophisticates, in particular Parisians, who are blinded by the discourse of convention and incapable of moral emendation from books, but rather the rural provincials whose isolation from the fracas of urban culture makes them more susceptible to the contemplation of virtue: "il n'y a point, selon moi, de lecture utile aux gens du monde. Premièrement, parce que la multitude des livres nouveaux qu'ils parcourent, et qui disent tour à tour le pour et le contre, détruit l'effet de l'un par l'autre, et rend le tout comme non advenu. Les livres choisis qu'on relit ne font point d'effet encore: s'ils soutiennent les maximes du monde, ils sont superflus; et s'ils les combattent, ils sont inutiles: ils trouvent ceux qui les lisent liés aux vices de la société par des chaînes qu'ils ne peuvent rompre" (p. 577) (I believe that all kinds of reading are useless to people of the world: first, because the number of new books which they run through, so generally contradict each other, that their effect is reciprocally destroyed. The few choice books which deserve a second perusal, are equally ineffectual: for, if they are written in support of received opinions, they are superfluous; and if in opposition, they are of no use; they are too weak to break the chain which attaches the reader to the vices of society).

22 It should be noted that Saint-Preux himself refers to Julie as a tableau at the end of this same letter.

23 See Rousseau's discussion of the reception of *Julie* in *Les Confessions*, pp. 545–8.

24 See pp. 462–3, 5:8.

13

Ironizing History (*Tristram Shandy*)

I have argued that in *Julie, ou la nouvelle Héloïse*, Jean-Jacques Rousseau redefines the boundaries and functions of narration and narrative in two directions, by making the generalized emulation and rearticulation of shared usage the foundation of society but attributing the formulation of the original cultural script to an enlightened dispassionate author figure who stands outside of the communal transactions he prescribes. The law-giver's account of how men and women live together has a prescriptive force far in excess of biographical narration or even personally manipulative narration. Wolmar's, and later Julie's and Saint-Preux's, account of ideal social relationships does not just express identity on the individual level, it prescribes a set of collective usages grounding an entire community's social and ethical organization. So that at the same time the right to devise accounts of reality is restricted to an initiated elite, the field of effect of the narrative produced by that elite expands to encompass the whole range of transactions between collective account and personal recounting, shared discourse and selfhood, which we identify with the economy of culture.

In *Julie*, authority over culture is lodged in exemplary narratives which are introduced into the collective discourse of the community and melded into the range of practices which that discourse continually elaborates. Rousseau thus implicitly states the case for the shaping of history by literature and for a fictional narration ultimately, if proleptically, referential in its thrust: once a fiction insinuates itself into a larger cultural narrative, the social order it narrates eventually becomes part of historical reality, even if it does not, at the moment of its "original" articulation, refer to any currently existing reality. This proleptic referentiality works itself out through secondary agents: readers who, like Saint-Preux, appropriate and reiterate the narrative, thus modulating its particular effects in a given society or period and confirming its enactment into culture. In that sense, the literary work envisioned by the author of *Julie* attains its end and meaning only within the ongoing flux of history it helps shape, and through the mediation of a reader whose responses it foresees.

Rousseau's *Entretien sur les romans* and the Author's chapters in *Tom Jones*, like the Préface-annexe in Diderot's *La Religieuse*, or the far more elaborate discussions of author-reader relationships in *Tristram Shandy* and *Jacques le fataliste*, testify to an increasing interest in this textual economy during the third quarter of the century. Overlying the plot of individuality and selfhood within society, we find in the novels of this period a "meta-plot" of sorts, a discussion of the way in which authors (and readers) construct the fictional plot and effect its assimilation into the collective text of culture. This metaplot examines the same paradigms of self-definition, dialogical rivalry, narrative titillation, and manipulation which we have seen thematized in conjunction with social discourse in the earlier novels of the century, but it does so from the perspective of literary expression, focusing on the way these paradigms are embodied in the transactions of literary writing and reading. In the works of Sterne, Diderot, and Laclos, the writing of fiction, and its reciprocal, reading, expand to displace romance and personal interaction as the paradigmatic mode of self-realization and the most immediately accessible vehicle of social influence. This is entirely predictable: when best-selling novels such as *Clarissa, Tom Jones*, and *Julie* underscore the centrality of narration and shared narrative to social manipulation, it becomes difficult to avoid looking at the mechanisms and motives of *professional* narration as embodied in the genre of narrative acknowledged to be the period's most influential.

Of course all novels are more or less metanovels to the extent that they can be read as commentaries on their own production and the economies that regulate it; but the novels I designate by that term, and in particular Laurence Sterne's *Tristram Shandy* and Diderot's *Jacques le fataliste*, focus explicitly on their own production and they do so in abstract terms. These are not attempts to represent in realistic terms the social reality of the times, but rather philosophical speculations on the problems of representation itself, and particularly representation in language, as it relates to history – works, in short, where "the dramatic presentation of the act of writing is the chief element of cohesion."[1] They deliberately foreground the event(s) of their own narration – the authorial act to which they owe their formal consistency as a narrative, and the corresponding act of that narrative's reception by the reader – rather than the material being narrated or experiences that pre-date the narration.[2] As one critic puts it, paraphrasing Sterne, *Tristram Shandy* is a work "where everything is known in the doing, not in the thing seen as done."[3] *Jacques le fataliste* is similarly preoccupied with the process of its own narration, and even more attentive to the role of the reader in this process.

As part of their increased attention to the mechanism and function of narration, both of these books take up the question of *time*, as it relates to representation, focusing on the distinction between narrated time and narrating time, between the representation of time, if you will, and the time of representation, or, finally, between history as an organized construct of past experience, and history as a lived time and duration. The reconciliation of these two concepts of history, as well as the writer's and the reader's experience, and the relationship between personal narrations, whether writer's or reader's, and the larger order of history which frames such narrations as a master narrative, forms the thematic armature of the metanovels.

Laurence Sterne's *Tristram Shandy*, published in nine volumes between 1761 and 1767, confirms the historical development covered in the preceding chapters, but in an ironic mode, foregrounding the difficulties of narration, the *work* involved in making sense out of the world, in finding a pattern in one's experience and using that pattern as a guide for future behavior. It starts from the premise that reality is only known as a product of the knower's mind, and that the processes of the mind, rather than some "objective" structure, are what bear investigation as the structuring force of history. "It is not things that disturb men, but their judgments about things" declares the epigraph to *Tristram Shandy*, and the novel promises not just the life, but also the "opinions" of its author, "who intrudes into his novel to comment on himself as writer, and on his book, not simply as a series of events with moral implications, but as a created literary product."[4] This is first and foremost a book preoccupied with the play between the events it recounts and the event of that recounting (and its reading) – one might say between Tristram Shandy's story and the story of *Tristram Shandy*.

But while *Tristram Shandy* explicitly addresses the relationship of narration to both experience and narrative, it does not do so systematically or straightforwardly. Fascinated by the capacity of his mind (and his narrational machine) to associate almost any episode or text to almost any other and to filter his account through a variety of styles, the narrator, Tristram, gives himself over to a parade of digression, leading his reader on a wild chase through philosophical speculations, parodies of other genres, satiric jibes, typographical innovations, nonsense chapters, and interpolated stories, few of which have any direct connection to the story of his life, but all of which dramatize some aspect of the process of rhetoric.[5] "Not doing, but expressing oneself, is the texture of life in this world,"[6] and narration for this narrator is an end in itself – a game of digression, expansion, appropriation, synthesis, and innovation, intertextual reiteration and reformulation, which, delighted with its own mechanism, ultimately displaces the historical experience it is supposed to relate. Rather than telling his own story, or even formulating and demonstrating a simple thesis about self-representation, Tristram explores and embodies the excesses to which self-conscious writing lends itself. The result seems narration for narration's sake, a display of pure production, "that turns our consciousness not to the end of the argument, but to the process."[7]

Ironically, in his narrational frenzy, Tristram frustrates his announced agenda. As he relates more anecdotes and provides more sidelights, he moves ever further from a simple account of his own identity: "there is never a new perspective; no new ground is reached from which to look back on the conflict past."[8] This is but one of the ironies of the book, which is structured according to a series of contrasts which frequently co-exist without resolving themselves into a dialectic or resigning themselves to paradox. *Tristram Shandy* proposes a variety of incompatible ways to organize experience, but unlike Diderot's "sequel," *Jacques le fataliste*, it does not synthesize these opposed approaches into a single dialectic scheme.

Within the context of this study *Tristram Shandy* presents a limiting case of what we might call one-sided narration, that is, a narrational gesture that in reaction to the dominant current of the times redefines the ground of reality and identity as the activity of narrating, rather than a stable narrative or world order. Whereas previous realistic narrators deferred to a referential framework of shared social, psychological, and material reality – either directly, by claiming to recount actual experience (Defoe, Marivaux, Richardson), or indirectly, by claiming to present an essential distillation of human nature (Fielding, Rousseau) – *Tristram Shandy* rejects the indenture to verisimilitude and grounds both the identity and the authority of its protagonist entirely within the *process* of narration. Tristram exists *because* he *relates*: his voice sustains and consolidates itself through the ingenuity of its transitions from one topic to another, rather than through the careful reconstruction of its past experience. More than any previous narrative voice, he succeeds in constituting himself through sheer force of imagination. Indeed, by linking his own story to an apparently limitless set of other narratives, he *personifies* relation in its least constrictive form. His story continually disperses itself into scores of other stories, rather than cohering into a single plot line susceptible to assimilation with the larger conventional vision of society which previous authors chronicle and Rousseau attempts to prefigure.

As the personification of a process of expression, Tristram is felt rather than depicted. He pervades the text as a distinctive narrational style, an ongoing self-conscious mentation divorced of any social framework or historical texture, rather than as a character like Marivaux's Jacob, who relates his adventures from a distance and thus plays a double role of narrator and actor.[9] Tristram attains no thematic consistency in the world he relates. When he mentions himself, it is seldom with respect to his past experience, but rather his current narrating activity, which becomes the sole ground of his identity in the book. He is in this respect similar to the Author in Fielding's comic novels, but he is far less discrete in his narration. Rather than allowing his descriptions of other individuals and their actions to become confused with a historical order above that of the storyteller's whim, he continually disrupts his story with intrusions that remind us to what degree the entire drama is a product of authorial fabulation. In this respect he dramatizes a purely "narrational" consciousness which undercuts its narrative's re-presentation of historical events with its own tireless assertion of selfhood.[10]

In stark contrast to this processual narrating consciousness are the "realistic" characters whose stories Tristram relates, principally his father Walter and his uncle Toby, both of whom are present at his birth, and in the description of whose previous lives, opinions, and experiences his account eventually exhausts itself. Toby and Mr Shandy are polar opposites in temperament and interest, and they present contrasting caricatures of the relationship between expression and reality: Toby satirizes the process of association gone berserk on a single theme, and a vision of history as a compendium of concrete data susceptible to objective re-presentation; Walter satirizes the converse idea of history as an abstract grammar whose laws can be derived from past experience in the form of texts. Both characters share a common goal, namely to make sense of reality, to order the world in which they find themselves, but each has his own idiosyncratic narrational practice, and together they form the background against which Tristram's ironic posture acquires its force as a negative affirmation of mastery.

Toby is a man dominated by his hobby-horse, or obsessive interest. He relates every conversation, every event back to the single subject that interests him: the art of military fortification and siege. His discourse is noteworthy not only for its lack of a speculative or creative dimension and its narrow propositional compass, but also because of the way it attempts to stabilize language and subordinate narration to objective master narratives. Rather than recounting the past in(to) the present, Toby's energy is mobilized entirely by the project of relating the present to an unvarying past, which he attempts to represent not just linguistically, but also materially, in the form of model earthworks.

The primal scene in this program is the siege of Namur, where Toby received some shrapnel in the groin, an injury that rendered him only partially ambulatory and perhaps, Tristram hints, otherwise dysfunctional as well. "The history of a soldier's wound beguiles the pain of it" (p. 100, 1:25),[11] we are told, and as a means of alleviating his suffering during his long convalescence Toby undertakes to reconstruct the circumstances of his incapacitation. From the outset, however, he is plagued by language:

the many perplexities he was in, arose out of the almost insurmountable difficulties he found in telling his story intelligibly, and giving such clear ideas of the differences and distinctions between the scarp and counterscarp,—the glacis and covered way,—the half-moon and ravelin,—as to make his company fully comprehend where and what he was about. (P. 103, 2:1)

As Tristram tells it, the cause of Toby's dilemma is "the unsteady uses of words" (p. 108, 2:2): he possesses no terminology precise enough to convey to his auditors an adequate idea of the course of the battle and his part in it. Yet more than most people, he depends on a clear narrative for his identity. His injury has made him "unfit for the service" (p. 100, 1:25), and his recovery "depending . . . upon the passions and affections of his mind, it behoved him to take the nicest care to make himself so far master of his subject, as to be able to talk upon it without emotion" (p. 109, 2:3). To this end, Toby purchases a map and undertakes the study of military science by plunging himself into the histories of its great theoreticians. Each of these gestures proposes to overcome language in a different way.

On the one hand, Toby trains himself in a technical discourse so limited in its application as to remain essentially free of the uncontrollable perversions that normal language suffers (and which Tristram exemplifies in his continual use of double-entendres and puns). On the other, he supplements his account with a non-linguistic representation designed to eliminate the imprecise referential mediation of that account. His map of the battle of Namur soon gives way to miniature earthworks on his estate, in which he reconstructs entire battlefields modeled on the siege.

Toby's goal is to re-present a perfect mirror image of the past in its material specificity, not in view of extracting some larger truth about human behavior, but only in accordance with an obsession for reproducing history (and his story) free of the confusion intrinsic to common-language narration. The reconstruction of the Namur siege, like the other sieges which Toby will elaborate subsequently, differs from the personal histories of previous novels in that it suffers no reformulation at the hands of a present selfhood re-counting the past in order to advance future objectives. Toby inverts the typical eighteenth-century paradigm of self-definition by coercing present discourse to relate to the past, rather than adopting his past to the present. Inevitably, he draws every conversation toward a military reminiscence, as his brother points out: "talk of what we will, brother, —— or let the occasion be never so foreign or unfit for the subject, — you are sure to bring it in" (p. 129, 2:12).[12]

During the entirety of the episode of Tristram's birth, for instance, he displays an interest only in bringing the conversation around to military science. When Dr Slop arrives to attend the delivery, Toby tries to draw him into a discussion of curtins, ravelins, and half-moons, although, as Tristram's father exclaims "I cannot see what kind of connection there can be betwixt Dr Slop's sudden coming, and a discourse upon fortification" (p. 128, 2:12). Later, when Trim reports that Dr Slop is making a bridge (for Tristram's broken nose), Toby concludes, against all probability, that the physician is repairing a broken footbridge in his model earthworks (p. 215, 3:23). When Mr Shandy laments the disfiguration of his son's nose, Toby's mind wanders to an episode of military punishment (4:3). When his brother is discussing the question of radical heat and radical moisture with respect to health, Toby remembers a particularly rainy bivouac in Limerick (5:37). When Trim attempts to tell him the tale of the King of Bohemia, Toby interrupts with extensive discourses on geography, chronology, and the invention of gunpowder (8:19). And when widow Wadman decides to court him, she must go to extremes to get his attention, since he otherwise "would have sat quietly upon a sopha from June to January . . . with an eye as fine as the Thracian Rodope's besides him, without being able to tell, whether it was a black or a blue one" (pp. 550–1, 8:24). Toby's response to arguments is even more infuriating: he simply stops talking and whistles.

Dysfunctional conversationally, Toby is passive with regard to his own fate: totally preoccupied with re-creating that which was, he is incapable of structuring the present or preparing the future. We are told, for instance, that when Toby fell in love with the widow Wadman, he "took it like a lamb – sat still and let the poison work in his veins without resistance," while Mr Shandy in a similar situation "was all abuse and foul language, approaching rather towards malediction . . . cursing himself in at the bargain, as one of the most egregious fools and coxcombs, . . . that ever was let loose in the world" (p. 553, 8:26). And when faced with the task of declaring himself, Toby, a man "having no talents for amplification," quite literally has nothing to say: "when he had told Mrs Wadman once that he loved her, he let it alone, and left the matter to work after its own way" (p. 603, 9:The Eighteenth Chapter).

Finally, Toby is linguistically crippled on the most fundamental level, for his monomania and his compulsion to reduce the past to an aggregate of objective data blind him to figurative language and make it impossible for him to follow complex speculative arguments. The only lexical meanings he records are those that pertain to his hobby-horse; words used figuratively are registered literally or simply misunderstood. For example, when Tristram's father launches into an intricate philosophical discussion with him, he hears only that term which relates to his field of interest:

> with all the semblance of a deep school-man intent upon the *medius terminus*,
> — my uncle Toby was in fact as ignorant of the whole lecture, and all its pros
> and cons . . . But the word *siege*, like a talismanic power, in my father's

metaphor, wafting back my uncle Toby's fancy, quick as a note could follow the touch, — he open'd his ears... (P. 243, 3:41)

Yet the ideal of unambiguous representation eludes him, even within the discourse of military fortification. His straightforward offer to put widow Wadman's finger on the very spot (on the map) where he was injured meets with misunderstanding, just as the elements of his earthwork reproduction take on identities and trigger events which he cannot foresee: his "mortar-pieces" turn out to be Mr Shandy's favorite boots (3:22); his cannon are sash weights, which, having been removed from all the windows by Toby's man Trim for their lead, bring about the accidental circumcision of young Tristram (5:17–19).

Thus in spite of the frequent praise of his gentle character, "the benignity of whose heart interpreted every motion of the body in the kindest sense the motion would admit of" (p. 176, 3:5), Toby remains throughout the book a parody of narrational dysfunction, obsessed with recounting the past, but oblivious to the communal fashioning of reality and truth to which such narrational efforts pertain. Reproduction and sterility form a thematic axis of the book, and Toby's fanatical re-creation figures a particularly fruitless attempt to compensate for an invalid present through the recovery of a lost past. In his endeavor to recoup the concrete texture of his history, Toby renounces productive social discourse and the possibility of constructing an authentic future: "the normal life movement which carries a thick past towards the open future to which it is connected by some active project has become altered to a closed world of memories."[13] His attempt to fashion the perfect stable narrative forces him to abandon productive engagement in culture, both narrational and otherwise.

If it is clear that Toby, like the other men in the book, "substitutes a situation of potential mastery" for the sexual situation over which he has less control,[14] his agenda of mastery, like that of Tristram and Walter Shandy, involves the melding of his story with history. The historiographic-al epistemology Toby parodies is that of naive historicism, the narrative epistemology that of realism. He remains convinced that reality precedes his gesture, that it is somehow simply "there," and that historical truth lies in its objective re-creation. His enterprise turns around the possibility of subordinating his story(telling) to history – of creating for his public a rendition of the past that will bear no trace of subjective manipulation according to personal motive, but merely reflect objective reality. Objective reality, however, manifests itself through a particular narrative form to which Toby's need for facts indentures him: Tristram explains how the old soldier and his man Trim follow the campaigns preceding the peace of Utrecht through the news reports, "regulating their approaches and attacks, by the accounts my uncle Toby received from the daily papers" (p. 429, 622). In its function of providing society with the material "facts," the news report (as opposed to fiction) downplays the act of narration which produced it and purports to re-present for its public the compendium of military and political "events" which we refer to as "history" in the most vulgar sense. This narrative of historical events speaks in the anonymous voice of reality, not private consciousness, presenting itself as collectively held knowledge, unmediated and objective, and it quite literally guides Toby's representation, which differs from the normal use of such accounts by social individuals only to the extent that he exaggerates beyond all measure its role in the construction of his personal identity, allowing, as it were, history in the crudest sense to usurp his story.

Toby's brother, Walter Shandy, personifies an entirely different conception of history, not unlike that of Wolmar in its pretentions to analytic clarity and control; and he likewise satirizes the ordering of reality according to personal hypothesis which Wolmar, and by extension the novelist, embodies. "A man of deep reading — prompt memory — with Cato, and Seneca, and Epictetus, at his fingers' ends" (p. 354, 5:6), Mr Shandy regards history as a text which the individual can interpret and refashion according to current needs. Where Toby relates all present discourse to the past, Walter continually reworks the past into the present. "Never at a loss what to say to any man, upon any subject" (p. 387, 5:34), he is "a philosopher in grain, — speculative, — systematical" (p. 91, 1:21), a permanently cogitating, permanently synthesizing mind, "whose way was to force every event in nature into an hypothesis, by which means never man crucified TRUTH at the rate he did" (p. 613, 9:32).

Like Toby, Mr Shandy has a hobby-horse, but his is that of the hypothesis or explanation: "he was systematical, and, like all systematic reasoners, he would move both heaven and earth, and twist and torture everything in nature to support his hypothesis" (p. 80, 1:19). Where his brother seeks only to recreate physical events, Tristram's father formulates laws to regulate such events, and he sees in scientific nomenclature such as that which furnishes Toby his precision of reference only a further occasion for interpretation and theorizing. While Toby subordinates all current narration to a single static narrative, his brother devours all existing narratives in an insatiable narration: writings from all domains and periods nourish his ongoing synthesis, which addresses questions of virtually all sorts, from the wisdom of circumcision or the influence of noses, names, and modes of birth on an individual's later life, to the concept of life's "radical heat" and "radical moisture," the value of the auxiliary verbs, or the nature of love.

The texts which govern Walter's hypotheses are, unlike news stories, openly personal and subjective. Their vision of reality is born of the individual author's narrational response to the world as conditioned by previous narratives. Such responses carry the name of their author as an acknowledgment of the fact that they are mediated by private consciousness; they know that the vision of reality they proffer the reader is never limited to the brute material facts of the geopolitical timeline but includes by definition the traces of narrational configuration.

Events in such a framework do not exist in any state of pure materiality, but rather as lived experience and knowledge, shaped by individual reaction, and Mr Shandy, like the authors he cites, imparts his own personal configuration to the "reality" that surrounds him. For example, his tactic for dealing with the misfortunes that befall him – most of which involve his progeniture – is to re-evaluate the situation in the light of historical precedents. Thus when his eldest son Bobby dies, he takes solace by citing to himself "Servius Sulpicius's consolatory letter to Tully" (p. 350, 5:3), and when Tristram is more or less circumcized in an accident, he consults his history books regarding the practice in other cultures and concludes:

— if the EGYPTIANS, — the SYRIANS, — the PHOENICIANS, — the ARABIANS, — the CAPPADOCIANS, — if the COLCHI, and TROGLODITES did it — if SOLON and PYTHAGORAS submitted, — what is TRISTRAM? — Who am I, that I should fret or fume one moment about the matter? (P. 377, 5:27)

This reliance on *textual* precedence implies no participation in the economy of social discourse. Walter's opinions are as remote from the collective norm as is Toby's frame of association:

his road lay so very far on one side, from that wherein most men travelled, — that every object before him presented a face and section of itself to his eye, altogether different from the plan and elevation of it seen by the rest of mankind. — In other words, 'twas a different object, — and in course was differently considered (P. 375, 5:24)

Reiterating a paradigm we have seen in various guises throughout the period under consideration, the character of Walter Shandy *construes* the world according to individual motives and personality, disputing by his example the concept of a brute material reality which his brother personifies. Walter differs from previous characters, though, in that he does not elaborate his world in dialogue with his social peers, but within a purely textual transaction. Inspired by, synthesized out of, and reinforced by allusion to, previous writings, his ongoing discursive theorization finds its Other in the text of history. Where Defoe's, Marivaux's, Richardson's, or Rousseau's characters create new identities in their negotiations with sexual and social rivals, Mr Shandy finds his "originality" in the hermeneutic synthesis of reading – twisting and torturing what he finds, in order to get a better grip on reality.

This process attains its apogee in Mr Shandy's project for a "Tristrapæ-dia," or program of education for the childhood and adolescence of his son, which the narrator distinguishes from Toby's more passive use of narrative precedent:

> my father gave himself up to it with as much devotion as ever my uncle Toby had done to his doctrine of projectiles. — The difference between them was, that my uncle Toby drew his whole knowledge of projectiles from Nicholas Tartaglia. — My father spun his, every thread of it, out of his own brain, — or reeled and cross-twisted what all other spinners and spinsters had spun before him, that 'was pretty near the same torture to him. (P. 366, 5:16)

Mr Shandy's ideas are his in a way that Toby's are not, since he has developed them through a process of reinterpretation, compilation, and combination:

> my father stood up for all his opinions; he had spared no pains in picking them up, and the more they lay out of the common way, the better still was his title. — No mortal claimed them: they had cost him moreover as much labour in cooking and digesting as in the case above, so that they might well and truly be said to be of his own goods and chattels. (P. 229, 3:34)

We have here an abstract formulation and parody of a pattern underlying many of the plots of earlier novels, where by dint of narrational energy, a character comes into possession of certain property. But where Pamela, for example, gains an estate and title by virtue of her narrational tenacity, Mr Shandy gains knowledge.[15] His enterprise is significant, though, not because his motivations and rewards are abstract, but because his purely textual dialogue implicitly renounces culture broadly defined in favor of a more narrow literary authority. He not only does not rely on collective discourse for his opinions, he actively shuns it:

> Mr Shandy, my father, Sir, would see nothing in the light in which others placed it; — he placed things in his own light; — he would weigh nothing in common scales (P. 160, 2:19)[16]

His ideas hold weight for him not because they emerge from collaboration with his peers – indeed, he sees his brother as no more than a "simpleton" (p. 350, 5:3), albeit a loveable one, while his wife refuses any discussion whatsoever, always bowing to his intuitions – but because they are grounded in a private transaction with a textual corpus considered *a priori* authoritative. His is the conviction of the solitary reader, who arrives at understanding through the hermeneutic reconstitution of narratives, rather than by exchanging ideas with his contemporaries. And to the extent that his theories have any validity, they promote the authority of literature over that of society, reading over conversation. Indeed, Tristram, who as we shall see momentarily is in many respects a more sophisticated version of Mr Shandy, makes this displacement explicit, stating emphatically that "writing, when properly managed, . . . is but a different name for conversation" (p. 127, 2:11).[17]

"Turning . . . to his advantage . . . every . . . thing, which the ancients did or said" (p. 420, 6:17), Walter appropriates and refashions (the text of) history to explain (the course of) history, suggesting that it is through "conversations" with the writings of previous authors that one attains mastery over one's identity and one's destiny. Were this shown to be an effective way of dealing with life, the effect of his character would be to elevate the literary transaction and literary text to a position of pre-eminence among narrations and narratives, respectively.

Unfortunately, his story never turns out the way he writes it: he is systematically "baffled and overthrown in all his little systems and wishes" (p. 82, 1:19). Having determined that a physician should deliver his son, he must cede to his wife's desires for birth with a midwife; having decided that noses are a crucial indicator of future happiness, he is confronted with the disfigurement of his son's; convinced that Tristram is the worst name any man can carry, he discovers to his horror that his son has been inadvertently baptized with precisely that name; determined to compensate for Tristram's misfortune with the Tristrapædia, he spends so much time writing that he neglects his son's elementary education; having an insatiable appetite for debate and philosophizing, he must spend his life in non-dialogue with his single-minded brother and passive wife.

Mercilessly ironizing Walter Shandy's entire program, this sequence of setbacks leaves little doubt as to whether the active narrational practice of reading provides any grip on history. To the extent that Shandy's agenda parallels Wolmar's in its educational objectives, the systematic crushing of his plans can be read as a satirical commentary on the kind of enlightened rational authoritarianism which *Julie* advances.[18] Tristram himself remarks of his father, that the "train of events [are] perpetually falling out against him, and in so critical and cruel a way, as if they had purposely been planned and pointed against him, merely to insult his speculations" (p. 82, 1:19). If Toby's earthworks parody the reduction of history to a concrete narrative, immune to the vicissitudes of language and narration,[19] Walter's failures parody the theoretician's conversion of history into science: history is as resistant to knowledge – and by extension to the authority of literature – as it is to representation.

The two central "characters," then, in Tristram's narrative actually function as symbolic embodiments of failed conceptions of narration and the narrative of history. Neither finally can establish a firm connection between his own story or story-telling, and his evolving history. Toby can no more negotiate the courtship of widow Wadman than can Walter program the future of his offspring. Their different but equally pathetic gestures underscore what the book continually demonstrates in all of its lesser anecdotes: the fallacy of seeking a simple link between expression and reality. *Tristram Shandy* dramatizes the processes by which we structure the world and persuade our peers, but it dissuades us from deluding ourselves into thinking that those processes lead to any certain reality, either private or public.

Much the same lesson emerges from Tristram's multifaceted irony. On the simplest level of analysis, Tristram seems to combine the divergent impulses of his uncle and father, ironizing the excesses of each with a self-consciously excessive practice all his own. He shares with Toby, who is in this sense his "parabolic equivalent,"[20] the ostensible goal of wishing to reconstruct his past, but he expands his narration to include all manner of subjective experience: not only portraits of his family, their personal histories, beliefs, foibles, virtues, but even the stories they told or heard. Far from coercing his gesture of self-expression into a single lexical and thematic domain like his uncle, whose narration answers to the pre-ordained agenda of a single referent, he allows the flow of his narration to predicate its reference: in the event of telling he discovers what must be told, and in this sense his ongoing act of representation defines the represented reality as much as the converse.

Like Walter, Tristram flaunts his erudition and peppers his accounts with citations of, and references to, previous authors; both have a penchant for theorizing and hypothesis; both find the play of wit irresistible; both generate their understanding and build their identity within a literary dialogue rather than a social one – although Tristram's is with the reader, not just the text; and both fail in their attempts to outstride history – a point to which I shall return. But more explicitly than his father, Tristram confronts the pressure exercised by narrative precedents, exploring ways in which the individual can find an identity within and against those precedents, using their formal and thematic conventions as a springboard for his own narrational innovation. However, he never takes his formal innovations so seriously as to think they could enclose or control the flow of history of which they partake. He recognizes that all attempts to impose a formal order on the flux of reality occur at the expense of prior orders they disrupt, and that the merely provisional grasp on the world which they provide is itself doomed to disruption. Walter, conversely, is *serious* in his hypotheses, which, although they enter his mind in the form of mere whim, frequently end "in downright earnest" (p. 80, 1:19) by dint of being wittily defended. The comic irony in his situation comes from the fact that he actually believes names and noses to be of the utmost importance in determining a person's fate and is therefore grief-stricken when "his little systems and wishes" are thwarted.

The comic element in Tristram's account comes rather from his self-ironization. Even as he perfects his narrational mastery, he acknowledges the impossibility of systematizing or getting "outside of" history and the impossibility of ever finishing *his* history, turning the gap between the enormity of his pretentions and the reality of his predicament into a source of laughter. He knows that he can never exhaustively account for his past life, much less get a handle on the future, and that the more allusions, references, and innovations he produces in the attempt, the more deeply he becomes mired in both his history and the historical intertext. But rather than despair, he makes this paradox the centerpiece of an exuberant self-mocking narrational virtuosity. Unable to master history, he makes his gesture the personification of its workings; unable to encapsulate the narrated experience, he displaces it with the experience of narration.

Tristram's most celebrated move is to make the disfiguration of extant literary conventions the very foundation of his identity. He muddles the chronological sequence of his episodes, mis-numbers and omits chapters and reinserts them later; interrupts his stories or suspends them in midstream to pursue other questions or parody other genres, such as legal judgments, travel accounts, sermons, or Ernulfus' curse (3:11); mingles narrative voices and levels (as when the reader or the narrator's friends intervene in Tristram's account, or the account is disrupted by events in the author's life); plays narrating time off of narrated time;[21] and embellishes his narration with typographical innovations such as mixed typefaces, symbols or lines, entirely black or blank pages, and pages taken up by the marbling used in bindings.[22]

Most all of these formal "innovations" can be found in earlier works, but *Tristram Shandy* is unique in that it makes them the explicit subject matter of its narrative.[23] Tristram's intrusive techniques, like his scorn for continuity, reflect a narrational self intent on asserting its freedom to reconfigure tradition as it goes, imposing the author's technical mastery on the readers whose responses it shapes, but they also underline the author's indebtedness to, and inscription within, literary conventions.[24] *Tristram Shandy* hardly attempts to structure society in its particulars along the lines of *Julie*, but its obsession with convention obliquely reveals a fascination even more intense than Rousseau's with the individual's paradoxical enclosure within, and influence over, the unwritten rules of "the natural." Like Wolmar, Tristram founds a world on usage, but unlike the lawgiver, he shares his project with his reader, using the logic of convention to foreground and subvert specific conventions:

The deuce of any other rule have I to govern myself by in this affair — and if I had one — as *I do all things out of all rule* — I would twist and tear it to pieces, and throw it into the fire when I had done... is a man to follow rules — or rules to follow him? (P. 282, 4:10, my italics)

Rules, as novels from Richardson to *Julie* have shown us, derive from, and are reinforced by, the collective narrative of past and current behavior which every society maintains as its culture; rules can be ephemeral and unwritten, as in the case of fashion and style, or more permanent and formally inscribed, as in the case of moral codes or laws. In telling a story at odds with his culture's rules of narration – in making it a rule to disobey them – Tristram establishes a private Shandyian convention to fight conventions. He uses the historical paradigm of culture to resist the draw of his culture, most notably the subcategory which prescribes how books should be structured. But by making it a rule not to do anything "as a rule," Tristram both triumphs over and reinforces that paradigm. He triumphs over it in the sense that he has found a means to subvert tradition and outpace his own history – to keep a step ahead of the accretion of convention that consistent use of a single formal innovation might precipitate. He reinforces the historical paradigm in that he must resort to a rule in order to break free of rules.

This double bind is most blatant in Tristram's use of digression, which he qualifies early on as "the sunshine... the life, the soul of reading" (p. 95, 1:22) and which he adopts as a stratagem to forestall the accumulation of a story line. Unfortunately, as digression is piled upon digression a pattern emerges that is as consistent and predictable as the convention the narrator seeks to disrupt. As we have seen, this is a problem with agendas of mastery from *Clarissa* onwards: individuals intent on overcoming their subjection to a cultural or moral grammar find themselves unable to formulate a program of resistance that does not itself inscribe the self within a framework of rules (and roles). These roles are frequently more coercive, because less explicit, than those they displace. *Tristram Shandy* differs from its predecessors in that it correlates such rules explicitly with the laws of narration, thereby situating the problematics of self-determination squarely within the relationship of the writing self to the written self, current story to past history, or personal narration to public narrative, rather than simply within a framework of familial or interpersonal rivalry.

Formal conventions are not the only arena in which written selfhood confronts history, though; the writing self must also contend with the textual embodiment of those rules: the existing corpus of similar narratives, or literary intertext into which the self is necessarily inscribed, the context within which it will be evaluated. Tristram's formal revolution is doubly ironic in that it is framed by, and frames, an extravagant use of intertextual references that seems intent on confusing any evaluation of its author's originality. As if to impress upon the reader the author's reliance on textual precedents at the same time that it insists on his innovation, the book choreographs its formal twists and turns against a background of literary citations, imitations, parodies, and verbatim borrowings of texts ranging from the classics to works of Sterne's day. One can of course attribute this patchwork of allusion to the practice of literary wit, of which it is a primary constituent. But that is to neglect its function within the conventions of *Tristram Shandy*, which is, after all, structured according to a principle of continual newness and constant originality.[25]

Like his father, Tristram loads his discourse with references, but unlike Walter, he purposely muddles them, mixing citations of actual sources with fictitious references, fabricated sources, and covert plagiarism. He flaunts his appropriation of passages from earlier sources, but only when those sources are fictitious, leaving for the erudite to ferret out instances of real plagiarism. Slawkenbergius' tale (volume 4), Yorick's sermon (2:17), the legal judgment of the Sorbonne on pre-natal baptism (1:20), or Toby's tale of Le Fever (6:6–11), to name just the most obvious examples, are presented as the works of some "other" author, while the great majority of Sterne's verbatim borrowings, such as the description from Rabelais of "Gymnast," or the many passages adapted from Burton's *Anatomy of Melancholy*, slip by unreferenced, although presumably not unnoticed by readers of the period.[26]

It becomes impossible in such a situation to decide whether Tristram (and Sterne) is an inventive genius or simply a derivative clown. But that is precisely the point: by attributing his own parodies to others even as he pillages tradition, Tristram undermines any simplistic version of originality or property, insinuating that all of the words he (or anyone else) writes have already been used or will ultimately be used by someone else.[27] *But not in the same context.* Since meaning is a function of individual judgment, and hence specific context, to reiterate in a new context a passage from Rabelais is to give it a new meaning. It is this newness of recontextualization that Tristram is after, and like his disfiguration of convention it depends for its effect on the recognition of the old or original context: we can only appreciate the use he makes of Rabelais if we know it is *from* Rabelais. This is originality based on the impossibility of originality.

Tristram's originality, in other words, lies in the way he thematizes his enclosure in the intertext, in the way he foregrounds his entrapment in tradition as a means of going beyond that tradition. Were his wit merely incidental, he would simply be one more hack in an established tradition. But by making the lack of originality an explicit theme of his work, he ironically attains a measure of originality. Accepting the fact that he is already inscribed in history, and powerless to avoid the associations and contexts of the western European classical intertext which enables his gesture, he manages to get one step ahead of his own history.

Walter Shandy at one point compares language, particularly the auxiliary verbs, to a "great engine . . . to open new tracks of enquiry, and make every idea engender millions" (p. 395, 5:42), which in a sense states the strategy of the narrator. While Toby and his brother struggle against history – for Toby a constantly evolving linguistic ambiguity, for his brother a perverse destiny intent on thwarting all his ambitions – Tristram discovers in the interweaving of historical precedents a powerful machine of narrational engenderment. By making the strictures of history explicit and grounding his own narration and identity in their recombination and disfiguration, he appropriates their authority and energy even as he reaffirms it. His strategy is to free himself from the tyranny of the past by simultaneously citing and rewriting the rules laid down by tradition. He puts history in his story and usurps its voice by substituting for his biographical history (the story of his past experience) the chronicle of his story-telling activity as literary history (the account of his act of narration as a recombinatory process enabled by the traditions it resists).

There is another substitution in *Tristram Shandy*, though, that goes beyond this appropriation of history – that in fact suspends and redefines it. What really sets off Tristram from the caricatures that frame him – and from previous heroes and authors we have considered – is his conception of reality (and history) in temporal terms. Previous novels conceive of reality and identity almost exclusively in terms of an *order* which conditions all human experience, grants the individual identity, and provides a context for his or her endeavors. As the century progresses, this order is increasingly understood to have an historical dimension, inasmuch as it accrues through usage and is validated by reiteration, but it remains nonetheless essentially spatial in nature. Whether cast as a providential scheme (*Robinson Crusoe*), a social hierarchy (*Moll Flanders, Le paysan parvenu, Pamela*), a cultural constant (*Tom Jones*) or the political system of an enlightened lawgiver (*Julie*), the context of human experience is consistently *schematized* as a field of relationships, functions, or laws, each component of which is defined in terms of its position with respect to the others. The individualist agenda emplotted in the early novels of our period generally involves shifting ranks within this scheme (*Moll Flanders, Roxana, Le paysan parvenu, La Vie de Marianne, Pamela*) or disputing its authority (*Robinson Crusoe, Manon Lescaut, Pamela*), while in the later works (*Clarissa, Tom Jones, Julie*), the preoccupation shifts to mapping the scheme from the outside as an abstract grammar or altering it through narrative manipulation. In all of these cases, the idea of change is synonymous with that of *progression*, which is to say advancement within a matrix the coordinates of which have been plotted up to the present, but whose future design hinges on human action. Reality and history are in these works like a large picture, continually being retouched by the narrational efforts of its figures, who, by relating and redefining their experience, alter not only their appearance and place in the overall design, but the design itself.

It is this concept of history as order and progression which is satirized in the characters of Toby and Walter, who parody concrete and abstract schematization, respectively, in their attempts to reduce reality to objective fact and systematic law. From the perspective of Tristram's narration, the ostensible plot plays a similar role: the coherent scheme of cause and effect which he promises us, corresponds precisely to the dominant contemporary paradigm of history as a causally organized progression of events. Tristram subverts this concept of history by undercutting and disrupting the order of his narrative with the digressive stream of his narration. Enclosing and ultimately suspending the *developing order* of his story within the permanent non-progressive *flow* of his narration, he counters the structural progressive notion of history with one predicated on directionless duration. The "events" in *Tristram Shandy* merely extend an ongoing process of association which, answering to the laws of rhetoric and expression rather than referentiality, prolongs itself indefinitely and constitutes an identity in its duration. This is what Tristram discovers after a year of narrating:

> I am this month one whole year older than I was this time twelve-month; and having got, as you perceive, almost into the middle of my fourth volume — and no farther than to my first day's life — 'tis demonstrative that I have three hundred and sixty-four days more life to write just now, than when I first set out; so that instead of advancing, as a common writer, in my work with what I have been doing at it — on the contrary, I am just thrown so many volumes back — was every day of my life to be as busy a day as this — And why not? — and the transactions and opinions of it to take up as much description — And for what reason should they be cut short? as at this rate I should just live 364 times faster than I should write . . . (Pp. 286, 4:13)[28]

Beneath its light tone, this wry analysis reverses the eighteenth-century's consistent subordination of the activity and moment of narration to the external field of experience it is supposed to organize. Whether conceptualized as an account of the past or a structuring of the future, the act of narrating has always defined itself in terms of a duration other than its own, namely that of the narrated plot. In temporal terms, we could call this the narration *of* time. It is an activity of schematization that defines experiences, assigns them a place in the structure of reality and plots the self's progress.

Here, however, Tristram stresses that the narration of a life is itself part of that life, and by its mere duration it generates an excess of experience ("three hundred and sixty-four days more life") for which it must yet account. This is narration-as-duration, or narration *in* and *as* time, and it puts into question the feasibility of any autobiography, since the attempt to gain a grip on one's personal history is necessarily self-defeating in proportion to its thoroughness: to transcribe the "transactions and opinions" of a day itself takes more than a day.

The same of course holds true for the realistic agenda in general: the representation of contemporary culture inevitably lags behind its object, if only because during the course of the fictional work's composition, the cultural order does not suspend its economy of reconfiguration. Indeed, unless we are willing to grant Rousseau that authors have a prescience unavailable to other members of society, we have to assume that the same cultural "prise de conscience" which animates the novelist's representation of social reality will have already reverberated through – and altered – the cultural order by the time its narrative has been published. Walter Shandy parodies this dilemma on a microcosmic scale in his struggle to complete the Tristrapædia:

> he was three years and something more, indefatigably at work, and at last, had scarce completed, by his own reckoning, one half of his undertaking: the misfortune was, that I was all that time totally neglected and abandoned to my mother; and what was almost as bad, by the very delay, the first part of the work, upon which my father had spent the most of his pains, was rendered entirely useless, — every day a page or two became of no consequence. (Pp. 368–9, 5:16)

The work is of no consequence because its schematic view of history blinds it to its own history as duration: intent on pre-scribing a particular course of events *over* time, Walter ignores the consequences of his own immersion *in* time. His narrative of Tristram's early years is overtaken and rendered obsolete by the years of its narration. Broadly taken, his pathetic gesture can be understood as a commentary on what I would call structural mimesis — that form of literary representation which focuses on the ordering of experience, as opposed to the experience of ordering.

Tristram Shandy responds to this bias by parleying its narrational duration into a rival form of realism – one which re-presents reality as lived time by immersing the reader in a stream of impromptu mental peregrinations which cohere over time into experience in spite of their heterogeneity. Tristram's autobiography is as much that of his reader as of Tristram himself, since its narration refuses to subordinate itself to his narrative and cannot, in fact, be overtaken by the life it describes precisely because it comes to constitute that life in the course of its writing. As Tristram points out:

> It must follow, an' please your worships, that the more I write, the more I shall have to write – and consequently, the more your worships read, the more your worships will have to read.
>
> Will this be good for your worships' eyes?.
>
> It will do well for mine; and was it not that my OPINIONS will be the death of me, I perceive I shall lead a fine life of it out of this self-same life of mine; or, in other words, shall lead a couple of fine lives together. (P. 286, 4:13)

Tristram has discovered that through its duration the historiographical enterprise can come to rival the experience it objectifies: in time, the attempt to render an account of one's life becomes constitutive of that life. The time it takes to narrate accumulates into a duration, constitutes an identity-as-process which, since it is not predicated on a specific end, is by definition always sufficient and complete, yet never finished. Each instant of the narrational flow, each component or association, is susceptible to retrospective organization – that is, it can be assessed as part of a directed endeavor to re-present an order; but it is felt in the present as an extension of the moment's expression, and not merely a sequence in an obvious larger agenda. In terms of causality, each moment in Tristram's stream of narrational associations is as much the product of the preceding sentence – or sentence fragment – as it is an episode in a larger narrative plan.[29]

This state is as representative of human reality as any form of social portraiture. *Tristram Shandy* is realistic, not because of the charming portraits of uncle Toby or the attention to Trim's posture, as some critics have suggested, but because it reflects the identity of temporal consciousness. At the same time, the novel plays this lived temporal reality against its schematic counterpart by framing Tristram's enduring yet aleatory identity within the literary intertext, the lexicon of conventions he distorts, and the satirical caricatures of his uncle and father.

The most profound irony in *Tristram Shandy* derives, finally, from the play between these two senses of reality – as a developing structure and as an enduring stream of experience.[30] And it is an irony that embraces the reader as well as the writer. We, like Tristram, are at every moment conscious of the predictable unpredictability of the events that flow past us – of the fact that all is being orchestrated by a narrator intent on undercutting the structural bias implicit in narrative organization, and of the fact that our comprehension of the narrative is conditioned simultaneously by the accumulating patterns of that narrative and the traditional conventions against which we perceive them. Tristram addresses the reader's predicament only indirectly, as an aspect of his own predicament of trying to read his story in the experience of others. In spite of the book's pyrotechnics, conversational rhythms, and frequent references to a hypothetical reader, it remains largely a monologue.[31] As John Preston puts it, "Tristram is reading himself; that is, he is reading the story of writing his book, and that story is the record of how he discovers himself in the lives of others."[32]

What we discover in Tristram's life is a series of ironies or mutually suspending propositions: that it is impossible to escape the flow of time or reduce it to an order, but also that we cannot *not* attempt to impose an order on it and thus transcend our own historicity, because that very gesture of ordering is constitutive of identity; that we can neither elude the existing grammars for making sense of the world nor avoid subverting them, since our every attempt at self-expression necessarily reaffirms, if only negatively, the Other of convention; that whatever we relate necessarily relates us, functioning first and foremost as a manifestation of our individuality, even though our story can never be told other than through the intertext of stories already told by and about others.[33]

Tristram Shandy, finally, is as emphatic in its repudiation of any reduction of historical consciousness or self-expression into simple, self-sufficient categories, as it is in its determination to understand and express the function of narrative self-representation in the affirmation of identity. Tristram's digressive but enduring gesture of consistent (self) disruption constitutes a captivating and persistent argument that selfhood must be understood in terms of an historical dialectic between self and Other, but it also refuses steadfastly to conceptualize that dialectic or reduce it to a structure. The narration of selfhood discovers its self in a variety of Others, ranging from the formal grammars of convention or the intertextual matrix within which all expression occurs, to the other characters through whose stories the narrator's personality emerges, and even to the image of the writing self and its predicament, which gradually assumes a central position in its own ironic consciousness. But the narrator never advances a theoretical model of this dialogical relationship or attempts to situate it with respect to the patterns of irony in which he delights. In a book overflowing with theoretical speculations, the one strategy that escapes conceptual scrutiny is, necessarily, that of narrator's persistent irony. Clearly, the narrator cannot provide an overt theoretical model of his irony without compromising it. This is the advantage of adopting irony as a strategy of expression: it contains a justification for its own unwillingness to say what it means. And to that extent, Sterne's novel reiterates the claim of cultural mastery in a particularly slippery way, asserting the authority and autonomy of the author not merely negatively, in the proposal that we accept as a definitive model of historical selfhood the text's vertiginous self-suspensions, but also in the sense that we cannot finally even know whether that model is advanced seriously.

This ironic form of representational manipulation is all the more powerful for its refusal to acknowledge its power. But it also risks being dismissed as trivial: unable to provide an account of its own functioning, it is *a fortiori* excluded from demonstrating its relevance to *non-literary* history. As we have seen from Marivaux onward, this is a central question for the emerging genre of fiction, and it is one to which subsequent writers return – although with a new sensitivity to both the conventional grammars of literary and non-literary expression and the temporal constitution of reality. One author strongly influenced by Sterne is Diderot, whose *Jacques le fataliste* explicitly takes up where *Tristram Shandy* leaves off, complementing the ironization of the Author's authority with a powerful conceptual model of history conceived as dialogue and dialectic.

NOTES

1 Wayne Booth, *Rhetoric of Fiction*, p. 229.
2 As shall become apparent in the chapter on *Les Liaisons dangereuses*, Laclos' novel also fits this definition, although its ostensible format is not that of a metaliterary novel.
3 Denis Donoghue, "Sterne, our Contemporary," in *The Winged Skull. Papers from the Laurence Sterne Bicentenary Conference* (London: Methuen, 1971), p. 46.
4 Wayne Booth, "The Self-Conscious Narrator in Comic Fiction Before *Tristram Shandy*," *PMLA* 67 (March, 1952), pp. 163–85; p. 165. There is substantial disagreement as to whether *Tristram Shandy* is a novel at all; cf. for instance, John Traugott, *Tristram Shandy's World*, (Berkeley: University of California Press, 1954), pp. 38, 148; Helen Moglen, *The Philosophical Irony of Laurence Sterne*, (Gainesville: University of Florida Press, 1975), pp. 29–30.
5 The metaphor of narration as a machine is Tristram's; cf. p. 95, 1:22; p. 459, 7:1.
6 Traugott, *Tristram Shandy's World*, p. 113. Traugott presents a detailed reading of *Tristram Shandy* as a dramatization of rhetorical processes.
7 Traugott, *Tristram Shandy's World*, p. 81. The lack of a progressive plot is also linked to the book's apology for wit, and it has been interpreted as part of a strategy of indirect discourse consistent with the author's wariness as regards unambiguous linguistic communication. According to Locke, to whose analysis of wit and judgment Sterne alludes, the former consists primarily "in the assemblage of ideas, and putting those together with quickness and variety, wherein can be found any resemblance or congruity, thereby to make up pleasant pictures and agreeable visions in the fancy," whereas judgment involves "separating carefully, one from another, ideas wherein can be found the least difference, thereby to avoid being misled by similitude, and by affinity to take one thing for another"; cf. *An Essay Concerning Human Understanding*, ed. Alexander Campbell Fraser, 2 vols (New York: Dover Press, 1959), vol. 1,

p. 203 (II, 11.2). Sterne maintains that judgment and wit are mutually complementary; like the two knobs which decorate his chair, they are "indubitably
both made and fitted to go together, in order as we say in all such cases of
duplicated embellishments, – *to answer one another*" (p. 209, 3:20). For differing views of Sterne's use of Locke, see Traugott, pp. 3–61, and Moglen, pp.
9–30, 49–50. For his place in the tradition of wit, see Traugott, pp. 62–75,
and D. W. Jefferson, "*Tristram Shandy* and the Tradition of Learned Wit," in
Essays in Criticism, 1 (1951), pp. 225–48. For a particularly ingenious reading
of the novel as an allegory of linguistic indirection, see Sigurd Burckhardt,
"*Tristram Shandy's* Law of Gravity," *ELH*, 28 (1961), pp. 70–88.

8   Traugott, *Tristram Shandy's World*, p. 116.

9   Sterne himself notes in a letter to Robert Dodsley, October, 1759, that "all
locality is taken out of the book – the satire general"; *Sterne: the Critical Heritage*,
ed. Alan B. Howes (London: Routledge and Kegan Paul, 1974), p. 39.

10   Patricia Meyer Spacks, *Imagining a Self*, gives a penetrating analysis of Tristram's recuperation of selfhood through an act of the imagination that displaces
all historical reference with a declaration of "the self-reference of all happening" (p. 135).

11   All citations are from the Penguin edition, ed. Graham Petrie (Penguin Books,
1985) which reproduces the text of the first London edition of *Tristram Shandy*,
with minor punctuation normalizations. Book and chapter numbers are given
for the convenience of those using other editions.

12   As Traugott notes, Toby's need to relate everything to military science personifies the irrational association of ideas which Locke decried as madness;
Tristram Shandy's World, pp. 46–7.

13   Jean-Jacques Mayoux, "Variations on the Time-Sense in *Tristram Shandy*," in
The Winged Skull. Papers from the Laurence Sterne Bicentenary Conference (London: Methuen, 1971), pp. 5–6.

14   Spacks, *Imagining a Self*, p. 131.

15   In fact, the shift away from material gain and towards abstract profit is surprisingly consistent in the period we are studying, from Defoe's characters, who are
clearly motivated by monetary gain, to Rousseau's, who are obsessed with
virtue. Again, Clarissa is the watershed figure, as the first in the series to forego
personal wealth in favor of freedom and authority over her destiny.

16   See also p. 489, 7:27.

17   The Abbé Trublet concurs in this assessment, going so far as to propose that
the best and most informative book might well be obtained by simply posting a
secret stenographer in the proximity of great wits, to transcribe and publish
their conversations; *Essais*, pp. 70–1.

18   I am not maintaining that Sterne was writing in response to *Julie* – although
that is a possibility, given the publication history of *Tristram Shandy* – but only
that in its implications his work runs counter to Rousseau's novel.

19   Toby's earthworks are not, of course, the only master narrative to which he
attends: besides being a devoted soldier he is also deeply Christian, and he sees
in the scriptures an immutable prescription of how he should behave. As he
tells Trim, "At the great and general review of us all, corporal, at the day of
judgment, (and not till then) — it will be seen who has done their duties in this

world, — and who has not; and we shall be advanced, Trim, accordingly" (p. 408, 6:7). This allegiance to the scriptures explains not only Toby's extraordinarily active intercession in the fate of Le Fever (6:6–13), but even, as he sees it, his military past and his current obsession: "the pleasure I have taken in these things . . . has arose within me, and I hope in the corporal too, from the consciousness we both had, that in carrying them on, we were answering the great ends of our creation" (p. 444, 6:32).

20 Burckhardt, "*Tristram Shandy's* Law of Gravity" p. 74; cf. also John M. Stedman, *The Comic Art of Laurence Sterne* (Toronto: University of Toronto Press, 1967), p. 120.

21 As Mayoux puts it: "It has been the characteristic effort of his admirable willfulness to blend and confuse the time-structure of the story with the time-infrastructure of the writing, for the delight of extricating them again, of analyzing their relations, of arranging them into telling patterns"; "Variations on the Time-Sense," p. 3.

22 Michael Vande Berg, in "Pictures of Pronunciation: Typographical Travels through *Tristram Shandy* and *Jacques le fataliste*," *Eighteenth-Century Studies*, 21 (Fall, 1987), pp. 21–47, sees many of Sterne's typographical innovations as part of a more widespread attempt in English writing of the time to simulate the flow of conversational rhythms through punctuation. Vande Berg contrasts such usage to that of the French, and in particular Diderot, who had already adopted the contemporary convention of using punctuation to mark off grammatical structures. This contrast fits in well with the argument I make below concerning Sterne's rejection of structural or schematic conceptions of history and reality in favor of a model based on flow and duration.

23 Wayne Booth, in "Self-Conscious Narrator," finds precedents in previous authors – among them Marivaux and Fielding – for most of the author intrusion techniques which *Tristram Shandy* made famous, arguing that Sterne's genius consisted less in discovering new techniques, than in making the activity of narration the very subject matter of the novel.

24 Stedman, *The Comic Art of Laurence Sterne*, pp. 9–10.

25 Tristram/Sterne's preoccupation with originality is manifest not only in his work's structure, and the character of Walter, from whom ideas are property not to be trifled with, but also in the comments he periodically inserts into his musings, such as the tirade against imitators, in the first chapter of his fifth volume, or his statement at the beginning of 4:13, that "I have made an observation upon the strange state of affairs between the reader and myself, just as things stand at present — an observation never applicable before to any one biographical writer since the creation of the world, but to myself . . ."

26 Stedman, *The Comic Art of Laurence Sterne*, pp. 166–8, has compiled a list of some 31 separate instances of verbatim borrowing, involving at least 51 different passages.

27 At one point Tristram/the Author laments: "Shall we for ever make new books, as apothecaries make new mixtures, by pouring only out of one vessel into another? Are we for ever to be twisting, and untwisting the same rope? for ever in the same track — for ever at the same pace?" (P. 339, 5:1).

28 Elsewhere Tristram remarks that he actually has "five minutes less, than no

time at all" to relate several chapters worth of material, if he is to stay on schedule (p. 240, 3:38).

29 It is in this context that I would situate the frequently noted tension in *Tristram Shandy* between order and chaos. Cf. for instance, Stedman, *The Comic Art of Laurence Sterne*, p. 9.

30 The play between various orders of time in *Tristram Shandy* has received much critical attention in the past, and is too vast a topic to cover here. See, for instance, Traugott, *Tristram Shandy's World*, pp. 38–44, or Moglen, *The Philosophical Irony of Laurence Sterne*, pp. 56–61.

31 Stedman, *The Comic Art of Laurence Sterne*, p. 62.

32 Preston, *Created Self*, p. 180.

33 Spacks, *Imagining a Self*, pp. 153–4, casts *Tristram Shandy*'s irony in propositional terms: "As a novel, *Tristram Shandy* denies what it affirms and affirms what it denies." She compiles a slightly different, but related set of mutually suspending conclusions embedded in the novel.

14

The Great Scroll of History
(*Jacques le fataliste*)

Like Fielding's *Joseph Andrews*, Diderot's philosophical metanovel *Jacques le fataliste* candidly acknowledges the extent to which it is a response to an earlier best seller.[1] The book takes as its point of departure an episode lifted from *Tristram Shandy* – that of Trim's wound in the knee and subsequent love affair (8:19–20) and the ensuing "plot" is articulated around a relationship strikingly reminiscent of Trim and Toby, namely that of the loyal, resourceful servant Jacques and his rather slow-witted master (who is never named). As in Sterne's work, however, it is hardly accurate to speak of a plot, since the ostensible storyline – the account of Jacques' first love – is interrupted with endless intrusions and digressions on the part of both the narrator and the narrating characters. Finally, for the reader unfamiliar with Sterne's work, Diderot includes, near the end of the work, some episodes taken directly from *Tristram Shandy*, and, in the guise of the "editor," points out the extent to which the "author" has plagiarized his English predecessor.[2]

However the link between the two works is less a function of plot details than of treatment. Diderot's comic novel, like Sterne's, is metanarrative, self-conscious, digressive, and at least as much preoccupied by the activities and beliefs of its Author and Reader as by the characters it depicts.[3] It is riddled with narrative intrusions, framed stories and storytellers, conventional innovations, and discussions of its own composition. Its most striking formal feature is its insistence, evident from the opening paragraph, on the dialogical compact linking the narrator or Author to a responding, pressuring Other:

> Comment s'étaient-ils rencontrés? Par hasard, comme tout le monde. Comment s'appelaient-ils? Que vous importe? D'où venaient-ils? Du lieu le plus prochain. Où allaient-ils? Est-ce que l'on sait où l'on va? Que disaient-ils? Le maître ne disaient rien; et Jacques disait que son capitaine disait que tout ce qui nous arrive de bien et de mal ici-bas était écrit là-haut. (P. 521)[4]

How had they met? By chance, like everybody. What were their names? What difference does that make to you? Where were they coming from? From the nearest place. Where were they going? Does one know where one is going? What were they saying? The master wasn't saying anything; and Jacques was saying that his captain used to say that everything good and bad that happens to us down here was written up there on high.

By commencing his narration *in medias res* and immediately enabling the Reader's voice with a series of pertinent questions, Diderot locates his narration and narrative squarely within the dialogical framework so typical of earlier novels but which *Tristram Shandy*, in spite of its frequent superficial references to the reader, had abandoned in favor of intertextual monologue.[5] The pattern of demand and response evident in this opening paragraph reinstates the dialogical paradigm by transferring the burden of intrusion to a Reader. Throughout the book, and at all the various levels of framing, from the Author/Reader relationship on down to the characters in the told stories, human action is portrayed as a two-party affair modeled on narration, in which the completion of the action or story hinges on the behavior of both the initiator of the action and the accomplice or victim, on both the narrator and the narratee. The insistent interruption of the Reader in this opening scene is but one note in a general pattern of reciprocity, rivalry, domination, and narrational coercion which informs the human relationships in *Jacques le fataliste*. It is this recurrent paradigm that makes Diderot's work more thematically coherent than *Tristram Shandy*: although it is composed of multiple interspersed stories similar to those in Sterne's work, which, moreover, are told by a greater variety of narrators, all of the stories turn around questions of social interaction and hierarchy, whether at the informal level of friendship, love, and professional camraderie, or at the level of the formal contracts which link husband and wife, servant and master, or authority and subject. At all levels, the relationship between individuals frames itself in terms of a conflict between dependence and mastery, and a struggle for power or superiority the mechanisms of which are essentially narrative.

On the face of it, the stories appear quite varied: a young priest muddles the records of his abbey in an attempt to make himself indispensable and gain influence; an eccentric husband defrauds his spouse of her rightful property by suing himself by proxy and appropriating his household goods; a noblewoman avenges herself on her unfaithful lover by duping him into marrying a prostitute; a young peasant is seduced by and seduces the wives of the two town braggarts; the debauched head of a monastery turns the tables on two young priests intent on exposing his licentious ways; two military officers of disparate backgrounds, but sharing a common love of dueling, become fast friends and find themselves unable to live apart and unable to keep from dueling when together; a baker foils an attempt by his wife and her lover to have him imprisoned, succeeding instead in imprisoning the lover; a young aristocrat in pursuit of the favors of a bourgeois girl discovers that his closest friend and ally has been sleeping with her and defrauding him of his money, but when he attempts, with the help of the same friend, to avenge himself on the girl, he finds himself entrapped into a breach of promise suit and the support of his rival's offspring.

These tales address the whole gamut of society, from peasant to aristocrat, soldier to clergyman, merchant to miser; and they argue collectively that human interaction is regulated by narrational manipulation and interdependence. Whatever the relationship between the parties in the stories, it involves, at a minimum, managing one's interlocutory partner to one's advantage, and more frequently, outright deceit, duping, fraud, or seduction. Diderot's work not only reasserts the primacy of the dialogical model of self-expression through the wealth of dyadic relationships that make up its plot; it also explicitly formulates dialogical interdependence and rivalry as a law of human behavior and dramatizes its repercussions for all manner of social and cultural phenomena. The literary author's simultaneous manipulation of, and dependence upon, a cooperative reader provides the clearest theoretical expression of such dialogical reciprocity, while its practical ramifications for political power find expression in the master/slave dialectic relating Jacques to his master.

As a correlate to its dialogical paradigm of social interaction, *Jacques le fataliste* also elaborates a dialectical explanation of the relationship of individual action to the course of events that frames human activity, playing its dramatic sequences off of an abstract model of history which its characters and narrator elucidate. At issue is how particular events relate to human volition and/or larger patterns of history, a variation on which question resonates in the first paragraph already, in the tension between two explanations of how things occur: "by chance" and according to a predetermined plan "written on high." Similarly, a debate between Jacques and his master over the possibility of free will furnishes the thematic armature of the novel. Jacques holds that everything occurs according to a pre-ordained pattern or overarching script, into which all human action is inscribed. His master contends that events are the consequence of our actions and the exercise of our free will. That neither of these views entail particular behavior is made clear in the course of the novel: in spite of his avowed fatalism, Jacques is the active member of the partnership, his master a relatively passive companion. Nor do their opposed philosophies imply incompatibility: the two travelers are as inseparable and interdependent as the Author and Reader – indeed, like most of the characters in the stories they tell, they reverse roles for a substantial portion of the novel.

So too do their divergent positions concerning human destiny converge in the novel's abiding metaphor of history as a great scroll, or script, which only progressively unrolls and reveals itself, but in which all human action is always already inscribed. Since the scroll of history unrolls over time, and therefore constitutes historical events simultaneously as events in time and as inscriptions in an unfolding textual pattern, both Jacques and his master's theories can find expression within the same metaphor: the question boils down to whether *we* write the script of history as we go, or merely act out its pre-existing plot line. In either case, it is clear that we cannot know far in advance where we are going ("Does one know where one is going?"). As a metaphor that is both temporal and spatial, Diderot's central figure expresses Jacques' vision of an inexorably unrolling, pre-inscribed historical plot as well as his master's sense of enduring selfhood and a constant revelation of new possibilities at every instant.

Diderot is more successful than Sterne in integrating the transaction of reading and writing with the other dialogical economies in his novel, if only because the figure of the unrolling scroll governs both the situation of the characters within the novel and that of the Reader and Author, for whom *Jacques le fataliste* itself appears as progressive inscription (which from the point of view of the Reader is already written, and from that of the Author, the product of an ongoing decision). In fact, writing and reading become in a sense the master metaphor for the conflicted historical consciousness caught up in its own passivity and activity, inscription and description: all of the major characters alternate between the role of narratee and narrator, recounting and relating their own stories to Others, structuring and being structured by the verbal constructs of their rivals and accomplices. One might say that the *temporal* regress of *Tristram Shandy*, which is brought on by Tristram's attempt to account for his account of himself, finds a *structural* counterpart in *Jacques le fataliste*'s hierarchical regress of characters recounting characters recounting characters. The result is not overt irony, or the suspension of narration by the narrating self, but a series of narrative Chinese boxes or framed stories, each of which simultaneously frames and is framed by other accounts, and is thus suspended by the very principle from which it derives its authority. To the extent that every story teller has authority over the events he or she relates, each level in the regress is both in control of and controlled by the pattern of the narrative: in control of it because responsible for relating a portion of it; controlled because enclosed in the telling of a metanarrator further up the chain of command. The framed narrator's story seems, from his or her immediate perspective, to be the product of his or her narration, but by the same token it appears from the perspective of narrators higher in the framing hierarchy as the result of *their* structuring gesture, which also encloses and guides the account of the inferior narrator's accounting.

At the top of this hierarchical regress, the story of the novel's reading and writing, as enacted by the Author and the Reader, emerges as the master trope for history, narratively conceived as a progressive articulation and enactment. Yet this in no way implies that the novel, or any other instance of writing, can comprehend or get "outside" of history. For, as the plagiarization of Sterne and other references to previous books emphasize, *Jacques le fataliste*, like any text, is always enclosed in a vaster intertextual economy which is the condition of its meaning. Like all of the gestures of comprehension it frames, the Author/Reader exchange is dialogically limited and contingent on the larger historical-cultural Other whose order it challenges and acknowledges.

Thus, while *Jacques le fataliste* may be the most clearly metaliterary and metahistorical of the works we have examined, in the sense that it attempts to dramatize the mechanisms which enable it, the model which the novel elaborates in no way allows for its own privileging. The work in fact systematically undercuts all relationships of priority (or finality) that might be assigned to its act of ordering and the order it depicts, doubling every suggestion that the fictional world is the product of Author-ity with an assertion of the Author's indenture to history. As we shall see, the same suspension of causal attribution and finality extends to all of the framed episodes as well. The notion of story and history that emerges from this text is one that defies breaking down into oppositions between cause and effect, event and record, and for that very reason it thwarts straightforward conceptualization. Instead, it is *figured* or allegorized in a series of secondary transactions involving various specular pairs or doubles: master and slave, narrator and narratee, narration and narrative, history as event and history as script or narrative.[6] Bodied forth in a series of interwoven anecdotes that put into question any finality or definitive authority by systematically posing, then inverting, the derivation of one term from the other, these paradigmatic reciprocals collectively allude to history's "inconceivable" double identity as permanent structuring event and structure of events, and in so doing implicitly demonstrate the role of fiction for Diderot. Rather than merely *describe* history, which would imply its transcendence or at least the delimitation of its scope, fiction, and particularly *Jacques le fataliste*, *inscribes* it, consigning its (fiction's) own identity to the process and structure of history by reenacting that structure/process an indefinite number of times for an indefinite number of readers.

We have seen in previous chapters that the exercise and appropriation of authority, first over one's own identity and later over the actions of others, functions in some respects as the archetypal plot of the eighteenth-century novel. *Jacques le fataliste* retains this thematic focus, but abstracts it into a struggle for narrative power that pervades all of society. Subsuming the many institutional forms of authority debated by earlier novels – scriptural, paternal, social, judicial, political, "natural," and narrative – Diderot's work proposes an archetypal relationship of mutual dependance and relentless rivalry that characterizes all social interaction. In its crudest manifestations, this relationship degenerates, as in the novels of Fielding, into outright jealousy, hostility, and deceit; but in its most refined and socially effective versions, it evolves into a mutual attachment that *grows out* of rivalry. The overarching incarnations of such a relationship are those which frame the major anecdotes of the novel, namely that of the Author and Reader, that of Jacques and his master, and that of Jacques and the hostess who relates the story of Mme de la Pommeraye.

The Author sets the terms of this contest for narrative authority in the opening pages of his story, when he pauses in his anecdote to vaunt his limitless prerogatives:

> Vous voyez, lecteur, que je suis en beau chemin, et qu'il ne tiendrait qu'à moi de vous faire attendre un an, deux ans, trois ans, le récit des amours de Jacques, en le séparant de son maître et en leur faisant courir à chacun tous les hasards qu'il me plairait. Qu'est-ce qui m'empêcherait de marier le maître et de le faire cocu? d'embarquer Jacques pour les îles? d'y conduire son maître? de les ramener tous les deux en France sur le même vaisseau? Qu'il est facile de faire des contes! (P. 523)[7]

> You see, Reader, I am well on my way, and I could perfectly well make you wait a year, two years, three years, for the story of Jacques' loves, by separating him from his master and subjecting each of them to all of the fortunes that should please me. Who is to stop me from marrying the master and making him a cuckold? from embarking Jacques for the islands? from taking his master there? from bringing them both back to France on the same boat? How easy it is to make stories!

In a similar vein, Jacques and his master quarrel extensively over their respective roles in the servant/master relationship, finally agreeing that while the master may retain the title of master, Jacques makes most of the decisions (pp. 687–94). Their relationship embodies the reciprocal authority which is intrinsic to any narrative situation, and it serves as a permanent emblem of the momentary reversals that occur within all of the framed stories whose characters vie for dominion over their rivals or partners.

Continual jockeying for advantage is a universal fact of society, as Jacques sees it, and most people are from one point of view masters, while from another, slaves:

> tout dans la nature songe à soi et ne songe qu'à soi. Que cela fasse du mal aux autres, qu'importe, pourvu qu'on s'en trouve bien? (P. 784)

il conclut que tout homme voulait commander à un autre; et que l'animal se trouvant dans la société immédiatement au-dessous de la classe des derniers citoyens commandés par toutes les autres classes, ils prenaient un animal pour commander aussi à quelqu'un. Eh bien! dit Jacques, chacun a son chien. Le ministre est le chien du roi, le premier commis est le chien du ministre, la femme est le chien du mari, ou le mari le chien de la femme ... Lorsque mon maître me fait parler quand je voudrais me taire, ce qui, à la vérité, m'arrive rarement, continua Jacques; lorsqu'il me fait taire lorsque je voudrais parler, ce qui est très difficile; lorsqu'il me demande l'histoire de mes amours et qu'il l'interrompt: que suis-je autre chose que son chien? (Pp. 695–6)

everything in nature thinks of itself and only of itself; no matter if something should hurt others, as long as it does us good.

he concluded that every man wanted to command another; and that, animals holding the place in society immediately beneath the last class of citizens commanded by all the others, those last citizens took an animal so that they too could order someone around. So, said Jacques, everyone has his dog. The minister is the king's dog, the aide the minister's dog, the wife the husband's dog, or the husband the wife's. . . . When my master makes me talk when I would like to be quiet, which in truth happens to me rarely, continued Jacques; when he makes me be quiet when I want to talk, which is very difficult; when he requests of me the story of my loves and interrupts me: what am I other than his dog?

Yet if society is a generalized struggle for dominance, each one of whose players at all moments strives to obtain or maintain the upper hand over his peers, the very fact that *everyone* is at all moments dog and master prevents power from becoming the privilege of a minority: each in his own arena of action plays the role of master as often as he plays that of dog, and in the most evolved relationships, such as those that make up the subject matter of the longer anecdotes, or that of Jacques and his master, or the Reader and the Author, each party alternates with the other in the exercise of mastery. The purest example of such a relationship is that of Jacques' former master, the "captain," and his dueling partner. Complete opposites in character and background, yet inseparable comrades, united by their common love of dueling, they are unable to live together peacefully and condemned to their endless series of duels in which the winner nurses the loser back to health so that he may once again try to kill him (pp. 577–80).

As Jacques' characterization of his own plight in the canine analogy reveals, the narrator/narratee relationship is for Diderot the most fundamental version of this paradigm. It owes its primacy to the fact that narration is available to all. As the Author explains, paraphrasing Jacques' further thoughts, recounting events is the most generalized means of self-elevation for the lower classes, a "manie qui les tire de leur abjection, qui les place dans la tribune, et qui les transforme tout à coup en personnages intéressants" (p. 697) (mania that draws them out of their abjection, that places them on the podium, and transforms them suddenly into interesting figures). Narrators achieve status by making themselves interesting as the agents of transmission of news: by recounting stories they transform themselves into the center of attention for a public.[8]

Yet this exchange only succeeds to the extent that the narrators can bring the auditors to corroborate the version of reality contained in the story: Jacques' account of his suffering from a wound to the knee succeeds in enlisting the sympathy of his master only when the latter injures his own knee and agrees that such wounds are particularly painful (pp. 525, 536–7). As the Author remarks to the Reader, ironizing his own frequent boasts of power, fabulation is a mutual endeavor: "Il faut sans doute que j'aille quelquefois à votre fantaisie; mais il faut que j'aille quelquefois à la mienne, sans compter que tout auditeur que me permet de commencer un récit s'engage d'en entendre la fin" (p. 584) (No doubt I sometimes have to proceed according to your whims; but I also need to go according to mine sometimes, not to mention that every listener who permits me to start a story commits himself to hearing its conclusion). The same mutual give and take characterizes Jacques' relationship to his master. Jacques is forced to admit that "au moment où l'on prend maître, on descendra, on montera, on avancera, on reculera, on restera et cela sans qu'il soit jamais libre aux pieds de se refuser aux ordres de la tête" (p. 691) (as soon as one accepts a master, one has to go down, come back up, advance, back up, remain, and all without the feet ever being free to refuse the head's orders). At the same time, however, he points out to his master that "attendu qu'il est écrit là-haut que je vous suis essentiel, et que je sens, que je sais que vous ne pouvez pas vous passer de moi, j'abuserai de cet avantage toutes et quantes fois que l'occasion s'en présentera" (p. 692) (given that it is written on high that I am essential to you, and that I feel, I know, that you cannot do without me, I will exploit this advantage every time and as many times as I shall have occasion). In spite of the constant bickering between servant and master, the one is inconceivable without the other – indeed, when they are definitively separated, the dialogical circuit that defines the book is broken and the narrative abruptly comes to an end.

Thus while *Jacques le fataliste* confronts the social implications of narration and links it to generalized political behavior, it does not underwrite the version of an all-powerful, manipulative narrator that the Author, in his most parodic moments, repeatedly embodies and which earlier authors explored, either seriously, as in Rousseau, or facetiously, as in Fielding. The fundamentally dialogical nature of narration makes absolute authority impossible in a world governed by narratives.

There is a more subtle way in which *Jacques le fataliste* checks the drive to authority. By making narration the most fundamental and universal tool of self advancement and extending to all of society the potentially manipulative, self-serving activity by which he earns his living, Diderot involves every member of the social hierarchy in a multiplicity of narrative transactions and authoritative perspectives. Because every attempt to structure reality is itself inscribed within a larger narrative which can construe the sense of such structures in unforeseen ways, absolute mastery of the economy remains by definition beyond the reach of any individual.

This inscription of local story within broader history is at the heart of the longer framed stories of manipulation, such as those of Mme de La Pommeraye (the woman who tricks her lover into marrying a prostitute), le père Hudson (the lascivious abbot), or Jacques' master (who is led into debt and "cuckolded" by his best friend). In each of these anecdotes a strong calculating character uses his or her skill in role-playing to manipulate a weaker or more gullible one. Reiterating a hypothesis enunciated most clearly in the *Paradoxe sur le comédien*, where Diderot correlates the intensity of an actor's affective impact on his public with the actor's detachment and lack of personal sentiment regarding the role, these stories all seem to stress the value of detachment and rhetoric over simple sincerity in obtaining desired ends, and to confirm the potential for abuse in the careful creation of a fiction. We are far from the correlation of narrative and character that the works of Marivaux, Prévost, and Richardson assume: refined discourse and the expression of exemplary values do not necessarily denote good breeding and moral character. Purely fictive self-narration, and by extension fiction in general, proves as efficient as the truth in the structuring of reality. Severed from its presumed link with the real state of the world, narration at first glance seem to take on an ominous aspect, particularly the narration of professional narrators.

Still, the stories in question, like that of Jacques and his master, evoke no unitary meaning. They are all subject to revision at the various levels of the narrative hierarchy – by the story's narrator, its narratee, the Author, the Reader, or, by extension us, the real readers. Like the "dogs" in Jacques' figure for society, each plot elaborated by a would-be "master" takes on different meaning when evaluated in a new context or further level of the hierarchy. Thus Mme de la Pommeraye's treatment of the Marquis d'Arcis appears as one thing to its naive victim, quite another to the agents of his ensnarement, and still another to Jacques and his master, who condemn both Pommeraye's perfidy and the Marquis' infidelity from a comfortable distance. Similarly, in the account of Jacques' early sexual encounters, his feigned innocence as an adolescent makes him a subject of ridicule for the town braggarts, an object of concupiscence for their wives, who "read" his virginity in quite a different light than their spouses, and an absolute scoundrel for the master and Reader, who know full well that it is part of a strategy of seduction.

The metaphor of the great scroll meanwhile reminds us that the multiple identities of such events derive as much from the temporality of reality as from the social extension of the narrative. As history "unrolls," the events which make it up are continually reframed, placed in an ever broader context that compels reassessment of their identity and meaning, just as the meaning of individual episodes in the book shifts with the expansion of the narrative. The status and meaning of any action or individual is not simply multiple by virtue of its inscription within a hierarchy of conflicting motives and readings of other people, but infinite, by virtue of its inscription in time. Even within the context of a single individual's experience, the meaning of every action shifts over time. This is the lesson of the Marquis d'Arcis, who upon realizing that he has married a prostitute, is at first disconsolate, but then subsequently rewrites the vengeance of Mme de la Pommeraye into a personal triumph by "rereading" his adventure in a positive light and concluding that she actually did him a favor by uniting him with the most charming, grateful, and obedient wife one could desire (p. 676). Similarly, Jacques' master, who at first appearance seems destined to marry the woman who tricked him and claim as his own the child of his treacherous friend, suffers a far milder fate when that friend is subsequently re-identified as a notorious scoundrel; and even this "conclusion" suffers revision near the end of the novel when the master happens upon his "friend" and kills him.

Such events, like the other reversals in the framed anecdotes, underscore the susceptibility of personal history to revision by the individual, but they also underline the limits of that control. Unlike the individualists earlier in the century, Diderot's characters do not narrate against a stable order into which their own stories can be assimilated as exempla. Once we accept our historicity – that is, our enclosure in a larger narrational hierarchy and narrative that change over time – we both accede to self-determination and foreclose on the delusion of absolute mastery over ourselves, others, or events. It is axiomatic that if events are continually being "written" by all ranks of society, we, too, participate in the construction of our identity and our reality; but it is equally clear that we can never dominate this process or be certain of closure. Definitive meaning is impossible as long as the story is not finished, and it will never be finished as long as there are narrators. As Jacques retorts when his master suggests his lot is inferior to that of Rousseau, "qui sait cela avant que d'être arrivé au dernier mot de la dernière ligne de la page qu'on remplit dans le grand rouleau?" (p. 785) (who can know that before coming to the last word of the last line of the page which one occupies in the great scroll?).

History, in short, occurs as a dialectic between and within individual agendas of mastery: between the personal attempts to formulate the world according to the self – as embodied in the novel's countless dramatizations of ambition, manipulation, and rivalry – and the larger, continually evolving script which results from and enables those agendas; and between one's own evolving horizon of understanding and its successive revisions with experience.

The interpersonal or intercultural dialectical transaction is most obvious in *Jacques le fataliste*, where numerous reinterpretations of events within the framed stories underscore the lesson that there is always a larger plot enclosing the minor plots we fabricate.[9] In a world where everyone is empowered with – indeed bound up within – the relating of experience in a self-serving manner, the determination of "what happened" in any given episode is in a constant state of contention. In theory, at least, everyone has the potential to be both reader and narrator, and every reading has the potential of being altered over time – a point which the Reader's continual interruptions and redirections of the plot make clear, and which the Author drives home near the end of the book when he grants the Reader the prerogative to finish the plot as he sees fit, and then assumes the role of reader himself, evaluating three further textual fragments which provide alternate conclusions to the story (pp. 805–8).[10]

However, the intrapersonal dialectic of present gesture and past experience carries a larger burden of the philosophical issues in the text, and in particular the question of free will versus determination, both as it pertains to personal action and to the question of novelistic invention and authority. Although presented as a metaphor for history, the scroll also functions as an analog for the story within which Jacques and his master are "written" and thus justifies a rapprochement of the historical and literary transactions. Specifically, it invites us to resolve the paradox of Jacques' ardent fatalism and his consistent, and generally ethical, behavior, by consulting the comportment of the Author with regard to *his* conflicting claims of arbitrary authority and historical fidelity. Indeed, the Author and Jacques share a common incongruity: each claims to be bound by a higher order, even as he asserts his right to do as he pleases. The higher order for Jacques is simply the great scroll; for the Author, it is the concept of historical truth, which, he insists, dictates his writing by restricting his account to things that actually happened. The literary correlative of fatalism appears to be meticulous historicism. Yet this should not be taken literally, no more than Jacques' insistence that his actions are all predetermined should lead us to conclude that he has no latitude of decision. To understand how fatalism and freedom, truth and fiction, can be compatible, we need only examine the literary transaction which the Author so consistently brings up in his digressions.

Fundamental to understanding the Author's apparently inconsistent claims is the assertion that *Jacques le fataliste* is not a novel in the traditional sense of the word – which is to say, in Diderot's own words, "un tissu d'événements chimériques et frivoles" (a fabric of fanciful and frivolous events).[11] Intent on linking his story to the broader script of the *grand rouleau*, the Author reiterates on several occasions that his narrative is an *histoire* and not a *conte* or *roman*.[12] What he means by this gradually emerges from the novel's free and frequent appropriation of anecdotes from its Author's lived experiences, as well as from other literary, dramatic, or popular sources. If the point of narration is to enlist the corroboration of one's vision of reality by the narratee, and if, as the Author believes, "on ne peut s'intéresser qu'à ce qu'on croit vrai" (p. 805) (we can only get interested in what we think to be true), then the successful author will be the one who re-counts that which already counts as real, that which is already written in the great scroll of our cultural patrimony and personal experience, that which we have in a sense already read and which therefore informs our own narrational gestures.

Jacques makes the same point for his master in the simple terms of sensation: "Il cherchait à faire concevoir à son maître que le mot douleur était sans idée, et qu'il ne commençait à signifier quelque chose qu'au moment où il rappelait à notre mémoire une sensation que nous avions éprouvée" (p. 537) (he tried to make his master understand that the word pain was lacking any specific idea, and that it only commenced meaning something at the moment it recalled to our memory a sensation that we had experienced).

To ensure that his own text recalls familiar meanings to the reader, and to be certain that the reader does not miss the point that *all* meaning functions by referring to previous experiences and previous meanings, the Author assembles his narrative out of a wide variety of texts, ranging from popular proverbs, to classical literature, from contemporary works of literature like *Tristram Shandy* or the numerous plays cited in the text, to philosophical theories. To be truly compelling and attain a position of real authority within one's culture, a narrator must know how to reiterate the intertexts of that culture. To read is to actualize as personal experience a script which, like the great scroll, is in a sense "already there," but this script is multiple, encompassing not only the novel being read, but all of the previous novels which influence the reading act; the collective experience or culture which determines, in general, how we read fiction and what its standard repertoire of forms mean; and, finally, the individual reader's idiosyncratic personal experiences which might find resonance in the narrative.[13] Diderot alludes to these various private and shared texts in his "Eloge de Richardson," where he associates the amazing effect the English novelist has on him with the fact that

> Le monde où nous vivons est le lieu de la scène; le fond de son drame est vrai; ses personnages ont toute la réalité possible; ses caractères sont pris du milieu de la société; ses incidents sont dans les mœurs de toutes les nations policées; les passions qu'il peint sont telles que je les éprouve en moi; ce sont les mêmes objets qui les émeuvent, elles ont l'énergie que je leur connais; les traverses et les afflictions de ses personnages sont de la nature de celles qui me menacent sans cesse; il me montre le cours général des choses qui m'environnent.[14]

> The scene is set in the world in which we live; the fundamentals of his drama are true; his characters have all possible reality; his personality types are taken from the midst of society; his incidents are in the usage of all civilized nations; the passions he paints are such as I feel within myself; they are moved by the same objects, they have the energy which I know them to have; the problems and afflictions of his characters are of the kind that threaten me constantly; he shows me the general course of those things which surround me.

Diderot here reiterates ideas about fiction's relationship to contemporary culture which we have previously encountered in English essayists such as Johnson.[15] He assumes that reading is a private re-presentation within the framework of past experience, and that an episode or story which expresses itself within the terms of that experience, which on the collective level can be identified with the script of culture, will appear particularly true for the reader even as it expresses the vision of its author. The fictional representation bodies forth a structure of reality which expresses both reader and author.

It follows that the most powerful expression of literary authority, the one most likely to succeed in promoting the decisions of its author, will be the one which re-presents most thoroughly that which counts for both author and reader as truth – truth not in the sense of something which actually occurred, but in the sense of a construct which is representative of dominant cultural currents. A successful narrative necessarily reconfigures the already written; regardless of the historical veracity of its content, it is by definition "true" to the extent it reiterates the cultural intertext of its readership. Indeed, fiction in this light has a greater potential for historical truth than history. As Diderot exclaims,

> O Richardson! j'oserai dire que l'histoire la plus vraie est pleine de mensonges, et que ton roman est plein de vérités. L'histoire peint quelques individus; tu peins l'espèce humaine: l'histoire attribue à quelques individus ce qu'ils n'ont ni dit, ni fait; tout ce que tu attribues à l'homme, il l'a dit et fait . . .[16]

Oh Richardson! I daresay the truest history is full of lies, and your novel full of truths. History portrays a few individuals; you portray the human species: history attributes to a few individuals things they neither said nor did; man has said and done everything which you attribute to him . . .

Novels, following this logic, are closer to philosophy than history: they represent human nature and articulate general truth – as Fielding and Aristotle would concur. Their authority goes beyond that of past experience to embrace the delineation of current cultural practice. However, they do not *invent* the laws of culture. For like Jacques and his master, and all of the other narrators and listeners in *Jacques le fataliste*, the novelist and novel reader are inscribed within the evolving story they tell: they are enclosed, far more than Rousseau's author-lawgiver figure and his exemplary vehicle of instruction, by the cultural assumptions they help articulate. The same point might be made concerning the form of the novel. No matter how original the narrational gesture, it is necessarily fueled by the conventions of the culture that frames it, and it invariably reiterates those norms even as it modifies them. Through its re-presentation of "reality," the narrative expresses both the individual volition of its reader and author, and the larger, pre-existing cultural matrix the conventions of which empower, and are validated by, that narrative. It is in this sense that the Author, like any author, can indeed do anything he wishes, while at the same time claiming to be true, since any moves he makes will reflect the larger culture narrative within which his writing is inscribed.

Of course this analysis hinges on the assumption that culture is historical, and that rules of usage accrue through reiterated use. This is indeed the assumption of *Jacques le fataliste*, which establishes its own local conventions about the relationship of Author to Reader – and the impossibility of terminating the story of Jacques' loves – through repetitions of the same contestatory engagement which began the novel. It is also the assumption of Jacques, who bases his right to contradict his master on the fact that his behavior has been validated over time: "stipulé ou non stipulé, cela s'est fait de tous les temps, se fait aujourd'hui, et se fera tant que le monde durera. . . . soumettez-vous à la loi d'un besoin dont il n'est pas en votre pouvoir de vous affranchir" (pp. 692–3) (stipulated or not, it has always been done, is done today, and will be done as long as the world shall last . . . submit to the law of a necessity which it is not in your power to abrogate).

Laws of behavior, like rules for reading, find their sanction in reiteration. And the particular elegance of *Jacques le fataliste* lies in the way it uses this principle to validate its own vision of reality. The novel does not just articulate its message within a broad spectrum of cultural styles, character types, and narrative traditions; it also infuses its various episodes with an aura of familiarity by replicating the same paradigmatic situations on each successive level of narration, such that each anecdote appears to confirm a previously read pattern. Hence the paradigm of the duped manipulator, which informs all of the longer stories; or the pattern of interdependent rivalry, which extends from the Author and Reader through Jacques and his master down to nearly every anecdote in the book; or the notion of the duel, which regulates nearly all of the interpersonal confrontations in the plot.[17] By reiterating within the proliferating framed anecdotes the same paradigm of complicity and rivalry that is constantly before our eyes in the double framing dialogue of Jacques and his master, and the Author and Reader, the novel brings the represented world into conformity with the postulates of the representing consciousness.

Ultimately, of course, the validation of those postulates requires their acknowledgement and accreditation by the real reader. *Jacques le fataliste* procures this acknowledgement by underscoring the analogy between the activity of the characters in the anecdotes and that of the novel reader in general. By making the Author and Reader characters within the narrative; by multiplying the narrative frames so as to put into question the privilege normally accorded the framing narrator; by making the leitmotif of his fiction the relationship of interdependent rivalry he explicitly likens to that of the real reader and author; Diderot not only correlates the "plot" of his work to the "plight" of the reader, he also directly implicates the latter in the process of fabulation.[18] We can scarcely dispute the "reality" of the narrative/interpretive activities depicted in the plot, for they reproduce our own. The representational transaction they persistently reiterate is an extension of ours.

If *Jacques le fataliste* reconciles authorial prerogative with collective truth, it also argues that individual action, however freely initiated, necessarily expresses the larger sequence of events, both personal and collective, which informs it. For Jacques, free will is a meaningless concept, if only because the context of one's acts, and hence their ultimate meaning and consequence, is beyond our ken. We cannot act in accordance with our wants because we cannot know what we want in the long run:

> C'est que, faute de savoir ce qui est écrit là-haut, on ne sait ni ce qu'on veut ni ce qu'on fait...
>
> ... y a-t-il un homme capable d'apprécier juste les circonstances où il se trouve? Le calcul qui se fait dans nos têtes, et celui qui est arrêté sur le registre d'en haut, sont deux calculs bien différents. (P. 531)

> It's just that without knowing what is written on high, we cannot know what we want nor what we do...
>
> ... is there any man capable of evaluating perfectly his circumstances?

> The calculation which occurs in our heads and that which is set down on the record up there are two very different calculations.

One should not be misled by Jacques' use of the expression "là-haut" into thinking the unknowability of the scroll of history inheres in some theological gap between individual plans and global design. As the Author specifies, "le destin, pour Jacques, était tout ce qui le touchait ou l'approchait, son cheval, son maître, un moine, un chien, une femme, un mulet, une corneille" (p. 548) (destiny, for Jacques, was everything that touched or came near him: his horse, his master, a monk, a dog, a woman, a mule, a crow). It is not necessarily the result of a supernatural motive, nor does it really precede the historical events in which it is manifest. When the master asks Jacques whether human action determines the script of the scroll or vice versa, Jacques replies without hesitating: "Tous les deux étaient écrits l'un à côté de l'autre. Tout a été écrit à la fois. C'est comme un grand rouleau qui se déploie petit à petit" (p. 527) (Both were written alongside each other. Everything was written at once. It's like a big scroll unrolling little by little). If destiny is unknowable on the individual level, it is for the simple reason that one can neither situate one's story nor know its conclusion – *a fortiori* the meaning of its individual episodes – while still within that story: knowledge is also inscribed within the great scroll, and historical knowledge is by definition provisional and retrospective.[19]

What one can know, however, is that every moment in one's story will quite literally follow on those that precede it. For Jacques, this means that all of one's actions are inscribed in a great causal chain, and that for every supposed act of free will, there is a cause. Most frequently the cause or immediate motivation for our actions can be found in the actions of another, as Jacques slyly demonstrates to his master:

[JACQUES]
Mon capitaine disait: «Posez une cause, un effet s'ensuit; d'une cause faible, un faible effet; d'une cause momentanée, un effet d'un moment; d'une cause intermittente, un effet intermittent; d'une cause contrariée, un effet ralenti; d'une cause cessante, un effet nul.»

LE MAITRE
Mais il me semble que je sens au dedans de moi-même que je suis libre, comme je sens que je pense.

JACQUES
Mon capitaine disait: «Oui, à présent que vous ne voulez rien; mais veuillez vous précipiter de votre cheval?»

LE MAITRE
Eh bien! je me précipterai.

JACQUES

Gaiement, sans répugnance, sans effort, comme lorsqu'il vous plaît d'en descendre à la porte d'une auberge?

LE MAITRE

Pas tout à fait; mais qu'importe, pourvu que je me précipite, et que je prouve que je suis libre?

JACQUES

Mon capitaine disait: «Quoi! vous ne voyez pas que sans ma contradiction il ne vous serait jamais venu en fantaisie de vous rompre le cou? C'est donc moi qui vous prends par le pied, et qui vous jette hors de selle . . . . » (Pp. 785–6)[20]

[JACQUES]

My captain used to say «given a cause, an effect will follow; from a weak cause, a weak effect; from a momentary cause, the effect of a moment; from an intermittent cause, an intermittent effect; from a countered cause a decreased effect; from a cause that stops, a negligible effect.»

THE MASTER

But it seems to me that I feel deep inside of myself that I am free, just as I feel that I am thinking.

JACQUES

My captain used to say: «Yes, now that you don't want anything; but would you want to fall off of your horse?»

THE MASTER

Well! If I did, I would fall off.

JACQUES

Cheerfully, without hesitation, effortlessly, as when it takes your fancy to dismount at the door of an inn?

THE MASTER

Not exactly; but what's the difference, as long as I fling myself off and prove that I am free?

JACQUES

My captain would say: «What! you don't see that without my provocation it would never have occurred to you to break your neck? It is therefore I who am taking you by the foot and flinging you out of the saddle . . .»

The two thematic strands of *Jacques le fataliste* merge here in the idea that the causal chains of destiny are expressed through the actions of other people. The ubiquitous struggle for control which drives people to manipulate each other or causes readers to dispute the word of authors, like the dialogical rivalry which accompanies any form of self-expression, is nothing other than a play of causes and effects, the microcosmic human manifestation of the patterns which globally we call destiny. But ultimately, "cause" and "effect" are nothing more than mechanical tropes for the servant/

master exchange. As the Author explains to the Reader, we do not, in our everyday affairs, perceive ourselves to be pursuing our destiny, but merely to be responding to the demands of others:

> Jacques suivait son maître comme vous le vôtre; son maître suivait le sien comme Jacques le suivait. — Mais, qui était le maître du maître de Jacques? — Bon, est-ce qu'on manque de maître dans ce monde? Le maître de Jacques en avait cent pour un, comme vous. (Pp. 565–6)

> Jacques followed his master as you do yours; his master followed his own master just as Jacques followed him. — But who was the master of Jacques' master? — Well, is there any lack of masters in this world? Jacques' master had a hundred of them to one, as do you.

The drive to mastery which saturates the world of *Jacques le fataliste* can in this light be likened to an attempt to become pure "cause," to shape the destiny of others, rather than be shaped by them. Conversely, the repeated duping of the dupers in the framed anecdotes, like the reversal of roles among the narrators and readers/listeners, demonstrates the folly of trying to exclude "effect" from one's actions. And if identity seems bound to dialogue, it is merely because in a world where one attributes effects to causes, and identifies causes with the acts of others, the mapping of one's personal destiny requires at least one partner with whom one can form a chain of dialogic provocation.

From another point of view, though, consistency of character can also be explained causally. Since each successive moment of one's destiny finds a cause in all of its precedents, there is a tendency toward replication built into each individual's destiny – an accumulation of like causes susceptible to eliciting like effects. Again, all that prevents us from perceiving this unity, which functions like the psychological notion of personality, is our limited perspective:

> [Jacques] croyait . . . que, si l'enchaînement des causes et des effets qui forment la vie d'un homme depuis le premier instant de sa naissance jusqu'à son dernier soupir nous était connu, nous resterions convaincus qu'il n'a fait que ce qu'il était nécessaire de faire. Je l'ai plusieurs fois contredit, mais sans avantage et sans fruit. En effet, que répliquer à celui qui vous dit: Quelle que soit la somme des éléments dont je suis composé, je suis un; or, une cause une n'a qu'un effet; j'ai toujours été une cause une; je n'ai jamais eu qu'un effet à produire; ma durée n'est donc qu'une suite d'effets nécessaires. (P. 698)[21]

> [Jacques] believed . . . that if the concatenation of causes and effects forming the life of a man from the first instant of his birth to his last sigh were known to us, we would be convinced that he had merely done what had to be done. I contradicted him frequently, but to no advantage and no avail. In effect, what can you reply to someone who says to you: Whatever the sum of the elements

of which I am composed, I am one; now a unitary cause has but one effect; I have always been a unitary cause; I have never had but one effect to produce; my duration is thus nothing but a series of necessary effects.

More simply put, the determining frame constituted by our past accumulates over time into an identity which necessarily defines each of our acts. One cannot act "out of character" since everything one does is written into one's identity: Puis-je n'être pas moi? Et étant moi, puis-je faire autrement que moi? Puis-je être moi et un autre? Et depuis que je suis au monde, y a-t-il eu un seul instant où cela n'ait été vrai?" (p. 526) (Can I be other than myself? And being myself, can I act other than myself? Can I be myself and an other? And since I have been in the world has there been a single instant when this hasn't been true?). From the perspective of our accumulated causes and effects, we are merely confirming our identity when we act "freely," while from the perspective of the interpersonal social mechanism, we are responding to the "causes" of Others, and eliciting, in those Others, our own effects. Just as the great scroll of culture and the intertext underwrites the merger of fiction and truth, the notion of history as a collectively enacted chain of causes and effects, within which are written both private and shared designs, brings together the freedom to follow personal impulse and the subordination to a larger pattern.

Finally, the easiest way to understand the complex status of individual acts and stories within history more broadly conceived is through the analogy of writing inherent in Diderot's metaphor of the scroll. A single act is like one word of a text. It has both a paradigmatic and a syntagmatic axis and derives its identity as particular meaning both from its inscription in a larger semantic matrix and from the words that immediately precede and follow it. Thus when Jacques' new horse repeatedly bolts for the nearest gallows, or when he sees a coffin with the coat of arms of his former captain, a variety of interpretations present themselves, some generated by the symbolic (paradigmatic) value of the gallows and coffin, others by the (syntagmatic) context of the events. And just as the ultimate explanation of the horse's behavior comes only with the melding of its symbolic value and the context of further experience (its previous owner turns out to have been the hangman) so too will the particular value of *any* act be contingent on the successively larger textual bodies within which its reader frames it. Every act or word evolves with other similar instances in other (con)texts, although from the perspective of any given interpretation, it seems both to be a statement unique to its situation and to embody the larger stable system of which it is an instance.

Identity thus conceived is the intersection of an evolving structure of reference and a constant process of reinstantiation, in which both the individual instance and the framing context reciprocally effect each other. Just as each new word and sentence contributes to the ongoing reformulation of the meaning of the larger text of which it is a part and from which it derives its value, so too does each individual action, above and beyond its immediate dialogical repercussions, in some small way change the private and public patterns which it reflects. The answer to the master's question "which comes first" is that we write history as it writes us. Neither can precede the other since each is the other's precondition and cause.

The model of selfhood and history outlined by *Jacques le fataliste* leads to no obvious agenda – indeed, it both invites and disqualifies attempts to seize destiny or "write" history, leaving the subject in an ambivalent position, the only logical expression of which is Jacques' active passivity. But I would argue that therein lies its peculiar appropriateness. For the novel demonstrates that however inevitable the will to mastery, it can never disrupt the order of things. *Jacques le fataliste* persuades us of the absurdity of cultural or historical subversion and thus authorizes the continuation of the fictional enterprise. Unlike Rousseau, Diderot postulates the suspension of his Author figures in the flow and structure of history, and he does so in order to retain his own narrational prerogative.

Diderot's novel implicitly relieves the novelist of the charge of tampering with history by reaffirming, in its tremendous cast of social rivals and would-be manipulators, the universality of such tampering and its ultimate futility. The legacy of the individualism that dominates the first half of the century would seem to be a generalized drive for metahistorical mastery, fueled by an understanding of social protocols, to which the new genre of fiction contributes. As adumbrated early on in *Clarissa* and fully dramatized in *Julie, ou la nouvelle Héloïse* and the story of Mme de la Pommeraye in *Jacques le fataliste*, the comprehension of cultural codes and the authority of tradition leads inevitably to delusions of authority: tradition can function as law only when it is cited, and citation implies a detached abstraction of the script of one's culture – and hence the placing of oneself above, or outside of, that script, in a position of mastery vulnerable to upset. Mastery and iteration imply each other in much the same way as the specular economies of hierarchy and succession that inform *Jacques le fataliste*, and like those economies, they can only be expressed as a dialectic of supersession: to master one's culture is to extract patterns from its script and to reiterate those patterns in a personally advantageous reformulation of experience, but the same logic of successive framing which authorizes that reiteration foretells its enclosure in further, other formulations. Conceived as a product and process of continual reordering, a constantly evolving narrative/narration, history carries the promise of both empowerment and subjugation for its agents, and as this version of history gains currency in the century, we might expect more extravagant agendas of mastery to lead to more dramatic reversals. The most extreme of these are dramatized in the works of the marquis de Sade, where lengthy dissertations on the authority of natural order frequently alternate with the demented programs of personal coercion for which that author is best known. But Choderlos de Laclos' phenomenally successful *Liaisons dangereuses* provides an equally perverse, and infinitely more complex, demonstration of what occurs once the exchanges regulating society have been totally codified and incorporated into agendas of manipulation.

As we shall see in the next chapter, Laclos' work in one sense stands as an extraordinarily rigorous dramatization of Diderot's theories and an extension of his interest in codification. Within a framework of exaggerated narrative manipulation and interpersonal rivalry, *Les Liaisons* pushes to its logical extreme the double identity of historical inscription by showing how the absolute mastery of a culture's scripts leads to enclosure within the script of mastery. This merger leads to both the most extravagant versions of selfhood and its virtual disappearance, since once it is put into application, the theoretical mastery of the code confines the self to a set of roles and actions which it by definition no longer authors.

The most unnerving aspect of *Les Liaisons dangereuses*, though, is the way it plays out this imperative in its reader by eliminating any middle ground, in the form of a narrator, from which to view the action. Composed entirely of personal letters, the work goes further than *Jacques le fataliste* in performing its thesis, for it coerces its readers into re-enacting the presumptions and errors of its characters, and it makes this coercion appear *agentless*, thus carrying to its logical conclusion the implication of the reader which characterizes the metanovels. Diderot's generalization of narrative jockeying, like his realignment of the narrator's and reader's function in his novel, is part and parcel of a trend toward disseminating the representative agendas of the novelist throughout culture and associating the activity of the reader with the ethical consequences of the fiction. This is a move we have already seen in Rousseau's disclaimers in the *Entretien sur les romans*, and it goes hand in hand with a gradual evasion of the novelist, who, behind the screen of the thematized Author and the rhetoric of self-ironization, becomes increasingly difficult to locate beyond the fiction. Even as the idea of fictional authority moves to the center of the novel's thematic field, the precise claims of the novelist at hand become more difficult to assess.

Eventually, in the nineteenth century, personal narration as such disappears from the novel, leaving the reader to interact with an impersonal narrative system. This shift stems, I think, not just from the conviction that systems transcendent of individual volition are at work structuring the world, but also from a growing desire on the part of novelists to dissociate their activity from the world they claim merely to represent but increasingly see themselves shaping. It is not simply that they fear being charged with specific effects on public morality – although that clearly does play a role in the defensiveness which Rousseau, Sterne, and Diderot display with regard to the possible repercussions of their work – but rather that having discovered the extent to which reality is malleable in the hands of a skilled narrator, and having dramatized in their works the various excesses to which such manipulation can go, the professional narrators have it in their own best interest to downplay their virtuosity – or, what amounts to the same thing, to redefine reality as resistant to manipulation by any individual. Their persistent articulations of collective reality or culture as a vast narrative economy beyond comprehension or tampering thus serve to rationalize the growing authority of fiction as just one particularly prominent instance of a widespread practice, and to exempt their own figurations of society from accusations of moral subversion.

By the time of Balzac, the novel will have refined its cloak of innocence still further: the responsibility for reality will have been transferred entirely to the impersonal order of science and nature; there will be no more talk of fiction as the author of history. But then, the notion of history will have changed as well, fracturing into two disparate orders: the course of events and the discipline-bound mode of discourse that purports to represent it. The remarkable thing about *Jacques le fataliste* is that it conveys a sense of history in its completeness, that is, prior to this schism. Neither merely the duration of reality (course of events) nor the story of that duration, the continually unrolling scroll is neither pre-verbal reality nor its representation – nor any combination of those terms that would subordinate one to the other – but rather both act and fact at all times. It is perhaps ungraspable prior to its differentiation into event and record, but it can nonetheless be sensed in the experience of Jacques (le fataliste).

NOTES

1   *Jacques le fataliste et son maître* was published in 15 installments in the *Correspondance littéraire* between 1778 and 1780, then reissued in 1796 and 1798, with additions made by Diderot before his death. It appeared in English as *James the Fatalist and His Master*, translated from the French of Diderot, 3 vols (London: G. G. and J. Robinson, Pater-Noster-Row, 1797).
2   For details on the plagiarized portions, see Diderot's *Œuvres romanesques*, ed. Henri Bénac, reviewed by Lucette Perol (Paris: Garnier, 1981), pp. 904–6,

n. 2. As Bénac points out, Diderot's entire novel plays itself out within a single episode from *Tristram Shandy*, the conclusion of which is constantly postponed by further digressions.

3   In keeping with the convention used in earlier chapters, I shall use the uppercase (Reader, Author) to refer to the reader and author thematized in the text.

4   All citations of novels by Diderot are from the Bénac edition cited above. Translations are my own.

5   The entire action of *Tristram Shandy* consists of talking, but with the exception of Toby and Trim none of the characters seem to have a valid interlocutor. Toby and Mr Shandy love each other but have little interest in each other's hobby-horse; Mrs Shandy remains throughout the book a passive voice of assent, refusing to participate in Mr Shandy's discussions; widow Wadman can hardly make herself understood by Toby, since they share no common field of reference. These characters no longer derive their identity from involvement in a collectively elaborated discourse, but from within their relationship to the past, most often personified as a text. And to the extent that we can associate the characters with various attitudes toward history, the novel allegorizes the inability of any of these orders to communicate with the others.

6   The figure of the specular pair is from Suzanne Gearhart, *The Open Boundary of History and Fiction*. In her incisive reading of *Jacques le fataliste* Gearhart uses the idea of specular pairing in order to distinguish Diderot's depiction of the master/slave relationship from the Hegelian dialectical version: "underlying all of the relationships depicted in the novel is a fundamental similarity between individuals who are all someone's master and someone's servant – who are all each other's doubles" (p. 216). I think it is equally useful as a means of characterizing the other conceptual pairs. Each "cause," in the novel, to cite but the most obvious example, is also always an effect; each narrational act but one episode in a larger narrative. This will become clear in the course of my argument.

7   For other similar boasts, see pp. 759, 774.

8   Samuel Johnson, *Rambler*, no. 188 (January 4, 1752), makes much the same point: "Almost every man listens with eagerness to contemporary history; for almost every man has some real or imaginary connection with a celebrated character; some desire to advance or oppose a rising name. Vanity often co-operates with curiosity. He that is a hearer in one place, qualifies himself to become a speaker in another; for though he cannot comprehend a series of argument, or transport the volatile spirit of wit without evaporation, yet he thinks himself able to treasure up the various incidents of a story and pleases his hopes with the information he shall give to some inferior society."

9   Suzanne Gearhart makes the point in terms of narrative's inability to transcend its own mechanisms: "narrative is limited by the fact that *no narrative can totally situate itself*, for just as a given narrator is always potentially a character in another story, so a given narrative is always potentially set within the context of still another narrative, and so on" (*Open Boundary*, p. 221).

10 Gearhart points out that there is even more to this turnabout at the conclusion

of *Jacques le fataliste*: in turning the narration over to an "editor," who is also by definition a reader, Diderot not only frames the Author and inverts the master/servant advantage he held over the reader up to this point, he also "situates *Jacques le fataliste* in terms of another narrative – *Tristram Shandy*" (*Open Boundary* pp. 219, 221).

11   The definition is from the "Eloge de Richardson" in *Œuvres esthétiques*, ed. Paul Vernière (Paris: Garnier, 1968), p. 29.

12   See for instance pp. 533, 535, 537, 742, 759.

13   There are of course an infinite variety of further scripts which we actualize when reading, the most pertinent in the context of this study being those which students of literature absorb from the discipline of literary study as it is practiced in western universities.

14   *Œuvres esthétiques*, pp. 30–1.

15   Cf. *Rambler*, no. 4 (March 31, 1750), and no. 60 (October 13, 1750).

16   *Œuvres esthétiques*, pp. 39–40.

17   Gearhart, *Open Boundary*, p. 216.

18   This implication is literalized in Diderot's short tale "Ceci n'est pas un conte," where the burden of narration is so completely distributed between a teller and a listener that it becomes difficult, near the middle of the story, to know which one is speaking (cf. *Oeuvres romanesques*, especially pp. 824–5).

19   Both Jacques and the Author repeatedly remind us that we cannot know where we are going as long as our journey continues; cf., for instance, pp. 521, 565, 601, 626, 631, 638, 785.

20   In this passage as elsewhere, Jacques' narrative technique mirrors that of Diderot's in that it confirms its own thesis: by framing his personal philosophy within an extended citation of his previous master's words, Jacques demonstrates at one and the same time the degree to which his current actions are inscribed within the text of past experience and the extent to which his own beliefs and reactions are the simple effect of another individual's actions.

21   It should be noted in passing that this passage, where the Author refers to personal conversations with one of his characters, is a prime example of how Diderot undermines the conventions of framing which ground his authority.

15
Self-Emplotment and the Implication of the Reader (*Les Liaisons dangereuses*)

Les Liaisons dangereuses ou lettres recueillies dans une société et publiées pour l'instruction de quelques autres by Choderlos de Laclos makes a fitting capstone to this study, not only because of its chronological position – published in 1782,[1] it is the last great novel of pre-revolutionary France and will be followed by a significant hiatus – but also because it encapsulates in its remarkable marriage of form and theme most of the concerns of the eighteenth-century novel that pertain to this study – parental authority, love and seduction, dialogical dependence and rivalry, interpersonal negotiation and manipulation, masks and role-playing, self-definition and individuality, and the role of the collective discourse in determining social identity.

However, Laclos' achievement is most remarkable for its brilliant dissection of the mechanisms of fiction, its analysis of how narrative contrivance relates to social intercourse and alters the lives of reader and author alike. Although less obviously a metanovel than *Tristram Shandy* or *Jacques le fataliste*, *Les Liaisons dangereuses* is more blatantly metanarrative, concerned primarily with the power which fictional accounts exercise over those for whom they are intended and, more importantly, over those who claim to control their effect. Taking as its central theme the elaborately conceived intrigues by means of which two brilliant libertines manipulate their peers, the novel transposes to the plane of social interaction the practice of detached analysis, systematization, and emplotment which I have identified with authorial mastery. Testing the hypothesis that interpersonal behavior can be reduced to a predictable series of story lines and narrative components, the mastery of which procures not only power over the destiny of others, but exemption from the social laws or mores which subordinate individual liberty to shared norms, *Les Liaisons dangereuses* dramatizes the attempt to transcend culture through its comprehension, to elude inscription in the history of the collective by emplotting that history in one's own fictions.

Ultimately this program of codification and mastery, which takes to its logical limits a tendency we have seen developing since Richardson, implodes upon its architects, foreshadowing the thematic devaluation, in subsequent novels, of narrative contrivance as an explicit mode of cultural mastery, as well as the gradual fading of the first-person narrative voice which embodies that mastery. In the great realistic works of the nineteenth century, social reality will emerge as a complex texture of material, geographic, religious, and political factors, moral codes, and disembodied systems of "natural" determination, the course and regulation of which narrators may claim to transcribe and understand, but no longer control. Coming to grips with this reality, indeed manipulating it, will persist as a central preoccupation of the novel – perhaps even as the primary function of the novel. But the novels which perform this function, and the authors behind them, will no longer do so overtly: they will no longer make their power the explicit theme of their works, teasing the reader into complicity with the offer of a share in the writing of the world. One of the reasons for this, I will argue, lies in the incompatibility between the dialogical compact upon which that power depends and the *explicit* claim of authority. And this is an incompatibility which *Les Liaisons dangereuses* will dramatize in the failed relationship between its two master authors/readers.

Coming a generation after *Clarissa* and *Julie*, from which it openly takes part of its inspiration, Laclos' novel portrays a world where the contrivances of Lovelace have been codified into a conventional script, where Clarissa's willful sublation of selfhood into public text has been perverted into a practice of ongoing self-fictionalization, and where the agenda of cultural authority implemented by Wolmar has degenerated into a self-centered will to power. As part of its foreclosure on all such strategies, *Les Liaisons dangereuses* stresses the *economic* dimension of narration, that is, the degree to which both the production of narratives and their interpretation are bound up in processes, structures, and laws of development which, embracing all levels of society and social interactions, and modulating and defining over time the shape and extent of individual claims to authority and self-determination, are to a large degree transcendent of individual volition. This larger impersonal economy not only frames and empowers, but, the outcome of the *Liaisons* suggests, even determines the histories which individuals enact.

A key step in this shifting of emphasis from the personal to the impersonal, from the individual to the all-inclusive, involves formalizing as a structure the dynamics of narration/narrative, that is, locating within the phenomenon of textuality itself the dialectic of misprision and revision which we associate with the progress of historical understanding. In *Les Liaisons dangereuses* personal initiative alone cannot account for the constant flux of factuality (and history) – that endless rearrangement and rearticulation of past accounts in light of present experience, the continual integration of shared record and private life whose development I have traced from the seventeenth century through the eighteenth. It is also bound up with an interference or tension between multiple and irreconcilable identities of the narrative act/text itself, which, as embodied in the notion of the personal letter, generate an endless series of reinterpretations and decisions analogous to the course of history more generally.

Composed entirely of realistic personal letters – the correspondence between a half dozen major characters and as many secondary figures – *Les Liaisons dangereuses* probably represents the purest version of that most successful of eighteenth-century genres, the epistolary novel.[2] The formal particularities of the epistolary mode lend themselves to a variety of theoretical analyses, but for our purposes the salient points are relatively obvious.[3] First, in a novel composed entirely of letters, all reality is by definition a function of narration: there is no information available to the reader within the course of the novel that is not filtered through the subjectivity, motives, and rhetoric of some character. The "reality" we constitute through our reading is blatantly one of contrivance, however laudable or accurate the motives of the particular letter writer might seem. Second, in a "dynamic" epistolary novel such as *Les Liaisons*, where "le héros, cessant de parler *de* son antagoniste, parle *à* son antagoniste" (the hero, no longer speaking *about* his antagonist, speaks *to* his antagonist), where "la trame, au lieu de progresser *dans* les lettres, progresse *par* les lettres" (the plot, rather than advancing *in* the letters, advances *through* the letters),[4] all significant events and initiatives are the direct consequence of narration and representation. One makes things happen first and foremost by writing them into existence. In the context of epistolary seduction, the letter itself becomes the significant event, and in *Les Liaisons dangereuses*, writing and reading form the primary, and in the case of the novel's central relationship, the *only*, mode of action and self-determination. To that extent, the novel takes to its logical limit the notion of narration as the ground of selfhood.

Less obvious but more important are the conflicting reactions which the presence of two very different sets of conventions – those of literary fiction and those of the personal letter – demand of the reader. The letters making up *Les Liaisons* differ from their counterparts in Richardson's or Rousseau's works in that they conform to the norms of intimate, everyday correspondence. With one minor exception, each letter writer in Laclos' work receives as well as writes, and what he or she writes is in response to the last letter received.[5] Less an extended reportage of all of the moments of the writer's experience than a precisely motivated expression of a desire and the solicitation of a response, the letters seldom exceed the bounds of verisimilitude:

their length is reasonable, the duration and moment of their composition is scrupulously accounted for, and each epistle is determined by a specific motive and designed to produce an effect on a *particular* reader. Consequently, there is no general narration in the novel addressed to an undefined or vague reader. Each phrase, be it a request for advice, a demand for support, an expression of desire, or a reproach, is formulated according to a specific strategy on the part of the letter writer in view of eliciting a precise response on the part of a particular recipient, whose character and relationship to the writer determines the letter's rhetorical tack.

Any uninvolved third-party reader who penetrates this closed circuit of intimate communication must necessarily choose between two possible roles. We can identify with the letter's writer, in which case we read the letter in the first person, as the elaboration of a desire, the ultimate effect of which we can only anticipate; or we can adopt the perspective of the addressee, in which case we read the letter in the second person and evaluate it as the expression of a previous state of mind of its writer and a solicitation to react. The epistolary format in this sense not only suspends us between two different subjectivities (me and you, self and Other), but between two different moments in time (future and past), two different emotional vectors (desire or solicitation and reaction or elicitation) and two different semiotic operations (self-*expression* and *interpretation* of the Other). *Les Liaisons dangereuses* thus situates itself at the very crux of the "double" identity of (hi)story as narration and narrative, present ordering and past order. Every major character in the novel is both a reader and a writer – not just figuratively, but literally, and every phrase in the novel is literally both a (current) event of narration and a (previously composed) narrative structure – so much so, in fact, that we can qualify our terminology, which provisionally separated these two supplementary faces/phases: in *Les Liaisons dangereuses* every moment/fragment of text is at all times *explicitly* both "narrative" and "narration."

By its very form then, *Les Liaisons dangereuses* invests narration/narrative with a self-differing, plural identity which, incapable of finding expression within a single meaning, necessarily plays itself out in time: although both of the perspectives available for understanding a given letter are permanently available, they cannot be reconciled within a stable unitary meaning: one cannot *simultaneously* read the text as the expression of the self and the Other, as a prescription for the future and a description of the past, as manipulation and representation, as motivated story and unmediated history. Infinitely plural, the meanings of the text, like the characters of its *dramatis personae*, only elaborate themselves through an ongoing process of rereading and rearticulation that is structurally equivalent to history, conceptualized as both a form of understanding and the course of experience, in that it inscribes its own present experience under the guise of recapitulating and reinterpreting the past, in that it articulates its own (readerly) selfhood within an ambivalence between the I and the Other, the (writing) subject who structures the world and the subject prefigured by the world already written.

The historicization of meaning and selfhood which *Les Liaisons dangereuses* performs through the mediation of its reader can be attributed in the first instance, perhaps, to what we might characterize in structural terms as the letter/narrative's difference from itself, but the fundamental historicity of meaning and identity also makes itself felt within the plot of the novel, which is to say, by the letter writers and readers themselves. Even for the characters who animate the closed epistolary circuit, meaning is neither stable nor unitary; it varies, to start with, according to the meta-narrative detachment of the particular writer/reader and according to the moment of that individual's (re)assessment of the text, which is to say, according to the context of that (re)assessment. Like *Jacques le fataliste*, *Les Liaisons dangereuses* figures the process/structure of history in terms of hierarchical and interpretive regress, various crucial events being shown to assume different identities according to their level of narrative framing and the stage, moment, or context of their reinterpretation.

One can distinguish at least three levels of plot in the novel, each of which presents a different version of the struggle for narrative authority and each of which invites a reassessment of the work's meaning: that of the seduction of the narratively naive victims by the libertines; that of the libertines' mutual self-delusion and destruction at the hands of their plot; and that of the apparent privileging and subsequent suspension of the reader's authority. The successive relationships of selfhood to narration and narrative which these different plots inscribe can be read not only as an allegory of the eighteenth-century novel's thematic progression from stories of self-expression to those of social management and cultural authority, but also as an undoing of the delusive epistemological privilege of author and reader to which that progression leads and an enclosure of both firmly within the textual dialectic of history.

At the simplest level of analysis, the plot of *Les Liaisons dangereuses* is simply that: a plot. The letters depict the seduction and humiliation of a series of innocent people at the hands of two libertines, the marquise de Merteuil and the vicomte de Valmont, who, working separately but in concert and using their superior command of the cultural code and their understanding of how private and public account can shape individuals' acts, entrap their victims in a web of vicious fictions which ultimately destroy their lives. Valmont is primarily occupied with the seduction and humiliation of a virtuous young wife, the présidente de Tourvel, through a protracted epistolary campaign in which he rehearses the entire repertoire of the conventional lover; but Merteuil involves her ex-lover in her own project of debauching the young debutante, Cécile Volanges, in order to take vengeance both on Cécile's self-righteous mother and on the intended husband of Cécile, one of Merteuil's former lovers.

These two projects differ in their means, but they both have as their goal the possession or control of others and the enhancement of the plotters' image of mastery within the subculture of the libertines. Libertine society, according to its variation of the double standard, respects and fears men known to have, or suspected of having, seduced great numbers of women; admires women suspected, but not known, to have subjugated great numbers of men; and ostracizes anyone caught *in flagrante delicto* and any woman whose seduction can be proven.[6] Power, in such a context, is explicitly narrative, since the destruction of a rival's reputation automatically brings an enhancement of one's own. To write another's story is always also to embellish one's own, as even the prudish Mme de Volanges concedes: "pour avoir l'empire dans la société, il [suffit] de manier, avec une égale adresse, la louange et le ridicule" (32, p. 65) (to have power in society it [suffices] to wield praise and ridicule with equal skill).[7]

For the woman, that mastery consists primarily in manipulating others into positions of vulnerability while concealing her own behavior and relations from the public eye. This she must do by constructing and maintaining fictional identities that elicit the respect and trust of her rivals and allow her to influence their decisions. Thus under various masks Mme de Merteuil orchestrates the behavior of not only her current lover, Belleroche, but Cécile, Cécile's lover Danceny, her mother Mme de Volanges, the rake Prévan, and eventually Valmont, while maintaining for the public eye a reputation of irreproachability.

For Valmont, mastery also involves the construction of fictional identities. His most elaborate one is directed at the limited public of Mme de Tourvel, whom he must convince of the sincerity of his love, but he establishes a secondary identity as the friend and helper of Danceny and Cécile. His ultimate goal, though, is the enhancement of his own reputation of mastery, toward which end he undertakes the seduction of Tourvel, who is known for her austere morals and will thus provide a superb addition to his list of conquests.

Both the male and the female versions of the libertine project involve the possession of others in the sexual sense, but sexual possession is only one moment in a general will to power that ultimately seeks to transcend enclosure in history by assuming an authoritative role in the articulation of the public record. The libertine takes possession of his or her victim by recounting his/her deeds and those of the victim, by fashioning a private account of the self with which to beguile the weak, and a public account of one's triumph with which to humiliate the victim and dazzle one's rivals. *Les Liaisons dangereuses* dramatically underscores the narrative dimension of this agenda by restricting its protagonists to epistolary modes of action. Not only is the greater part of Valmont's seduction of Tourvel performed by letter, but his relationship to Merteuil evolves entirely through narrative, namely the running account he provides of his progress (and she of hers).[8]

Unlike previous versions of individuality we have encountered, then, the protagonists of *Les Liaisons dangereuses* do not construct fictions about themselves in order to obtain some material advantage, such as acquiring a spouse or fortune (Defoe), advancing one's estate (Marivaux), cheating a half-brother out of his rightful inheritance (Fielding), or founding a culture (Rousseau), but rather as part of a more abstract compulsion to overcome subordination to the collective voice and the rules that govern it.

An essential component of this program is the distancing of oneself from the network of behavior one manipulates. The libertine's erotic and narrative objects must remain just that: *objects*, and not individuals, identifiable components in a mechanism whose manipulation insures that one is not subject to it.[9] Should the libertines lose their distance and become personally involved, they risk incorporation into the text of gossip and, consequently, disgrace. As Valmont notes, early in his campaign to possess Tourvel: "j'ai bien besoin d'avoir cette femme, pour me sauver du ridicule d'en être amoureux" (4, p. 14) (I need to have this woman to save myself from the ridicule of being in love with her).[10] To maintain their sense of detachment, they reduce all individuals to types, all behavior to conventional codes, the mastery of which allows the libertine to simulate an unlimited number of characters. Thus Valmont, who is intimately familiar with the code of the pious Christian woman, or dévote, knows precisely which fictional postures to assume in order to win Tourvel's love and draw her into behavior that violates this code: he gains access to her esteem initially through a contrived act of Christian charity (21, pp. 43–5; 23, pp. 48–51) and uses the fiction of his conversion as the final strategy in his assault (123–5, pp. 288–300). Conversely, the ignorant Cécile – "une jeune fille qui n'a rien vu, ne connaît rien" (4, p. 13) (a girl who has seen nothing, knows nothing) and therefore "n'a ni caractère ni principes" (38, p. 78) (has neither character nor principles) – can be initiated into the code of libertinage without even realizing what she is doing, since she lacks any competing rules by which to evaluate her actions.

Constructing each of their letters according to the code of its recipient and interpreting those they receive in line with the codes of its author, the libertines assume they are both immune to exposure and privy to the thoughts of others: their own letters, they think, represent only what they are designed to, while those of others unabashedly reveal their writer's soul. Similarly, the plotters view their social interactions as an aesthetic work, a performance to be savored, analyzed, recounted and refined, but in which the performer never loses sight of his or her real underlying identity. Merteuil's long biographical letter is the clearest testimony to this commitment to selfhood as pure performance (letter 81).

In its selection of libertines as its central protagonists, and its identification of their subculture as a major component of society, *Les Liaisons dangereuses* generalizes the idiosyncratic practice of self-configuration as art which we first noted in *Moll Flanders* and *Roxana*, and which defines the character of Lovelace in *Clarissa*. Lovelace is an innovator, a self-proclaimed artist in a world of hypocrisy that denies the role of art in the formulation of social identity. He finds his identity in his difference from his peers, in his singular commitment to "art" in a society that condemns artfulness of all kinds, and his inventions stun us all the more for the fact that they have few equals or models. The world of Valmont and Merteuil, on the other hand, not only acknowledges but esteems masks, deception, and manipulation as the hallmark of the superior being. Accordingly, the true master is the one who takes on the most difficult projects, the most skilled opponents, and finds the most elegant solutions.[11] This requirement, which is built into the social fabric, with its generalized aspiration to narrative mastery, dooms the partnership of Valmont and Merteuil. But their relationship to each other can only be understood in the context of their different strategies for controlling others.

Valmont's seduction of Tourvel occupies by far the greatest portion of the novel. It demonstrates how narrative reality can become experienced reality through reading – how the "facts" depicted in a story are assimilated into the world of the reader's lived experience merely by virtue of being read repeatedly. Inverting Merteuil's warning that a seduction by letter is a difficult enterprise, since, among other things, it allows the victim too much time to reconsider any feelings the letters might inspire (33, p. 67), Valmont uses Tourvel's energetic resistance to his narrative of passion as a means of anchoring the idea of that passion in her mind. His strategy assumes that however repulsed by the idea of adultery the prude may be, her vanity will not allow her to leave unchallenged his grossly distorted interpretations of her actions and his passion. He needs only to relate their story from a biased perspective in order to provoke a lengthy indignant response from his victim that enmeshes her ever more deeply in the co-authorship of their affair. Intent on refuting his version of events, she unwittingly contributes to the consolidation of its central fiction, that of Valmont's love, by acknowledging and addressing its argument. A typical opening from one of his letters, and her response:

Par où ai-je donc mérité, Madame, et les reproches que vous me faites, et la colère que vous me témoignez? L'attachment le plus vif et pourtant le plus respectueux, la soumission la plus entière à vos moindres volontés: voilà en deux mots l'histoire de mes sentiments et de ma conduite. Accablé par les peines d'un amour malheureux, je n'avais d'autre consolation que celle de vous voir; vous m'avez ordonné de m'en priver; j'ai obéi sans me permettre un murmure. Pour prix de ce sacrifice, vous m'avez permis de vous écrire, et aujourd'hui vous voulez m'ôter cet unique plaisir. Me le laisserai-je ravir, sans essayer de le défendre? Non, sans doute: eh! comment ne serait-il pas cher à mon cœur? c'est le seul qui me reste, et je le tiens de vous. (58, pp. 117–18)

On what grounds have I merited, Madame, the reproaches which you make me and the anger you express? The most lively and yet the most respectful attachment, the most complete submission to your every will: there in two words is the story of my sentiments and conduct. Overwhelmed by the pain of an unfortunate love, I had no consolation other than that of seeing you; you ordered me to deprive myself of it; I obeyed without permitting myself so much as a murmur. In return for this sacrifice you gave me permission to write you, and now you want to take this single pleasure from me. Will I allow myself to be robbed of it, without trying to defend it? No, surely not: how could it not be dear to my heart? it is the only pleasure left me, and I have it from you.

Je ne voulais plus vous répondre, Monsieur, et peut-être l'embarras que j'éprouve en ce moment est-il lui-même une preuve qu'en effet je ne le devrais pas. Cependant je ne veux vous laisser aucun sujet de plainte contre moi; je veux vous convaincre que j'ai fait pour vous tout ce que je pouvais faire.

    Je vous ai permis de m'écrire, dites-vous? J'en conviens; mais quand vous me rappelez cette permission, croyez-vous que j'oublie à quelles conditions elle vous fut donnée? Si j'y eusse été aussi fidèle que vous l'avez été peu, auriez-vous reçu une seule réponse de moi? Voilà pourtant la troisième; et quand vous faites tout ce qu'il faut pour m'obliger à rompre cette correspondance, c'est moi qui m'occupe des moyens de l'entretenir. Il en est un, mais c'est le seul; et si vous refusez de la prendre, ce sera, quoique vous puissiez dire, me prouver assez combien peu vous y mettez de prix.

    Quittez donc un langage que je ne puis ni ne veux entendre; renoncez à un sentiment qui m'offense et m'effraie, et auquel, peut-être, vous devriez être moins attaché en songeant qu'il est l'obstacle qui nous sépare. Ce sentiment est-il donc le seul que vous puissiez connaître? et l'amour aura-t-il ce tort de plus à mes yeux, d'exclure l'amitié? (67, p. 136)

I did not want to reply to you, Sir, and perhaps the discomfort I feel at this moment is itself proof that I ought not. However, I do not want to leave you any subject of reproach against me; I want to convince you that I have done everything I could do for you.

You say I gave you permission to write? I admit that; but when you remind me of this permission, do you think I have forgotten under what conditions it was given you? If I had been as strict in observing them as you have been lax, would you have received a single response from me? And yet here is the third one; and while you are doing everything you can to oblige me to break off this correspondence, I am concerning myself with the means to maintain it. There is one way, but it is the only one; and if you refuse to take it, you will prove to me, whatever you might say, how little you value the correspondence.

Leave off, therefore, this language that I neither can nor want to hear; give up this sentiment that offends and frightens me, and to which, perhaps, you should be less attached, realizing that it is the obstacle that separates us. Is this sentiment the only one you can understand? and is love to have yet this further fault in my eyes, that it excludes friendship?

Much as a novelist initiates his reader's belief in a fictional world, Valmont accustoms Tourvel – and she accustoms herself – to the "fact" of his love through sustained narrative reference.

Of course, to maintain his position of superiority, the meta-narrator must himself remain immune to the seduction of his fiction. And that is indeed Valmont's assumption: more intent on forcing his victim to acknowledge defeat than on simply seducing her quickly – "qu'elle se rende, mais qu'elle combatte; que, sans avoir la force de vaincre, elle ait celle de résister; qu'elle savoure à loisir le sentiment de sa faiblesse, et soit contrainte d'avouer sa défaite" (23, p. 50) (let her surrender, but may she also fight; without having the strength to win, may she have the strength to resist; may she slowly savor the sense of her weakness and be forced to admit her defeat) – he flaunts his privileged understanding of what his letters "really" mean in his correspondence with Merteuil. The most famous embodiment of this presumed semiotic mastery is the elaborate double entendre he pens for Tourvel from a prostitute's bed, describing in exact detail his erotic situation, but in language she can only understand as that of his sentimental attachment to her (48, pp. 100–1). Later, after having obtained her submission, he risks an even more extreme version of the same *tour de force* by persuading her, through a careful reconstruction of events, that her sighting of him in the company of the same prostitute does not mean what it seems (135–7, pp. 320–6). Even when it conflicts with her own direct perception of events, Tourvel prefers Valmont's version of reality, convinced that the character he paints for himself in his narrative is the true one, that his public image as libertine no longer corresponds to his inner identity.

Valmont's conviction that only he understands the "true" meaning of his letters extends to his grasp of the entire protracted relationship with

Tourvel as a script. While the présidente blindly follows what she takes to be the dictates of her conscience, unaware of the extent to which her every move, virtuous or otherwise, is encoded within the norms of her culture, Valmont understands their interaction in terms of a familiar scenario, the variations in which he relishes as an opportunity to hone his virtuosity and render his performance more impressive.

On a first level of analysis, then, *Les Liaisons dangereuses* seems to argue the possibility of metanarrative mastery – at least as regards interpersonal relationships. To the extent that we accept Tourvel's characterization of herself as being incapable of guile, we can read her capitulation as a validation of detached narrative craft over unmediated self-expression.[12] And to the extent that Valmont's art derives its rules from the script of its culture, the plot suggests that given sufficient analytic discipline, a determined metanarrator can master the grammar of culture, turning its conventions and encoded scripts of behavior to personal advantage and displacing providential agency as the author of individual destiny. Such godlike semiotic omnipotence is indeed the goal of Valmont:

> J'aurai cette femme; je l'enlèverai au mari qui la profane; j'oserai la ravir au Dieu même qu'elle adore. Quel délice d'être tour à tour l'objet et le vaiqueur de ses remords! Loin de moi l'idée de détruire les préjugés qui l'assiègent! Ils ajouteront à mon bonheur et à ma gloire. Qu'elle croit à la vertu, mais qu'elle me la sacrifie.... Je serai vraiment le Dieu qu'elle aura préféré. (6, p. 18)

> je vis en effect cette femme adorable à genoux, baignée de larmes, et priant avec ferveur. Quel Dieu osait-elle invoquer? en est-il d'assez puissant contre l'amour? En vain cherche-t-elle à présent des secours étrangers; c'est moi qui réglerai son sort. (23, p. 51)[13]

> I will have this woman; I will take her from the husband who profanes her; I will dare to steal her even from the God she adores. What delight to be in turn the object and the vanquisher of her remorse! Far be it from me to destroy the prejudices that assail her! They will add to my happiness and to my renown. Let her believe in virtue, but may she sacrifice it to me.... I will truly be the God she will have preferred.

> in effect, I saw that adorable woman bathed in tears, kneeling and praying with fervor. What God could she dare invoke? Is there one powerful enough to resist love? In vain does she now seek help from beyond; it is I who will determine her fate.

Eventually, this vision of omnipotence will be woven into the public record alongside Valmont's other exploits to commemorate his glory:

> Si pourtant on aime mieux le genre héroïque, je montrerai la Présidente, ce modèle cité de toutes les vertus, respectée même de nos plus libertins, telle

enfin qu'on avait perdu jusqu'à l'idée de l'attaquer! je la montrerai, dis-je, oubliant ses devoirs et sa vertu, sacrifiant sa réputation et deux ans de sagesse, pour courir après le bonheur de me plaire, pour s'enivrer de celui de m'aimer; se trouvant suffisamment dédommagée de tant de sacrifices, par un mot, par un regard, qu'encore elle n'obtiendra pas toujours. Je ferai plus, je la quitterai; et je ne connais pas cette femme, ou je n'aurai pas de successeur. Elle résistera au besoin de consolation, à l'habitude du plaisir, au désir même de la vengeance. Enfin, elle n'aura existé que pour moi; et que sa carrière soit plus ou moins longue, j'en aurai seul ouvert et fermé la barrière. Une fois parvenu à ce triomphe, je dirai à mes rivaux: «Voyez mon ouvrage, et cherchez-en dans le siècle un second exemple!» (115, p. 272)

If, however, they prefer the heroic genre, I will depict the Présidente, this exemplary model of all virtues, respected even by our most debauched, so much so, in fact, that they had even given up the idea of taking her on! I will depict her, I say, forgetting her duties and her virtue, sacrificing the reputation she has earned by two years of propriety, in order to pursue the happiness of pleasing me, to intoxicate herself on that of loving me; finding herself sufficiently compensated for such sacrifices by a word, a glance – which even then she will not always obtain. I will do still more. I will leave her; and if I know this woman I will have no successor. She will resist the need to console herself, the habit of physical pleasure, even the desire of vengeance. Finally, she will only have existed for me; and whether her career is long or short, I alone will have opened and closed it. Once I have achieved this victory, I will say to my rivals: «Look upon my work, and try to find a second example of its kind in the century!»

Merteuil's pretentions are even more grandiose. Where Valmont is content to measure his success against the conventional norms of the rake, she aspires to nothing short of virtual cultural transcendence. Scorning Valmont's traditional scripts, she does not simply excel at the game prescribed for her by her society, she elaborates one of her own, based on a unique personal code of behavior which permits her to understand and manipulate virtually everyone in society while remaining impervious to their gaze.[14] She is the consummate author figure, expressing herself obliquely through the scripts she devises for others to act out.[15] She is not herself the agent of Cécile's infatuation, debauchment, and retreat into the convent, but she orchestrates it, by maneuvering not only Cécile, but Danceny, whom she directs in the role of Cécile's lover; Valmont, who deflowers the young girl; and Cécile's mother, whose decisions concerning the education and marriage of her daughter the marquise oversees. In addition, she engineers the satiation of the chevalier Belleroche, her current lover, of whom she wishes to be free; the disgrace and imprisonment of the famous rake Prévan, whom she entraps into a charge of sexual assault; and her own seduction by Danceny, whom she decides is too good for Cécile. In all of these plots her own role and desires are concealed from the public eye by the actors whose moves she premeditates, and in this sense she exceeds the epistemological ideal of the libertine woman: even as they unwittingly answer to her direction, her peers are maintained in a permanent state of uncertainty, respectful of the exploits they surmise, but unable to prove them and thus incorporate them into the economy of public gossip Valmont seeks to dominate.

Essential to this program is a systematic analysis of society, a codification of social roles and behavior from which Merteuil can extract a grammar of gestures and expressions that permits her to simulate virtually any emotion and disguise any true feelings she has. From earliest adolescence she takes her distance from the behavior she sees around her, recording its patterns, while feigning disinterest: "tandis qu'on me croyait étourdie ou distraite, écoutant peu à la vérité les discours qu'on s'empressait de me tenir, je recueillais avec soin ceux qu'on cherchait à me cacher" (81, p. 175) (while they thought me absentminded or distracted, barely listening, it was true, to the discussions they were eager to make me attend to, I was carefully noting those which they tried to conceal from me). This attention to the hidden discourse of the collective is doubled by a conscious practice of dissimulation: "forcée souvent de cacher les objets de mon attention aux yeux qui m'entouraient, j'essayai de guider les miens à mon gré.... je tâchai de régler de même les divers mouvements de ma figure" (81, p. 175) (often forced to conceal the objects of my attention from the eyes that surrounded me, I tried to guide mine at will...I similarly attempted to control the various movements of my face). Even on her wedding night Merteuil maintains her dispassionate analytic perspective: "cette première nuit, dont on se fait pour l'ordinaire une idée si cruelle ou si douce, ne me présentait qu'une occasion d'expérience: douleur et plaisir, j'observai tout exactement, et ne voyais dans ces diverses sensations, que des faits à recueillir et à méditer" (81, p. 176) (that first night, which we ordinarily imagine so cruel or so sweet, presented me only with an occasion for experimentation: pain and pleasure, I observed everything precisely, and saw only in those various sensations facts to be gathered and considered).

Finally, considering all of culture a text to be studied, the marquise supplements her practical observations with a systematic study of the texts which take in that culture – above all, the novel, which in her view defines the limits of action:

> J'étudiai nos mœurs dans les romans; nos opinions dans les philosophes; je cherchai même dans les moralistes les plus sévères ce qu'ils exigeaient de nous, et je m'assurai ainsi de ce qu'on pouvait faire, de ce qu'on devait penser, et de ce qu'il fallait paraître. (81, p. 177)

> I studied our behavior in novels; our opinions in the works of the philo-
> sophers; I even sought in the most severe moralists an idea of what they
> demand of us, and I thus determined what one could do, what one was
> supposed to think, and how one should look.

Because she not only knows the scripts of her culture but also understands
the grammars of action, thought, and appearance according to which they
are articulated, Merteuil can assume any identity at will, while perfectly
concealing her true thoughts and feelings: "non contente de ne plus me
laisser pénétrer, je m'amusais à me montrer sous des formes différentes
. . . ma façon de penser fut pour moi seule, et je ne montrai plus que celle
qu'il m'était utile de laisser voir" (81, p. 175) (not content with no longer
being penetrated, I amused myself with showing myself under different
forms . . . my way of thinking was for me alone, and I showed only what was
useful for me to show). Having mastered both her own facial expressions
and the social repertory, she adjusts her identity to that of her interlocutor,
making every individual see in her what she wishes: all of the members of
society with whom she has commerce, from the prudes to the libertines,
think her unique and all think her to be one of their own. Valmont is no
exception: it is not at all clear that he knows her real motives and feelings
any better than her other victims, since although she claims to have revealed
to him alone all of her secrets (81, p. 180), she also notes that one of her
standard tactics is to make every one of her lovers think himself unique (81,
p. 179).

In sum, the marquise aspires to nothing less than transcendence of social
and cultural determination – or absolute control of her own history. She
does not inherit her moves from her culture, but devises them according to
her needs of the moment, and her constant measured control of her public
identity, her superb detachment from emotional entanglement, her immunity to spontaneity, are the fruit of her own agenda. She writes her own
character, and that character is one of unique authority:

> Mais moi, qu'ai-je de commun avec ces femmes inconsidérées? Quand m'avez-
> vous vue m'écarter des règles que je me suis prescrites et manquer à mes
> principes? je dis mes principes, et je le dis à dessein: car ils ne sont pas,
> comme ceux des autres femmes, donnés au hasard, reçus sans examen et
> suivis par habitude; ils sont le fruit de mes profondes réflexions; je les ai créés,
> et je puis dire que je suis mon ouvrage. (81, p. 175)

> But I, what do I have in common with these rash women? When have you
> seen me stray from my self-prescribed rules and go against my principles? I
> say *my* principles, and I say it intentionally, for they are not, like those of
> other women, given randomly, received without scrutiny, and followed by
> habit; they are the fruit of my profound reflections; I created them, and I can
> say that I am my own work.

This is self-definition in its ultimate form: an ego profoundly cognizant of the determining role culture plays in personal behavior and identity, who through a carefully laid-out program of analysis and self-discipline aspires to abstract herself from the conventions of her culture and the embrace of collective discourse which determines personal identity according to those conventions. Merteuil strives to be at once her own creator and creation, to transcend the ambivalence between activity and passivity, mastery and enslavement, which normally accompanies an awareness of one's inscription within culture.[16] She recognizes that social identity in her world results from a dialectic between personal account and public record, but she is determined to substitute for that dialectic a closed circuit of self-historicization, all phases of which remain under her control. This is why she never writes any letters in her own hand, but rather has them transcribed by her servant, of whose discretion she can be certain, thanks to incriminating information in her possession. Even should one of her accounts fall into the wrong hands, it could never be shown to be hers. In theory, at least, she is outside of the history of her times.

If the surface plot of *Les Liaisons dangereuses* seems to glorify such pretentions, it also ultimately discredits them: Merteuil and Valmont destroy each other and themselves. Increasingly, as their plots gain in complexity, the master figures lose control over their dialogical relationship and over the fictions they have set in motion. The first of these developments is a predictable consequence of the libertine agenda of mastery. Valmont and Merteuil must ultimately clash. Defined by their seductive expertise, they are enslaved to it as well – they must demonstrate with ever more extravagant programs of manipulation their mastery of the game: "conquérir est notre destin, il faut le suivre" (4, p. 12) (to conquer is our destiny, we must pursue it), Valmont declares, and Merteuil echoes this conviction with "il faut vaincre ou périr" (81, p. 181) (we must triumph or perish). And as Merteuil's destruction of the celebrated rake Prévan attests, the most challenging victim is not the one who swears allegiance to an alien code of conduct, but the forewarned co-practitioner of libertinage as an art form. Since the strength of one's identity is directly proportional to that of one's opponent, Valmont and Merteuil are doomed, sooner or later, to challenge one another: their own principles and scenarios for glory demand it of them. As the best, they are each other's ultimate test.

Beyond the inevitability of their confrontation lies their more absolute desire to possess or destroy the Other on which they depend. The final stage of mastery for the supernarrator who claims to have transcended the dialectic of history, or inscription within the text of culture, is to refute one's dialogical dependency on the interpersonal level by eliminating or absorbing the Other against whom self-representation plays itself out. Merteuil initially seeks to accomplish this by incorporating Valmont into her story, seducing him into the leading role in her plot in exchange for the illusion of being privy to her true plans. Her strategy emerges in the opening lines of their epistolary relationship:

> Revenez, mon cher Vicomte, revenez.... Partez sur-le-champ; j'ai besoin de vous. Il m'est venu une excellente·idée, et je veux bien vous en confier l'exécution. Ce peu de mots devrait suffire; et, trop honoré de mon choix, vous devriez venir, avec empressement, prendre mes ordres à genoux.... Je veux donc bien vous instruire de mes projets: mais jurez-moi qu'en fidèle chevalier, vous ne courrez aucune aventure que vous n'ayez mis celle-ci à fin. Elle est digne d'un héros... (2, p. 9)

> Come back my dear viscount, come back:... Leave on the spot; I need you. An excellent idea has occurred to me, and I am willing to entrust you with its execution. These few words should suffice; and, overly honored by my choice, you should eagerly rush to receive my orders on bowed knee.... I am willing to instruct you concerning my plans: but swear to me as a loyal cavalier, that you will undertake no affair until you have brought this one to a conclusion. It is worthy of a hero...

The vicomte's plans for possessing his Other are rather more literal. Resisting Merteuil's demand that he abandon his plot to enact hers, he tempts her with a vision of their pre-lapsarian happiness and proposes they renew their liaison: "laissez-moi l'espoir de retrouver ces moments où nous savions fixer le bonheur" (15, p. 34) (leave me the hope of rediscovering those moments when we knew how to secure happiness). Though she agrees to entertain his attentions on the condition that he dispose of Tourvel, Merteuil knows that Valmont's goal of mutual seduction is a contradiction in terms, since both members of the dialogic transaction cannot simultaneously be master: "mais, dites-moi Vicomte, qui de nous deux se chargera de tromper l'autre?" (131, p. 311) (but, tell me, viscount, which of us two will take responsibility for deceiving the other?). Once enclosed in the grammar of absolute mastery, there can be no subordination, however provisional, to the Other whose complicity and rivalry validates the self's accomplishments.[17] The libertine can neither accept the Other nor do without it; mastery can only confirm itself in its self-destruction.

Thus Merteuil, in spite of her claims of cultural transcendence, feels compelled to convince Valmont of her difference from all other women. Her identity, she argues, is founded on her uniqueness:

> Si... vous m'avez vue, disposant des événements et des opinions, faire de ces hommes si redoutables les jouets de mes caprices ou de mes fantaisies; ôter aux uns la volonté de me nuire, aux autres la puissance;... si, au milieu

de ces révolutions fréquentes, ma réputation s'est pourtant conservée pure,
n'avez-vous pas dû en conclure que, née pour venger mon sexe et maîtriser le
vôtre, j'avais su me créer des moyens inconnus jusqu'à moi? (81, p. 174)

If . . . you have observed how, arranging events and opinions, I turn these men
that are so dangerous into the toys of my whims and fancy; depriving some of
the desire to harm me, others of the capacity; . . . if, in the midst of these
frequent upheavals, my reputation has nonetheless retained its purity, should
you not have concluded that, born to avenge my sex and to master yours, I
have succeeded in creating for myself means unknown before me?

Yet this uniqueness is also a delusion. Like those she despises, indeed like
all of the master figures of her century, the marquise reiterates a pattern of
dialogical dependency: she requires for the confirmation of her superiority
the validation of her story by an Other. For the libertine more than for any
previous type of character, identity derives entirely from the transaction
with the Other, whether conceived individually as the object of one's erotic
triumphs, or collectively as the public opinion which one molds by means of
such triumphs. That Merteuil feels compelled to persuade Valmont of her
uniqueness, stands as an ironic disproof of her difference: she may claim to
be above convention, but she remains determined by the deep structure of
the libertine script. She cannot confirm her mastery in solitude; as much as
Valmont, she requires an appreciative, initiated public. That is why she
relates all of her exploits to the vicomte, including her duping of Prévan,
which he cautioned her against attempting, and that is why, when she
senses that he does not grasp the extent of her accomplishments, she goes
against her own principles and relates to him the story of her entire life, the
details of which are specific enough to allow her subsequent identification.[18]
Ironically those two letters which were designed to convince Valmont of her
control of the laws of her culture – the account of her life story and her
tale of how she engineered the rape charge against Prévan – bring about
her disgrace and banishment when Valmont makes them public and their
precise detail permits identification of the marquise.[19] Merteuil cannot
finally control the readership she needs for her sense of superiority. Once
she loses control of her Other, she loses hold of her identity as well. Like a
textual fragment that is reread in a new context, she is both figurally and
literally dis-figured: repudiated by the society that adored her and scarred
by an attack of smallpox.

Valmont's downfall is also ironic, in that it comes about in part because
of his very success as an author: he writes himself into two opposing plots
and characters, only to find the characters interfering with each other and
the plots increasingly restricting his range of options. The character he
elaborates for Tourvel is that of the totally infatuated lover; for Merteuil he

presents himself as the completely detached artist. Each of these roles corresponds to the character of the women he addresses, and each implies a different relationship to narrative: the infatuated lover, like Tourvel, reads and writes naively, says what he means, and is a pawn of rhetoric; the detached artist never says what he means, is immune to the surface arguments of texts, and exercises complete control over his reader.

As Valmont's narrative seduction of Tourvel develops, his ability to resist the positional force of his own discourse becomes increasingly questionable. At the outset of his campaign, he notes that technically speaking his behavior suggests he is in love: "si l'amour est de ne pouvoir vivre sans posséder ce qu'on désire, d'y sacrifier son temps, ses plaisirs, sa vie, je suis bien réellement amoureux" (15, p. 34) (if love is not being able to live without possessing that which one desires, sacrificing for it one's time, pleasures, and life, then I am indeed really in love). As the story progresses, his commentary on his reactions to diverse episodes leads us to suspect he might well have lost control and assumed the character he paints for Tourvel:

> Je l'avoue, je cédai à un mouvement de jeune homme, et baisai cette lettre avec un transport dont je ne me croyais plus susceptible. (44, p. 94)

> Mais quelle fatalité m'attache à cette femme? cent autres ne désirent-elles pas mes soins? . . . Pourquoi courir après [le plaisir] qui nous fuit, et négliger ceux qui se présentent? Ah! pourquoi? . . . Je l'ignore, mais je l'éprouve fortement. (100, pp. 230–1)

> J'ai besoin de me faire violence pour me distraire de l'impression qu'elle m'a faite; c'est même pour m'y aider, que je me suis mis à vous écrire. (99, p. 225)

> Serai-je donc, à mon âge, maîtrisé comme un écolier, par un sentiment involontaire et inconnu? (125, p. 292)[20]

> I admit it, I gave in to an adolescent's impulse and kissed that letter with a transport I no longer thought myself capable of.

> But what fatality attaches me to this woman? do not a hundred others desire my attention? . . . Why run after the pleasure which flees us and neglect those which present themselves? Ah, why? . . . I know not, but I feel it strongly.

> I need to force myself not to think about the impression she made on me; indeed, it is to help me do so that I set about writing you.

> Am I to be thus at my age overcome like a schoolboy by an involuntary and unknown feeling?

At one point, Valmont will even compare his behavior to Danceny's innocent love for Cécile (57, p. 116) – a comparison not completely ludicrous, in light of his state following the consummation of the affair:

L'ivresse fut complète et réciproque; et, pour la première fois, la mienne survécut au plaisir. Je ne sortis de ses bras que pour tomber à ses genoux, pour lui jurer un amour éternel; et, il faut tout avouer, je pensais ce que je disais. Enfin, même après nous être séparés, son idée ne me quittait point, et j'ai eu besoin de me travailler pour m'en distraire. (125, p. 300)[21]

The intoxication was total and reciprocal; and, for the first time, mine outlived the carnal pleasure. I left her arms only to fall at her feet, in order to swear eternal love to her; and, I must admit all, I believed what I said. Finally, even after having separated, the thought of her would not leave me, and I had to work at it to distract myself from it.

For Merteuil, who, as we shall see, increasingly disputes Valmont's readings of his story, such descriptions leave little doubt that the libertine has lost his detachment and succumbed to love.

Whether or not one assumes Valmont to have become completely absorbed by the passion he claims to emulate for Tourvel, it is clear that he entraps himself in the part he plays for Merteuil. Having staked his identity on his "art," he is compelled to live up to the role of the ultimate seducer even when he no longer relishes that role. Like history, or the great scroll in *Jacques le fataliste*, the totality of his story at all moments frames his current behavior, determining the meaning which any action will take. Valmont is in a sense free to do anything he wishes, but he can only control the significance of his acts for others – which is, after all, the heart of the libertine project – if he attends to the context of their interpretation. In that respect, his developing adventure, whether it be fiction or fact, encloses him in a ever more limited script of possibilities. Having committed himself to the character of the heartless seducer and enriched this role with a panoply of secondary anecdotes intended to confirm it in the eyes of his readership, he finds himself excluded from any behavior that would be "out of character." As he protests to Merteuil, "je ne suis point amoureux; et ce n'est pas ma faute si les circonstances me forcent d'en jouer le rôle" (138, p. 326) (I am not in love; and it is not my fault if circumstances force me to play that role).

This is the risk of merging selfhood with narrative: the versions of one's self which one puts into circulation remain in circulation permanently, accruing interest, as it were, over time, as they frame, and thus effect the meaning of, the new stories which in turn modify them. To the extent that this historical accretion of identity – this personal history – perpetuates itself in the consciousness of the Others for whom it is devised, it resists government by the individual whose identity it determines. Unlike the early novels of self-determination, Laclos' novel no longer tolerates the delusion of an individual identity which is based in collective discourse but answers to the dictates of a single author: the shape of history cannot be traced to any one intentionality or located in any specific moment or fragment of narration; it is a permanently evolving collective story that *takes into account* the individual's version but need never account to the individual.

Even as Valmont struggles to maintain his two diverging characters and readerships, Merteuil becomes a progressively contentiousness reader, disputing, by means of a careful exegesis of his narratives, not only Valmont's actions, but his grasp of the truth concerning his feelings. Challenging his reading of Tourvel (letter 106), his understanding of women in general (letter 113), his assumptions about their own relationship and agreement (letter 127), and especially his grasp of his own situation (letters 134, 141), she bases her arguments on citations of Valmont's own narrative, which she italicizes to make her point:

> En effect, ce n'est plus l'adorable, la céleste Mme de Tourvel: mais c'est *une femme étonnante, une femme délicate et sensible*, et cela, à l'exclusion de toutes les autres; *une femme rare* enfin, et telle *qu'on n'en rencontrerait pas une seconde.* Il en est de même de ce charme inconnu, qui n'est pas *le plus fort*. Hé bien! soit: mais puisque vous ne l'aviez jamais trouvé jusques-là, il est bien à croire que vous ne le trouveriez pas davantage à l'avenir, et la perte que vous feriez n'en serait pas moins irréparable. Ou ce sont-là, Vicomte, des symptômes infaillibles d'amour, ou il faut renoncer à en trouver aucun. (134, p. 318)

> In effect, she is no longer the adorable, the heavenly Mme de Tourvel: but she is *a surprising woman, a delicate and sensitive woman*, and that to the exclusion of all the others; *a rare woman* finally, and such *that one could never encounter a second one like her*. The same applies to this unknown charm, which is not *the most remarkable*. Well, so be it! but since you had never found it up to now, it is to be believed that you would be no more likely to find it in the future, and the loss which you would suffer would be no less irreparable. If those are not symptoms of love, viscount, we might as well give up trying to find any.

Repeatedly confronted by his own words, Valmont will, ironically, disclaim control of their meaning: "ces mots, plus souvent pris au hasard que par réflexion, expriment moins le cas qu'on fait de la personne, que la situation dans laquelle on se trouve quand on en parle" (129, p. 307) (those words, more often chosen at random than deliberately, express less one's esteem for the person, than the situation in which one finds oneself when speaking of her), but such a claim is patently inconsonant with the claim of virtuosity and only serves to reinforce Merteuil's conclusion that he has lost control. Even on the lexical level, the economy of history puts the would-be master in a double bind: unable to disavow responsibility for his words, neither can he control their meaning or the stories they authorize. Reread in the framework of his own fiction, and in the context of a hostile motivation, Valmont's rhetoric turns against him, giving the lie to his pretense of mastery and entangling him in a series of contradictory claims.

The final step in his loss of control occurs when Merteuil literally takes over the duties of authorship from him. She composes a short parable about a man who has become bogged down in an adventure unworthy of him, and whose "embarras était d'autant plus grand, qu'il s'était vanté à ses amis d'être entièrement libre" (141, p. 333) (embarrassment was all the greater because he had boasted to his friends of being completely free). This she sends to Valmont along with a cruel letter for Tourvel, composed on the refrain of Valmont's own pathetic disclaimer ("ce n'est pas ma faute") (it is not my fault), which the vicomte dutifully recopies and sends off.[22] Only then does Merteuil reveal to Valmont the extent to which he has been the victim of his own fiction:

> Oui, Vicomte, vous aimiez beaucoup Mme de Tourvel, et même vous l'aimez encore; vous l'aimez comme un fou: mais parce que je m'amusais à vous en faire honte, vous l'avez bravement sacrifiée. Vous en auriez sacrifié mille plutôt que de souffrir une plaisanterie. Où nous conduit pourtant la vanité! (145, p. 340)

> Yes viscount, you loved Mme de Tourvel deeply, and you even love her still; you love her madly: but because I amused myself with making you ashamed of it, you dutifully sacrificed her. You would have sacrificed a thousand, rather than tolerate a jest. To what extremes vanity drives us!

Ultimately, it is not Valmont who writes the plot, but the plot which writes him. He cannot forestall its outcome or manage the readings which his peers impose on its episodes; yet he is subject to the identity those readings impose. By quite literally holding him to his word(s), Merteuil forces him to assume the destiny he prescribed for himself and deprives him of the freedom that script was supposed to confirm. She can rightfully boast, "je dirigeais vos coups" (145, p. 340) (I directed your blows): she has appropriated authority from the master author.

If the marquise and Valmont fail in their attempts to master each other and the epistolary machine that empowers them, there is good reason to suspect that the reader of *Les Liaisons dangereuses* might also be in a position of vulnerability. Although the struggle to absorb or possess the Other can be conceptualized in terms of a love triangle between Valmont, Tourvel, and Merteuil, it also explicitly involves reading, and the relationship between authors, fictions, and readers.[23] The two libertines relate entirely by letter, after all, and both of their projects fail, in the final analysis, because they cannot control their reader. Given that the relationship of the marquise and the vicomte is mediated entirely by texts, and that their reliance on detached analysis, characterization, plot construction, and close reading parallels that of the novelist and reader, it is difficult not to read their failed attempt at mastery as a commentary on the epistemological privilege of novelists and their readers which preoccupies the second half of the eighteenth century. All the more so since the libertines' most obvious advantage resides in a contextual advantage which mirrors that of the reader: by breaking one of the fundamental rules of private correspondence and conveying to each other all of the letters and private information that they receive, they can evaluate each letter within the context of its author's other statements. They consolidate this advantage by stealing letters, authoring letters attributed to another, and guiding others in the composition of their letters. By intruding on the epistolary economy and putting themselves in the place of the letter's author or reader, they can not only control the flow of information but assume multiple functional identities in the mechanism of exchange, thereby putting themselves in a position to determine the meaning of each text with more certainty than their adversaries.

The reader's position reiterates this advantage, but more absolutely: we have access to virtually all of the letters written by everyone in the novel. By comparing letters to different parties from the same writer, we can presumably obtain a more complete picture of that writer's personality and determine when he or she is telling the truth and to whom. More generally, our privileged access to all information gives us an insight into the complexity and "real" meaning of many of the episodes reported in the letters: events such as the discovery by Madame de Volanges of Cécile's secret correspondence reveal their significance only when we, like Valmont, learn how Merteuil engineered the whole affair. Similarly, we share in the smug irony of the libertines: Valmont's outrageous running pun in letter 48 can only be savored – or deplored – in the light of the explanation of his situation which he provides for Merteuil.

The book nurtures in its reader a growing conviction of semiotic superiority. Valmont's cynical stylistic analyzes of the love letters he pens to Tourvel provide us, and Merteuil, for whose amusement the commentary is designed, with the illusion of a certain readerly sophistication: unlike poor Tourvel, we are aware of the degree to which such love letters are merely formulaic and express nothing more than the rhetorical art of their authors, so that even once the commentary ceases, we will know enough not to take Valmont seriously. Similarly, we know, as Tourvel cannot, the true motives behind Valmont's "conversion." There are even moral repercussions to our omniscience: it is difficult not to conclude that even the most virtuous person has a devious side, when we see Mme de Tourvel conceal part of the truth from her confidante, Mme de Volanges – and ultimately change confidantes, when the truth becomes more than she can hide.

In short, we the readers know, as none of the characters can, what is "really" happening in the plot. Or at least that is what the epistolary mode tempts us into assuming. I would argue that while the narrative mode and plot structure of *Les Liaisons dangereuses* give us an exaggerated sense of "knowing what is happening," and thus promote us to a position of authority analogous to that of the Author in the works of Fielding, Rousseau, and Diderot, they also undercut that authority by making it virtually impossible to impose any closure on the text. The narrative seduces us into a delusion of detached mastery akin to that of its protagonists, only to suspend us in a proliferation of meanings which resist the closure they invite.

As in the case of the libertines, this turn of events is inscribed in the very grammars of control which give us our privileged viewpoint. To begin with, the proliferation of narrative viewpoints, access to all of which only we enjoy, also entails the lack of a single narrative ground. In a text explicitly structured by conflicting deceits, where determining the truth value of any given letter is crucial to understanding what is happening, this creates insoluble problems. Even if we could determine whether or not the vicomte is sincere when he declares "I am not in love" (which we cannot), we have no way of knowing whether or not it is the truth, since Merteuil, who carries at least equal authority in the narrative, unequivocally maintains that he *is* in love, and that his statements can only be read as self-delusion or lies: "vous faites-vous illusion à vous-même, ou cherchez-vous à me tromper? la différence entre vos discours et vos actions ne me laisse de choix qu'entre ces deux sentiments" (141, p. 332) (are you deluding yourself, or are you trying to deceive me? the disparity between your words and your actions leaves me no choice other than these two feelings). Narrative unreliability in previous novels is generally local: Clarissa does not initially know whether Lovelace is to be trusted, but the reader does. Here, the reader enjoys no more reliable means of ascertaining the truth than the two master narrators framed in the story: Merteuil draws her conclusions on the basis of the same texts by Valmont as we do, which she reads in approximately the same order and context.

Already complicated by this fundamental undecidability, our task is made considerably more difficult by the multiplicity of conventional fields which the novel invokes – even before the commencement of the correspondence. Two diametrically opposed prefaces, which echo both Rousseau's refusal to pronounce on the historicity of *Julie* and Diderot's insistence that the fiction of *Jacques le fataliste* is history, suspend the reader from the outset between two competing sets of conventions: those of fiction and those of real letters.

The first statement, the "Avertissement de l'éditeur" or publisher's preface, inverts the standard claim of historical veracity of the eighteenth century by warning us that, notwithstanding the claims of the editor which follow, there is strong reason to suspect the collection of letters to be a mere novel. To support this claim, the publisher points out, in strongly ironic terms, the lack of correlation between the behavior depicted in the work and the mores of his period, crowning his argument with the snide observation "que sans doute les mêmes causes ne manqueraient pas de produire les mêmes effets; et que cependant nous ne voyons point aujourd'hui de demoiselle, avec soixante mille livres de rente, se faire religieuse, ni de présidente, jeune et jolie, mourir de chagrin" (p. 1) (no doubt the same causes would not fail to produce the same effects; and yet we find no young heiress today with sixty thousand pounds income who chooses to become a nun, nor any young attractive wife of a magistrate dying of heartbreak).

Counterbalancing this eminently worldly warning, the "Préface du rédacteur," or editor's foreword, exposes in the humble terms of sober morality the story of how the editor came into possession of the letters and why he felt compelled to publish them. His arguments, which are implicit in the full title of the novel (*Lettres recueillies dans une société et publiées pour l'instruction de quelques autres*), rely on the familiar criteria of the useful and the agreeable to justify his publication: by negative example the book might teach mothers how not to raise their daughters; the exposure of the libertines' stratagems might forearm potential victims; the diversity of styles and voices should prove interesting to a reader who might be bored by the uniformity of a single author's tone.

Taken at face value, these two prefatory statements call upon us to read the text as both a fiction and as the truth, to read all of the letters as the work of one calculating mind and to read them as a complex melody of individual voices. The cynical reader may of course discount the claims of the second preface as a *pro forma* gesture, or even as a parody of the claim of historicity which nearly every eighteenth-century novel includes. But the first preface specifically invites us *not* to take its own claim at face value, by phrasing it in the language of heavy irony: how can we take literally a narrator who refers to the age of libertinage as "ce siècle de philosophie, où les lumières, répandues de toutes parts, ont rendu, comme chacun le sait, tous les hommes si honnêtes et toutes les femmes si modestes et si réservés" (this century of philosophy, where the universal enlightenment has, as everyone knows, rendered all the men so honest and all the women so modest and reserved)? Moreover, the publisher's admonition to read the letters as fiction, imposes on the reader a task that goes against the very form of the novel: to read all of the texts as the work of a single authorial intention requires that we try to overlook the obvious stylistic differences of the letters and evaluate them exclusively in terms of their role in some larger scheme or moral lesson. This is not only to resist precisely the identification with the author or recipient which the epistolary format invites, but also to defuse the question of truth and deceit which lies at the heart of the plot.

Reading the letters *as* letters, however, in no way obviates these difficulties. As I mentioned earlier, the conventions of personal correspondence carry their own ambivalence with them, in that any given letter can be read as either expression or interpretation, either a document of the writer's state of mind or an anticipation of the receiver's future reaction. Strictly speaking, this binary structure makes it impossible to determine exactly when or where a given event occurs, since every letter not only exists in two intentions, two moments and two places, but displays two functions: it is necessarily both a response (to the previous letter) and the elicitation of a response; its ultimate effect is permanently deferred and, to that extent, it only provisionally confirms the effect of the letter it answers.[24] There is no way of determining precisely how the election of one of these functions or identities of the letter affects a given reader, or in general which readers will elect to read whose letters from which viewpoint. It is clear, however, that the possibility of two different perspectives, either of which is permanently available, but not simultaneously with its converse, opens the possibility for an endless number of permutations within the multi-authored correspondence of *Les Liaisons dangereuses* – particularly when these conventions are crossed with those of the novel, which pressure us to read the letters in the *third* person, as the contrivance of some uninvolved party.

At the same time, our privileged viewpoint on the entire epistolary network entraps us into making discriminations that are not necessarily justified. For example, because we have access to Valmont's letters to Merteuil and to the fact that he sends her copies of his letters to Tourvel, we tend to discount his love letters to the latter: instead of documents of his feelings, we read them as masterpieces of deceit and subversion. We suspend, in other words, our interpretative apparatus, since we already "know" where the libertines stand. When Valmont exclaims to the présidente "il suffit de vous voir, pour désirer de vous plaire" (83, p. 184) (seeing you is enough to make one want to please you), we do not for a minute assume this statement to represent his inner feelings. There is no way of deciding whether or not this is the correct way of reading Valmont's letters, since, as we have seen, his subsequent behavior raises questions about his own knowledge of his emotional state – as Merteuil points out. However, that is not the point. What is crucial is that the novel's structure guides us towards an interpretive bias which not only contradicts the principles of narrative mastery upon which it is based, but undercuts the novel's moral agenda it claims to serve.

Should we succumb to Valmont's delusion that we can stabilize the value of the letters, separating sincerity from ruse, we ironically relinquish our own detachment in a novel that consistently preaches the need for detachment if we are to perceive the truth: ludicrously enough, we identify with the viewpoint of a character whose every move is calculated to discredit identification; we take at face value the statements of someone who delights in deceit. This is particularly ironic given that the letters disclaiming true love could not really say anything other than what they do, given the identity of their addressee, Merteuil.

Second, to privilege Valmont's viewpoint and his reading of himself over Tourvel's is to lend greater credence or truth value to letters that deny sincerity of emotion, simplicity of expression, and moral honesty. This is a questionable position at best in a novel whose perverse displays of erotic cruelty are justified by the claim that "c'est rendre un service aux mœurs, que de dévoiler les moyens qu'emploient ceux qui en ont de mauvaises pour corrompre ceux qui en ont de bonnes" ("Préface du rédacteur," p. 5) (it is rendering a service to public morality to reveal the means used by those of bad morals to corrupt those of good morals). We cannot exercise our mastery of the novel's complex schemes and appreciate the means by which Valmont victimizes Tourvel without devalorizing the honest discourse she represents in favor of his cynical rhetoric of detachment. In our attempt to read the text morally, distinguishing good from bad, we subvert the moral position it defends.

Other such paradoxes abound in the text, particularly as regards Merteuil's relationship to Valmont – one need only think of the problems involved in taking at face value Merteuil's evaluation of Valmont, when she has patiently explained that the fundamental principle of her survival is *never* to reveal what she is thinking. To attempt to sort such double reversals out is to involve oneself in an infinite regress, given the context of their articulation and the conventional ambivalence of their narrative mode. Between the fictions of a rake whose identity is founded on deceit and whose control of his story is uncertain, and the interpretations of a master author who personifies the paradox of the liar, the reader has no solid ground upon which to stand, no stable context within which to evaluate any portion of the text.

Finally, it is not just the character of Merteuil or Valmont which causes the problem, but the dynamic epistolary structure with its multiple, conflicting frameworks of interpretation. As the two prefaces imply, with their divergent invocations of fiction and real correspondence, the interpretive regresses which *Les Liaisons dangereuses* provokes have less to do with authorial intention than with the conventions framing the book's reception. This is an idea we encountered in Rousseau and the works of Sterne and Diderot, where the parameters of the dialogical paradigm are redefined to include the relationship of individual instance of meaning to the grounding conventions of shared discourse, and where the meaning of the work is explicitly linked to the conventions governing its reception.[25] But *Les Liaisons dangereuses* goes one step further than its predecessors in that rather than simply thematize the framing of the reader by convention, it enacts it.

In the earlier metanovels, as in all novels that incorporate "the reader" into their plots, the explicit thematization of a reading consciousness exempts the real reader from what one might call profound implication: the thematized Reader takes his/her place among the characters of the book and his/her reactions, as outlined in the narrative, are manifestly distinct from ours. To the extent we feel involved in such reactions, it will only be through an identification with this "reader" within the confines of the plot. This is involvement by choice, dictated by our recognition that the conventions regulating the activity of the thematized Reader also, in principle, regulate ours.

Quite different is the mechanism of profound implication in *Les Liaisons dangereuses*, where we do not necessarily perceive the parallels between our plight and that of the characters. Rather than pointing out a similarity between our presumptions and those of the characters – and then offering us disinvolvement through the insertion of a proxy Reader's reactions – the text channels us into a pattern of behavior that approximates the characters' precisely to the extent it remains unaware of its own precariousness. Deluded by the privilege which the conventions of the epistolary novel seem to offer, we overlook the more fundamental assumptions that frame and define our gestures. That a given reader may remain totally unconvinced of this precariousness and persist in believing she or he controls the text's ambiguity only illustrates the subtlety of the system. The example of Merteuil prefigures this possibility, in that it illustrates how one may lose control of the system and become its victim rather than its master without ever acknowledging that fact. Even when confronted with her own downfall, the marquise remains unmoved, giving no evidence that she has accepted her fallibility or is even aware of it.

Les Liaisons dangereuses invites any number of arguments condemning or defending various characters, all of which will find substantiation in the text, but none of which can ever impose closure by appealing to a mediating authority beyond the event of their own articulation. By multiplying the conventional frameworks in which every textual fragment can be read, the author does away with the primacy of the single narrative voice, absents himself from the text, and extends to the reader the authority he declines. By prefacing the collection of letters with contradictory evaluations of its intent and origin, he obscures his own position, and shifts responsibility for the effect of his work to a system of semiotic exchange and the interpretive activity it grounds. That activity, however, can never completely master the text, since both text and reading are suspended between contradictory conventional fields, one of which – that of the personal letter – compels by its very nature a *partial* reading. Our only option is to deploy our different evaluations of the letters in successive readings, renouncing the certainty of knowing exactly what is happening or exactly what any letter means in favor of a continually evolving understanding of the text that is by definition provisional and unending. In this sense, though it may not talk about the historical imbrication of the reader, *Les Liaisons dangereuses* enacts it. The reading gesture that sets out to master the story finds itself suspended in history, asserting itself through its gradual progress toward an end it can never know.[26]

If the reader's implication in the novel's history coincides with the Reader's disappearance from its roster of major characters, the Author's (and author's) disappearance in *Les Liaisons dangereuses* can be correlated to a negative assertion of authority. In effect, the two prefaces, with their oblique allusions to convention as the ground of meaning, foreshadow the indirect strategy by which authors in the nineteenth century will exercise their mastery. To acknowledge the suspension of meaning in a semiotic economy that defies closure is to dissociate oneself from the repercussions of one's text, while at the same time asserting a form of mastery through knowledge. And this is a particularly apt strategy for Laclos: having demonstrated the power and uncontrollability of fictions, and predicated the impossibility of a narrative that is not bound up in some form of self-serving motivation, it would hardly be in his best interests to claim the text as his own. By adopting the metaperspective that characterizes all agendas of mastery, by telling us he *knows* he cannot control the meaning of his text, Laclos reasserts his grasp of the economy, while at the same time disavowing any responsibility for its effects. His is a willing renunciation of control that counters the text's negation of narrative mastery with a suspended claim to the paternity of that negation. Faced with the inevitable absorption of individual volition within the system that enables it, he gives himself over to the system and leaves open the possibility that it is his own creation.

NOTES

1 *Les Liaisons dangereuses* was published in English in 1784 as *Dangerous Connections, or Letters Collected in a Society and published for the instruction of other societies*, by M. C∗∗∗ de L∗∗∗, 4 vols (London: T. Hookham, 1784).

2   Frank Gees Black lists no less than 816 works published between 1740 and 1840
    which exploited variations on the epistolary mode; *The Epistolary Novel in the
    Late Eighteenth Century*, Studies in Literature and Philology, no. 2 (Eugene,
    Oregon: University of Oregon Press, 1940). For other histories of the epistolary
    mode, see Godfrey Frank Singer, *The Epistolary Novel* (Philadelphia: Univer-
    sity of Pennsylvania Press, 1933); Charles E. Kany, *The Beginnings of the
    Epistolary Novel in France, Italy, and Spain* (Berkeley: University of California
    Press, 1937); and Laurent Versini, *Laclos et la tradition* (Paris: Klincksieck,
    1968).

3   For theoretical studies of the epistolary form, see François Jost, "Le Roman
    épistolaire et la technique narrative au XVIIIe siècle," *Comparative Literature
    Studies*, 3 (1966), pp. 397–427; Janet Gurkin Altman, *Epistolarity: Approaches
    to a Form* (Columbus, Ohio: Ohio State University Press, 1982); Jean Rousset,
    Forme et signification, pp. 65–108. Further analyses with specific reference to *Les
    Liaisons dangereuses* can be found in Christine Belcikowski, *Poétique des Liaisons
    dangereuses* (Paris: José Corti, 1972); Jean-Louis Seylaz, *Les Liaisons dangereuses
    et la création romanesque chez Laclos* (Paris: Droz-Minard, 1958); Dorothy R.
    Thelander, *Laclos and the Epistolary Novel* (Geneva: Droz, 1963); Ronald
    Rosbottom, *Choderlos de Laclos* (Boston: G. K. Hall, 1978); Tzvetan Todorov,
    Littérature et Signification (Paris: Larousse, 1967); Peter Brooks, *The Novel of
    Worldliness* (New Haven: Yale University Press, 1969); Vivienne Mylne, *The
    Eighteenth-century French Novel: Techniques of Illusion* (Manchester: Manchester
    University Press, 1965), and Peggy Kamuf, *Fictions of Feminine Desire* (Lin-
    coln, Nebraska: University of Nebraska Press, 1982).

4   Jost, "Roman épistolaire," p. 411. Jost distinguishes between dynamic epistol-
    ary novels and passive, or static ones, such as *La Vie de Marianne*, where the
    protagonist merely relates his or her experience through letters to a passive
    reader; see p. 406. See also Mylne, *Novel*, p. 150.

5   That exception is the comte de Gercourt, whose short informative note to
    Madame de Volanges is unanswered (111, p. 262). There is also one mute
    "post-box" character, who receives letters but never writes: Sophie Carnay,
    who serves as Cécile's sounding board before the latter is involved with Dan-
    ceny, Valmont, and Merteuil. Neither Gercourt nor Sophie play any significant
    role in the action of the novel.

6   This definition seems contorted, but it corresponds to the usage portrayed not
    only in *Les Liaisons dangereuses*, but in other famous libertine novels such as
    Crébillon's *Les Egarements du cœur et de l'esprit* and Duclos' *Les Mémoires du
    comte de M***. Although men, particularly men "à la mode" as Duclos puts
    it, are assumed to have seduced large numbers of women, they cannot with
    impunity be caught in the act: Valmont's uneasiness over Cécile's nocturnal
    squealing, and his desire to hush up her miscarriage indicate as much. Indeed,
    his death is ultimately the result of being figuratively caught in the act with
    Cécile, since the duel with Danceny is motivated by the latter's learning of their
    affair. Prévan almost suffers a similar fate at the hands of the "inseparables'"
    lovers, and, of course, his imprisonment and dismissal from his post results
    from being caught with his pants down (literally) in Merteuil's bedroom. It is

also clear that women *suspected* of having monopolized the attentions of the stylish men, but who cannot be *shown* to have had an affair, enjoy remarkable prestige in the libertine world. Duclos' stylish comte de M∗∗∗ is quite explicit about the prestige his suspected affairs confer upon the women involved. Similarly, Mme de Merteuil's status comes not from a record of flawless virtue – Mme de Volanges notes "quelques inconséquences qu'on avait à lui reprocher au début de son veuvage" (9, p. 23) (a few slips which could be held against her at the beginning of her widowhood) and Prévan openly disputes her virtue (70, p. 140) – but from the fact that no one can prove anything. She benefits from the prestige of having been courted by Valmont, but there exists no evidence that she succumbed to his charms.

7   References are to the letter number and page in the Yves Le Hir edition (Paris: Garnier Frères, 1961). Translations are my own. As Peter Brooks points out, there is a strong implication in *Les Liaisons dangereuses* that the values of the marquise de Merteuil apply to all of the women of *le monde*, or fashionable society. Those women who delight in the marquise's ultimate exposure and disgrace differ from her "only in the lesser success and daring of the exploits; their present advantage comes only from their being luckier in their disguises, and their love is not of morality but of *médisance*, which they can now direct toward the previously inviolate Mme de Merteuil" (*Novel of Worldliness*, p. 212).

8   They only come into physical proximity once, near the end of the novel, when Valmont forces his way into Merteuil's house to discover her with Danceny (letter 151). Ironically, this brief reunion, which was originally proposed as a means of celebrating their respective triumphs, precipitates their confrontation and mutual destruction. Substituting unmediated communion for the dialogic ambiguity of epistolarity is not the final step in the mastery of history; rather, it confirms that one cannot achieve such mastery.

9   See Brooks, *Novel of Worldliness*, p. 177: "... to reduce social relations to erotic relations, human behavior to erotic comportment, as Valmont and the Marquise continually try to do, is to operate an important mechanization of social laws and human existence".

10 As Jean Rousset points out, the entire plot of *Les Liaisons dangereuses* can be read as the triumph of love over principle, both for the prude, Tourvel, and the libertines; *Forme et signification*, p. 98. Such a reading is not incompatible with the one I propose, since love as Rousset characterizes it is precisely a loss of control over one's behavior and the disruption of one's plans.

11 The interpolated story of Prévan, the rake/artist who manages to seduce and humiliate three inseparable friends simultaneously, is paradigmatic of the value system in question, as are, of course, Valmont's and Merteuil's various secondary triumphs, including the latter's destruction of Prévan; cf. letters 47–8, 71, 79, 85, 96, 138.

12 Tourvel characterizes herself as completely incapable of guile in letter 26. Her subsequent behavior, particularly her change of female correspondents once she is involved with Valmont, puts this assessment into doubt.

13 Similarly, Valmont's justification of his excitement over Tourvel focuses on her

role as an embodiment of the moral and religious values of her culture – the product of precisely those institutions most opposed to his megalomaniacal practice.

14 For Merteuil's criticism of Valmont's conventionality, see 106, p. 248; 113, p. 267; 141, p. 332.

15 Merteuil and Valmont frequently express their exploits in literary terms: the marquise refers to her plots as *romans*, and specifies in her first letter that she will include the seduction of Cécile in Valmont's *mémoires*, which she intends to write (2, pp. 9–10; 81, p. 181). Valmont sees himself as something of a legend in the making: in his first letter he boasts that "je vais vous confier le plus grand projet qu'un conquérant ait jamais pu former" (I am going to entrust you with the greatest project that a conqueror has ever formulated), an "entreprise qui . . . m'assure autant de gloire que de plaisir" (enterprise that assures me as much glory as pleasure) (4, p. 13). He amplifies this subsequently (letter 144) and rephrases his exploits in literary terms (letter 115).

16 The marquise de Merteuil's attempt at completely self-enclosed self-definition, at grasping herself simultaneously as creator and created, would seem an extreme example of what Marie-Paul Laden identifies as the fundamental paradox of self-representation: "the fact that the self cannot ever truly designate itself"; *Self-Imitation in the Eighteenth-Century Novel* (Princeton: Princeton University Press, 1987), p. 156.

17 That this is the case finds ample confirmation in the plot. When Valmont momentarily submits to Merteuil by allowing her to take command of his relationship with Tourvel, he loses control over Tourvel, the marquise, and his own plot in a single stroke. His desperate attempts to regain mastery over his situation and re-establish an equilibrium between himself and Merteuil lead directly to their final confrontation and ultimate mutual destruction.

18 Altman, *Epistolarity*, pp. 79–80, sees Merteuil as exempt from the need for an approving public and motivated entirely by a desire to have Valmont play "the lover's game" with her. I think the presence of the extraordinary biographical letter (81), which plays no role in advancing either of their plots, which has virtually no erotic value, and whose only motivation can be to elicit in Valmont an appreciation of the marquise's remarkable mastery, testifies quite amply to the contrary.

19 See Altman, *Epistolarity*, p. 81.

20 See also letter 6, pp. 18–19: "Vous le dirai-je? je croyais mon cœur flétri; et ne me trouvant plus que des sens, je me plaignais d'une vieillesse prématurée. Mme de Tourvel m'a rendu les charmantes illusions de la jeunesse" (Dare I tell you? I thought my heart withered; and finding in myself nothing other than my senses, I lamented my premature old age. Mme de Tourvel has restored to me the charming illusions of youth).

21 Brooks sees in this admission of intoxication the source of Merteuil's jealousy, since she too exhibits "a conscious desire to lose herself" but is unable to (*Novel of Worldliness*, p.198). In any case, narrating his rapture to a former mistress whose jealousy it is almost certain to inspire, does testify to a loss of prescience on Valmont's part.

22   Interestingly enough, Merteuil is also citing herself with the refrain "ce n'est pas ma faute," which she uses earlier to ironize Valmont's slow progress with Tourvel (106, p. 250). Were Valmont a keen enough reader to notice this, he might suspect that he is being manipulated through his vanity to appease that of his accomplice/rival.

23   This is no mere analogy; the great bulk of their correspondence consists of pure narrative: Valmont relating, in addition to the day to day progress of his campaign against Tourvel, his brief dalliances with Emilie (letters 47, 138), his adventure with the vicomtesse de M. (letter 71), his seduction of Cécile (letter 96), the latter's miscarriage (letter 141), and the story of Prévan's simultaneous triple seduction (letter 79); Merteuil relating her project to satiate Belleroche (letter 10), the ongoing Cécile–Danceny affair, her destruction of Prévan (letter 85), and, most important, the story of her life and principles (letter 81).

24   One can also correlate the letter's difference from itself with the dialogical structure of selfhood. As first-person narration, the letter is an expression of the self for the Other; as second-person narrative, it is an impression of the Other which the self elaborates. The writing self expresses itself as an image it projects onto the Other: foreseeing the reader's reaction, it takes it into account in its projected identity. The reading self expropriates its identity into an interpretation of the Other: the Other forms the locus of its attention even though that Other, emerging only through interpretation, constitutes an elaboration of the self. These two formulations do not correspond to two different entities, but rather to the two faces every narrative presents us at all moments. Letters are different from most texts in that they are the single form of everyday textuality in which we regularly experience both perspectives, whereas, with the exception of authors and academics, most readers treat literature as narrative.

25   This is particularly apparent in the *Entretien sur les romans* which accompanies *Julie, ou la nouvelle Héloïse*, and where the distinction between the *tableau* and the *portrait*, and the interest each elicits in the reader, is located squarely in the conventions of the two genres. See above, chap. 12.

26   To the extent that this paradigm of permanent recontextualization and reinterpretation coincides with the institution of literary criticism as it develops in the nineteenth century, *Les Liaisons dangereuses* can be said to prefigure its own assimilation into the economy of literary debate.

Bibliography

Adam, Antoine, ed. *Romanciers du XVIIe siècle*. Paris: Gallimard "Bibliothèque de la Pléiade," 1958.

Alter, Robert. *Fielding and the Nature of the Novel*. Cambridge, Mass.: Harvard University Press, 1968.

—— *Rogue's Progress*. Cambridge, Mass.: Harvard University Press, 1964.

Altman, Janet. *Epistolarity: Approaches to a Form*. Columbus, Ohio: Ohio State University Press, 1982.

Argens, Jean Baptiste de Boyer, marquis d'. *La Philosophie du bon sens ou reflexions philosophiques sur l'incertitude des connoissances humaines, à l'usage des cavaliers & du beau-sexe*, revûë, corrigée, & augmentée d'un examen critique des remarques de Mr. l'Abbé d'Olivet. 3 vols. The Hague: Pierre Paupie, 1747.

—— *Lettres juives*, nouvelle édition. 8 vols. La Haye: Pierre Paupie, 1754.

Aristotle. *Poetics*, trans. Thomas Twining, ed. T. A. Moxon. London: J. M. Dent, "Everyman's Library," no. 901, 1934.

Arnaud, F. M. Baculard d'. "Préface aux *Nouvelles Historiques*" (1774), in *Oeuvres complètes*, 5 vols. Amsterdam: Michel Rey, 1775.

Bakhtin, M. M. *The Dialogic Imagination: Four Essays by M. M. Bakhtin*, ed. Michael Holquist, trans. Caryl Emerson and Michael Holquist. Austin, Tex.: University of Texas Press, 1981.

Balzac, Honoré de. "Avant-propos," in *La Comédie humaine*, ed. Marcel Bouteron. 11 vols., Paris: Gallimard "Bibliothèque de la Pléiade" 1951, vol. 1, pp. 3–16.

Battestin, Martin. *The Moral Basis of Fielding's Art*. Wesleyan, Conn. Wesleyan University Press, 1959.

Bayle, Pierre. *Dictionnaire historique et critique* (1697), 3rd ed. 4 vols. Amsterdam: Michel Bohm, 1720.

Behn, Aphra. *All the Histories and Novels Written by the Late Ingenious Mrs Behn*, 7th edn." 2 vols. London: Published by Mr Charles Gildon, 1722.

Belcikowski, Christine. *Poétique des Liaisons dangereuses*. Paris: José Corti, 1972.

Bennington, Geoffrey. *Sententiousness & the Novel. Laying Down the Law in Eighteenth-century French Fiction*. Cambridge: Cambridge University Press, 1985.

Bissell, Frederick. *Fielding's Theory of the Novel*. New York: Cooper Square, 1933.

Black, Franck Gees. *The Epistolary Novel in the Late Eighteenth Century*. Studies in Literature and Philology, no. 2. Eugene, Oreg.: University of Oregon Press, 1940.

Blewett, David. *Defoe's Art of Fiction*. Toronto: University of Toronto Press, 1979.

Bolingbroke, Henry St. John, Lord Viscount. *Letters on the Study and Use of History*, a new edition, corrected. London: A. Millar, 1752.

Booth, Wayne. *The Rhetoric of Fiction*. Chicago: University of Chicago Press, 1961.

—— "The Self-Conscious Narrator in Comic Fiction Before *Tristram Shandy*," *PMLA*, 67 (March, 1952), pp. 163–85.

Bourdé, Guy and Martin, Hervé. *Les Ecoles historiques*. Paris: Seuil, 1983.

Brooks, Peter. *Reading for the Plot*. New York: A. A. Knopf, 1984.

—— *The Novel of Worldliness*. Princeton: Princeton University Press, 1969.

Brown, Homer O. "The Displaced Self in the Novels of Daniel Defoe," in *Studies in Eighteenth-century Literature*, vol. 4, ed. Harold E. Pagliano. Madison: University of Wisconsin Press, 1975, pp. 69–94.

Brown, John. *An Estimate of the Manners and Principles of the Times*. London: L. Davis and C. Reymers, 1757.

Burckhardt, Sigurd. "*Tristram Shandy's* Law of Gravity," *ELH*, 28 (1961), 70–88.

Burns, Bryan. "The Story-telling in *Joseph Andrews*," in *Henry Fielding: Justice Observed*, ed. K. G. Simpson (London: Vision Press Ltd., 1985), pp. 119–35.

Castle, Terry. *Clarissa's Ciphers*. Ithaca: Cornell University Press, 1982.

—— *Masquerade and Civilization*. Stanford: Stanford University Press, 1986.

Chamard, H. and Rudler, G. "Les Sources historiques de la *Princesse de Clèves*," *Revue du XVIe Siècle*," 2 (1914), pp. 92–131.

—— "Les Episodes historiques," *Revue du XVIe Siècle*, 2(1914), pp. 289–321.

—— "La Couleur historique dans *La Princesse de Clèves*," *Revue du XVIe Siècle*, 5 (1917), pp. 1–20.

Chasles, Robert. *Les Illustres Françoises* (1713), ed. Frédéric Deloffre. 2 vols., Paris: "Les Belles Lettres," 1967.

Coolidge, John S. "Fielding and the 'Conservation of Character.'" *Modern Philology*, 57 (1960), pp. 245–59.

Coulet, Henri. *Le Roman jusqu'à la révolution*. 2 vols. Paris: Armand Colin, 1967.

Cox, Stephen D. *"The Stranger Within Thee"*: *Concepts of the Self in Late Eighteenth-Century Literature*. Pittsburgh: University of Pittsburgh Press, 1980.

Crébillon, Claude Prosper Jolyot de. *Les Egarements du cœur et de l'esprit* (1735–8) ed. Jean Dagen. Paris: Garnier-Flammarion, 1985.

Defoe, Daniel. *The Life and Adventures of Robinson Crusoe* (1719), ed. Angus Ross. Penguin Books, 1985.

—— *Serious Reflections During the Life and Surprising Adventures of Robinson Crusoe: with his Vision of the Angelick World* (1720).

—— *The Fortunes and Misfortunes of the Famous Moll Flanders* (1722), ed. Juliet Mitchell. Penguin Books, 1985.

—— *The Great Law of Subordination consider'd; or the Insolence and Unsufferable Behavior of SERVANTS in England duly enquir'd into*. London: 1724.

—— *Roxana, the Fortunate Mistress or, a History of the Life and Vast Variety of Fortunes of Mademoiselle de Beleau, Afterwards call'd The Countess de Wintelsheim, in Germany. Being the Person known by the Name of the Lady Roxana in the Time of King Charles II* (1724), ed. David Blewett. Penguin Books, 1985.

Deloffre, Frédéric. *Marivaux et le marivaudage*. Paris: Les Belles Lettres, 1955.

Diderot, Denis. "Eloge de Richardson" (1762), in *Œuvres esthétiques*, ed. Paul Vernière. Paris: Garnier, 1968, pp. 29–48.

—— "Paradoxe sur le comédien," in *Œuvres esthétiques*, ed. Paul Vernière. Paris: Garnier, 1968, pp. 299–381.

—— *Jacques le fataliste et son maître* (1778–80) in *Oeuvres romanesques*, ed. Henri Bénac, revue par Lucette Perol. Paris: Garnier, 1981.

—— *James the Fatalist and His Master*, trans. from the French of Diderot. 3 vols. London: G. G. and J. Robinson, Pater-Noster-Row, 1797.

Donoghue, Denis. "Sterne, our Contemporary," in *The Winged Skull: Papers from the Laurence Sterne Bicentenary Conference*. London: Methuen, 1971, pp. 42–58.

Duclos, Charles Pinot. *Considerations sur les mœurs de ce siècle*. (1750) Nouvelle edition. Paris: Prault fils, 1751.

—— *Les Mémoires du comte de M**** (1741). Reprinted Lausanne: Les Editions Rencontre, 1970.

Eagleton, Terry. *The Function of Criticism*. London: Verso Editions and New Left Books, 1984.

—— *The Rape of Clarissa*. Oxford: Basil Blackwell, 1982.

Fielding, Henry. *The History of the Adventures of Joseph Andrews, and of his Friend Mr. Abraham Adams. Written in Imitation of the Manner of Cervantes, Author of Don Quixote* (1742), ed. R. F. Brissenden. Penguin Books, 1984.

—— *The History of Tom Jones, a Foundling* (1749), ed. R. P. C. Mutter. Penguin Books, 1985.

Furetière, Antoine. *Dictionnaire universel*. The Hague and Rotterdam: Arnout & Reinier Leers, 1690, reprinted Paris: S. N. L. – Dictionnaire Le Robert, 1978.

Gearhart, Suzanne. *The Open Boundary of History and Fiction*. Princeton: Princeton University Press, 1984.

Gibbon, Edward. *Essai sur l'étude de la littérature*. London: T. Becket and P. A. de Hondt, 1762.

Goldberg, Homer. *The Art of Joseph Andrews*. Chicago: University of Chicago Press, 1969.

Goldberg, Rita. *Sex and the Enlightenment: Women in Diderot and Richardson*. Cambridge: Cambridge University Press, 1984.

Goldsmith, Oliver. *Essays*, 3rd edn, corrected. Dublin: James Williams, 1772.

Gossman, Lionel. *Medievalism and the Ideologies of the Enlightenment: the World and Work of La Curne de Sainte-Palaye*. Baltimore: Johns Hopkins University Press, 1968.

Guetti, Barbara Jones. "'Travesty' and 'Usurpation' in Mme de Lafayette's Historical Fiction," *Yale French Studies*, 69 (1985), pp. 211–21.

Habermas, Jürgen. *Strukturwandel der Öffentlichkeit* (1962). 17th printing, Darmstadt: Hermann Luchterhand, 1987.

Hardy, Barbara. *Tellers and Listeners*. London: The Athlone Press, University of London, 1975.

Hatfield, Glenn W. *Henry Fielding and the Language of Irony*. Chicago: University of Chicago Press, 1968.

Howes, Alan B. *Sterne: the Critical Heritage*. London: Routledge and Kegan Paul, 1974.

Huet, Pierre Daniel. "(Lettre à Monsieur de Segrais) De l'origine des romans" (1670), in *Œuvres complètes de Mesdames de la Fayette, de Tencin et de Fontaines*, ed. Etienne et A. Jay. Paris: P.-A. Montardieu, 1825.

Iser, Wolfgang. *The Implied Reader*. Baltimore: Johns Hopkins University Press, 1974.

Jacquin, Armand–Pierre. *Entretiens sur les romans: Ouvrage moral et critique*. Paris: Duchesne, 1755.

Jefferson, D. W. "*Tristram Shandy* and the Tradition of Learned Wit," in *Essays in Criticism*, 1 (1951), pp. 225–48.

Johnson, Samuel. *The Rambler* (1750–2). *The British Classics*, vols 15–18. London: W. Suttaby, 1809.

Jones, S. Paul. *A List of Prose Fiction from 1700 to 1750*. New York: H. W. Wilson, Co., 1939.

Jost, François. "Le roman épistolaire et la technique narrative au XVIIIe siècle," *Comparative Literature Studies*, 3(1966), pp. 397–427.

Kames, Henry Home, Lord. *Elements of criticism* (1761), 11th edn. London: B. Blake, 1839.

Kamuf, Peggy. Fictions of Feminine Desire. Lincoln, Nebr.: University of Nebraska Press, 1982.

Kany, Charles E. *The Beginnings of the Epistolary Novel in France, Italy, and Spain*. Berkeley: University of California Press, 1937.

Kinkead-Weekes, Mark. "Out of the Thicket," in *Henry Fielding: Justice Observed*, ed. K. G. Simpson. London: Vision Press Ltd., 1985, pp. 137–57.

Laclos, Pierre-Ambroise-François Choderlos de. *Les Liaisons dangereuses ou lettres recueillies dans une société et publiées pour l'instruction de quelques autres* (1782), ed. Yves Le Hir. Paris: Classiques Garnier, 1961.

Laden, Marie-Paul. *Self-Imitation in the Eighteenth-Century Novel*. Princeton: Princeton University Press, 1987.

Lafayette, Marie-Madelaine Pioche de la Vergne, comtesse de. *La Princesse de Clèves* (1678), in *Romans et nouvelles*, ed. Emile Magne. Paris: Garnier, 1961.

—— *The Princess of Cleves. The Most Famed Romance. Written in French by the greatest Wits of France*. Rendered into English by a Person of Quality at the Request of some Friends. London: A. Bentely and M. Magnes, 1679.

—— *Histoire de Madame Henriette d'Angleterre*, suivie de *Mémoires de la cour de France pour les années 1688 & 1689*, ed. Gilbert Sigaux. Paris: Mercure de France, 1982.

Lenglet Du Fresnoy, Nicolas [pub. under pseudonym: C. Gordon de Percel]. *De l'usage des romans*. 2 vols. Amsterdam: chez la Veuve Poilras, à la Vérité sans fard, 1734.

—— *L'histoire justifiée contre les romans*. Amsterdam, 1735.

Locke, John. *An Essay Concerning Human Understanding*, ed. Alexander Campbell Fraser. 2 vols. New York: Dover Press, 1959.

Man, Paul de. *Allegories of Reading*. New Haven: Yale University Press, 1979.

Marivaux, Pierre Carlet de. *Œuvres de jeunesse*, ed. Frédéric Deloffre et Claude Rigault. Paris: Gallimard "Bibliothèque de la Pléiade," 1972.

—— *La Vie de Marianne* (1731–42), ed. Michel Gilot. Paris: Garnier-Flammarion, 1978.

—— *La Vie de Marianne*, ed. Frédéric Deloffre. Paris: Garnier, 1963.

—— *Life of Marianne: or Aventures of the Comtess of* *** . . . 3 vols. London: Charles Davis, vol. 1, 1736; vol. 2, 1741; vol. 3, 1742.

—— *Le paysan parvenu* (1734–5), ed. Michel Gilot. Paris: Garnier-Flammarion, 1965.

—— *Le paysan parvenu*, ed. Frédéric Deloffre. Paris: Garnier, 1959.

—— *Le Paysan parvenu: or the Fortunate Peasant. Being the memoirs of the Life of Mr* ——. *Translated from the French of M. de Marivaux*. London: John Brindley, Charles Corbett, & Richard Wellington, 1735.

Marmontel, Jean-François. "Fiction," in *Eléments de littérature* (1787). 3 vols. Paris: Firmin Didot, 1846, vol. 2, pp. 173–85.

Marrou, Henri-Irénée. *De la connaissance historique*. Paris: Seuil, 1954.

May, Georges. *Le Dilemme du roman au XVIIIe siècle*. New Haven: Yale University Press, 1963.

Mayoux, Jean-Jacques. "Variations on the Time-Sense in *Tristram Shandy*," in *The Winged Skull: Papers from the Laurence Sterne Bicentenary Conference* (London: Methuen, 1971), pp. 3–18.

McKeon, Michael. *The Origins of the English Novel 1600–1740*. Baltimore: Johns Hopkins University Press, 1987.

Miller, Nancy K. *The Heroine's Text: Readings in the French and English Novel, 1722–82*. New York: Columbia University Press, 1980.

Moglen, Helen. *The Philosophical Irony of Laurence Sterne*. Gainesville: University of Florida Press, 1975.

Montesquieu, Charles-Louis de Secondat, baron de la Brède et de *Lettres persanes*, in vol. 1 *Œuvres complètes*, ed. André Masson. 3 vols. Paris: Nagel, 1950.

—— *Pensées*, in vol. 2, *Oeuvres complètes*, ed. André Masson. 3 vols. Paris: Nagel, 1950.

Mornet, Daniel. "Les Enseignements des Bibliothèques Privées," *Revue d'Histoire Littéraire*, 17 (1910), pp. 449–96.

Mylne, Vivienne. *The Eighteenth-century French Novel: Techniques of Illusion*. Manchester: Manchester University Press, 1965.

Paulson, Ronald, and Thomas Lockwood, eds. *Henry Fielding: the Critical Heritage*. London: Routledge and Kegan Paul, 1969.

Poulet, Georges. *La Distance intérieure (Etudes sur le temps humain, II)* (1952). Paris: Editions du Rocher, 1976.

Preston, John. *The Created Self: the Reader's Role in Eighteenth-century Fiction*. London: Heinemann, 1970.

Prévost-d'Exiles, Antoine-François. *Histoire du Chevalier des Grieux et de Manon Lescaut* (1731), ed. Frédéric Deloffre et Raymond Picard. Paris: Garnier, 1965.

Price, Martin. *Forms of Life*. New Haven: Yale University Press, 1983.

[Ralph, James]. *The Case of Authors by Profession or Trade, Stated. With Regard to Booksellers, the Stage, and the Public. No Matter by Whom*. London: R. Griffiths, 1758.

Rapin, René. *Instructions pour l'histoire* (1677), 2nd edn. Paris: Claude Cellier, 1690.

Rawson, C. J. *Henry Fielding and the Augustan Ideal under Stress*. Routledge and Kegan Paul, 1972.

Ray, William. "Convergence et Equilibre dans *Le Paysan parvenu*," *French Forum*, 1, no. 2 (May 1976), pp. 139–52.

Reeve, Clara. *The Progress of Romance* (1785). 2 vols. New York: Text Facsimile Society, 1930.

Reilly, Patrick. "Fielding's Magisterial Art," in *Henry Fielding: Justice Observed*, ed. K. G. Simpson. London: Vision Press Ltd., 1985, pp. 75–100.

Richardson, Samuel, *Pamela, or, Virtue Rewarded* (1740–1), ed. Peter Sabor. Penguin Books, 1985.

—— *Clarissa, or, the History of a Young Lady* (1747–8), ed. Angus Ross. Penguin Books, 1985.

Richetti, John J. *Defoe's Narratives*. Oxford: Clarendon Press, 1975.

Rousseau, Jean-Jacques. *Julie, ou la nouvelle Héloïse* (1761), ed. Michel Launay. Paris: Garnier-Flammarion, 1967.

—— *Eloisa, or a Series of Original Letters Collected and published by J. J. Rousseau*. Trans. from the French. 4 vols. Dublin: James Hunter, 1761.

—— *Emile* (1762), ed. François et Pierre Richard. Paris: Garnier, 1961.

—— *Les Confessions*, in vol. 1 of *Œuvres complètes*, ed. Bernard Gagnebin et Marcel Raymond. Paris: Gallimard, "Bibliothèque de la Pléiade," 1959.

Rosbottom, Ronald. *Choderlos de Laclos*. Twayne World Authors Series. Boston: G. K. Hall, 1978.

—— *Marivaux's Novels: Theme and Function in Early Eighteenth-Century Narrative*. Rutherford, N. J. Fairleigh Dickinson University Press, 1974.

Rousset, Jean. *Forme et signification*. Paris: José Corti, 1962.

—— *Narcisse romancier*. Paris: José Corti, 1972.

Sacks, Sheldon. *Fiction and the Shape of Belief*. Berkeley: University of California Press, 1966.

Seylaz, Jean-Luc. *Les Liaisons dangereuses et la création romanesque chez Laclos*. Paris: Droz-Minard, 1958.

Showalter, English, Jr. *The Evolution of the French Novel 1641–1782*. Princeton: Princeton University Press, 1972.

Simpson, K. G. ed. *Henry Fielding: Justice Observed*. London: Vision Press, Ltd., 1985.

Singer, Godfrey Frank. *The Epistolary Novel*. Philadelphia: University of Pennsylvania Press, 1933.

Spacks, Patricia Meyer. *Imagining a Self*. Cambridge, Mass.: Harvard University Press, 1976.

Stedman, John M. *The Comic Art of Laurence Sterne*. Toronto: University of Toronto Press, 1967.

Sterne, Laurence. *The Life and Opinions of Tristram Shandy, Gentleman* (1760–7), ed. Graham Petrie. Penguin Books, 1985.

Stewart, Philip. *Imitation and Illusion in the French Memoir-Novel, 1700–1750*. New Haven: Yale University Press, 1969.

Tavor, Eve. *Scepticism, Society, and the Eighteenth-Century Novel*. New York: St Martin's Press, 1987.

Thelander, Dorothy R. *Laclos and the Epistolary Novel*. Geneva: Droz, 1963.

Todorov, Tzvetan. *Littérature et Signification*. Paris: Larousse, 1967.

Traugott, John. *Tristram Shandy's World*. Berkeley: University of California Press, 1954.

Trublet, Nicolas-Charles-Joseph. *Essais sur divers sujets de littérature et de morale*. Paris: Briasson, 1735.

Turnell, Martin. *The Rise of the French Novel*. New York: New Directions, 1978.

Valincour, Jean-Henry du Trousset de. *Lettres à Madame la marquise*** sur le sujet de la "Princesse de Clèves"* ed. Albert Cazes. Paris: Bossard 1925.

Van Ghent, Dorothy. *The English Novel: Form and Function*. New York: Rinehart and Company, 1953.

Vande Berg, Michael. "Pictures of Pronunciation: Typographical Travels through *Tristram Shandy* and *Jacques le fataliste*," *Eighteenth-Century Studies*, 21 (Fall, 1987), pp. 21–47.

Versini, Laurent. *Laclos et la tradition*. Paris: Klincksieck, 1968.

Voltaire (François-Marie Arouet). "Nouvelles considérations sur l'histoire," in *Oeuvres historiques*, ed. René Pomeau. Paris: Gallimard "Bibliothèque de la Pléiade," 1957.

—— *Lettres philosophiques* (1734), in *Mélanges*, ed. Jacques Van Den Heuvel. Paris: Gallimard "Bibliothèque de la Pléiade," 1961.

Warner, William. *Reading Clarissa*. New Haven: Yale University Press, 1979.

Watt, Ian. *The Rise of the Novel*. London: Chatto and Windus, 1957.

Index

Page numbers in italics indicate sections of book devoted to heading